THE
AFRICAN
FRONTIER

THE
AFRICAN
FRONTIER

The Reproduction of
Traditional African Societies

EDITED WITH AN INTRODUCTION BY
IGOR KOPYTOFF

Indiana
University
Press

BLOOMINGTON AND INDIANAPOLIS

Library of Congress Cataloging-in-Publication Data

The African frontier.

1. Ethnology—Africa—Addresses, essays, lectures.
2. Africa—Social conditions—Addresses, essays,
lectures.   3. Frontier thesis—Addresses, essays,
lectures.   4. Ethnic barriers—Addresses, essays,
lectures.   I. Kopytoff, Igor.
GN645.A362   1986   306'.096   85-45468
ISBN 0-253-30252-8

1 2 3 4 5 90 89 88 87

Contents

Contents

PREFACE

It is always difficult to reconstruct the genesis of an idea, especially an academic idea, and especially an idea that one elaborates in one's own work. One can only rely on uncertain memory and hope that forgetfulness and repression do not get too much in the way. The idea that an African society that has been formed relatively recently can be seen as having started on a "frontier" came to me when I was doing fieldwork, in 1969 and 1970, among the Aghem of western Cameroon—a society whose memory of its growth beginning in the mid-19th century was still fresh and whose customs and traditions still showed signs of its heterogeneous origins. Later, I realized that similar signs appear in most African societies and that the sheer facts among the Aghem were not very different from what they were among the Suku of Zaire, among whom I did my first fieldwork in 1957–59. But at that time—no doubt because of the dominant anthropological paradigm that stressed the "ethnographic present" and was skeptical of all systematic speculations about origins—it never occurred to me to see Suku society in this way.

The realization of the potential significance of such a frontier perspective was reinforced by a re-reading of Warren d'Azevedo's pioneering article on the Liberian-Sierra Leonean area (Annals, New York Academy of Science v. 96[2], 1962), which examines its ethnology as a product of frontier-like conditions. The impetus to organize these various ideas came when Ivan Karp and Emilio Moran, of Indiana University, organized a symposium on "frontier and inter-ethnic situations" at the November 1977 meetings of the African Studies Association in Houston and invited me to contribute a paper. The paper, "Speculations about the Internal African Frontier" (Papers, African Studies Association, 1977) attempted to generalize the frontier perspective derived from my Aghem experience to Sub-Saharan Africa as a whole. The present collective work is the result of trying to give further substance to these ideas. The other contributors to the book agreed to present data from the African societies with which they were intimately acquainted from the perspective of these societies' genesis in relation to a "frontier." As the reader will see, the data—coming from widely scattered areas of Africa—revealed a startling amount of convergence around certain themes. It is these themes that have given the Introduction to the volume whatever organizational consistency it possesses.

While working out these ideas and writing the Introduction, I benefitted from comments by various people, among whom Sandra Barnes, Nancy Farriss, Joel Jutkowitz, Barbara Klamon Kopytoff, and John Middleton are due special mention. I also benefitted from numerous other comments I received when I presented some of these ideas at the University of Pennsylvania Ethnohistory Program, at the anthropology seminars at the Université de Montréal, McGill University, and Université Laval, and at the African Studies seminar at the University of Toronto.

Outremont, Quebec   Igor Kopytoff
June 1985

PART ONE

Introduction

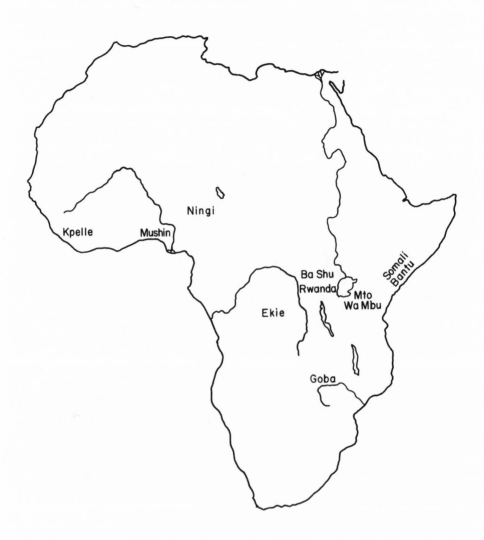

Kpelle   Mushin

Ningi

Ba Shu
Rwanda

Mto
Wa Mbu

Somali
Bantu

Ekie

Goba

Igor Kopytoff

1

The Internal African Frontier: The Making of African Political Culture

The aim of this book is to introduce a particular perspective on African societies and African cultural history—the perspective of the "frontier" from which we may better understand the formation of these societies and the perpetuation of a pan-African political culture. The germ of the idea, needless to say, comes from Frederick Jackson Turner's notion of the "frontier," to which he assigned a major role in the shaping of the American political character. But before Turner's ideas are carried to an African setting, some crucial points in them have to be revised. For example, the thesis sees the frontier as a natural force for cultural transformation. In this regard, our analysis stands Turner's thesis on its head, for we suggest that the frontier may also be a force for culture-historical continuity and conservatism.

The frontier perspective taken here is that of the local frontier, lying at the fringes of the numerous established African societies. It is on such frontiers that most African polities and societies have, so to speak, been "constructed" out of the bits and pieces—human and cultural—of existing societies. This posits a process in which incipient small polities are produced by other similar and usually more complex societies. This conception of political development is entirely opposite to those "evolutionary" theories that see small polities as arising out of some hypothetical archaic bands roaming over a hypothetical pre-historic landscape. Whatever the virtue of such speculations about a pre-historic "in-the-beginning," they have nothing to do with the formation of real, historic African societies.

ETHNOGENESIS AND THE TRIBAL MODEL

The frontier perspective suggests a particular model of the process by which many African societies developed—a model that calls into question the prevalent "tribal model" of African societies. Hence, we shall begin our discussion with a few words about this tribal model.

For some time now, the notion of the "tribe" has been under critical scrutiny, first in anthropology (e.g., Helm, ed., 1968) and then in African studies—and with good reason. One objection—that the term is seen by some Africans as pejorative—is social and political. The other objection—scholarly and hence more relevant to our discussion—is that the term is analytically inadequate and historically misleading.

The notion of the "tribe" that has embedded itself in popular and scholarly thought is above all a nineteenth-century European notion. It arose out of the struggle of a new Europe of self-conscious nations, rather than one of mere states, to construct a past appropriate to their new self-perceptions. In this notion, the tribe was a collectivity within whose boundaries one found a uniform "breed" or "race" (as the term was understood before modern biology gave it an exclusively genetic meaning). In its ideal form, the tribe embodied a uniformity of such traits as physique (what we now mean by "race"), custom, polity, language, character, mind, and group identity (what we now call "ethnicity"). The unity of the tribe resulted from common descent, common blood, and a common formative historical experience. To the many frustrated nationalisms of nineteenth-century Europe, this notion gave a sense of deep roots in the past and it made their history into a progression from tribes to peoples to nations. As the embryo of the nation, the tribe served as a charter for national independence—the nation being the natural historical self-realization of common descent, common blood, and common unique character.

To be sure, the tribal model fit the ideological demands of European self-perception rather better than the realities of European history. It is not surprising that it should fit the historical reality of non-European societies even less well (on this, see, e.g., Fried 1968). In Africa, as elsewhere, the conjunction within a "tribe" of physique, language, custom, polity, and group-identity is the rare exception rather than the rule. The term "tribe" was consequently applied by European explorers, administrators, and finally anthropologists to a variety of different groupings, with an emphasis on one or another criterion—in one place it was a polity, in another a linguistic unit, in a third, a cultural grouping. But the term has continued to carry its implicit meaning that, in turn, has presupposed a particular historical process: an ethnic germ, its beginnings lost in the mists of the past, growing through time, retaining its essential character, and becoming a people that, in turn, becomes or deserves to become a nation. At the heart of our problem, then, is the question: what is the model of ethnic formation—of ethnogenesis—that in fact applies best to Africa?

ETHNICALLY AMBIGUOUS MARGINAL SOCIETIES

One occasionally comes across African societies that do not fit the tribal model in a particularly glaring way, and they deserve more attention than they have received. In terms of standard ethnographic expectations, they are ambiguous, anomalous, marginal societies that nestle in the interstices between "normal" societies and ethnicities. Such a society does not quite hang together. It presents a mishmash of regional cultural traits. It is usually small and neither shows nor often claims much time-depth. The legitimacy of its political institutions comes periodically into question, as does its independence from nearby polities who may dispute the very territory it occupies. Such a society is apt to annoy the administrator (colonial or African) for whom the tribal model—with its essential unity, clear body of customary law, and unambiguous legitimacies—is better suited to the task of maintaining public tranquility. Such a society is also not very interesting to most anthropologists, for mainstream anthropological theories are more comfortable with groups that more or less approach the tribal model. Anthropological studies of such "anomalous" rural communities as, for example, Mto wa Mbu of Tanzania (Arens 1979; also Ch.9) are most unusual.

The collective, "official" history that such a society tells about itself may be unitary and straightforward. But it is belied by the individual histories of its separate kin groups that show their ancestors coming from different areas and at different periods—as refugees from war or famine, or as disgruntled kin group segments, or as losers in the succession struggles of their kin groups or polities, or in reaction to accusations of witchcraft. Some of them may continue to maintain relations with their relatives, taking part in their funerals and marriage rituals, and there may be lingering differences in customs, usually those of marriage and burial that are attributed to different ethnic origins. There may also be some linguistic differences. The collectivity may have a dominant "public" language, but some of its kin groups may privately maintain the knowledge of the language of their parent group and there may be recognized differences in speech and accent.

Having arisen at the fringes of the mature regional "metropoles," such not-quite-formed societies (reminiscent, but for their small scale, of the great immigrant nations of the world) are in effect societies that have emerged out of a frontier—but a local frontier. If they are rare in the literature, it is because they are apt to be ignored by the anthropologist, who usually prefers for his fieldwork site the unambiguous heartland of a society to its uncertain peripheries. But that is only part of the reason. They are also rare precisely because they are short-lived social formations on the way, potentially, to becoming full-fledged societies. They are rare for the same reason that in biology newly emergent forms at the point of becoming separate species are rare, both now and in the fossil record. And like emergent species, these societies are important—not in themselves perhaps but for the insights they can give us into the processes of ethnogenesis. For the events that have shaped them are not rare. They are very common in two contexts: in the everyday flow of African social life and in the traditions of origins of established (I shall call them mature) African societies and polities.

Anyone familiar with the routine workings of African social organization will recognize these events. An elder is accused of witchcraft, a disgruntled group of siblings feels mistreated by their deceased parent's successors, a chief's son loses the struggle over succession, an adventurous hunter or trader goes out in search of new game or profits—such people are forever leaving their settlement, accompanied by their brothers, sons, nephews, other relatives, retainers, and adherents. They move beyond the edge of the village, "into the bush," and sometimes into the no-man's land between established polities—that is, into the local frontier zone. Here, they set up a compound, or a hamlet, or a mini-chieftaincy of uncertain autonomy, or join a settlement already established by others like them. These recurrent events are usually of little lasting historical import: the embittered elder is wooed back, or merely founds a new hamlet among many; the group of siblings reintegrate into their lineage, or establish yet another new lineage segment; the new chieftain recoups his political fortunes or grudgingly accepts his vassalage; the adventurer settles down or moves on.

Such minor movements to the frontiers of existing societies may result in the extension of an ethnic group's territory. If consistent, they may represent the advance guard in the political expansion of a metropole—as, for example, in the case of Rwanda (Newbury, Ch.6). Or they may produce trade diasporas (cf. Curtin 1984:15-59), such as those of the Hausa or the Dyula (Cohen 1969, Lovejoy 1980, Launay 1982), or the military diasporas of "Swahilis" serving Arab slave traders or of African agents of Portuguese expansion (Isaacman and Isaacman 1975, Isaacman 1972), or the well-known pastoral diaspora of the Fulani that swept across the western Sudan over the centuries, or the more modest hunting diaspora of the Chokwe (Miller 1974).

But sometimes those events lead to something else. The new immigrant compound becomes the nucleus of a hamlet. In time, the hamlet grows into a village as it attracts relatives from back home and other settlers that have been similarly ejected from the surrounding societies onto the frontier. Sometimes the new settlement solidifies, joins with other settlements or establishes a hegemony over them, and finally crystallizes into a new polity and eventually a society. We recognize these processes of social formation from innumerable—and remarkably repetitive—oral histories of mature African societies which so very often attribute their foundation or transformation to immigrant aliens who came from other areas. Nor is the pattern simply a matter of some widespread mythology. It occurs in many historically recent, documented instances of the founding of polities that were, however, frozen by the arrival of colonial administrations. These range from such famous ones as Msiri's in the southeast of what was to become the Belgian Congo (Verbeken 1956, Reefe 1981) to small and relatively unknown ones that have lately been uncovered by historians (e.g., Roberts 1967, Cohen 1977, Cassanelli Ch.8); and they exhibit the "anomalous" configuration I have described. Their formation involved movements that anthropologists are apt to label as "migrations"—which indeed, they were, even if their scale was often smaller than the term "migration" usually implies.

This pattern of social formation is incompatible with the model of ethnogenesis implied by the classical notion of the tribe. Instead of a primordial embryo—a kind of tribal homunculus—maturing through history while preserving its ethnic essence, what we have here is a magnet that grows by attracting to itself the ethnic and cultural detritus produced by the routine workings of other societies. This kind of social formation also lacks the historical depth that the tribal model implies. And indeed, the formation of most African societies seldom dates back more than a few centuries. Rather than being exceptional, then, the ethnically "ambiguous" society is but another indicator of the general fluidity of ethnic identity in Africa, a fluidity that begins to reveal itself as soon as one brings history to one's investigations of ethnicity.

THE AFRICAN FRONTIER THESIS

The thesis being proposed here is simple. Its justification lies in the results of the last fifty years of Africanist scholarship. Contrary to a previously widespread stereotype of Sub-Saharan Africa as a continent mired in timeless immobility, its history has emerged to be one of ceaseless flux among populations that, in comparison to other continents, are relatively recent occupants of their present habitat. In brief, Africa has been a "frontier continent"—the stage for many population movements of many kinds and dimensions, ranging from such sub-continental proto-historic dispersions as that of the Bantu or the Nilotes to the local movements preceding the colonial era. In recent times, the urban and industrial expansion of the colonial and post-colonial eras gave rise to migrations to towns, mines, and plantations, and, in the process, to a continuing reorganization of ethnic identities, including the formation of what might be called new "colonial tribes" (see Wallerstein 1960). Population movements, now as in the past, have also been brought about by famines, civil wars, ethnic rivalries, despotic regimes, and conflicts between polities. In all these instances, displaced Africans have had to face the problem of forging a new social order in the midst of an effective institutional vacuum. But these movements, one must stress, represent the more dramatic eruptions on a surface continuously scarred by innumerable local movements to local frontiers—movements of more modest scale but of great systemic importance in the shaping of African culture history.

The thesis being explored here also proposes that many, indeed most, African societies were formed around an initial core-group developed under the relatively undramatic conditions of local frontiers. The process has been repeated again and again in the course of African culture history, giving African societies and their shared political culture a frontier cast. This political culture, in turn, has systemically led to the continuous reproduction of new frontier polities at the peripheries of mature African societies. At the same time, the continuous recreation of the frontier has maintained an African frontier-conditioned ideology in the political consciousness of African metropolitan societies.

The focus of this analysis is on the early stages of the process by which new polities emerged, polities out of which eventually grew new societies and new ethnicities. It is during these early stages that the fundamental principles underlying the construction of new societies were forged and re-forged in the course of African history. These principles persisted into the later stages of political development, but these later stages are, in themselves, beyond the scope of this analysis.

These propositions carry some implications for general "frontier theory" (if such a thing exists), and I shall comment on them at various points of the analysis. But the central concerns of this study remain African cultural history, African political culture, and the role the frontier has had in shaping them. The frontier perspective will allow us to account for at least some features of African political culture. Even a modest step in this direction is preferable to merely treating these features as historically given—which is what one does now and which is all one can do if one accepts the tribal model and the kind of ethnogenesis that it implies. These do not allow one to deal with an important culture historical question: why do we find such profound similarities among the political cultures of far-flung African societies? On this question the frontier perspective sheds some revealing even if flickering light.

THE NATURE OF THE AFRICAN FRONTIER

A frontier perspective on Africa immediately raises two questions: Is the idea of the frontier applicable to Africa? And if it is, what sort of frontier is it?

Frederick Jackson Turner's frontier thesis for the United States has endowed the general image of the frontier with peculiarly American characteristics: sweeping like a tidal wave or a succession of waves across a sub-continental or at least national landmass, such a "tidal" frontier brings with it settler societies engaged in colonizing an alien land from a base in a metropolitan society whose authority usually follows more or less closely on their heels. This image has tended to restrict the use of the term "frontier" to similar situations at other times and places: scholars have written extensively about the Canadian, the Australian, the Russian, the German, the Hungarian, the Latin American and other frontiers around the world (for overviews, see Wyman and Kroeber 1957, Gerhard 1959, Hennessy 1978).

In Africa, unsurprisingly, the term has been applied most often to the European intrusion into South Africa (notably De Kiewiet 1957, Neumark 1957, MacMillan 1963, Lamar and Thompson 1981) or in connection with colonial penetration elsewhere (McIntyre 1967), though an occasional study might delve deeply into the African side of the frontier (e.g., Isaacman and Isaacman 1975). Thus, a survey of the African historical literature (Deveneaux 1978) confines itself, of necessity, almost entirely to cases of external intrusion, even though its author suggests the applicability of the concept to internal African history. A pioneering examination of frontier expansion as a key to the understanding of an African ethnographic region is d'Azevedo's (1962) culture-historical analysis of the Liberia-Sierra Leone region, while another paper (Kopytoff 1977) represents a brief initial attempt to formulate the idea of an internal and entirely African frontier. Yet much of the anthropological literature on "expansion" and "migration" can be recast into a frontier perspective (a notable example being Bohannan 1954).

The term frontier conflates two meanings: of a region and of a boundary. The latter meaning is stressed in Owen Lattimore's *Inner Asian Frontiers of China* (1940), showing how the cyclical alternation of mutual dominance between Imperial China and its nomadic neighbors resulted over the centuries in what might be called an "oscillating frontier." And in anthropology, Bohannan and Plog (eds., 1967) gave the term "frontier" a nearly metaphorical cast by applying it to any kind of interaction across cultural boundaries. But in most anthropological usages, the frontier is a geographical region with sociological characteristics. However, unlike most historians, anthropologists have been more willing to see frontiers as operating on a more local scale (thus, Whitten 1974 on Ecuador or Helms and Loveland 1976 on Lower Central America). In this volume, we shall carry further this reduction in scale by making the frontier encompass even more narrowly local phenomena. The African frontier we focus on consists of politically open areas nestling between organized societies but "internal" to the larger regions in which they are found—what might be called an "internal" or "interstitial frontier."

What sort of frontiers has Africa known historically? Certainly, Africa is no stranger to the tidal frontier. The reconstruction of the ancestral distribution of African language families (Greenberg 1970), bolstered by culture-historical data (Murdock 1959) and archeology (Clark 1970, Fagan and Oliver 1975), suggests that from the beginning of the North African Neolithic, sometime about 5000 B.C., and until 2500 B.C. or so, most of the populations ancestral to the present population of Sub-Saharan Africa were concentrated in the northern half of the continent, specifically in the now barren but then fertile Saharan-Sahelian band that spans the continent from east to west. These populations—ancestral linguistically, culturally, and preponderantly biologically—were living in association and contact with one another in the kind of setting in which regional cultural syntheses and patterns are usually evolved. It is here that we must assume that the "incubation" of the ancestral pan-African culture patterns took place, often under frontier conditions and in contact with the kindred patterns of the pre-Islamic Near-East. From this ancestral "hearth" of African culture, after the onset of desiccation of the Saharan-Sahel belt sometime around 2500 B.C., a population tide crept slowly southward, out of the expanding Saharan desert and into the savannas, even while the savannas were themselves expanding southward at the expense of the equatorial forest zone that dominates the center of the continent. A second spurt in the occupation of the southern part of the continent by way of the central forests began during the first millennium B.C., leading to the spread of speakers of Bantu languages throughout most of the then very sparsely inhabited southern third of Africa.

The purpose of this lightning sidetrip into elementary African pre-history is to stress that the ancestral African population was relatively concentrated in the past, constituting what one may refer to as an "ecumene" which I would define as a region of persistent cultural interaction and exchange (see Kopytoff 1981). The result—cultural-ideological synthesis and homogenization—is to create a broad "culture area" of varying degrees of internal uniformity. Most of Sub-Saharan Africa has been occupied and culturally dominated by populations deriving from this Neolithic Saharan-Sahelian cultural ecumene. This process of occupation by Africa's present "indigenous" population has occurred relatively recently in comparison to the peopling of most other major continental areas of the world before the post-fifteenth-century European expansion. In many other areas—one immediately thinks of India or the Middle East—the sheer time-depth of occupation by different populations has led to pell-mell mixtures and mosaics of cultures and ethnic identities. In Africa, the immigrants did encounter small groups of Pygmoids, Bushmanoids and Cushites (and whatever other populations there might have been that have left no traces for scholars upon which to build their reconstructions of the past). But these original populations have scarcely left any traces on the present population, which reinforces the impression that they did not represent the kind of large bodies of ancient and culturally disparate pre-existing populations that might have deeply and differentially influenced within each region the culture of immigrants as these moved into the different regions. In this respect, the slate was essentially clean. As the initial tidal frontier crept across Africa, the frontiersmen were bringing with them a basically similar kit of cultural and ideological resources. It is thus not surprising that Sub-Saharan Africa should exhibit to such a striking degree a fundamental cultural unity.

This African tidal frontier, however, left the continent very sparsely populated—as much of it continued to be in historic times and even now. After the first thin spread of immigrants, large expanses remained available to settlement. Established societies were surrounded by large tracts of land that were open politically or physically, or both. Together, these tracts made up a continent-wide interstitial network of thousands of potential local frontiers. Settlers wishing to leave the established societies could move into this internal African frontier and set up their own social order in the midst of what was effectively an institutional vacuum. It was under such frontier conditions that the dynamic of African social and political formation was played out over the past centuries. Two features, often absent on other frontiers, characterized this one: (a) the frontier areas were unpoliced by the small metropoles from which the frontiersmen came, and (b) in most instances, the frontiersmen were not the advance agents of metropolitan expansion. Hence, the frontier could become a stage for the emergence of numerous new, small-scale, and independent political formations, most of which eventually faltered but some of which grew into larger polities that provided the nucleus for the emergence of new societies.

The effect of these early frontiers is perhaps fresher in some areas than others. The Bantu southern third of Africa, more recently and on the whole more sparsely populated than West Africa, may well exhibit more frontier-conditioned cultural patterns than do some of the more deeply-rooted societies to the north. I said "on the whole" because, as we shall see, the internal African frontier is characteristically a very local phenomenon. Nor is it a simple matter of geography and demography. It is also a matter of opportunities and, therefore, a matter of local history. Thus, with the appearance of the European sea-borne trade from the late fifteenth century on, many coastal areas of West Africa became active frontier areas rather recently (with important culture-historical consequences, as d'Azevedo 1962 demonstrates for the Liberia-Sierra Leone area). And with the new opportunities of the colonial and post-colonial periods, new frontiers beckoned, such as the urban frontier of Yoruba towns examined by Cohen (1969) in his study of Hausa migrants or by Barnes (Ch.10, and 1986) in her study of the growth of Mushin, a suburb of Nigeria's capital, Lagos.

If, then, one were to look down from on high upon an ethnographic map of pre-colonial Africa, one would observe what might be likened to a meteorological map projected from a weather satellite, in which mature societies and polities would be represented by numerous blotches of dense light clouds and frontier areas by the meandering dark channels between them. These channels might be narrow or wide, with abrupt or uncertain boundaries—depending on whether the control by the mature local metropoles of their peripheries extended far or near, whether it was strong or weak, whether it stopped suddenly at the boundary or petered gradually out beyond it. But this map metaphor requires an important emendation. The metaphor conveys an "objective" picture of the interstitial frontier as one of sparse population and weak or non-existent political institutions. But the frontier also arises out of subjective definitions of reality: societies often define neighboring areas as lacking any legitimate political institutions and as being open to legitimate intrusion and settlement—this even if the areas are in fact occupied by organized polities. In brief, the frontier is above all a political fact, a matter of a political definition of geographical space. Frontiers tend to be seen as geographical phenomena because empty or sparsely populated areas are usually also the areas that can offer little political resistance to intrusion. These are the easiest frontiers but they are not the only ones.

Finally, and the point is crucial, the map in question is not static, no more than a historically realistic ethnographic map of Africa would be. The clouds on the map, like African societies over the centuries, would move, reform, disappear, break-up into pieces; the pieces would reassemble and new distinct areas would form; and the channels between them would expand, contract, and shift. As new polities and societies emerge, other polities and societies would shrink or disappear and their populations would redistribute themselves among the new groupings.

FRONTIER DYNAMICS

Having revised the structure of Turner's frontier, let us now turn to the frontier dynamics that he postulated.

When Turner initially presented his thesis in 1893, he did so with a vigor that made the theoretical issue misleadingly unidimensional: boldly stated, the thesis seemed to say that the frontier more or less determined the salient features of the American national character. Turner's later re-phrasing of the central thesis (1922) was more careful and less deterministic. Nevertheless, the comparative questions inspired by the thesis tend to return to the problem of determinism: does the frontier everywhere produce the same results? or, less ambitiously, is the frontier generalizable as a cause? But, as anyone acquainted with history knows or should know, it does not and it is not.

The case for the frontier's uniform impact rapidly collapses when one considers other societies that grew out of a frontier, be it China, Russian Siberia, parts of Latin America, the Hungarian plain, East Prussia, Southeast Asian lowlands, or what have you. Even in culturally similar societies, the effects of the French Canadian (Eccles 1983), Western Canadian, and American frontiers have been notably different. If the frontier *per se* has not been a determining factor elsewhere, why should it be in the United States? Within American history, there have been innumerable critiques of Turner's thesis—critiques that have often been marked by their own kind of parochialism because so often based not on comparison with other frontier areas but on a deeper immersion into the details of the American experience. They need not concern us here (see Taylor 1956 and, for a concise assessment of the state of the thesis, Billington 1967). But the half-century of enthusiasm, argument, rejection, spirited defense, and revival does leave us if not with a thesis then with elements out of which a frontier "model" may be fashioned for Africa.

Most American historians would now agree that the frontier as such, *qua* natural setting, did not create the American national political character, as Turner strongly implied. Rather, the frontier as an institutional vacuum was a place where the frontiersmen could literally *construct* a desirable social order. They came to the frontier not with a sociological and political *tabula rasa*, to be shaped by its forests and plains, but with a mental model of a good society. The elements of the model went well into the past, and not merely the American past at that. Some of the elements have English roots that we can perceive through works such as those of E. P. Thompson (1963) and Christopher Hill (1965). Others sprouted in the soil of the earliest settlements. And some grew during the century and a half preceding the westward surge, invigorated by ideas of the Enlightenment—Scottish, English, French—in a society that was unusually literate for its time. Thus, the efforts to construct a new social order on the frontier were, from the beginning, informed by an ideal model that the frontiersman held—perhaps vaguely but certainly culturally.

In discussing the diffusion of manorialism and feudalism in Western Europe, Marc Bloch (1961:248ff) has noted that institutions often assume a form closer to the ideal when they have been transplanted. William of Normandy could design on the clean political slate that was conquered England a more faithful version of the feudal scheme than that which prevailed on the continent. Closer to home, Henry Steele Commager (1977) has recently argued that while Europe imagined the ideas of the Enlightenment, it was America that realized them because it could apply European ideas that in Europe itself ran counter to innumerable entrenched interests. One may argue that a similar situation prevailed in America itself in the relation between the western frontier and the eastern metropole. The American frontier allowed frontiersmen to apply the ideal model and produce a result that was indeed purer, simpler, more naive, and more faithful to the model than one could possibly have it in the East. For in the East, the model, even while it was being explicitly developed ideologically, had to contend in practice with much historical residue, many vested interests, and all the compromises that a successful maturing society embodies. As the frontier moved westward, the recently created local societies it left behind were soon enough "corrupted" (see, for example, Mitchell 1977 on the early Virginian frontier). But the model could be carried on to the next zone of the moving frontier. Not only was the model thus kept alive; its incorporation into living social forms in the West strengthened its place in the national consciousness as expressed in the culturally hegemonic East, which remained the dominant ideological articulator (though not practitioner) of the national political culture.

It is in such terms that Turner's original insights might now be reinterpreted into a model of a cultural process. The result is to synthesize Turner's views with those he fought against in his time—namely, the "germ" theory that saw the development of American institutions as the sprouting of transplanted European seeds. This reinterpretation also suggests how unusual among frontiers is the American one with its peculiar egalitarian ethic.

With important modifications, then, the frontier perspective can be usefully transferred from America to other frontiers. The main elements of this perspective seem to be as follows:

a) The frontier factor is permissive rather than determinant; it does not create a type of society and culture but provides instead an institutional vacuum for the unfolding of social processes.

b) An important variable in the structure of relations between frontier and metropole is whether the frontier is an area into which the metropole is itself expanding or one into which it merely sends out settlers who remain independent of the metropole.

c) A crucial factor in the outcome of the frontier process is the nature of the initial model carried from the metropolitan culture to the frontier.

d) The institutional vacuum perceived by the frontiersmen exists to the extent that the balance of forces gives them the freedom of action to express the model brought from the metropole—to express it more directly and forcefully in the course of social construction than it could be in the metropole.

e) If communications continue between the metropole and the frontier, the repetitive use of the model on the frontier maintains it in the regional cultural awareness, validates it, and constantly revitalizes it. The frontier may consequently act as a culturally and ideologically conservative force.

One need hardly stress that the last point—about the potentially conservative functions of some frontiers—represents a radical departure from the core of Turner's thesis for the United States. The point will be elaborated at some length for Africa, since it is Africa that concerns us here. Nevertheless, the point suggests that Turner's thesis for America may well be re-examined in this "conservative" perspective.

When one takes the frontier perspective from the United States to Sub-Saharan Africa, one must confront a glaring difference between the two areas. First, there is the matter of scale. Like the American frontier—a series of successive local frontiers moving uni-directionally westward—the historic internal African frontier also consisted of many local frontiers which, however, were discrete and not connected serially (the pre-historic and proto-historic African tidal frontiers excepted). Also, we have, in the American case, a unified nation-state, with some form of national culture. In the African case, we have a sub-continent where each society was aware of but a few of the innumerable societies that were kindred to it. Thus, the scale of cultural awareness, as of the frontier itself, was much more local. Moreover, the cultural interaction on the African internal frontier was quite unlike the meeting between European and Native American cultures and unlike the more complex confrontations on many other frontiers, sometimes involving layers of cultural syntheses and interaction between them (see, for example, Whitten 1974 on the Afro-American adaptation to the Hispanic-American adaptation on the Pacific frontier of northwestern South America, or Stein 1980 on Brahman and peasant expansion in medieval South India). In Africa, by contrast, the frontiersmen encountered culturally kindred or at least similar societies, with whom they already shared fundamental features of political culture.

In this analysis, I postulate—on good empirical grounds, I think—the existence of certain pan-African cultural principles, not least in the political sphere. These exist on the same level of generality as do certain European or Western cultural principles and I have already discussed the historical reasons for this cultural unity (whose precise dimensions remain largely unexplored). But that said, the continued existence of such common cultural patterns over the past couple of millennia still poses a problem whose solution depends to some extent on the kind of culture-historical model one chooses to adopt.

The tribal model, be it coupled to an evolutionary or a functionalist outlook, implicitly assumes relatively isolated ethnic corridors of development through time. The tribal model would, therefore, attribute pan-African patterns to common origins in some distant past, or to similar responses to similar outward conditions more recently, or to a combination of both. By contrast, a diffusionist model of culture-historical development assumes loose, permeable, and inconstant ethnic boundaries; and it would see similarities among African societies as being sometimes ancient and sometimes recent but, in most cases, as attributable to continued communication within a cultural ecumene. But the diffusionist model has always presented a problem: logically, continuous diffusion should create a spread across the face of the land of a mish-mash of cultural traits. But what we find is something else: a structured distribution of culture patterns, some being very widely distributed and others being more locally confined, with common traits being sometimes derived from a common historical past, sometimes from diffusion among kindred societies receptive to the same ideas, and sometimes from the convergence that occurs when kindred societies respond in similar ways to similar recurrent conditions.

The model adopted in this analysis takes the effects of common origins, diffusion, similarities through convergence, and a functional relationship among cultural features as having been equally powerful in the historical shaping of African societies. Many of the widely shared fundamental traits of African political culture must have initially been laid down in the Saharan-Sahelian Neolithic, often under frontier-like conditions. The existence in African societies of this common pan-African cultural base insured a relatively easy spread of local elaborations of these traits within the African cultural ecumene, especially in the absence of serious competition from preceding local cultural traditions. And this diffusion, in turn, has maintained and reinforced the cultural unity of the Sub-Saharan region. In this process, the presence of the internal African frontier played an important role. Most of the established societies being themselves products of the frontier, their founding charters and histories provided a legitimate and functioning model for new frontier societies (this embeddedness of the frontier ethic in the metropole is illustrated in Newbury's [Ch.6] study of Rwanda's political ideology). At the same time, the frontier provided a favorable setting in which these idealized models could be re-applied and validated in the construction of new societies on new frontiers. The process thus both re-injected frontier-conditioned features into the political cultures of the new societies and revitalized them in the wider cultural consciousness of established societies.

In brief, African metropolitan societies prefigured frontier ones as African frontier societies prefigured the metropolitan ones. The implications of this perspective may perhaps best be seen by contrasting it with a model that assumes an opposite perspective: if the different African societies, once formed, had remained separated from one another, each to develop independently in its own world, the result over a couple of millennia would have been a vast proliferation of very dissimilar cultures.

In the present analysis, even while reasonably postulating such a frontier process in the pre-historic and proto-historic past, we are interested in examining the process as a self-sustaining dynamic that we can detect in historical and anthropological data. We shall examine here historical frontiers and their relation to historical African cultures. The lack of time-depth is compensated for by the geographical spread of our data. When similar processes are seen to have occurred more or less simultaneously at the opposite ends of a continent and in many places in-between, and when recent diffusion or functional convergence cannot be advanced as a plausible explanation, the reasons for the similarities must then be attributed to the participation of all these societies in a common culture-historical stream in which similar historically-given features have interacted functionally in similar ways.

THE FRONTIER PROCESS

From the foregoing discussion a series of issues appears about what we might call the "frontier process" as it applies to Africa. These issues will provide the themes around which I shall organize the remainder of this essay.

a) *The Production of Frontiersmen.* Traditional African societies were characterized by a social dynamic that periodically ejected people out of their kin groups, communities, and polities. Some of these people became frontiersmen.

b) *Movement in Groups.* Those who disengaged themselves from their societies usually did so as a group.

c) *The Institutional Vacuum.* The definition of a frontier was political: the metropole defined an area at its periphery as open to legitimate intrusion. To the immigrant settlers it represented an institutional vacuum, although it usually contained other organized groups with which the settlers had to deal.

d) *Pre-Existing Social Models.* While most of the immigrants simply joined existing social groups, some proceeded to construct a new social order—a task to which they brought from the metropole a political culture and a model of a legitimate social order.

e) *Adherents as Kinsmen.* Social construction on the frontier called for entrepreneurship. Since power on the frontier lay largely in numbers, this meant attracting and retaining adherents and dependents; initially, this was done by resorting to a kin-group model of integration.

f) *Adherents as Subjects.* If the emergent polity grew in size, the kin group model for recruiting adherents became increasingly impractical. In this second stage, the polity moved from a corporate kin-group model of integration to one emphasizing the inter-dependence between rulers and subjects. Nevertheless, from the rulers' point of view, the polity continued to be the patrimonial estate of the founding kin group.

g) *Firstcomers and Latecomers.* In principle, authority was legitimized by being a "firstcomer." The principle had to be adapted to the reality that the polity was in fact dominated by the immigrant latecoming group.

h) *Patrimonialism.* Since the growing polity was a direct expansion of the founders' frontier hamlet, the patrimonial model of the latter became the basis for the rulers' constitutional ideology. By contrast, in the ideology of the subjects (who could always leave for other frontiers), the ruler was a creation of the subjects. This ideological duality gave a particular stamp to what has been called African "sacred chieftainship" and "divine kingship."

i) *Inter-Dependence.* As the polity matured, the ruler-subject division and inter-dependence were incorporated into the integrative symbolism of royal ritual.

j) *The Regional Context.* The charter of the expanding polity also sought legitimacy in the eyes of neighboring polities. This required it to abandon its parochialism and draw upon values, traditions, and legitimizing themes widely shared in the region.

k) *The Frontier as Historical Process.* The new polity, if stabilized into an integrated society, might then have entered another phase of growth— that of expansion at the expense of neighboring polities. Or, more commonly, it vanished, broken up by internal stresses or absorbed by similar but more successful frontier polities or regional metropoles. In this, too, it played a role in the political ecology of the frontier, which systemically generated small polities, endowed them with a frontier-conditioned political culture, and re-injected them into the regional system.

THE SYSTEMIC PRODUCTION OF FRONTIERSMEN

The mere existence of areas open to intrusion and settlement does not make a frontier. A frontier is made by frontiersmen and these have to be socially produced, so to speak, by the metropoles—something metropoles do not always do. The effects of such natural forces as famines or overgrazed pastures aside, the reasons for the continuous re-creation of frontiers in

Africa are cultural and sociological: African societies were so constructed that they systemically produced frontiersmen. Innumerable ethnographies support the commonplace observation that African social groups—be they kin groups, villages, cult groups, chieftaincies, or kingdoms—show consistently a tendency to fission and segment. As a result, the formation of new social groups as offshoots of old ones has been a constant theme in the histories of African societies—histories filled with the movement of the disgruntled, the victimized, the exiled, the refugees, the losers in internecine struggles, the adventurous, and the ambitious. Several cultural principles and social mechanisms are and were behind the centrifugal forces, many of them being themselves products of frontier conditions or at least consonant with them.

Among traditional African kin groups, the tendency to segment flowed in part out of the great autonomy they enjoyed within the larger social and political structures. Even in highly centralized polities, almost all internal affairs of kin groups were generally considered to be their own and not subject to outside interference. The burden of settling internal disputes was thus ultimately placed on the very people engaged in them— a situation that insured frequent splits.

Quarrels within kin groups were encouraged by the co-existence of two potentially contradictory principles. On the one hand, there was the principle of hierarchy—not least, that of age—so pronounced in all African social relations. This meant that authority in a kin group lay with a gerontocracy that controlled its collective resources and often used them to their own advantage (most notably in the acquisition of wives); and younger kin group members were treated in many societies as legal minors even when they approached an increasingly impatient middle age. Side by side with this hierarchical principle stood the conflicting principle of the essential equality of members of the corporate kin group. The ideology of the kin group stated that individual interests were transcended by the corporate interest: the kin group "owned" equally all its members. By the same token, they all ultimately held equal rights to the wealth and benefits of the corporation; every person, if he or she lived long enough, would become an elder, and every male (and, rarely, female) could, in principle, claim someday the headship (chiefship) of the kin group on equal terms with others. This principle is not an egalitarian one (as the term is used in the West) but rather one of equal potentiality, embodied in the equality of potential access to authority. The principle is frequently celebrated in sayings to the effect that "every man is a chief"—or, as the title of Henderson's study (1972) of an Igbo polity puts it, "The King in Every Man." The co-existence of the two principles of hierarchy and essential equality easily led to resentment by the younger members of the unarguably legitimate yet galling authority of the elders.

The more energetic solutions to these endemic tensions included ritual reconciliation, witchcraft accusations, and poisoning. Another solution might have been a clean and permanent break. But a definite split ran into its own difficulties. African social relations, once established, tend to acquire a functional autonomy of their own that makes it difficult to break them. One might call it the principle of "the primacy of structure over content." In her full-scale study of Mushin, a suburb of Lagos, Barnes (1985) points out how, in modern Nigerian politics, established political relationships and networks persisted even while their substance changed with political circumstances. A ritual alliance, once established, could change into a political one under one regime; and when party politics were forbidden under another regime, the alliance became an economic one. In traditional Africa, this autonomous persistence of relationships *per se* meant that when a relationship was broken, the break had to be ritually sanctioned. Yet even then, the relationship was often believed to linger and diviners would attribute misfortunes to the ritual mishandling of a relationship that was thought to have been terminated. This was all the more true of kin relations, based as they were on "blood" ties (which could be generated biologically or ritually).

These ideas illuminate the widespread African pattern of maintaining a continuity amid a break—most easily, by confining the break to some contexts but keeping the relationship itself alive by maintaining it, often in token ways. Strategically, the relationship was held in a kind of reserve out of which it could be resurrected when circumstances demanded it. A pragmatically effective resolution of a conflict within a group, then, lay in spatial withdrawal: this de-activated the relationship without taking any formal steps that might be interpreted as breaking it. The pattern is congruent with frontier conditions—"adaptive," some would say—for it left open the option of the prodigal's return to the *status quo ante* if the attempt at independent existence elsewhere failed. The prevalence of this pattern of withdrawal meant that occasionally the movement was into a frontier area.

Another source of displacement of people lay in the patterning of witchcraft accusations. Internal tensions within an African social group commonly expressed themselves in mutual suspicions and accusations of witchcraft. This, as LeVine (1976:125-27) points out, was part of a more general tendency to attribute misfortunes to the malevolent designs of human enemies. Once the accusations were made, who won and who lost in the ensuing struggle depended on the balance of forces within the group. The weaker faction might be expelled, or, outraged over the accusations, it might leave on its own.

Group fission and factional struggles, resulting in emigration, also arose from the ambiguity of rules of succession to political positions. Succession usually took place without great strain within small groups, such as extended families and minor kin groups (where the senior male usually took the headship). But in larger kin groups, such as major lineages and clans, and especially in political groups, such as chieftaincies and kingdoms, succession rules were usually ambiguous and indecisive. They typically appealed simultaneously to several criteria; each represented a cultural ideal but it was unlikely that all of them would be incontestably lodged in a single person. It is difficult to see, for example, how succession struggles could be avoided when the rules stated, as they so often did, that the successor was to be that candidate who was, simultaneously, the eldest, the most qualified, the official heir-apparent, and the one whom the ruler had named on his deathbed in secret to a few trusted councillors who, later, often disagreed on what they had heard. Indeed, succession struggles—covert or open, preemptive or after the fact—among the different claimants were a normal part of the political dynamics of most large kin groups, chieftaincies and kingdoms. Every successor thus carried an aura of potential illegitimacy. The illegitimacy would sometimes be confirmed *ex post facto* when the early demise of a new ruler would be attributed to the irregularities in his ascension to power. And the ever present possibility of illegitimacy could even be incorporated into the succession ritual, such as that of Goba kingship (Lancaster, Ch. 3). In the repetitive succession struggles fostered by these uncertainties, the unsuccessful claimants might lose their lives, or be exiled, or leave, or be deliberately pushed toward the frontier—there to languish or to found what eventually might become a new polity which, in turn, would suffer from the same problems and push other people out to its own frontiers.

Struggles between autonomous groups—as opposed to struggles within them—also resulted in periodically pushing people out of the metropoles. Self-help was a well-established means of redressing wrongs not only in "uncentralized" polities but also in most of the large and centralized ones as well. And (*pace* functionalist optimism) self-help generated new disputes as often as it settled old ones, leading to periodic withdrawal of one or the other side to a dispute—withdrawal to other areas within the polity, or to other polities, or to the frontier.

In all this, a general point needs to be stressed. Political consolidation in Africa, at whatever level, was not always followed by the disappearance of internal violence and peace-keeping was not always very high on the list of functions of formal political authorities. Like most pre-modern political systems, African polities could successfully exist amid a degree of public disorder quite incompatible with modern Western views of "normal" state functions (for one example, see Vansina 1978:127-71 on the political administration of the Kuba empire in what is now southern Zaire). There was a logic in this: the more autonomous the local groups and the less interference with them by the political center, the more combativeness the political system could tolerate among its constituent units. The term "centralization," rather easily bandied about in anthropological discussions of African political systems (including this one), does not in fact say anything precise about the political functions allocated and their hierarchy. Did peace-keeping, for example, have priority over tribute-collection? (For a particularly cogent critique of the term "centralization," see Lloyd 1965:81-2.)

Colonial regimes, to be sure, saw as one of their first tasks the imposition of their particular kind of *pax*, and anthropologists partly responded to these concerns by discovering institutions that kept social order in ways unimagined by the stolid colonial administrator. Yet, even in colonial times, peace-keeping *per se*, as an administrative value, was after all held mainly by the later, more mature, and more bureaucratized colonial administrations. In the earlier "heroic" stages of colonial occupation, things were different: it was not unknown to use warfare by one African polity against another as a way of arriving at the ultimate *pax*. What is constant in both the earlier and the later colonial stances is that the sovereign authority was expressed, here as everywhere else, through a judicious *control* rather than abolition of conflict. This included the right to authorize violence as well as to prohibit it and to choose the kinds of violence one wished to concern oneself with. The modern home-grown Western outlook sees the dampening of armed conflict as a necessary function of sovereign authority. But such an idea of authority is no more applicable to Africa than it is to pre-colonial southern Asia or medieval Europe. The Kuba empire illustrates the point: the Kuba sovereign's authority was expressed not in an absolute prohibition of warfare among his subordinate chiefdoms but rather in the requirement that it not occur without his knowledge and approval.

Other forces that ejected people out of African societies lay beyond the kin group, the local community, and the polity. Behind the stories of the building and the flowering of African kingdoms, great and small, stand—here as elsewhere—political upheavals, oppression, conquest, raids, pillage, and the displacement of huge numbers of people. Defeated rulers, with their relatives and adherents, sought new places to escape to and, if possible, to dominate, while ordinary people sought their own more modest refuge from the clash of opposing armies. We know of the enormous movements of peoples that followed, in domino fashion, the creation by Shaka of the Zulu empire. Yet, one suspects that as a source of population movement over the centuries, the less spectacular but steady little local quarrels and raids, involving far smaller forces and displacing far smaller numbers of people, have been more important. The various kin groups among the Kpelle, described by Murphy and Bledsoe (Ch.4), and those among the Goba, described by Lancaster (Ch.3), typically moved to new frontiers to escape the periodic outbursts of disorder in their parochial areas. And Patton's story (Ch.7) about Muslim divines fleeing heresy and unjust taxation by new conquerors—to establish, as it turned out, a new predatory state—is but a minor example of the dislocations that followed when local power changed hands.

We have so far emphasized factors that ejected people toward the frontier. But there were also some positive factors of attraction. In many societies in the world, to withdraw to some new frontier is an overwhelmingly unattractive and risky business. In Africa, however, the trauma was offset by a possible reward—the achievement of self-realization by "being first." The general value of "being first" appeared in many different contexts in Africa. One could be the first-born among siblings, the first wife in a compound, the first in age in the lineage, the first entrant into a ritual initiation, the first in the region to acquire a title, the first village to have set up a secret society or a cult house. All these were ways of being senior, of enjoying precedence in the etiquette of public events, and, not least, of being remembered after one's death.

Being the first settler in an area gave one a special kind of seniority—it gave one the right to "show the place" (as the common expression goes in many African languages) to those who came later. To found a new community made one "first" in it, even if that community were under a higher authority. To found a community which became autonomous and grew into a chieftaincy was even better. Within the crucial field of kinship, to found a new large segment within one's lineage was to grasp at social immortality. The segment, carrying one's name, might multiply forever, and one's name would be forever remembered by one's descendants. In the shorter run, the tangible evidence of a successful social career was to be the founder of a compound and to end one's days as the head of a large establishment of people—of wives, children, in-laws, relatives, "slaves," adherents, and dependents. Thus, unless one inherited an established position of primacy, the path to success lay in detaching oneself from one's own group and founding a new one, be it a kin group, village, chieftaincy, or even ethnicity. To the ambitious, the frontier could hold the promise of such achievements.

The configuration I have described is consistent with another attitude: the Africans' relative indifference to rootedness in physical space, together with an indifference to a permanent attachment to a particular place. The pattern, to be sure, is relative—it is striking when one contrasts it with the strong attachment to specific areas that one often finds in peasant societies around the world. African space is, above all, social space. Traditionally, a village, a region, or a chieftaincy was often referred to by the name of the social group that occupied it. And unlike, for example, the frequent naming of towns in the American Midwest after their founders, the African group usually took the place-name with it when it changed its emplacement (an excellent illustration of this domination of physical space by social space is found in Bohannan 1958, which discusses the social mapping of geographical space among the Tiv of Nigeria). African "roots" were not conceived to be in a place (as Westerners often define theirs) but in a kin group, in ancestors, in a genealogical position. And by projecting this notion into the future, one established one's future roots by becoming the founder of a group yet to come. Unlike, for example, the Chinese, Africans take their ancestors with them when they move, regardless of where these ancestors are buried. This capacity to carry, so to speak, with oneself the rootedness of one's own social structure—be it to a rural frontier, as in the past, or to a city, as now—gives African migrations a peculiarly "stable" flavor when compared with the often disruptive migrations one encounters elsewhere. This social transcendence of purely physical roots certainly contributes to the ease of movement into frontier areas—and it may itself be a frontier-conditioned trait.

Finally, and in harmony with this pattern, there is the general African "adventurousness": the eagerness to see new places, the curiosity about other societies, the avidity for travel, the readiness to migrate. The trait is, again, a relative one, best seen in contrast to, say, the singular unadventurousness of most European peasants (see, for example, the reticence by French peasants before the possibilities of modernization, described by Eugen Weber 1976, or even the notorious immobility of the British working class). In contemporary Africa, this adventurousness is one of the factors in the extensive labor migrations and in the general ease with which Africans move to cities and to other countries, and it undoubtedly also played a part in the past in the willingness to disengage from one's society and move to a new area.

DISENGAGEMENT FROM THE METROPOLE BY GROUPS

When African oral traditions speak of an individual appearing on the frontier—and that, stylistically, is a way of speaking of a kin group—the individual is soon transmuted in the course of the narrative into a group. The individual turns out to have been the symbol or the spearhead of a group. The narrative pattern reflects social reality: segmentation and fission in African social groups led, almost universally, to disengagement from existing groups by sub-groups rather than individuals. The reason lay in the social and ritual embeddedness of the individual in a hierarchy of groups (in contrast, for example, to the modern West, with its individualistic social identities and individualistic patterns of migration). Conflicts in Africa—even if individual in origin—always ran the risk of being pushed into a collective framework, pitting group against group. This does not mean it always happened; indeed, one of the notable things about life in African communities is the care given to containing individual conflicts as much as possible, precisely because of their tendency to become group conflicts if they are not contained. The point is that when the conflicts did expand, they did so in ways that involved social groups (by contrast to, say, willing friends, ideological sympathizers, and indignant partisans of "what's fair").

The pattern, fundamental to African social dynamics, extended beyond organized groups. Social categories, such as those of gender or age or occupation, would sporadically coalesce into ephemeral solidarity groups when someone of that category was attacked. Conflicts between individuals have been known to expand in a flash and involve all market sellers, or all women, or all youth, or all soldiers. (It says much about the nature of most African systems of "slavery" that "slaves" scarcely ever coalesced in this way—because they rarely saw themselves as a social category sharing in a common social identity.)

More regularly, the pattern involved those organized groups on which the structure of the society rested. Depending on who was the adversary, an attack against a man made for the closing of ranks around him by his sons, or brothers, or immediate kin group, or community, or age-group. In a conflict over succession, the losing claimant would withdraw with a group of close kinsmen, adherents, and retainers. A man expelled by his community for witchcraft left with his wives, children, grown sons, and perhaps brothers. A quarrel between two members of different lineage segments involved the respective segments as groups. A small lineage segment rent by quarrels would divide into groups of siblings. A conflict between two half-siblings engaged groups of full-siblings on each side.

In brief, each person was attached to several latent groups of solidarity. Depending on the context, one expected support from each and offered it to each of them. In times of conflict, one tried to mobilize the support of the maximum contextually relevant group. Since traditional African societies were largely structured in terms of corporate groups, individual survival was possible only by being under the protective umbrella of one or another such group, and the larger and more powerful it was, the safer one was. The most immediate and most secure groups of support were those based on ties of kinship.

Once on the frontier, these principles of organization became as relevant to group-building there as they had been to disengagement by groups back home. They defined the newcomers as constituting a corporate body, different from its neighbors; its relations with these neighbors, whatever their nature, had to be based on this fact. And the neighbors, of course, sharing these principles, would not allow it to be otherwise. Also, following the pattern I have discussed above, the break in the relations with the parent group, left behind in the metropole, was not irrevocable and these relations remained in limbo. Once established on the frontier, a kin-group segment could strengthen itself by reactivating this dormant network of kin relations and use it to draw additional kinsmen to itself. The process was not restricted to kinship: political relations could be similarly reactivated. A dissident immigrant from a chiefly lineage, once established on the frontier, could appeal for support and supporters from his erstwhile competitors. And a disaffected royal retainer, out on the frontier in the hope of carving out a chieftaincy of his own, could, when politically convenient, renew the tie from the new comfortable distance by sending ambiguous gifts to his former masters, which they might interpret as tribute.

Such lingering relations of frontiersmen with parent groups provided a continuing connection with the metropole and the metropolitan identity provided a basis for building an identity on the frontier. Even escaped Bantu slaves in Somaliland created pseudo-kin groups on the frontier on the basis of having belonged to the same Somali masters (Cassanelli, Ch. 8). The connection with the metropole also gave the frontier settlers a historical base outside the frontier—a base upon which they could erect their solidarity in the new area, to which they could resort in the recruitment of new members, which they could elaborate and tailor to local circumstances when creating a charter for the new polity, and to which they could even appeal for political help. This relationship to the metropole could sometimes make the frontiersmen into the spearhead of an expanding metropole. As Newbury (Ch. 6) shows for Rwanda, escapees to the frontier from Rwanda often became eventually the local agents for Rwandan expansion into the frontier areas.

Thus, outside historical origins—real or claimed, of greater or lesser time depth—represented for the frontiersmen a kind of social and political capital. It is not surprising, then, that we find a constant reiteration of outside origins in African oral traditions; one never allowed oneself and others to forget that "we are from . . ." elsewhere. At the same time, however, these claims of alien origin had to be reconciled with the equally important but contradictory contention: that of "being first" in the area—a matter which I shall discuss presently in some detail.

THE FRONTIER AS INSTITUTIONAL VACUUM

As usually employed in the literature, the term frontier implies a "no-man's land"—yet one that is almost always inhabited by some kinds of "aboriginal" societies. The American frontier was a frontier to American settlers; to the Indians, it was their home. By the same token, the aggressive Iroquois expanded into a frontier that their victims saw as a homeland under attack. And so too with the frontier in Africa. The definition of the frontier as "empty" is political and made from the intruders' perspective. To most African frontiersmen—as to others—a frontier was an area in which they felt they could aspire to establish themselves, free of their metropolitan ties and without being beholden to new political masters. In this sense, they saw it as an institutional vacuum in which they could consider themselves not to be morally bound by institutional constraints. This was the conception. Whether the frontiersmen could or did succeed in their hopes is another question.

The essence of the frontier as a historical phenomenon lies in this: once outsiders have defined an area as a frontier and have intruded into it in order to settle in it, there begins a process of social construction that, if successful, brings into being a new society. The central thesis of this analysis is that most African societies arose out of such a conjuncture of events. And, further, that this process of building new societies, paralleled by the demise of established societies, has been a continuous one in African history.

This view focuses on a process. But between the aspiration to succeed on the frontier and its fulfillment lay a host of factors—geographical, ecological, demographic, and political—that made this process more or less likely to take place. Some areas in Africa lent themselves easily to the frontier process; others resisted it. The frontier was seldom an institutional vacuum, even if the frontiersmen saw it as such morally. The outcome of the immigrants' attempts at social construction on the frontier was necessarily affected by the political and cultural relations between metropole and frontier, the relative population densities of the societies involved, and the organization and strength of the "aboriginal" societies.

Frontiersmen usually came from an established society, which I refer to here as their metropole, and their co-frontiersmen came from the same or other metropoles abutting more or less closely on the frontier. Such a metropole could be a large state or a set of states, such as the Luba-Shankadi state for the Ekie (Fairley, Ch.2), the northern Nigerian emirates for the Ningi Muslim divines (Patton, Ch.7), or the Rwanda kingdom for its western frontier (Newbury, Ch.6). Or the metropoles could be quite small, as in the case of the various Goba polities (Lancaster, Ch.3) or the even smaller Kpelle chiefdoms (Murphy and Bledsoe, Ch.4). Or, as with Bantu slaves escaping from Somali lineages (Cassanelli, Ch.8), the metropole could be an acephalous system of autonomous kin groups. Also, the metropolitan societies could be stable or in a state of crisis. But ideologically, each provided for its frontiersmen the main outlines of an overall model of civic organization; even if the metropole were currently strife-ridden, the model contained the criteria for a "normal," effective, and legitimate political system. Relations in the metropoles were not accidental and ephemeral but had historical depth and sanction, with institutional constraints that prevented their being solely instrumental.

When immigrants moved out of the metropolitan political system to the frontier, they left behind them institutions that had a moral legitimacy and entered what was, morally, an institutional vacuum. The institutional legitimacies they had brought with them were now confined to within their own group, which was already bound by a solidarity that had made it move as a body in the first place. But even these legitimacies—lacking any external supports on the frontier—had, sooner or later, to be institutionalized in the new setting. This task of re-institutionalization was not without problems. The political culture they had brought with them made them no less subject to the systemic forces of fission than their parent body had been back home, while the consequences of fission were apt to be more serious, given the political insecurities of the frontier. But initially, the divisive tendencies were apt to be offset by solidarity in the face of common danger on the frontier and, not least, by the small size of the group and the consciousness of its vulnerability.

If the immigrants' own relations had a certain moral foundation, such a foundation was lacking in their relations with their hosts—some of them immigrants like themselves, others living in long-established societies. To the frontiersmen, moving in among aliens, the host population was part of the new environment with which they had to cope; the challenge was primarily pragmatic rather than moral (though pragmatism, of course, includes pragmatic coping by means that Westerners may define as "ritual"). But while the moral distance between new and old settlers was great, the cultural distance was apt to be small. It was certainly smaller on the recurrent interstitial internal frontier that concerns us here than it has usually been, historically, on most of the world's tidal frontiers—including Africa's own pre-historic tidal frontier on which the ancestors of most present-day Africans met the culturally alien Pygmoids, Bushmanoids, and Cushites. On the internal frontier, immigrants usually encountered a population that was much like them in culture and often in language. At the least, they shared the basic elements of the general pan-African political culture and, most likely, the local regional variant of it. Thus, the immigrant group was on the one hand free of moral and social constraints in the pursuit of its interests and, on the other, capable of dealing with the surrounding population in terms of common cultural understandings.

In what kinds of areas in Africa did the frontier process usually take place? In its most local, almost microcosmic expression, the process may be glimpsed in the segmentation of kin groups in acephalous societies, so widely reported in the African ethnographic literature. Here, a segment detached itself from the parent body and moved out into the no-man's land nearby, to found there an independent settlement. This has usually been analyzed as a process of structural replication: if the segment survived and grew, it became like its parent body and eventually split in its turn. But one can also see the matter in a frontier perspective: a group from a very local metropole constructed according to a pre-existing model a new petty polity which, however, was never an exact replica of the parent body. A cumulation of such departures from each preceding model might have produced, in the long term, a somewhat altered structure. This kind of "structural drift" might indeed have been one of the mechanisms by which such segmentary systems produced variations within the overall pattern.

Such a view of kin group segmentation as a micro-frontier process emphasizes its creative, and usually rather neglected, side. But when we see it as a variant of the frontier process, segmentation-as-replication represents the frontier process at its most conservative. The process did not lead to a radical detachment of the segment from its parent body. The new lineage *qua* petty polity remained largely within the institutional constraints of the local political system. Its relations with its neighbors, as with its parent body, continued to be bound by a previous history. Even if the new segment were situated at the very periphery of the system, it merely extended the system's boundaries. In brief, the new segment did not find itself in what it could regard as an institutional vacuum in which it could be free to construct a new society. Nor, consequently, was there in this situation the germ of a new ethnicity. Thus, overall, the process of local segmentation and of social construction on this quasi-frontier would have only produced a kind of accelerated perpetual micro-frontier cycle, in which each detached segment followed the parent model very closely and preserved it very faithfully.

To engage in significant new social construction on a frontier, a group had to disengage itself radically from the controls of its parent society and find an area whose political system would not preclude the building of an independent settlement. A true geographical frontierland, empty or nearly empty of all inhabitants and presenting an objective political vacuum, would allow this, as it did, for example, to the escaped Bantu slaves of nineteenth-century Somalia (Cassanelli, Ch.8) or to the heterogeneous immigrants of Mto Wa Mbu in early twentieth-century Tanganyika (Arens, Ch.9).

On populated frontiers, the intruders could overcome the constraints by sheer military superiority. Such was the case on most of the tidal frontiers in history, where the intruders had to deal with fundamentally different populations, or as, for example, Russians did with Siberians, Spanish conquistadors with Indians, Boers with southern African populations, or southeast Asian farmers with "tribals." But the internal African frontier usually involved technologically similar populations, so that the intruders' success on the frontier depended less on physical superiority and more on organizational and political skills. In African ethnography, the classic example of this kind of organizational superiority are the Alur of the Zaire-Sudan border, who founded petty states at the presumed invitation of politically atomized populations because they possessed, and were recognized by their hosts as possessing, the skills of chieftaincy (Southall 1956). And throughout the savanna area of southern Central Africa, many small and large states owed their emergence to immigrant founders who took over local political systems and remolded them to their own purposes by skillful political maneuvering (Vansina 1966). The Ekie (Fairley, Ch.2), the Goba (Lancaster, Ch.3), and the Ningi (Patton, Ch.7) also illustrate the importance of political rather than military factors in the initial stages of the foundation of such frontier polities.

Whether an area could become a frontier, then, depended on the potential balance of forces and skills between intruders and hosts. In this respect, the relative political vacuum of the "no-man's lands," at the peripheries of large polities or wedged between them, probably offered some of the least problematic frontier prospects. Such areas were often a systemic product of the territorial organization of the larger African centralized polities. What one might call the "technology of reach" of African polities—that is, the available material and administrative technology of political control—imposed clear limits on the political penetration that the center could achieve both in geographical extent and, locally, in depth. Limitations in transport, in speed of communication, in methods of rec-ord-keeping, and in the flexibility and reliability of military resources—all these meant that even as a polity expanded, the center's control over the new peripheries was weaker and less direct.

These limitations of power by distance is at the root of the repetitive pattern that one finds in African centralized polities larger than the most petty ones (see, e.g., Vansina 1962a, Lloyd 1965; for a revealing example of the dynamics, see Vansina 1978). At its maximum extension, the pattern may be represented as a structure of concentric "circles" of diminishing control, radiating from the core. The core, usually the area of earliest politi-cal consolidation, continued to be ruled directly by the central authority. Then came an inner area of closely assimilated and politically integrated dependencies. Beyond it was the circle of relatively secure vassal polities and what Mair (1977:14) calls "subordinate allies" who enjoyed a certain degree of autonomy. This circle merged with the next circle of tribute-pay-ing polities straining at the center's political leash. Beyond, the center's control became increasingly symbolic, confining itself to fewer and fewer functions. Increasingly, the etiquette of domination prevailed over its sub-stance. And beyond a certain point, control became erratic, ineffective and, finally, impossible—in the way of classical "marches." The center could only practice political intimidation and extract sporadic tribute through institutionalized raiding or undisguised pillage. Finally, came the potential frontier—areas beyond the effective reach of the metropolitan power, which nevertheless sometimes conceitedly claimed to control it.

This deep frontier was often a political "no-man's land" separating a large metropole from neighboring metropoles, whose own zones of con-trol were similarly structured, and often serving as a mutually useful buf-fer between them. Had the contact between them been more direct (say in the manner imposed by the clear-cut lines of modern state boundaries), the frequent pretensions of African polities to "being first" among their neigh-bors would have easily led to unwanted continuous clashes.

On the above pattern, there also existed quasi-frontier areas within the boundaries of the larger polities, namely, in the interstices of their territorial structures. Each vassal and tributary polity usually had its own peripheral frontier-like areas into which immigrants could move. But the chances of constructing an independent polity so much within the sphere of the metropole's power were slim. The chances were better in areas just beyond the peripheries of metropolitan control. These were good areas for the incubation of new petty polities, close enough to the metropole to be bereft of powerful local competing polities (which the metropole would not tolerate) but far enough to be beyond its active concerns.

Above all, a new frontier polity had the best chance of survival as long as it remained modest in size and ambitions, was willing to feign subordination to more powerful neighbors, and, in the long run, bide its time. The early Ekie polity (Fairley, Ch.2), the Namainga kingdom of the Goba (Lancaster, Ch.3), the Mallam state in the Ningi mountains of northern Nigeria (Patton, Ch.7), and some of the escaped Bantu slave polities in Somalia (Cassanelli, Ch.8) insured their survival that way in the precarious early years of their existence. The frontier sustained them for periods that were long enough for them to solidify politically and to work out the necessary cultural syntheses that could result in new embryonic ethnicities. Their chances for further political expansion and their transformation into large states arose when the inevitable metropolitan troubles came.

In sum, frontier areas at the peripheries of metropoles were a recurrent phenomenon, a systemic accompaniment to the formation, expansion, and stabilization of successful African polities. Large polities—themselves often having risen on the frontiers of declining ones—created new frontiers that in turn nurtured their future rivals. This process of creation of societies and frontiers assured a continuing existence side by side of metropolitan and frontier cultures. And the communication and interplay between them made for the persistence, reproduction, and reinvigoration of the frontier pattern in African political culture as a whole.

So much for the broad picture. Within it, there are details worth a closer look, for the calculus of forces in any particular area was apt to be complex. For example, Verdon (1983:102ff) has pointed out, in his conceptually innovative study of political formation among the Ewe of Ghana, that new communities could more readily spring up within the boundaries of a state than within the neighborhoods of village polities; the reason was that states could control such new settlements, whereas small polities rightly saw them as potential rivals and therefore would nip them in the bud. Thus, states could also harbor within their borders potential political formations that might, some day, come into their own. But with respect to the frontier process being examined here, it is clear that what states would not allow within their boundaries was the creation of frankly autonomous settlements, either by their own subjects or by intruders from other polities. At the same time, the very far peripheries of large states were not necessarily hospitable to such autonomous settlements either. Such utterly autonomous areas had political systems of their own, and these systems varied in their tolerance of and their capacity to obstruct new independent settlements.

Regions occupied by uncentralized, acephalous political systems, embracing agglomerations of small-scale polities (sometimes as small as autonomous lineages), contained interstitial areas between the small polities which were open to intrusion—both as a near frontier for small offshoots of local polities and as a deep frontier for immigrants from outside. Some regions in Africa seem to have been characterized over the centuries by this kind of political ecology. A well-documented example is the Upper Nile area where Zaire, Uganda, and Sudan converge. Here, many groups show the ethnic ambiguities we have spoken about and the organizational features of emerging frontier polities examined throughout our analysis (for a striking example, see the agglomeration of groups known as the Madi, described by Middleton 1955). But, as Verdon shows, small-scale polities might be especially watchful about the emergence of new potential rivals. Unless the immigrant group were able to defy local organized groups, the solution for it was to be absorbed into the local political system. No frontier process would then take place.

Such absorption was often inescapable when the local political system was one or another variant of the widespread "segmentary" system, of which the classic and orderly ethnographic exemplars are the Nuer of the Sudan (Evans-Pritchard 1940) and the Tiv of Nigeria (Bohannan 1954, Bohannan 1958). Such a system encompassed the various autonomous segments within a large conceptual scheme: the segments were all related in different degrees to one another through a ramifying and mostly fictitious genealogy. This kind of political integration made the area unreceptive to intrusive settlement by independent immigrants from beyond the system's boundaries; the system allowed the small and otherwise divided polities to spring jointly into action when outsiders impinged on any of them or on their common territory. Small bands of strangers arriving from outside would be ejected, or "adopted" as junior and subordinate pseudo-kinsmen and fitted into their hosts' genealogy, or allowed to place themselves as clients under the protective domination of an established lineage or community, as happened among the Nuer (Gough 1971). In all these cases, instead of founding an independent settlement, the immigrants would find themselves incorporated into an established network of small polities acting as kin groups.

In what has become a classic article on the processes by which states may grow out of "stateless" systems, Horton (1972) shows that it is not areas with integrated segmentary systems such as the above but rather areas of independent small-scale polities that provided the best environment in which larger-scale polities might emerge. Instead of the pseudo-brotherhood of the segmentary systems, these areas provided a hierarchy in which resident "firstcomers" could claim superiority over immigrant latecomers. The kind of polity formation that interests Horton is one in which an established community grows politically by incorporating weak immigrants. What interests us here is a different and earlier stage of the process, involving a different perspective: how could an immigrant community get established in the first place, so that it might then grow by incorporating other groups (immigrant or established) in the locality—this in an area of small independent polities (as small as kin groups of several score members)? Many—probably most—groups moving into such an area would be forced to attach themselves permanently to local groups as clients. But if the area offered wide and empty interstitial tracts for autonomous settlement and the immigrant group were sufficiently strong (or the local groups sufficiently weak), it might become yet another small independent unit on the local political arena, thus fulfilling its frontier aspirations. Such indeed was the case with the BaShu (Packard, Ch. 5), the Ekie (Fairley, Ch. 2), and the Muslim mallams of Ningi (Patton, Ch. 7), and, on a more local scale of movement, with some of the Kpelle (Murphy and Bledsoe, Ch. 4) and the Goba (Lancaster, Ch. 3). Once established, such communities would have the possibility of growing through processes like those envisioned by Horton.

The above process presupposes that the area was not so physically overcrowded that any attempt at settlement would have led to immediate impingement on one or more established groups. For overcrowding might well result in an accelerated political consolidation and consequently the end of the local internal frontier, as Gluckman (1963) suggests in his theory of the rise of the Zulu kingdom in South Africa in the early 19th century. Before the late 18th century, the Natal was a region in which small pastoral polities co-existed in balance, if not always in peace, with one another. But increasing overcrowding led both to increasing impingement upon others' territories and fiercer resistance to such impingement. With the resulting rise in warfare, some polities came to dominate others, and of these the Zulu kingdom proved to be the most successful. This led to the end of the open frontier in Natal and to an expansion of the Zulu kingdom. It also led, in turn, to the creation of new frontier areas. In classic "domino-effect" fashion, the Zulu expansion set into motion the displacement, over thousands of miles of territory, of large numbers of people and polities into other lands that, to them, became frontier areas; in the process, new polities were founded, which in turn pushed other peoples on to other frontiers.

The repercussions of Zulu expansion represent an unusually dramatic acceleration of the frontier process, involving an unusually large area. Normally, the process has been more localized and discrete. What areas, then, were apt to have been most propitious to this latter process? They were areas of low or moderate population densities (within the range imposed by traditional African subsistence techniques), not so crowded as to preclude independent settlement in interstitial areas but populated enough to have potential followers available for incorporation in the course of future growth. To make new autonomous settlement in them possible, such areas would have had to contain either groups of truly negligible power (e.g., hunters and gatherers) or agglomerations of weak, independent, or very weakly integrated polities. Essentially, such areas would have had to offer both physical and political room in which one could proceed to the construction of a new polity. These conditions might have prevailed both over large continuous areas and in the interstices between large polities.

PRE-EXISTING MODELS OF THE SOCIAL ORDER AND ITS CULTURAL REPRODUCTION

While utopians (who usually live in metropoles) have often been attracted by the idea of the frontier, few frontiersmen are utopians. Many things push them out into the frontier, but the yearning to construct a designed and utterly new social order is very rarely one of them. Most often, the impulse that carries people to the frontier is culturally (if not necessarily politically) a conservative one—to secure a way of life that is culturally legitimate and desirable but that is, for some reason, unattainable at home. Hence, the main challenge in social construction on the frontier is usually to replicate metropolitan patterns in terms favorable to oneself. In this sense, and in a broad culture-historical perspective, the frontier may act to conserve, reinforce, and revitalize the central values of the regional political culture.

The general point being made here is obvious: frontiersmen bring with them pre-existing conceptions of social order and the society that they construct cannot be explained without reference to this model. The model of social order that American frontiersmen carried with them was radically different from that carried by African frontiersmen—and so were the societies that they constructed. All social arrangements, in brief, have a history behind them. The point would be trivial were it not so often denied in practice by the functionalist assumption that has often shaped anthropological analysis—the assumption that the explanation for the fundamental features of an existing social order is to be sought in the here and the now, in the workings of a social system treated as an isolate in space and time.

Let us take, for example, the rather "despotic" official cast of even small-scale chieftaincies in Africa. The prevalence of this "despotism" is something of a puzzle from a functionalist perspective, for the elaborate symbolic accoutrements of its absolutism are quite out of keeping with the frequently small scale of the political systems in which it is found. From a functionalist standpoint, one would assume *a priori* that the realities of power relations in small face-to-face societies should result in far more egalitarian systems, all the more in societies created under frontier conditions. Yet the non-functionalist alternative explanations are not very satisfactory either. One such explanation of this "despotism" is given by the anthropologist Murdock (1959), who sees it as the result of the diffusion of what he calls "African despotism." Some historians (e.g., Oliver and Fage 1962) have also attributed to diffusion the prevalence in Africa of "divine kingship" (which Murdock subsumes under his "despotism")—with the improbable touch of deriving it from ancient Egypt. But modern

anthropology is uneasy about making simple diffusion account for the
occurrence over such large distances of such complicated phenomena as
the character of chieftaincy, as if institutions diffused in the same way as
pottery styles. Principles of political rule, though they do "diffuse" in
some sense, have a tight functional relationship with other cultural com-
plexes. Which takes us back full circle to functionalism.

The answer must go beyond both the mechanistic assumptions of continent-wide diffusionism and the nearsighted vision of parochial functionalism. The similarities across Africa are too complex to have simply arisen
from direct diffusion, yet they are too great to have developed through
repeated coincidence, again and again, independently. The explanation
must be sought in some kind of functionalist historicity. We must see the
societies in question from a new perspective, as having been *constructed*—not
out of whole cloth but from a cultural inventory of symbols and practices
that were brought from a metropole and that pre-dated any particular society being observed. Much of this construction-to-a-model has usually been
quite conscious, for the model was near at hand and fresh in memory. Thus,
a "despotic" model—though pragmatically tempered in its workings in a
mature polity by developed checks and balances—may be resurrected in
stark form as an ideology in the institutional vacuum of the frontier (though
there too tempered by various factors that will be examined below). In this
perspective, the small scale of a polity, rather than determining its ideological flavor, imposes limits on the application of the "despotic" model which,
under different conditions, can bloom more fully (we shall return to this
"despotic" pattern, which is better dealt with as a variety of patrimonialism, in the section on " 'Sacred Chieftainship' and the Inter-Dependence of
Rulers and Subjects").

All this argues for the necessity of a regional cultural perspective and,
beyond that, a Sub-Saharan one, and it argues for the use of functionalist
analysis *within* the givens of a culture-historical tradition. This requires an
essentially Boasian view of culture as a sociological variable which is a
historical and regional product. And it means the abandonment of the
Malinowskian illusion that general explanations of social facts can be directly built on the data from one or many specific societies, without first
passing the data through the filter of a regional culture-historical analysis.

Cultures and societies are historical and regional products, local variations of regional patterns. We take this for granted when we deal with
Europe. It goes without saying, for example, that events in an Occitan
village in the 14th century, such as Montaillou, involving Catholic and
Albigensian convictions (Le Roy Ladurie 1978), are not *sui generis* and do
not come into being merely to "serve" locally some general sociological
function. That is, in Europe, where we know there was a history, we
automatically begin with the region and see communities in it as local,
sometimes idiosyncratic, expressions of the regional culture and history.
In Africa (and wherever else we had to "discover" history), we had been

forced by necessity to proceed in reverse order. We began with each society as a unique "tribe" and then, having noticed the similarities among neighboring tribes, discovered cultural regions. And we have let the sequence of our discoveries order the direction of our explanations.

Once we accept that the African frontiersmen brought with them a cultural model of the society they wished to construct, we make the resulting society a product of the region. The frontier process then becomes one of cultural self-reproduction on a regional scale, all the more so since frontier societies are apt to derive not from a single society but to draw upon and re-synthesize several idiosyncratic local expressions of common cultural principles. At the sub-continental level, cultural reproduction occurred through the constant interdigitation, over time, among the regional frontier networks. Thus, overall, the numerous local internal frontiers provided the means for the self-reproduction of certain cultural principles of organization that are shared throughout Sub-Saharan Africa. Some of these principles, as we have seen, underlay the mechanisms by which people were ejected onto the frontier. They also shaped the emergent frontier societies. And as these societies matured, they worked to eject new people onto new frontiers.

In a superb summation of the patterns of African personality, LeVine (1976) has presented certain commonalities of African behavior and thought. Unfortunately, no comparable delineation of a pan-African pattern of cultural principles exists in the literature. The task, if rigorously done, would require a combination of enormous scholarship, enormous boldness, and enormous theoretical sophistication. At present, one can only note pragmatically certain themes that appear again and again in the African ethnographic literature and that would form part of the cultural "baggage" that African frontiersmen would have repeatedly brought with them to their new settlements. Some of them are mentioned by LeVine, who casts them in a psychological rather than, as here, in a cultural idiom. It is this "baggage" that made these frontier societies specifically African, in contrast to frontier societies constructed within other cultural traditions. We have already discussed above those organizing principles that served specifically to eject people out of their groups. Here are some others.

It has often been remarked by ethnographers, more often in informal talk than in print, that African cultures are suffused with a sense of hierarchy in social, political, and ritual relations (for a general statement, see LeVine 1976:119-20). This holds true even for those "segmentary" or "acephalous" or "stateless" African societies that are sometimes labelled (or rather mislabelled) as "egalitarian." What appears to be egalitarianism was a product of the relative smallness of politically sovereign groups. Relations among them were inevitably non-hierarchical and attempts by one group to dominate another were resisted—by the potential victim. But such structural equality is no more a sign of an egalitarian ideology than a balance of power among nations is a sign of an ideological renunciation of domination. Even such notoriously "egalitarian" peoples as the Tiv were not impervious to the appeal of the trappings of chieftaincy, which some of them sought in the Jukun kingdom (Bohannan 1953:35ff). And, as Gough (1971) has stressed, the "egalitarian" ethic governing the relations among Nuer kin groups was not extended to their dependent immigrant clients.

The measure of hierarchy in such "acephalous" societies lies not in the relations between autonomous groups but in relations within them. Within families, kin groups, civic and "secret" societies, for example, seniors stood over their juniors and patrons over their clients as clearly as they did in other African societies. Structurally, the hierarchical ethic was expressed in the pattern of "being first" (on which I shall say considerably more later). One could be "first" in a great variety of contexts—age, gender, sequence in polygynous marriages, order of initiation, and so on. Even among the Igbo, to whom the term "egalitarian" has so often been applied, the sense of hierarchy was such that "even seniority by a day" in the order of birth was taken into account (Njaka 1974:59); and the hierarchical "title societies" provided the stage on which people competed for status (Uchendu 1965:16ff).

A hierarchical ethic means that one finds it normal to be at either side of a culturally sanctioned hierarchical relationship. Behaviorally, it means that whether one is subordinate or in command is accepted as being a matter of circumstance, maneuver, and optimizing strategy. Psychologically, it means that one is both comfortable about exercising authority and not discomfitted by subordination to authority. In the realm of values, it means that one prizes both one's standing over others and one's being attached to a superior power—hence, the inherent value that was usually granted to chieftainship and kingship in Africa. To be under no one at all, and dependent on no one, was to be utterly without status, in effect, to be like a "slave" (in sharp contrast to the Western idea of "slavery" as a denial of autonomy). The Suku of Zaire, who had a king, would taunt their Mbala neighbors, whose largest sovereign unit was the independent community, that they were "like slaves because they had no king" (Kopytoff and Miers 1976:17). In a broader context, Mazrui (1967) has referred to this pattern as "the monarchical tendency in African political culture."

In brief, hierarchy imposed itself upon any relationship involving any degree of dependence. This precluded the emergence, on the African frontier, of the kind of egalitarianism that Turner saw, mistakenly, as flowing more or less directly out of the frontier experience. African frontier communities began with some internal hierarchy and as they grew the hierarchy expanded in range.

Another principle of African political culture was the tendency for certain positions of authority to be held for life. Heads of kin groups and cult groups, incumbents of political and ritual offices, heads of civic and "secret" societies, and chiefs and kings (and nowadays presidents)—all were expected to remain in authority until they died. This applied, it may be noted, not to any position of authority but to what might be called the "terminal position" within a given structure—a position whose incumbent could move no higher within, say, the lineage, or the chieftaincy, or the cult group (and, in modern Africa, a church or a country). The principle is related to the principle of hierarchy: he who had been the most senior within a given context could not drop down, as he would have had to do if he had to give way, while alive, to a junior as successor. This made removal from office, and especially demotion, a culturally difficult operation. One consequence was that the easiest option for a junior competitor was to secede from his superior or to kill him. For the same reason, a king wishing to remove the head of a subordinate chieftaincy would often find it easiest to kill him (which, in turn, meant that the chief's offense had to be very serious indeed, and minor transgressions and abuses of power were tolerated). On the frontier, the principle of life-tenure meant that the founder of a settlement remained its senior member for life, making equality with any subsequent settlers impossible. New settlers had to come in as subordinates, or take over, or try to establish their own autonomous settlement.

Hierarchy in relations within a group was accompanied by corporate unity in its relations without. We have already discussed the submergence of the social identity of individuals in the group, above all the kin group. This also meant that social and political positions held by individuals— chiefships, titles, administrative posts, councillorships, ritual offices, etc.— tended to become vested in the kin group of the first incumbent and to remain so vested, becoming part of the corporate estate of the kin group. Similarly, rights and wealth acquired by persons in their individual capacity tended to become absorbed into their corporate kin group's estate. There was, however, a variant to this pattern: a person's individually acquired estate could also provide the base for the estate of a new corporate group of which he then became the founder; that is, private property was still transformed into corporate property, but the corporation in this case consisted of the individual's descendants. As Barnes (1986) points out in her study of the politics of the Lagos suburb of Mushin, this principle resulted in the founding of new corporate property-holding groups in the city by immigrants from rural areas. On the African frontier, the principle had a similar effect: what the first settler created on the frontier—the settlement, the control over land, the title, the headship over other immigrants—became the corporate estate of the new kin group that he founded. Thus was replicated on the frontier—including the modern urban frontier—the structure of metropolitan corporate kin groups and, with it, the rest of the apparatus of authority.

Another widespread African pattern (to be sure, not only African) was the use of the kinship idiom as an appropriate metaphor for political relations, including relations of authority. In the modern West, metaphors of kinship convey intimacy, closeness, and nurture. In African usage, the range of connotations carried by kin terms is much wider and the connotations tap dimensions that are quite different from Western ones. To give a modern African example, when President Amin of Uganda told President Nyerere of Tanzania in a telegram that he thought of him as his "wife," it is obvious that the metaphor was conveying other than Western meanings. Among the Ekie (Fairley, Ch.2), the old ritual chief, the *tshite,* who had been coopted into a subordinate role by the immigrant Luba king, was also referred to as the king's "wife," in the sense of "helper." In both cases, the metaphor of "wife" emphasizes status in a way that it could not in Western usage.

In Africa, such terms as "mother" and "sister" convey sentiments of warmth, nurture, and attachment (and a man can thus be said to be "a mother" to someone). Other terms—such as "father," "mother's brother," "brother," or "brother-in-law"—tap such formal dimensions of status as authority, subordination, obligation, obedience, alliance, etc. (for an especially suggestive examination of these dimensions, see Fernandez 1971). Thus, kin terms lend themselves very well to metaphorical use in African political discourse. Relations of subordinates with superiors, of residents with village heads, of tenants with landlords, of "slaves" with masters, of subjects with chiefs, of chiefs with chiefs, of subordinate chiefs with high chiefs and kings—all these were easily and very subtly expressed in the idiom of kinship. Murphy and Bledsoe (Ch.4) analyze the intricate political uses to which the metaphor of the "mother's brother-sister's son" relationship can be put among the patrilineal Kpelle. The relationship connotes a multiplicity of meanings: hierarchy but also a degree of equality, supportiveness but also potential competitiveness. Hence, the "mother's brother-sister's son" metaphor is simultaneously appropriate to the authority relationship between chief and subject, to the hierarchical but mutually supportive alliance between a patron and the client he wishes to attract, and to the potentially competitive relationship between people in a politically ambiguous environment, such as that of the frontier. The range of meanings embedded in the metaphor thus accommodates itself to subtle shifts in the content of the relationship and also allows for its rhetorical manipulation.

A pattern often referred to in the literature, and first formally described and named by Cunnison (1951:33ff), is that of "perpetual kinship" in the relations among rulers. To state it briefly: when, for example, the founder of a new segment of a polity was in a certain relationship—say that of brother or son or nephew—to the head of the polity, their respective successors continued to stand in that relationship to one another. In effect, the original kin relationship subsequently defined the relationship between the two offices. In practice, of course, the political relationship need not be based on an actual historical kin relationship. The original kin relationship might have been a metaphor in the first place, and relationships with new polities could also be cast in the idiom of kinship and so perpetuated. The significance for political dynamics is that political relations can be stated in terms of kinship and vice versa, that each can suggest the other, and that there is therefore a tendency for political relations to merge and overlap with kinship relations. When my real son is called my "son," he obeys me and pays me tribute, and when someone pays me tribute, I can metaphorically call him my "son." But when a subordinate pays me tribute and is called my "son," it is not always clear which side of the equation generated the other: is the tribute the result of a relationship of real "perpetual kinship," or did the tribute lead to the relationship via a metaphor? There were here possibilities for ambiguities and for their political exploitation. For example, Packard (Ch. 5) shows how among the BaShu of Zaire, different interpretations of a founding myth could hinge on this fact that "son" is often a metaphor for "servant" or "slave"; a group said to have been founded by a "son" of a chief could be seen either as a worthy descendant of the parent chieftaincy or as its inferior offshoot.

It is a commonplace in the modern West to advise one to avoid doing business with friends. In much of the rest of the world, friends are precisely the ones with whom one seeks to do business. Within a small community in which lives are intertwined with respect to most activities, the Western advice is in any case impossible, while outside the moral community, where business relations are an amoral free-for-all, to deal with strangers is inherently dangerous. Consequently, the modern Western tendency to separate the realm of sentiment from the realm of economic relations and material exchange did not exist in traditional Africa (see LeVine 1976:121-23 on what he calls the "emphasis on material transactions in interpersonal relations"). Rather, the network of kinship relations intermeshed with a network of precisely measured material transactions, of obligatory gifts and counter-gifts that could be analogous to (and conceptualized in the same way) as tributary relations. A similar intermeshing existed between politics and material exchange, and this further facilitated the integration of political and kinship relations through the common medium of material transactions. On the frontier, new relations could thus be initiated within any one of the three realms—of kinship, of politics, and of material relations—and later redefined into one or both of the others.

Unlike some of the themes I discussed earlier, these particular cultural themes do not seem to be easily attributable to frontier conditions and one can only treat them in an analysis as cultural givens of hoary antiquity and undeterminable origin. What they did do was to provide some of the constants on which on-going African social relations rested and on which any new social relations were built. On the frontier, their role in the construction of a new social order gave that order the most elementary kind of legitimation—the shaping of the society into something that is perceived, culturally, as "normal" and "human."

ADHERENTS AS KINSMEN: AFRICAN KIN GROUPS
AS A FRONTIER PHENOMENON

To be a frontiersman is to be an entrepreneur. On the American frontier, where, typically, independent individuals and small nuclear families lived an isolated existence in a wilderness, the entrepreneurship was largely technological and economic. On the African frontier, the contrast with the homeland was not so great as to call for technological innovations, and the immigrant kin group's ways of making a living were similar to its neighbors' (which may not be irrelevant to the relative weakness of technological innovation in Africa, discussed by Austen and Headrick 1983). Entrepreneurship on the African frontier was above all social and political, devoted to achieving independence or favorable terms of dependence, acquiring adherents, and making alliances. In this section, we shall examine the acquisition of adherents in the early phases of the settlement, when the small immigrant group faced the imperative of surviving and growing as a group of kinsmen and pseudo-kinsmen. In the next section, I shall turn to the problem of adherents when the settlement had begun to grow into a significant polity.

The drive to acquire relatives, adherents, dependents, retainers, and subjects, and to keep them attached to oneself as a kind of social and political "capital," has often been remarked upon as characteristic of African societies and of African political processes (see, on this, Goody 1971, Kopytoff and Miers 1977). The mirror-image of this drive is the search for patrons and protectors and a readiness to attach oneself to a superior power. The two pursuits may, of course, be often conducted at the same time. Indeed, the oral traditions about the establishment of polities usually show the founders to begin their career on the frontier by placing themselves under the patronage of their hosts even while seeking adherents of their own. But eventually, one of the two paths had to predominate: that toward independence and that toward attachment to an existing polity. If attachment were chosen, the safest course was to subordinate oneself to the strongest polity around. But this placed a weak immigrant group as "latecomers" at the bottom rung of the polity's hierarchy. An incipient or middling polity might, so to speak, offer better terms; but here, the greater equality of forces made probable an eventual competition for primacy or fission and independence. Oral traditions often speak of such an initial alignment, followed by separation and conflict leading to independence. Once independence was chosen, frontier entrepreneurship had the task of increasing the group's size.

The search for adherents as a source of power has obviously existed in various forms in innumerable societies. Nevertheless, the pattern is particularly congruent with conditions on a frontier which is uncontrolled and unpoliced by a metropole—the larger the group, obviously, the more secure it is. It has often been remarked that in their largely underpopulated continent, African societies have usually faced a shortage of people amidst an abundance of land; and the latter allowed them to secure their livelihood by mobile and extensive exploitation of the land through shifting cultivation or, less often, pastoralism. Goody (1971:30ff) has persuasively argued that the result of this in the political sphere has been that "chiefship tended to be over people rather than over land; these a leader had to try to attract as well as restrain." The effect of the shortage of people, it should be stressed here, was most pronounced under frontier conditions; and once the pattern established, it would, in turn, be reinforced by the periodic recurrence of these conditions. There is undoubtedly a relationship between this emphasis on social rather than geographical control and the lack of a rigid "rootedness" in physical space, previously mentioned as a pan-African cultural feature that made for the recurrence of the frontier.

All of this would perhaps hold for frontier areas on any continent. However, what we must account for here is the specifically African version of the pattern, a version in which the gathering-in of adherents is so closely interwoven with the kinship system. It would be futile to search for the origins of this African pattern, hidden as they are in an unrecoverable past. Nevertheless, the anthropological literature—notably Fortes (1953)—has suggested some of the elements that would enter into an explanation of the pattern and we shall elaborate further on these suggestions.

The point at issue is the prevalence and overwhelming importance in African social systems of the corporate kin group. This group has been commonly referred to as the "lineage," but this term carries with it so strong a connotation of "lines" of genealogical "descent"—which is how Westerners see these things—that its usefulness may well be coming to an end. One solution is to cling to this genealogical meaning but question whether "lineages" have really existed in Africa—as, e.g., does Kuper (1982). We prefer the less drastic solution of speaking instead of the corporate kin group, whose characteristics include corporate control of a body of resources, including in most cases the "ownership" of its members, and an ideology that makes ties modelled on kinship ties ("blood" being the usual idiom) the basis for its existence and for the induction of new members.

Fortes (1953) has drawn attention to the fact that African societies that are organized into such kin groups have traditionally been horticultural or pastoral and in "the middle range" of economic and technological development—neither hunters-gatherers nor societies with pronounced occupational specializations. It is, indeed, to such middle-range societies that the African frontier under discussion here had offered open land and open resources.

These middle-range societies were unlike hunting-gathering bands, where adding people after a certain point increased the strain on local resources and made it necessary to move on with inconvenient frequency.

Depending on transient circumstances, such a band would need at one time to acquire more members and at another to shed those it already had; hence, inflexible kinship-based rules of membership (for example, permanent membership by birth) was not congruent with the band's existence. Nor were frontier groups like the societies on the other side of complexity, with a great deal of individual economic specialization. In such societies, individuals produced wealth at clearly unequal rates, and this militated against a collective control of most resources. The group preferred to pull in the more productive and push out the less productive members; but the more productive for their part preferred to become more autonomous, while the less productive insisted on their rights to the group's resources. Here too, the situation militated against inflexible rules that automatically and with no further discrimination inducted people into the collectivity. When corporate kin groups do exist in such societies (as, e.g., in Korea—see Janelli and Janelli 1978), their corporateness is narrowed to a few specific matters (such as trade cooperation, hospitality, defence, or the maintenance of resources for ritual) rather than being functionally diffuse and totalistic, as it normally is in African corporate kin groups.

The conditions on the African frontier for immigrants from horticultural and pastoral middle-range societies were quite different. With the relative lack of differentiation in economic roles (sexual division of labor aside), every person was, *qua* unit of labor, more or less equal to every other person of the same sex; on the whole, each labor unit essentially supported himself or herself and produced a slight surplus beyond that. At the same time, given open resources, the addition of each new person brought with it no extra pressure on resources and did represent a slight economic gain. In brief, the marginal economic utility of each additional individual remained more or less constant, even if slight, so that each group could theoretically contemplate an endless expansion in its numbers. Consequently, recruitment of new members could be essentially undiscriminating.

Moreover, this economic calculus dovetailed with a similar social and political calculus. For in any uncentralized society, where political power hinges very directly on numbers, the search for adherents becomes a primary political impulse and competition for people a primary concern of political interaction. But competition for people by groups is inevitably inflationary: there is always someone who goes the last winner one better. Also, given endemic diseases, epidemics, warfare, and raiding, any given group's security in numbers was always precarious and never to be taken for granted; even the winners had to go on running for fear of falling back.

These conditions were most pronounced on the frontier, where, we claim, many of the central features of African social organization at the domestic and near-domestic level were forged and reforged in the course of African history. But many of these conditions also prevailed in mature and even politically centralized societies that enjoyed plentiful land resources and lacked pronounced full-time occupational specializations. As I have noted before, in these mature societies kin groups were also strikingly autonomous and engaged in political competition with minimal interference from the center. Thus, once again, we find a continuity between the pattern of the frontier and that of the metropole, each processually reinforcing the other. (To be sure, these conditions did change in some African societies, most particularly in the urbanized societies of the Sudanic belt, with consequent alterations in the relationships both within and between kin groups. But these alterations proceeded from an already established cultural base and with an expected cultural lag.)

All this makes it understandable why, traditionally, African kin groups had an almost insatiable demand for people and jealously guarded those they already had. Socially, this meant the existence of corporate groups of kinsmen, collectively holding resources, carefully enforcing their rights in persons, and being always on the lookout for new ways of increasing their membership. Thus, a very high proportion (usually over half) of customary court cases in Africa have to do with disputes over marriage, divorce, and bridewealth—matters that above all involve the social appropriation of progeny. In pre-colonial times, such concerns and such disputes gave substance to much of the relationship among kin groups. Every newborn was legally spoken for and eagerly appropriated at birth by one or another autonomous kin group; and the various rights over the child by the respective kin groups of each of its parents had to be clearly, often tortuously, defined. Similarly, the reproductive capacity of every woman was a resource to be appropriated from birth, later to become the subject of transactions—all the more so on the frontier, with its tendency to suffer from a shortage of women. Culturally, all this has produced a variety of elaborations of systems of rights in persons, so that these appropriations could be accomplished unambiguously, flexibly, and with a minimum of conflict.

The argument so far does not entirely answer the question of why the recruitment of people into these fundamental corporate units should have been done by way of kinship. In fact, it was not—especially not if we take kinship in its Western meaning. For kinship was one of several mechanisms. But what kinship did was to provide the model and the idiom for the others. The reason, we would suggest, lies in the sociology of group expansion on the frontier.

Once a new frontier group chose the path of autonomy, it faced simultaneously two problems in the early stages of expansion. On the one hand, to establish its independence, the new group had to assert its exclusiveness as "firstcomers" in its particular territory; on the other hand, it needed to expand its numbers to be able to stand up to neighboring groups and the readiest pool of people to draw upon for adherents was the local population. This posed a dilemma. There was little that a recently arrived group could offer to induce any but the very miserable to adhere to it; but if it did attract many adherents, the group might easily be swamped by them. The safest course, then, lay in expanding the kin group internally, by acquiring adherents who could qualify as kinsmen rather than by bringing in mere followers who, in time, might become competitors. Compared to the allegiance of strangers, rights over kinsmen were more reliable. At the same time, externally, one also sought alliances with other local groups, and these were best achieved through ties of kinship and marriage. In both instances, kinship provided a ready-made pattern for binding relations in a frontier area that otherwise represented an institutional vacuum for the newcomers.

Thus, the brunt of all the complexities of the social relations with one's frontier hosts was borne by transactions in kinship, that is, in various rights in persons. The African uses of kinship have been congruent with these complexities, showing a striking diversity in the ways in which rights in persons could be acquired, in the varieties of these rights, and in the ways in which different rights in the same person could be shared among different groups (for a discussion of this pattern in connection with African "slavery," see Kopytoff and Miers 1977:11ff).

Anthropologists have a set of terms, more or less agreed upon, that define the different kinds of reproductive arrangements by which kingroups perpetuate themselves by establishing their rights over the newborn—terms such as "matrilineal," "patrilineal," "non-unilineal," "cognatic," and so on. These reflect the anthropologist's need for an orderly typology and also satisfy the Western concern, when it comes to kinship, with "lines" and "descent." And, as typologies are meant to do, this one seeks to transform empirical variations into analytical uniformities. But one of the fundamental characteristics of African kinship systems lies precisely in the great variety of means by which rights-in-persons can be acquired and in the great proliferation in the variety of these rights. African kinship systems are best understood not in terms of norms but in terms of the range of actions that the systems permit.

The tendency throughout Sub-Saharan Africa has been to elaborate rights to the things that people can offer, to keep these rights flexible, separate, and divisible into subsidiary rights, and to transact in them in a great number of different ways. These rights have, at various times and places, been rights to people's domestic labor, to their agricultural labor, to portions of hunting produce, to residence, to exclusive or partial or transient sexual services, to sexual exclusion of others, to fertility, to total or sequential progeny, to marriageability of the progeny—to name but those that come most readily to mind. Much of this elaboration ultimately stems from the elaboration of rights over the reproductive forces—namely, women and their fertility, through which progeny is acquired.

A good example is provided by the Tiv of central Nigeria, studied by the Bohannans (1953:69-78) at a time when they had been engaged for a century in frontier expansion, and who would, in textbook categories, be simply classified as "patrilineal." In various places and at various times, the Tiv could call upon a large repertory of ways in which rights to the newborn could be acquired by kin groups. New kin group members could be born to wives that one had exchanged for women of one's own kin group, or born to wards, or to wives exchanged for wards, or to wives exchanged for a promise of women later, or to wives obtained by "cashing in" on a debt in women, or to wives acquired by payment in cattle (and, later, money), or to wives whose progeny was "divided" with another kin group. Among the Ijaw of the Niger delta, one could, depending on the size and mode of the marriage payments, acquire a consort whose progeny one had the right to affiliate to one's own kin group or one whose children went to her own kin group, or one whose children were divided by complicated formula between the two kin groups (Williamson 1962, Leis 1972). And in the Zambezi area, Lancaster (1971) has shown how the same ethnic group may shift back and forth, depending on circumstances, between marriages that, in one case, produce what anthropologists call "patrilineal descent" and, in another, "matrilineal descent."

Similar elaborations existed in the rights over women, both as daughters and wives. Not every frontier was likely to have a shortage of women as pronounced as, for example, in the communities of Bantu former slaves in Somaliland (Cassanelli, Ch.8); but many African systems of rights over women were as incomprehensibly complex to ordinary Westerners as were those elaborated there. In Dahomey (Herskovits 1938, I:300ff, Bohannan 1949), a half-score different kinds of clusters of such rights existed, each depending on minor variations in the nature of the transactions. One of these included the so-called "woman-marriage," in which a woman acquired the formal conjugal rights in another woman and, while allowing her to co-habit with a man, retained for herself the roles of legal husband and father to her progeny. Variations on "woman-marriage" appear sporadically throughout Africa, having been also reported, among others, for the Igbo (Uchendu 1965:50), and, across the continent in eastern Africa for the Nuer (Evans-Pritchard 1965:106ff) and the Nandi (Oboler 1980). In yet another permutation of these principles among the Lele of Zaire (Douglas 1951), a whole village, through its males, could corporately acquire similar "husband-father" rights in a female. As to transactions in sexual rights in women, their elaboration into strikingly complex and flexible systems has been most intensively studied in the Jos plateau of Nigeria and the Cameroon highlands; here, anthropologists have sought to convey the variety of arrangements by resorting to terms such as marriage by abduction, marriage by elopement, secondary marriages, serial or polyandrous marriages, brides on credit, and so on (Smith 1952, Sangree 1969, Tardits 1970, Muller 1976, Chalifoux 1979, Collard 1979).

These sometimes baroque elaborations on rights focusing on sex, labor, and progeny reflect a cultural readiness to allow for a great variety of very precise ways of securing various kinds and degrees of control over people. Most of the transactions involved the exchange of one or another kind of right-in-persons for wealth. And, indeed, the greater the wealth in a kin group, the greater was its capacity to expand its human "capital" and maximize its control over people. Wealth also allowed one to acquire not only selected rights in persons but entire persons as well, namely, in the acquisition of "slaves." African "slavery" was part of the larger system of the acquisition of rights-in-persons, of which kinship transactions were also a part, and kinship could, and did, overlap and even merge with "slavery" (see Kopytoff and Miers 1977). But their affinity was most pronounced in that both were part of a repertoire of ways of expanding one's group, of acquiring people whose diverse statuses merged, often imperceptibly, into one another—relatives, quasi-relatives, adoptees, dependents, adherents, retainers, and clients.

Some readers will note that the set of frontier conditions we are speaking about here—namely, open resources and a sparse population—are also the conditions postulated by Nieboer (1910), in an often quoted book, as the prerequisites for the development of slavery. According to Nieboer, since open resources allow people to pursue an independent existence, labor is not available to those who wish to exploit it except through compulsion—hence, the development of compulsory labor and therefore chattel slavery. What the theory lacks is a political dimension. As classical frontier theory has so often stressed, it is precisely the open land and resources of the frontier that make compulsion of adherents extremely difficult. Rather than being compelled, followers more often have to be seduced. Thus, while it is true that such conditions are likely to make social groups desire more people, only rather complex societies, with well-developed systems of compulsion and control over movement, can resort to slavery to satisfy this desire. For small autonomous groups, including those on the frontier, the means of acquiring and retaining people have to be rather more subtle. And the goals in acquiring people involved political considerations no less, and often more, than economic and labor considerations. On the African frontier, culturally and historically, kinship ties served in this as both the means and the ends.

All the African varieties of incorporation had a ritual side to them, and the rituals were similar to and sometimes identical with those of kinship: they established some kind of "blood" affinity. The model of the group as an association of ritually connected "blood-kinsmen" thus remained, giving African kin groups the shape, ideologically if not structurally, of what we have classically come to call by the rather irrelevant term "lineage" or "descent group" and which is more realistically referred to by the looser term "kin group."

For a kin group on the frontier, indefinite expansion was desirable for external reasons, namely, those of competition with other kin groups. But the expansion posed some internal problems for the group. The principles of its internal cohesion were of a kind most appropriate to groups of intimate, face-to-face interaction. Once the kin group reached a size in which sub-groups within it began to crystallize into potential factions, it inevitably ran into administrative problems. The cultural forces that, back home, had led to conflicts within the parent group and to the ejection of a segment to the frontier, were now coming to the fore in the new setting and tearing apart the grown kin group.

One solution was, once again, to "segment," that is, to split the group into two or more smaller kin groups that replicated it structurally. The other solution was to introduce a greater hierarchy within the group. Thus, the true "blood" descendants of the original core group, or the elder line among them, might arrogate to itself greater authority, and the power of junior, or adopted, or "slave" lines might be reduced. But given the availability of resources on the frontier, this solution did not always work—those who continued to be formally defined as "brothers" might prefer to split off rather than to submit to the weakening of their position. Another solution was to begin acquiring adherents that, at the outset and unambiguously, would have a clearly subordinate status. This strategy was more appropriate after the frontier group had established itself sufficiently well that it could offer enough protection to new adherents to be attractive to them yet be sufficiently sure of itself not to be too anxious for their support. Strangers seeking a haven or acquired "slaves" (and their descendants) could be frankly treated as permanent legal juniors and dependents. The group could then expand, yet shield itself from the dissensions that would normally accompany expansion in a less differentiated group.

Thus, the institutional emphasis, both on the frontier and in mature societies, on acquiring persons—by reproducing kinsmen, adopting adherents, purchasing "slaves," and attracting strangers—was congruent with conditions of competition among small autonomous kin groups and it also could bring about considerable formal inequality even at very petty levels of political organization. This gave African frontier societies an authoritarian flavor that Turner's American frontier so clearly lacked.

The inequality, however, had to be instituted and maintained with circumspection, for frontier conditions also made it relatively easy for dissatisfied adherents to leave. Hence, no matter how low their formal status in crucial matters of authority, the adherents had to be well treated in everyday life—usually as quasi-kinsmen. An important aspect of good treatment was to make knowledge of their precise status a strictly internal matter. A secret guarded by autonomous kin groups, particularly in the uncentralized African societies, has always been the secret of "who is" and "who isn't" a real relative, as opposed to a "stranger" or "slave." Vis-à-vis the outside world, the strangers could hold their heads high by being publicly defined as relatives. But in all this there remained an unimplemented authoritarianism that could come to the surface once the pragmatic conditions changed. In mature societies, organized on a larger scale, escape by slaves and adherents was more difficult, and one could afford to let the formal inequality manifest itself more openly in everyday life. (With the arrival of colonial control in these societies, when the dissatisfied dependents could again easily leave, circumspection about dependent statuses and the camouflaging of them in the idiom of kinship reasserted itself).

Thus, kinship as the idiom and the template for political relations was built into the frontier process, reinforced by the nature of the need for adherents. When one was in search of group-members, one looked for total persons, so to speak, who could offer a generalized loyalty rather than a functionally specific one; the "services" one sought could not be hired on a temporary or contractual basis. For such a relationship, the kinship model is most appropriate. In this respect, the typical African structures of political dependence were fundamentally different from the feudalism of Western Europe, where many of the relations were strictly contractual and functionally specific, permitting a vassal, for example, to owe obligations to more than one suzerain. By contrast, in the African pattern (as also in the misnamed "feudalisms" of such places as Japan), there was a primary political allegiance that was functionally diffuse and indivisible and exclusive—involving the kind of "primordial" allegiance to which kinship ties easily lend themselves.

But the kinship model for relations of authority carried with it some built-in ambiguities and dangers, for the model made an equation between political distance and kinship distance. Retainers whose subordination was expressed by their status of junior pseudo-kinsmen might in time demand to share power by claiming to be real kinsmen of junior status. And, in a reverse process, the dominant kin group might claim that a junior branch of the kin group had no legal claims whatever to political power because it was in fact a line of incorporated aliens. Both the Kpelle and the Goba (Murphy and Bledsoe, Ch.4; Lancaster, Ch.3) show how this ambiguity of kinship ties was exploited with every new turn in political fortunes. In societies without written records and in which the internal affairs of kin groups were treated as a private matter, each contending party could claim to be of "true blood." As Africans have often pointed out: "the slaves sometimes became the masters, and the masters slaves." Given the acceptance of the difference between public fiction and privately guarded truth, each party to a dispute could plausibly accuse the other of having misrepresented the truth in the past. In the end, the current balance of forces resolved the contradictions. But no case need ever be finally settled and every case could remain forever problematic.

On the whole, then, for a new group on the frontier the kinship model was the most useful one to follow in its earliest stages of growth. But if the settlement continued to grow, the use of the model began to threaten the authority of the founding group, which had to turn to other models to shape its political relations with its dependents.

ADHERENTS AS SUBJECTS: AFRICAN POLITIES AS A FRONTIER PHENOMENON

An immigrant autonomous kin group, once established on the frontier, need not, of course, have continued toward political autonomy. It might have stopped at this stage of development and attached itself to a local more powerful kin group or become yet another segment among others in an acephalous segmentary system. Not every frontier group grew into a polity. What interests us here, however, is what happened when such a kin group did follow the course of independent political growth. Such a growth would require, first, that the group establish a local hegemony on the frontier. The group would be at the core of an emerging, ethnically "anomalous" community of the kind we discussed at the beginning of this analysis as discomfitting to the notion of the "tribe." The group's continued growth would lead to a gradual consolidation of customs from the disparate but kindred customs of its constituent units. And one of its languages would become dominant—a process facilitated by widespread African regional multi-lingualism (for a case study of the sociology of such multi-lingualism, see Warnier 1980).

In many of the oral historical accounts of traditional African polities, ranging from innumerable petty polities to those as large as Oyo, Dahomey, Asante, or Rwanda, two plots recur in the stories of how they came to be established. The two plots may exist side by side, one told by rulers and the other by subjects. Or one or the other of the plots may dominate a single narrative. Or the two plots may be intermingled.

The rulers' story is one of political entrepreneurship and it is apt to touch on several out of a set of widespread themes. The story begins in a foreign land which the rulers' ancestors leave after an incident, such as a quarrel over some resources or over succession; or they leave in search of new hunting grounds, or new pastures, or trade, or subjects; or they are sent out as agents of their seniors or rulers. They often travel a considerable distance, and may split up into several groups on the way. When they arrive in the present area, they find it empty, or occupied by a few people whom they expel outright, or by people too strong to be subdued or dislodged. In the latter case, after a period of co-existence, or submission to their hosts, and inter-marriage, the newcomers eventually clash with their hosts. They then expel them, or conquer them, or co-opt their rulers, or at least secure the hosts' acceptance of their autonomy.

The clash is usually triggered by a dispute of seemingly petty origins: the hosts ask for a token part of the harvest, or forcibly appropriate a newcomer woman, or demand the skin of a wild cat or the leg of an antelope after a hunt. In fact, the demands involve the visible symbols of precedence in the land: to yield to them is to recognize the "firstcomer" status of the host; to refuse is to deny this precedence. (Later, the emergent polity would similarly insist on such payments from latecomers.) Sometimes, however, there is no early quarrel. Instead, the newcomers' leader insinuates himself into power—for example, by marrying the daughter of the local ruler. And he may also bring to his hosts some new crops or techniques that raise them to a new level of civilization. In the end, the newcomers establish their rule by superior knowledge, or intrigue, or trickery, or force. The new rulers bring in a new organization (and perhaps, again, new crops or technology), thereby ushering in a new social order where before, the story claims, a true or at least a civilized society scarcely existed. In time, another chapter in the story may begin, when the new rulers expand their polity to incorporate other neighboring peoples. But that has to do not with the expansion of the immigrant group but of the established polity they had founded.

So much for the rulers' story. What of the subjects'? One can obtain the stories of individual kin groups, as variable as any set of family histories would be in any society. But there is also the subjects' collective story—the history of "the people" or, specifically, of the ethnic group or groups that had preceded the rulers in the area. This story speaks of their having "always" been in the area, or of having arrived in it as immigrants (and here the story recapitulates, for its earlier period, the themes found in the rulers' story), and of having, in any case, preceded the present rulers. The ancestors of the present rulers arrive meekly on the scene, on their own or in response to a request to come because they can offer something new. The newcomers' meekness then gives way to ambition and they assume power, with varying degrees of assent by the people.

In both the rulers' and the subjects' plots, there was a point when the newcomers assumed power. For the subjects, this event ushered in the birth of the new polity. For the rulers, it represented the first expansion of their already existing frontier settlement—the beginning of another stage in the process by which an original kin group, grown into a kin-like group, continues on its course toward founding a polity. In this polity, an unambiguous distinction existed between the kin-like ruling core and those over whom it now ruled. A crucial change in the model of integration has taken place: the frontier community had moved from a corporate solidarity modelled on kinship to a solidarity of inter-dependence modelled on political contract.

The rulers' group at the core of the newly established polity faced new conditions. First, being better able to provide a safe haven, the community could attract increasing numbers of frontiersmen and refugees from neighboring polities and the metropoles. And second, the dominant group could afford to be more selective about whom it wished to admit and could more easily set the terms for admission. It did not have to entice newcomers by treating them as pseudo-kinsmen but could frankly deal with them as outsiders seeking protection. Some of them might even be kept out, as the Goba kingdom of Namainga tried at one time to keep out new immigrants (Lancaster, Ch. 3). The rulers could indeed regard weak new settlers as being little better than squatters on the estate of their hosts, there only at the pleasure of their hosts and subject to expulsion at any time. Each successive group of newcomers would find itself at the very bottom of an emerging hierarchy of "firstcomers" and "latecomers," and the polity's increasing size added to the social distance between rulers and the later latecomers. As the community became divided into sub-units, such as wards or sub-chiefdoms, it smoothly assumed the overall "pyramidal" structure of most African polities, in which the original unit was replicated by subordinate sub-units that grew under it. The heads of these sub-units became, in turn, the local "firstcomers" who "showed the place" to newcomers and mediated between them and the rulers.

This mode of expansion in size carried with it certain peculiarities. In its simplest paradigmatic form, the original compound grew into a hamlet, the hamlet into a village, the village into several wards, and the whole into a small polity. Concomitantly, the newcomers' compound head also became transformed, step by step, into a hamlet head, a village head, and a chief, while remaining what he was at the beginning—the head of his kin group (cf. Kopytoff 1977). In contrast to political mobility in which one "climbs" over the existing rungs of a political structure, or to mobility by conquest in which one appropriates control over more and more individuals by force, there was here a kind of "mobility by levitation," in which the rulers were gradually raised higher and higher as new layers of immigrant adherents voluntarily "inserted" themselves under them—a process vividly exemplified in the growth of chieftaincies in the Lagos suburb of Mushin (Barnes, Ch.10). This process of mobility did not require great material resources on which to build the resulting stratification; rather, the stratification rested on the insubstantial currency of precedence in residence and the more substantial but non-material currency of political and ritual power. The increasing size of the structure led smoothly to a delegation of power and responsibility to the lower levels without greatly affecting the ideology and symbolism at the top. In the polity that emerged, the chief continued to be a kin group head, the administrative apparatus was an expansion of household and kin group management, and the polity itself was the founding kin group's enlarged estate and private "patrimony." There was little room here for a distinction between the polity's concerns, or its purse, or its fortunes, and the concerns, purse, and fortunes of the ruling kin group.

To the extent that African political culture was being continuously shaped and re-shaped in these smaller frontier polities, the effects of the frontier pattern were also visible in the larger polities, usually called "kingdoms." Though products of a later stage of political growth, and integrated by conquest (rather than kinship or contract), their early origins usually lay in such frontier polities and the "patrimonial" model continued to shape their organization from the perspective of the rulers. Thus, expanding polities generally tended to incorporate, at each successive line of conquest, conquered peoples as adherents; reciprocally, the defeated and the conquered expected to be so incorporated. The pattern was not unadvantageous to the conqueror—each new conquered enemy became an interested party in the enterprise of the next conquest. This could allow a very rapid expansion of the kind that marked the growth of the Zulu and related kingdoms or, on a smaller scale, of the Ngoni kingdoms which grew out of what Barnes (1954:13) estimates to have been an original core of about a thousand warriors. (The pattern, it is worth noting, contrasts radically with the position that Africans later found themselves in after European conquest, the ideology of colonial rule precluding their incorporation as clients and adherents.)

The continuity of conception that led from kin group elder, to village head, to chief, and to king, could also lead one in the reverse direction. Just as elders were easily transmuted into kings, so did the rulers of shrinking kingdoms became easily demoted into elders while continuing to play essentially similar functions, but on a reduced scale. Hence, a village chief easily took on the poses and paraphernalia of greater chiefs, in what to non-African outsiders easily appeared as an exhibition of pretentiousness and vanity. And heads of formerly large but now diminished kingdoms could carry on with the royal ritual in ways that an outsider might see as a meaningless grasping at a vanished past. This similarity of stance, spanning village chieftaincies and "kingdoms," is at the root of the extraordinary confusion and inconsistency in the terms applied by Europeans to the African rulers they encountered: the same ruler would be called "chief" by one observer and "king" by another, and rulers over small towns would be called "kings" in some places, while rulers of large polities would be called "chiefs" (see on this Lemarchand 1977:7).

This continuity between small-scale and large-scale organization made all the easier the transmission of political culture between frontier and metropole, discussed earlier. The ideology of power could easily survive the radical change of scale implied by a move from a metropole to the frontier. And a rising frontier polity could no less easily and "prematurely" assume the trappings of far larger states.

THE AUTHORITY OF FIRSTCOMERS OVER LATECOMERS

We have referred in various contexts to the authority that, in Africa, was conferred on the firstcomer to a locality. We shall now examine this principle in greater detail, for a great deal of the local politics was conditioned by it.

In the hierarchy of firstcomers and latecomers, the earlier strata of adherents had greater claims than later strata to kin-like relations with the dominant core. The logic of these relations implied both the closeness and the potential competition endemic to African kin groups. The longer, then, a kin group had been in residence, the more local rights it acquired and the greater its potential as a rival to the founding group—a rival likely to have a power base, a network of connections, and local roots old enough for making ambiguous claims to great antiquity of residence and even to hint at primacy. Consequently, a dynamic reminiscent of the one we had seen at the level of the kin group was replayed, with some of the same subtleties, at the level of the polity.

In contrast to the earlier strata, a late arriving kin group posed fewer threats to the rulers. If small in numbers, it furnished adherents whose price was low while control over them was high; this made them an attractive resource in counter-balancing the earlier comers. But to secure their permanent loyalty, one had, as usual, to resort to the cementing metaphor of kinship and phrase their dependence in that idiom, even while keeping from them the rights that the idiom implied. The dilemma is similar to the one Barnes (Ch. 10) finds in established Yoruba polities: to insure widespread satisfaction through participation, the rulers stressed achievement as the road to influential titles; yet, to preserve their own power, the "firstcomer" dominant groups countered the potential threat from achievers by insisting on ascribed criteria for holding the more important titles. Thus, toward their subjects—be they early or late arrivals—the dominant kin group's policy had to be subtle, fluid, reversible, and ambiguous—a judicious mixture of appeasement and bullying, of assertion of relationship and its denial, of power-sharing and exclusion from power. The policy, in brief, had to be as contradictory as the dynamic with which it had to contend.

At the center of the dynamic was the general concept of the "firstcomer" and the special prestige and legitimacy that it carried (see Cohen and Middleton 1970:12). To claim prestige from the fact of being a firstcomer is, to be sure, a quintessentially frontier idea. One certainly finds it among the first settlers in American towns, from Philadelphia to Kankakee and on to Bakersfield, California. But it is not a universal idea. In areas of multilayered conquest and occupation and of centuries of mobility, such as Ireland or India or Southeast Asia, the earliest inhabitants do not necessarily enjoy the greatest prestige; often, quite the opposite. And in the United States too, the historical precedence of American Indians did not grant them special prestige, except in some areas of the East and South where they had been largely absorbed and where a dash of Indian blood provides a kind of genealogical flourish.

In Africa, the principle of precedence—which ties firstcomers to latercomers to lastcomers into a chain of hierarchy—is intimately intertwined with the legitimacy of authority. It does not determine authority, but authority must accommodate to it in some way. The first occupant was in some sense the "owner" of the land, with a special ritual relationship to it and its spirits. To be sure, Americans, too, have often attributed to Indians a special relationship with the land, be it in the romantic version of a James

Fenimore Cooper or the mystical "ecological" one of recent vintage. But nineteenth-century expanding America took inevitable progress through science for granted; to it, a quasi-mystical relationship to land was an anachronism, an irrelevancy, and even, in evolutionary terms, the sign of belonging to a dated past. What sincere regret there was over the passing of the Indian—and such a regret was always an aspect of American thought—was tempered by the belief in its historical inevitability. By contrast, in traditional African societies, untouched by progressivist rationalism, the notion of a special relationship to land was a hard fact of life to be dealt with politically.

To recognize the firstcomer was, in Africa, to recognize his authority and his special ritual position in the local scheme of things. This constrained the legitimacy of whatever claims to authority might be made by latecomers bent on establishing their own polity. Since newcomers to a frontier seldom found it empty of inhabitants, the latter would, according to this principle, automatically lord it over them. There is a paradox here. A principle so obviously derived from frontier conditions would, if mechanically applied, have taken away from the frontier its essential attraction, that of an environment devoid of legitimate political authority.

The principle of the primacy of the firstcomer also implied an infinite regression of ever earlier comers going back into the mists of the past. No one, that is, could ever claim to be really first. The endless regression had therefore to be shortened and a beginning point established. The shortening was achieved by collapsing together the earlier layers of the population, who had, in any case, usually achieved some degree of homogeneity. Thus, we find among the Goba of Namainga (Lancaster, Ch.3) that while the two most recent immigrant groups are differentiated, all the preceding layers of population are lumped into the single category of "Tonga." But there still remained the problem of dealing with one's predecessors. Broadly speaking, two approaches were possible here: to claim to have displaced them or to recognize their early presence but redefine its significance.

An obvious strategy for newly arrived immigrants was to chase the previous inhabitants out. This is not an uncommon theme in African oral traditions: "We came and we found the such-and-such, and they fled." Sometimes, indeed, they did. When the Ekie say that the pygmoid Twa fled before them (Fairley, Ch.2) or when the Bantu ex-slaves in Somaliland say the same thing about local hunters-gatherers (Cassanelli, Ch.8), they are stating what numberless other African groups have said. But the claim that the early inhabitants are completely gone was always as much a political as it was a historical statement. The Goba (Lancaster, Ch.3) are not unique in showing some genetic traces of an earlier population. Sometimes the evidence is more direct: in the midst of assertions about the expulsion of the original inhabitants, the anthropologist or the historian may stumble, while collecting genealogies, upon kin groups descended from them and disentangle secretly nurtured claims to primacy of occupa-tion out of uneasy silences and shamefaced revelations. But everyone could still subscribe publicly to the myth of a single ethnicity and a single origin.

Sometimes, however, the pretense that the previous inhabitants had altogether vanished could not be sustained in any case—their presence was simply too glaring a fact. If the rivalry involved merely a kin group, one might simply dispute their precedence over oneself; thus, Goba contenders for local power would claim genealogical connections with some ancient local dynasty (Lancaster, Ch.3). But with large local ethnic groups, such a claim was difficult. Throughout Africa, there were several patterns in dealing with the problem.

In some cases, one recognized the existence of a prior population but tamed them structurally; one simply kept them at the margin of one's own society, restricting one's relationship with them, or one put them into a special niche as providers of specialized services. We find socially "out-cast" groups of blacksmiths in northern East Africa and in the Sudanic belt, living as quasi-ethnic groups in the interstices of the dominant social order. In other cases, while keeping the earlier inhabitants at a social and political distance, one incorporated them into the ritual order, by assigning to them a particular ritual role based on their special relationship to the land. Thus, various Pygmy groups in Central Africa, living in parallel autonomy beside their Bantu neighbors, were asked periodically to play their indispensable part in the rituals of the latter.

Sometimes, the sheer numbers of the conquered precluded any possi-bility of expelling them, or ignoring them, or making them into a margi-nal parallel society. For example, among the Goba (Lancaster, Ch.3), a distinction was made between the older "Tonga" inhabitants, considered to be the "owners of the land," and the later conquering intruders from Korekore, said to be the "owners of people." The distinction attempted to allocate ritual power to the oldtimers and political power to the new-comers. But when the numerical preponderance of the conquered made their exclusion from the political sphere impossible, the distinction might become an integral part of the political system. Thus, the various Lunda conquerors of the southern savannas of Central Africa incorporated the conquered chiefs into their administration as titled "owners of the land."

What is common to all these arrangements is this: once the earlier settlers are recognized to exist, the newcomers attempt to co-opt their mystical powers in relation to the land. The institutional means of this co-optation may be quite direct, as when Tutsi conquerors attached to themselves the priest-like chiefs *abiru* of the conquered (Vansina 1962b). Similarly, the Ekie king of alien origin, like the new Namainga dynasty among the Goba, directly appropriated the ritual institutions of their re-spective subjects by subordinating to themselves the ritual heads of the previous political order (Fairley, Ch.2; Lancaster, Ch.3). In a region of

continuous movements of people, a succession of such appropriations resulted in a structure of several layers each of which saw itself as a political
authority over the previous stratum but was seen as having ritual authority
by the next stratum above. The strata might then be perpetually at logger-
heads over their roles in the system, as Binsbergen (1979:162ff) shows for
parts of Zambia.

All these maneuvers reveal the supremely legitimizing meaning of
firstcomer status. In the pursuit of this status, one sometimes attempted to
redefine, in culturally acceptable terms, the concrete meaning of primacy
of occupation. Such redefinitions are not confined to Africa. We have
discussed above, in very simple terms, the American indifference to Indian
precedence on the land. But on closer inspection, the story is not so simple
as it appears. That at some level of consciousness Indian primacy mattered
is clear from the fact that ideological arguments over it did take place. The
children of the Puritans could be seen themselves as the first occupiers of a
de-Indianized New England (sic) that was God's gift to the Righteous of a
new Land of Canaan; but something else was required by the children of
the Enlightenment. From the Bible, the justification shifted to archaeology: the mounds of the Ohio Valley were taken as proof that the contem-
poraneous Indian presence was but a savage interlude in the continuity of
civilization beginning with the Moundbuilders—who were, according to
different theories, lost tribes of Israel, or Vikings, or Danes on the way to
becoming Mexican Toltecs (for a summary treatment of this scholarship,
see Willey and Sabloff 1980:41ff). Later, when this history became untenable, a more subtle view came in, one more consonant with the evolutionary outlook of an industrializing nineteenth century and also (perversely
for any simplistic sociology of knowledge) similar to the prevailing African ideology of precedence.

In this view, precedence is not an absolute fact of chronology. The
claims to primacy by the founding families of frontier American communities, as of African communities, were not based on the fact that they
were the very first inhabitants but that they had wrested a civilized social
order out of a socio-political wilderness and that those before them were
part of the savagery that had preceded civilization. A vivid example of this
is provided by the Kpelle of Liberia (Murphy and Bledsoe, Ch.4). Here, a
newcomer would found a "new" political area by giving his chiefdom
new boundaries and a new ritual existence; in this way, he could claim to
be the firstcomer in it by virtue of having introduced social order into
what he asserted was previously an inexistent territory in the civic sense,
one that was politically disordered and ritually untamed. By similar logic,
the newer immigrants to the Lagos suburb of Mushin claimed political
rights because, like the older "sons of the soil," they too had participated
in the founding of the "new" modern Mushin, if not of the old Mushin
settlements (Barnes, Ch.10). And at the other end of the continent, among
the Goba (Lancaster, Ch.3), we see a similar re-definition of territory by

ritual means: founders of new chiefdoms install new central shrines to serve as the ritual foci for their "new" territories. The principle behind these actions is echoed in the advice supposedly given to Sundiata, the legendary king of ancient Mali, by a sage when Sundiata, having won over his rivals, asked him how he should go about becoming king: "Cut the trees, transform the forests into fields, for then only will you become a true king" (quoted in Lemarchand 1977).

Even if original inhabitants were neither remembered nor seen, the principle of infinite regression in settlement still implied that one's claims to firstness were uncertain. A widespread mythical solution to this problem took the form of a story, found among innumerable African peoples, about how they discovered, upon arrival in their present locality, various kinds of "little forest people," or deformed beings, or dwarfs, who quickly fled. Scholars have sometimes seen in these stories an echo of an early encounter with some original population of Pygmoids who, one assumes, were once ubiquitous in the forest areas. But these stories may echo more ideology than history. On the one hand, they concede to logic that there was always someone preceding those who had arrived within living memory. And on the other hand, the stories sweep away the implications of this fact by completely deculturizing these "very first" inhabitants and making them non-human. In effect, the stories take the idea of "pre-civilized" predecessors to its logical extreme.

To establish in these various ways a "new," hitherto non-existent territory was to usher in a new period of history—a period separated from what went on before by a boundary that changed the significance of previous historical events for the political present. This boundary was marked by what Murphy and Bledsoe (Ch.4) call a "pivotal event." They show that much of Kpelle political rhetoric is devoted to defining one event rather than another as pivotal. It is a way of being historical (as Africans deeply are), but within a selected historical universe.

The importance of being first meant that when several groups had to co-exist, all had to engage in certain kinds of historical games. A radical remolding by each group of past events into a favorable form could not entirely mask the reality. One could not claim that people had "run away" at the time of occupation if they were in fact around and in strength. Nor could one deny the existence of the founders of the polity when everyone knew who they were. The present rulers, even while insisting on their role of founders, were co-opting their predecessors into the political rituals precisely because they were predecessors. And the predecessors agreed to their formally subordinate ritual status precisely because their participation in the ritual kept the memory of their original position publicly alive; someday, the ritual could become an argument in reviving their own now dormant claim to primacy. Throughout all this, the different versions of the past were collectively suspended in the public arena in the interests of a *modus vivendi*. Yet, each party could continue to maintain its own view of which among the many events everyone agreed upon was the "pivotal" one historically.

In a community ruled by outside authority—as, for example, the twentieth-century frontier community of Mto wa Mbu was by the colonial administration of Tanganyika (Arens, Ch.9)—this public suspension of disagreement may reflect the fact that "being first" is in any case irrelevant to power. In independent communities, the suspension may reflect a balance of power. An example of this kind of *modus vivendi* is provided by the BaShu of eastern Zaire, with their several ethnic layers of immigrant population (Packard, Ch. 5). Each ethnic group defined its own arrival as the pivotal event marking the passage from the disorder of nature to the order of society. The earliest inhabitants saw it as the opening of the land—by them. The next comers claimed that it lay in the first serious clearing of the forest for agriculture—by them. The comers after them held it to be the introduction of "civilized" food crops—by them. And finally, the last comers, the now dominant pastoralists, dwelt on the installation—by them—of a "real" and "civilized" political system. Each group held to its own version, but without publicly denying any of the others. This agreement to disagree allowed the parties to coexist and operate pragmatically the political system that bound them together. At the same time, the ritual power of the earlier inhabitants was dealt with in various ways. The middle layers disputed locally, though not regionally, the ritual primacy of the earlier inhabitants; the pastoralists assured themselves of the ritual benevolence of the earliest agriculturalists; and these, in turn, asserted that their ritual primacy stemmed from the fact that it is they who had expelled the original Pygmy inhabitants.

But if ambiguity helped in the enterprise of co-existence, it could also lend itself to manipulation. As has been pointed out before, a multiplicity of meanings was attached to the African concept of "seniority." One could be "first" and "senior" in a variety of ways (through age, achievement, length of residence, precedence in initiation, etc.) and in a variety of contexts (such as the kin group, the settlement, an age-set, a civic society, a cult group, etc.). The multifarious semantics of seniority allowed considerable room for "sliding" from one context to another and for argument as to which context was the cause and which the consequence. Does the seniority of authority—say, in village government—imply the seniority of precedence in its rituals, or does it issue from it? Does precedence in ritual ranking more or less reflect precedence in the chronology of settlement, or does it prove that chronology? The semantic sliding was made all the easier because the common way to express different kinds of seniority in different context was by way of the same kinship terms (such as "father," "mother," or "mother's brother"). Murphy and Bledsoe (Ch.4) show how among the Kpelle the "mother's brother/sister's son" relationship—the common metaphor of authority—tied together the seniority in territorial organization, the definition of pivotal events, the meaning of marriages, and the hierarchy in ritual relations; this allowed the creation of new facts in one context by appealing to the facts of another.

In a growing frontier settlement, the kinship metaphor also provided an almost imperceptible transition and a bridge between two systems: the earlier one, in which real kin and quasi-kin relations held together the founding group and its close adherents, and the later system in which political relations between rulers and subjects (though still often expressed in the kinship metaphor) were more contractual, more formal, more distant, and more instrumental. In the course of political maneuvering, this semantic bridge allowed one to distance oneself from others—by claiming that the kinship idiom of the relationship was purely metaphorical, putting it into the later system—or to move oneself closer to others—by claiming that the kinship was real and the relationship belonged in the earlier system. One could thus push a branch of a chiefly lineage out of the competition for the chieftaincy by insisting that its kinship relationship to the chiefly line was but a metaphor for political dependence. And in a reverse process, an originally alien dependent group could in time claim that its position of "junior kinsmen" was real and proceed to make appropriate political demands. Thus, arguments about kin relations—their presence or absence—were never far below the surface of arguments over political claims and would periodically erupt into the open.

The sliding between the different contexts of seniority was often the stuff of community politics, of the kind that Barnes (Ch. 10) shows among the Yoruba. But one should not overemphasize the manipulation. The semantic ambiguities also gave rise to quite honest and sincere arguments and twentieth-century psychology should surely make one hesitate to draw too rigid a line between sincerity and self-interest. Westerners—including social scientists—should be able to empathize with the extent to which thought may be conditioned by semantics. The term "primitive" misled anthropological thinking for a century or so by confounding chronology (its original meaning) with social substance (its extended meaning) and by conflating chronological precedence and social "simplicity." In the same way, after the Second World War, two decades of thinking about "development" in political science, sociology, and policy-making foundered on the ambiguities of the term "modern," with its suggestion of something that is simultaneously recent and complex. These confusions occurred within intellectual disciplines in societies with written historical records, fixed chronologies, and the ability of making lists and interdigitating the sequences of events. One can understand then how, in societies without such means of analysis and comparison, the semantic confusions could be an intellectual burden as well as a political opportunity.

The principle of the authority of the firstcomers operated in many contexts, from the broadest—as in inter-ethnic relations—to the narrowest—as in the hierarchy of a hamlet. The principle meant that, once one has managed to achieve actual authority, one sought to legitimize it by claiming on the public stage that one was, in some significant sense, a "senior." Thereafter, one engaged in what one might call an "accumulation of symptoms" of seniority: one tried to extend signs of seniority to as many contexts as possible, and each new context made the extension to yet other contexts that much more plausible. In effect, one was engaged in the creation of a "tradition" to which one could later appeal. This strategy was consonant with the pattern, discussed above, of the primacy of structure over content in African social relations.

Arguments, such as those among the BaShu over who "showed the land" to whom, were above all over seniority and the authority it conferred. They were not about chronology per se but about chronology as an indication of seniority; not about who brought in what crop but about what this says about civilization and therefore seniority; not about who gave an antelope leg to whom but about the context and meaning that made it into a gift between equals, or a tribute by a dependent, or a reward by a superior; not about a marriage but about the authority relationship the marriage implied. In brief, the arguments were not about history as raw events but about the meaning of events for a history that sanctions political relations.

All this makes it understandable why, in the study of traditional African political systems, anthropologists and historians so often encounter what appear to be games that informants play, in which political reality is defined and redefined in seemingly contradictory ways as one moves from one context to another. To the anthropologist especially, whose training usually inculcates strong notions about logically integrated social and cultural systems, such contradictions may be disturbing. To the Africans, who have a political life to live, the different versions are part and parcel of the process of adjusting claims by different political forces and of avoiding a breakdown of a working *modus vivendi*—at least for the time being, one must hasten to add.

In addition to the current official history justifying the existing order, the researcher discovers what might be called "underground histories," inactive but biding their time. The conquered may cooperate with the conquerors but they do not forget their own past. Thus, both among the Ekie (Fairley, Ch. 2) and in the NaMainga Goba kingdom (Lancaster, Ch. 3), we find the former ritual heads letting themselves be co-opted by the new alien rulers while at the same time their lineages demonstratively removed their settlements away from the rulers' settlements in order to preserve visibly their singularity in an unpredictable future. For were they to be able later to contest the legitimacy of those who replaced them, they could in this way avoid the embarrassing question: "If the rulers were not legitimate, why were you living with them?" Among the Kpelle (Murphy and Bledsoe, Ch. 4), we see decisions about where to build a settlement being similarly made with an eye to a possible future reversal of political fortunes.

With a change in circumstances, the private versions of history, carefully nurtured for generations or recently created, may emerge from the "underground" onto the public stage. One of the problems with many structural-functional analyses by social scientists in the past lay precisely in accepting at face value the oral rendering of the current surface balance in an African political system. Not only did such analyses freeze the systems in time—which is an intellectual problem—but they also implicitly imputed a great deal of stability to the current arrangements—which creates a predictive and practical problem. Hence the shock when, for example, the seemingly well-balanced and long-standing relationship between the Hutu and their Tutsi overlords in Rwanda rapidly gave way, in the changed circumstances of decolonization, to wholesale massacres.

The principle of firstcomer authority also generated a series of potential conflicts at the advancing borders of the emerging polity. The logic of firstcomer status as a political charter was such that one who claimed to be first could not stop merely at securing one's independence. For once one declared oneself to be a firstcomer (in whatever sense), one had placed oneself in authority over the other inhabitants. By the same token, not to claim to be first was to accept implicitly one's subordination to someone else. To be sure, the claim to superiority was tempered, in actual relations, by a variety of subtle mechanisms (of the kind of social non-aggression contract analyzed by Colson 1974). But the claim remained embedded in the ideology of a rising polity. When circumstances changed, the temptation was there to assert it; and when conflicts arose, it gave one heart to fight for superiority by giving legitimacy to one's claims. The pattern imposed a logic upon relations between groups by which, fundamentally, one was either a superior firstcomer or a subordinate latecomer. This inter-group logic of inequality meshed with the logic that prevailed in other relations within African social groups, where, as it has so often been pointed out, there were seldom any equals—one was either a senior or a junior, a superior or a subordinate. On the frontier, with its numerous incipient polities, this logic gave every such polity a latent expansionist and hegemonic cast. Ultimately, one either absorbed or one got absorbed.

In all the processes described, being (in whatever sense) the "founder" of the polity was a crucial marker of seniority, and that, in turn, was connected with a "time of arrival" from somewhere else. The result was a constant reiteration of claims that had to do with movements and migrations of oneself and of others and this reinforced the frontier flavor of African notions of political legitimacy. It made present political relations, even in mature societies, flow out of what happened "in the beginning," when people were moving in, when the land was "first" being settled, when different groups confronted one another and clashed over their different claims to territory, and when the present society could be said to have come into being. In brief, the frontier was the legitimizing historical model in shaping relations within the polity.

PATRIMONIALISM AND AFRICAN SACRED CHIEFTAINSHIP

In the growing frontier polity, we have said, the solidarity of a corporate kin group gradually gave way to the solidarity of contractual inter-dependence between rulers and ruled. The change introduced a duality of perspectives on the polity, corresponding to the two paradigmatic stories— or, if you will, myths—about the foundation of the polity, that of the ruler and that of the subjects and a duality in its constitutional legitimation. The duality is vividly illustrated by Bradbury (1971) in his analysis of Benin political culture, whose central tenet was that while the king had an intrinsic right to rule, the kingship had come into being by the will of the subjects. The duality has also been analyzed by Heusch (1982) in its symbolic dimensions; he shows its relationship to two themes—the original uncouthness of the subjects and the refinements of an intrusive kingship— and examines how they are contrasted yet also welded together in the constitutions of African kingdoms. One of the principal contentions of our analysis here is that this duality in the ideology of kingship did not arise within kingship itself but is a continuation of the duality that inheres in the far more modest embryonic polity shaped by the frontier.

The standard myth of the founding of most African polities depicts the founders as leaving their place of origin, entering a frontier, confronting local inhabitants, and instituting a new political order that was at the origin of the society currently in being. In the subjects' perspective on this myth, the polity had issued out of the acceptance by the subjects of the ruler and it continued to exist because of it. The rulers were intruders, outsiders, aliens, latecomers. Thus do the common Goba conceive of all their rulers as quintessential aliens and therefore in the same class of beings as slaves and wandering homeless ghosts (Lancaster, Ch. 3).

The rulers, for their part, saw the subjects in the metaphor of latecoming adherents to the polity the rulers had founded; the subjects were the strangers, squatters, even "slaves," who had been outside a valid civil order and to whom one "had shown" a civilized place to live in. But the rulers had to be careful with this image. On a frontier with its open resources, the subjects could easily leave and they had to be enticed into remaining in the polity—hence the prevalence, in the ritual paraphernalia of African chiefs and kings, of special "medicines" to attract and retain adherents. Pragmatically, then, the rulers' public etiquette in dealing with their adherents gave the latter a status higher than the one they possessed in practice and higher still than the one they possessed in the rulers' ideology. In the prevalent metaphor of kinship, the adherents were like relatives, the polity like a kin group, authority relations like those in a family. For the frontier rulers knew that their rule was in no mean sense the creation of their subjects. The subjects knew it too. As the Sherbro proverb has it: "One cannot be a chief and sit alone" (MacCormack 1977:192).

These founding myths often emphasized a common theme in African political culture—that, as Mair (1977:22) baldly puts it, "it is 'uncivilized' to be without a ruler." The view was in harmony with the self-perception of the rulers as "firstcomers" because they were the founders of the polity that really mattered. It was they, therefore, who in reality "had shown" the place to their subjects. This accomplished a crucial reversal of chronological primacy—the original inhabitants of the area could be seen as "immigrants" into the new society, for they were incorporated into it after its creation.

This chronological contradiction between the two perspectives meshed with a chronological gap, since from the rulers' perspective the polity had been founded earlier than it had been from the subjects'. For the rulers, it began with their arrival on the frontier or even earlier, with their detachment from the parent body in the metropole; the emergence of the larger polity was a later episode in its political history. By contrast, the subjects naturally saw the founding of the polity in the installation of the new rulers over them. The two events would normally have been separated by a considerable gap in time and might have taken place under different leaders. From this arises the frequent two-founders pattern in African dynasties: a rather shadowy and sometimes mythical founder—the one who first arrived and founded the dynasty—and an outstanding successor who is remembered more "in the round" as the great consolidator of the polity. Thus, we have the mild immigrant father and the energetic son among the Ekie (Fairley, Ch.2), the prophetic founder followed by his warrior brother in Ningi (Patton, Ch.7), the expansionist great-grandson of the first Luba king (Vansina 1966:70ff), or the immigrant "leopard" as the ancestor of the effective founder of Dahomey (Newbury 1961:10). The chronological disjunction—by which the rulers could see their polity as coming into being earlier than the subjects would grant—reinforced the rulers' view of their subjects as latecoming strangers "joining" an already existing polity.

The difference in chronological perceptions corresponded to the difference in the conception of the essential character of the polity. In the ruling group's view, the polity was, from its humble beginnings as a frontier household, their private estate that had been growing larger. Not only had the kingdom issued out of the hamlet, it was the hamlet enlarged by the addition of "latecoming" subjects. That is, to use Max Weber's term (and one which Bradbury uses for Benin), the ruler's ideology of rulership was patrimonial: the polity was an extension of the ruler's household. In this patrimonialism, we suggest, lay the functional origins of African sacred chieftainship and of its outgrowth, African "divine kingship."

It is a truism that in any political system in which much power is vested in the leader, the fate of the polity will be seen to depend a great deal on the individual behavior of that leader. This holds for absolute monarchies, modern dictatorships, and, among democracies, presidential systems. It also holds for a patrimonial polity, where the ruler's personal and public spheres are fused—provided that the ruler is actively engaged in ruling it. The ruler's personal character, intelligence, weaknesses, vigor, and health visibly shape the destinies of the polity. A pragmatic equation is therefore readily made in such systems between the ruler's state and well-being and those of the polity; once made, it is then presented in an appropriate cultural idiom. Outside of Africa, the presentation has included the traditional quasi-sacred idiom of stable monarchies and, in much of the contemporary world, the manufactured secular mysticism and personality cults of transient dictators.

The pragmatic equation between the ruler's state and that of the polity was particularly realistic in the small patrimonial enterprises that grew into the chieftaincies of the African frontier. The pragmatic proposition was elaborated into a legitimizing and culturally believable complex. As a constitutional proposition, it was present in almost every African traditional polity. To capture its essence, scholars, focusing on the cultural strangeness of the idiom, have made it more religious than political by resorting to such terms as "sacred chieftainship" or, in the case of its more dramatic and very specialized manifestation, "divine kingship."

In its main outlines, the complex is well-known ethnographically (for one version, see Murdock 1959, listing eighteen features). The ruler's well-being was taken to insure that of the society. The ruler and the polity were conceptually merged and the success of the polity was seen to depend on the preservation of various aspects of the ruler's being: his personal vigor, his health, his sexual potency, the state of his ritual paraphernalia (that usually included remains of preceding rulers, such as their hair, nails, or bones), and so on. When the ruler died, so did the land, the country, the society, and the law; and only the installation of the new ruler revived them. Between the two events was the interregnum—a period of institutionalized lawlessness, with the law literally in suspension; and the chaos was regarded as a demonstration of what it was like to be without a ruler.

Though subscribed to by ruler and subject alike, the sacred chieftainship complex derived its essence from the ruler's perspective on the polity. But what of the perspective of the subjects? Their paradigmatic myth spoke of them as local people who had been visited by a stranger whom they allowed to settle; the outsider, or his heir, reinforced by more supporters from outside, then insinuated himself into power, took over its trappings and symbols of legitimacy, and began a new political era. It should be noted that the new regime was not illegitimate precisely because it was legitimized by appropriated local ritual symbols, even if the appropriation often involved trickery (in this respect, the logic was similar to what we find in European kingly quarrels, with their attention to the physical appropriation of symbols of power, as in the English abduction of the royal Scottish Stone of Scone). The crucial point in Africa was that legitimacy had been conferred by the people by way of the "consent" of their symbols (a notion that modern secular democratic ideology finds difficult to grasp). In the constitutional perspective of the subjects, then, the people existed before rulership existed since they were the grantors of authority; this was congruent with the subjects' paradigmatic myth of their precedence. Here, political chronology dominated "real" chronology in yet another way. As a collectivity, the people included even those immigrants who came after the polity had been established, for they too made it possible for the ruler not to be "sitting alone."

The ambiguities in the origins of the rulers' authority—making him into a kind of legitimate usurper—were paralleled by a certain cognitive ambiguity in the essence of this authority. The ruler was seen as necessary for the social order and therefore desired by the people. But by embodying a power that, to be effective, had to be unquestioned, he was also potentially dangerous. For, being unquestioned, the power was subject to abuse and it could betray the expectations of those who conferred it. The ambiguity affected both the ruler, in his perception of the limits to which he should exercise his powers, and the subjects, in their perception of the limits to which they must tolerate the ruler's actions. The ambiguity reflected a frontier conundrum, not unlike the conundrum of the captain's authority over a ship on the high seas. And it was also congruent with the "Shaka complex," suggested by Fernandez (1967, 1971) as the paradigmatic myth of African relations of power.

Once established and embroidered with culturally powerful symbols, the pragmatic proposition underlying "sacred chieftaincy"—that of the ruler-polity equation—endowed rulership with a special ritual potency, which reinforced the view of the inherent desirability of chieftainship. The classic example of this in the literature occurred on the Nile-Zaire divide (Southall 1956). Here, small chiefless polities would request the chiefs among the Alur people to furnish them with their sons and thereby with the benefits of chieftaincy, which insured the well-being of the society through control of rain and the prevention of certain natural disasters. The spread of chiefly institutions, titles, and associated ritual paraphernalia as a function of their attractiveness is also attested to for the southern savanna in what is now Zaire, Angola, and Zambia (see Miller 1976, Reefe 1981). And the story of the foundation of Benin—in which Edo elders are said to have requested the Oni of Ife to send them a king—has parallels outside of Africa: according to its founding myth, the Russian Kievan state came into being when the small local Slavic tribes invited the Vikings to "come and rule over us, for our land is vast but the disorder in it is mighty."

Modern historians are, to be sure, unwilling to take the Kievan story completely at face value—it sounds too convenient for the reputation of both the conquerors and the conquered. African stories of this kind also evoke a measure of scepticism, yet it should be a tempered one. There must have been an inherent pragmatic attraction in an institution that promised to give greater social order than one could manage on one's own (for, *pace* introductory textbooks in anthropology, people do not always consider their culture to provide them with the best of all possible worlds). As Colson (1974:62ff) shows, people in uncentralized and anarchic societies do often welcome the peace brought by an overarching authority, even if they may later regret some of the lost freedom of action. But whatever the nuances in the conquest-by-invitation stories, one must beware of the utterly modern Western axiom that the value of political independence is so self-evident a truth that submission to a greater outside power can never be voluntary. In the perspective of African subjects, it is precisely this voluntary element that is stressed, thereby making the ruler the creation of his subjects.

Being the creation of subjects, the African ruler's legitimacy rested on an implicit contract that could be withdrawn. The ruler was accepted because of what he did for the people—ideally, nurturing them, protecting them from misfortune, and insuring order in the society. As the extreme—or merely excessively frank—ideology of the Goba commoners stated it, the kings, *qua* rootless immigrants, were useful "slaves" and descendants of "slaves" (Lancaster, Ch.3). In this perspective, the ruler's sacredness, which made his well-being co-terminous with the polity's, had another logical side to it: when misfortune struck, it was the ruler who was held accountable, much as on the frontier the founder-entrepreneur was held accountable for the settlement's troubles. If the ruler were too weak to serve his subjects, he could be legitimately eliminated. (As mentioned previously, African political values tend to preclude simply discarding a person in a "terminal" position of authority; this at least partly accounts for the much-discussed "killing of the king" as an element of African "divine kingship".) But even the ruler's everyday life was loaded with socially useful burdens. The outward signs of his sacredness were onerous personal tabus, which he had to keep in the interests of the polity. His sex life, symbolically fused with his fertility and vigor, might be severely restricted. His most elementary physical functions, such as crying, eating, drinking, or defecating, were ritually controlled. And his movements were hemmed in by tabus, such as those against touching the soil in fields or seeing a corpse. And sometimes he might not even be allowed to reach the frailty of old age or, when at the point of death, to expire naturally by himself. Tabus of this sort applied, it should be noted, not only to secluded and unmistakably "sacred" kings but to all African chiefs and kings.

This overall configuration, varying in its details but consistent in its cultural logic, was pan-African and it has often been dubbed by the generic term "divine kingship" (for a review and a psychological interpretation of the complex, see Vaughan 1980). The term has been used for certain kinds of "sacred" kingships throughout the world, but we should not, for that reason, assume their cultural and socio-psychological roots, though perhaps similar, to be the same. The African configuration was an accentuated form of the "sacred" aura that suffused all African authority: kin group elders, village heads, chiefs, and kings were all in some sense "priests" ritually bound to the group they headed. The symbolism of this boundedness was at its most elementary in the ritual duties of the heads of kin groups. Not unexpectedly, the symbolic elaborations were most florid in the royal ritual of large polities.

This takes us back to the continuum we spoke about between hamlet head and king. But within the continuum there was also a crucial dividing line, having to do with the changing nature of the polity. We have summarized this change as a move from a solidarity based on a corporate kinship model to one based on an implicit contract between the rulers and the subjects. This affected the nature of the ruler's "sacredness." The ideology of a corporate kin group denies the possibility of a divergence of interests among its members. Thus, in African kin or quasi-kin groups, it was normally assumed that actions by the kin group's head and elders were taken in the interests of the group as a whole, even if appearances might suggest otherwise. If, however, appearances could no longer be denied, the blame on the elders took the moral and very personal form of an accusation of betrayal—typically, the form of an accusation of "witchcraft" or "sorcery," in which the accused was said to be impelled by evil motives. Alternatively, misfortunes in the group could be blamed on dissensions within the group, on a failure to live up to its corporate nature. Then the solution was a ritual act of collective reconciliation in which all "confessed" to all and all were "forgiven" by all (for a detailed study of this pattern, see Harris 1978).

By contrast, when, in a larger polity—in which the kinship model no longer held—failures were blamed on the ruler, the blame was more akin to an accusation of a breach of contract than to one of betrayal. Such an accusation was impersonal, raising issues of action and not of motive. In this, it partook of the ideology of traditional African "restitutive" law, applying to conflicts that involved people not sharing a common corporate identity. The patrimonial chief, in brief, was expected by his non-kin subjects to live up to his side of the bargain, and the subjects were not interested in his motives but in his performance. This indifference to motivation was congruent with the fact that many of the tabus which the ruler might breach were quite beyond his volitional control—tabus against physical weaknesses, illnesses, and old age. Personal moral blame and punishment for moral transgression were beside the point here. What was expected was outwardly visible performance and an essentially mechanical correction of failure. As Muller (1980) shows in a meticulous study of "divine kingship" among the Rukuba of the Nigerian Jos Plateau, while the sacredness of the king made him "divine," it also made him into a "scapegoat king."

The ultimate ritual blooming of the pragmatic ruler-polity equation was found in the larger established polities, in the classic and utterly specialized kind of "divine kingship." Here, the sacredness of the kingship had been cut away from its pragmatic roots by having been detached from all real politics and real political power. The king had become a remote, secluded, depersonalized, politically powerless, and utterly ritual figure. Thus totally desecularized, it served as pure symbol and scapegoat. Paradoxically, this detachment from pragmatism was the last step in a development that began in its very opposite—the high measure of personalization of active politics in the small frontier polity out of which the mature polity had grown.

RULER-SUBJECT INTER-DEPENDENCE AND POLITY INTEGRATION

The two perspectives on the polity, rooted in the different outlooks of the rulers and the subjects, might remain separate and be expressed by separate bodies of myth in those polities that remained embryonic states (for examples of this phenomenon in such polities, see Piault 1970, Feierman 1974). Or the separateness may be formally frozen into an institutionalized balance of power between chief and people (as among the Yako of southeastern Nigeria, described by Forde 1961, where it was frozen into an institutional opposition between the rulers and the subjects' secret societies). Or the separateness may express itself in an endless oscillation in power between the chief and the subjects (as Geary 1976 shows it for We, in western Cameroon). But the separateness was transcended as the polity matured into a kingdom, where it became less a matter of two perspectives and more that of a dual perspective (indeed, the transcendence of the separateness is what often leads us, as observers, to call such a polity a "kingdom"). What in a small polity might appear to be two separate self-interested views of the constitution by two contending parties had now become as single theory. To be sure, a theory with some ambiguities, but then what political theory is not? Both perspectives were now simultaneously held by both the rulers and the ruled. Both of them, for example, would expound to the investigator one or the other aspect, depending on the situation and context. Under a satisfactory ruler, who had lived up to his nurturing obligations, the subjects would present the patrimonial perspective on rulership, in which the ruler is the absolute "owner" of everything. Similarly, the good ruler would state publicly that his rule rested on the happiness of the people and on their consent. In this respect, the early colonial observers of Africa, who tended to focus on the ideology of the rulers' despotism, and the later liberal observers, who tended to stress the reciprocities between the rulers and the ruled, each gave half of the correct story.

The firmest integration of the two perspectives occurred in fully mature polities at a point of their development that lies beyond the main concerns of our analysis. Nevertheless, a modest exploration "forward" is worthwhile in order to see the working out of frontier themes. In these mature polities, the line between rulers and ruled became blurred, given the networks of kinship and marriage alliances that united the rulers with many of the subjects. The interests of many of those who were formally (and symbolically) among the subjects lay entirely on the side of the rulers; and some branches of the ruling group, with no hope of ever exercising power, had interests allied with the commoners. This blurring made it all the more easy for the duality to be part of a unified theory—the contradiction was spared from being confirmed by real political divisions. The duality could thus acquire an unchallenged integrative function in the constitutional realm (or, if one prefers another analytical idiom, the duality could successfully serve an "ideological"—that is, socially justifying—function).

This integrative function was vividly expressed in the way the two perspectives were woven into the single fabric of royal rituals (for a descriptive summary of these rituals, see Mair 1977:39ff). The ethnographic literature shows strikingly similar themes in royal rituals across the map of Africa, even if there are arguments among scholars about the specific nature of their integrative action (e.g., on the Swazi, see disagreements among Kuper 1947, Gluckman 1954, Beidelman 1966, Apter 1983). Similar themes occur among peoples as widely scattered as the Swazi, the Asante (Rattray 1923), the Fon of Dahomey (Herskovits 1938, Argyle 1966), the Yoruba (Lloyd 1960), the Jukun (Meek 1931), the Ndembu (Turner 1969), the Nyakyusa (Wilson 1959), the Nyoro (Beattie 1971), and the Shilluk (Evans-Pritchard 1948)—to give a very random sample. The royal installation ceremonies always involved the active participation of the symbolic representatives of the people whose role it was to admonish the new king on his responsibilities and to remind him that he was king by the will of the people; sometimes, the king was dressed in rags, or beaten, or made to crouch before the people's elders and harangued by them (leading Gluckman 1954 to refer to them as rituals of rebellion). At the same time, however, it was clear—from the very intensity of these preventive harangues—that the power, once conferred on the new incumbent, was in theory absolute and, publicly at least, unquestioned.

Our analysis contends that there are, roughly speaking, four stages in the growth of frontier settlements that develop into chieftaincies and kingdoms: (1) The initial immigrant settlement, organizing its limited expansion on the model of a corporate kin group. (2) The growth of the latter into a chieftaincy that incorporated new subjects and neighboring settlements into an integrated polity built on the recognition of the separateness and interdependence of rulers and subjects; this was done according to a model of an implicit contract which glossed over the role of force in the making of the polity. (3) The maturing of the preceding chieftaincy into a "kingdom." And (4) the further expansion of the kingdom through open conquest and frank domination of peripheral areas; this created an outer circle of vassal polities and subordinate allies, over whom—as Fairley (Ch.2) points out—control was achieved by pragmatic means, including force, rather than by symbolic means.

Our analysis has confined itself to the first two stages, which are the ones directly conditioned by the frontier dynamic. These are also the stages that produced the building blocks out of which the larger African political units were constructed, be they states, "segmentary states," or confederations. In polities that proceeded to the subsequent stages, other forces came to the fore, involving processes usually considered under the rubric of "state formation" (and which do not exclude an extensive use of the kinship model, as the structural skeleton of the state, as in the striking example of the Bamum state analyzed by Tardits 1980). But these processes are beyond our concerns, for by this time the frontier was no more. (An introduction to state formation may be found, for African polities, in Mair 1977, Forde and Kaberry 1967, Lloyd 1965, and, in worldwide perspective, in Balandier 1970, and Cohen and Service 1978.)

The ritual reflecting the dual perspective of the rulers and the ruled arose in the second stage of frontier political formation, when the division between rulers and subjects could no longer be glossed over by the kinship model, and it performed integrative functions in the third stage, that of the mature kingdom. The division was recognized and ritually accommodated to, without being abolished. But in an expanded patrimonial polity, in which the rulers conflated the various stages of the polity's expansion into a simple increase in the size of their estate, all chiefly rituals were—from the rulers' point of view—varieties of household rituals, regardless of their historical emergence at, and functional appropriateness to, the different stages in the polity's growth. Just as the rituals to the founders' ancestors—appropriate to the first frontier stage—continued to be performed at later stages, so the rituals reflecting the different perspectives of the rulers and the ruled continued after the polity's expansion had moved into its third stage. And they were also performed in the large conquest kingdoms, with their outer circle of uncertain vassals even though the integration promoted by them continued to apply only to the second and third level of the polity's integration, now represented by the kingdom's core.

This allows us to return to the question of the "tribal" model, posed at the beginning of this analysis. The earlier phases of the second stage ushered in those culturally mixed "anomalous" societies that I mentioned as being so uncomfortable for the "tribal" model. But this was also the stage out of which, as the integration of the mixed frontier society continued, there emerged—in the third, mature stage—the kinds of cultural-political-ethnic formations that approached the "tribal" model of African societies, with its uniformities of custom, language, and polity. In this third stage, the ruler-subject division in its simple original form was transcended. This transcendence did not mean that internal tensions had been abolished but, precisely, that they were now of another kind, involving different kinds of interests (such as regional chiefs, factions among councillors, different segments of the royal kin group, and so on).

All this leads one to some tentative thoughts. It may be that such a formation represented the largest integrated structural unit that the political-symbolic resources of traditional African societies could yield. Its solidarity, in Durkheimian terms (Durkheim 1915), was the "mechanical" social solidarity based on common belief and outlook. This was also the solidarity that characterized the initial frontier settlement and it was the solidarity that the emerging polity sought to reproduce as it grew, not least through ritual means. But the resulting formation—the "kingdom" of the third stage—reached the outer limits of its possibilities. Beyond it, the large political formations were perforce pragmatic and fragile assemblages of disparate political units, forever threatened with secession and held together by force or cunning. The "tribal" model became again increasingly inapplicable. Whatever the new means of integration that held the very large African states together, they were not of the kind postulated in the tribal model.

THE REGIONAL CONTEXT

Innumerable conquerors in the history of the world—from Arabs to Russians and from Scandinavians to Zulus—have cheerfully ruled over others, desiring no legitimizing charter but the fact of conquest itself. And so have innumerable small societies, in Africa as elsewhere, though their predatory histories are less well known. One must consequently resist the nineteenth-century bourgeois temptation, to which Marxists often succumb, of assuming that legitimation needs to be couched in a moral idiom—and, as a corollary, that most moral political statements must have the hidden purpose of legitimation. What is more certain is that legitimation is couched in a culturally valued idiom, as is the manipulation of legitimizing claims. In areas of relative cultural homogeneity, such as Sub-Saharan Africa, one expects that the legitimizing arguments will consistently exhibit such common, culturally attractive themes.

The principal theme in the legitimation of African rulers vis-à-vis their subjects and immediate neighbors on the frontier was that of "first-comer"—in one of its many senses. But the founding group also needed two other kinds of validating charters, one providing an existential validation of the group to itself, the other providing validation in the eyes of other regional polities. In traditional Africa, political independence did not provide self-evident validation, as it has in modern Western thought. Like "titles," "medicines," or cults, which could not be taken seriously if simply produced locally by creative invention, one's status had to be legitimized by an established authority.

The first validation—of oneself to oneself—had to come from one's dependence upon ancestors. Thus, among the Ekie, we see the independent king of Luba origin continue to sacrifice to his Luba ancestors as part of his royal ritual (Fairley, Ch.2). Since for immigrants such ancestral validation could not be local, it had to reach out beyond the immediate area. In contrast to the "firstcomer" charter, which attempted to root the immigrants locally, this charter established the rulers as outsiders and further reinforced the paradox that we have discussed—that of the rulers being simultaneously firstcomers and latecomers.

The need for the other validation—the one to regional polities—began as the polity grew and acquired a regional stature. "Being first" in one's own corner of the region was not enough anymore—such a charter carried little weight with neighbors whose own expansion had been on the frontier. To have any regional standing, the polity needed a charter that drew upon widespread regional values, themes, and traditions, and upon historical events and memories that carried prestige in the region as a whole. It is not surprising that, within a given African cultural ecumene, accounts of state origins tend to be strikingly repetitive as one moves from society to society, consisting of re-combinations of the same thematic elements, in much the same way that folktales combine and re-combine the same motifs—a pattern exhaustively documented by Heusch (1982) for the southern savanna belt in his theory of Central African kingship. In these accounts, legitimacy is sought by associating one's origins with mythical events, prestigious historical figures, and grand polities known in the region but often rooted outside of it.

Whether or not distance in time and space lends enchantment, it does make close scrutiny of historical claims difficult. Thus, in southwestern Zaire and northwestern Angola, many polities have claimed descent from the ancient kingdom of the Kongo or one of the other historical kingdoms remembered in the area. To the east of this region, links with the Lunda and Luba empires were asserted over many hundreds of miles. To the north, around the area where now meet the Sudan, Zaire, and the Central African Republic, similar links were claimed to the Zande "empire." In the Benue River region of Nigeria, one alleged a historical connection with the defunct Jukun empire. And so also elsewhere: one claimed links with the "Tikar" in western Cameroon, with Benin in southern Nigeria, with Monomotapa in the Zambezi region, and with the shadowy Kitara kingdom of the legendary Chwezi or with the Bito in East Africa. Modern African states and rulers have in the same way sought political blessings from the past by claiming some connection with ancient Ghana, or Mali, or Benin, or Zimbabwe, or even with the nineteenth-century ephemeral and predatory "empire" of Samory Toure. And so also on the more local stage with which we are concerned here: we find Rwanda dissidents on the frontier claiming to be Rwanda agents (Newbury, Ch.6), the chief of the former slaves on the Somali frontier taking on the title of "Sultan" (Cassanelli, Ch. 8), and even the poly-ethnic "anomalous" frontier community of Mto wa Mbu associating its ethnic mixture with the "progressive" ideal of non-ethnicity favored by the new Tanzanian state.

The pattern is reminiscent of the claims to political descent from the Roman Empire, asserted for a good millennium of European history by rulers on the make, from Charlemagne to Ivan the Third. But in Africa, such claims carried their own implications, for descent here imposed a subordination to the parent, if only token or ritual. For, as we have stressed before, a tie once in existence was not easily broken and it tended to linger on. This is one reason for the often many-layered "ethnic" identities one finds within a single African society: new identities do not wipe out old ones but are added to them. Given this, it was possible to assert what was culturally plausible—that one was reviving old lingering ties.

When the claimed link was to dead heroes or defunct dynasties and polities, it posed no problems. But when the famous polity, or its direct descendant, was politically alive, one's enjoyment of the prestige of association was tempered by the double need to validate visibly the connection and to deal with one's subordinate status. One might validate the connection by occasional token tribute payments to a distant polity—something the latter was unlikely to refuse. Thus, in southern Zaire and northern Angola, chieftaincies claiming Lunda connections would occasionally send, or locally claim to send, token tribute to the distant Lunda king. Or one might have the ruler of a prestigeful kingdom do the ritual installation of one's own rulers—which added to the prestige of both polities within their respective regions. Or one might claim a status historically senior to the source of the prestige, thus avoiding the need for tribute. In southwestern Zaire, many a petty chiefdom has claimed to have been founded by an "older brother" of an ancient king of the Kongo. While all these stories were in one sense "charters of separation" from parent polities, they should not be viewed exclusively as charters for independence. The very act of bringing up a link from the past, even if only to show how it was discarded, was a way of asserting that there was such a link. And, as we have stressed, severed relations were seldom seen as being permanently broken.

When the derivation from an existing polity was relatively recent and real, and the polity not very distant, both the problems and the possibilities were more concrete. On the one hand, association with a strong regional polity gave one an extra chip in the local game of power: one could appear to be under the protection of a superior metropole, with access to its aid. On the other hand, this placed one in formal subordination to the very metropole from whose jurisdiction one had escaped by moving to the frontier. One solution was to keep one's distance from the metropole while giving recognition to it by way of occasional symbolic payments whose meaning, oscillating between tribute and gift, could be redefined with changing fortunes. The uncertain arrangement was not without appeal to the metropole: by receiving nominal recognition of its seniority, its symbolic jurisdiction was spread to an area that was in fact beyond its control. This dynamic of ambiguous sovereignty makes it foolhardy to project the size of kingdoms and empires directly from oral traditions. For, paradoxically, the inferences about the great size of these empires have to be made from reports of their numerous links with outlying polities—links that may bear witness merely to the divisive forces of secession within them and to the parochial politics of prestige in neighboring areas beyond their control.

It is a commonplace observation that, in Africa as elsewhere, historical accounts often contain contradictions because various elements and factions in a polity advance those versions of the charter that are most favorable to them. But the contradictions in the charters of African polities went beyond that. Some of their consistent inconsistencies were systemic responses to the contradictory needs embedded in the very genesis of the polities as frontier formations: their charters sought to embody both independence and links with other polities, much as they embodied the contradictory perspectives of the ruler and the ruled. The two features were not unrelated.

The perspective of the subjects emphasized the primacy of their physical occupation of the land rather than their outside links, for the latter could undermine the only useful local claims they had. If one were a subject, one had best maximize one's rights by claiming to be an aboriginal conquered subject. The alternative was to be a latecoming subject, whose status could be perilously close to that of an alien and a "slave." And while emphasizing one's own local rootedness, one also stressed the non-local origins of the rulers.

For the rulers, their claim to primacy of occupation was best phrased in political rather than physical terms—as primacy in the establishment of a valid social order. This was not only because (as we have previously stressed) a claim for real chronological precedence was rarely feasible. Unlike the subjects, who had primarily parochial political interests, the rulers had to present themselves on a regional stage that included other polities. In the regional context, primacy of local occupation conferred no advantage while outside links did. The rulers' definition of primacy of occupation in other than purely chronological terms could satisfy both the internal and the external political requirements: it gave legitimacy at home and allowed for claims to outside ties abroad. The overall result was, yet again, to emphasize the foreignness of the rulers and the aboriginality of the subjects, and thus to reinforce the role of their two perspectives in the constitution of a growing frontier polity. To the extent that earlier generations of anthropologists and historians often took the rulers' history to be that of the ethnic group as a whole, this strengthened the "migratory" flavor of African ethnic history. And to the extent that their theories predisposed them to see conquest as the prime factor in the formation of states, they had no difficulty finding conquest in oral histories. Conquest there certainly was—but later, after the small-scale polities formed on the frontier moved (when they did at all) into the next phase of their expansion.

The recognition by emergent polities of links with established metropoles was one of the mechanisms that provided a historical continuity between frontier and mature societies in Africa. To validate visibly the link, the frontier society would strive to reproduce the political forms of its metropolitan "parent," as, on the material plane, it imitated its paraphernalia (thus, the "horned" Lunda beaded cap worn by chiefs claiming Lunda origin or, in the eastern Nigerian "Middle-Belt," the feather on top of the head worn by petty chiefs to indicate some connection with the defunct Jukun empire, or the increasing modern use of the assumedly "Tikar" term *fon* by local chiefs in the Grassfields region of western Cameroon). The result was, so to speak, a continuous "feeding" of the frontier areas with sophisticated metropolitan patterns. The reproduction of these patterns on the frontier perpetuated some of the fundamental features of the regional variant of pan-African political culture.

This back-and-forth mechanism of diffusion-through-time of political ideas, symbols, and structures, as well as broad cultural patterns, stands in sharp contrast to those frontier societies on other continents that saw themselves as radically breaking away from their metropoles. When the United States and South American countries were shaping their charters of legitimacy, they based them on a negative revolutionary disjunction from the mother countries and, appropriately, they appealed for positive validation to timeless universalistic political values. The specific political order of the mother country was not something they sought to reproduce, even if (as we have suggested in the case of the United States) some of the mother country's cultural aspirations were in fact being put into practice. African polities, by contrast, sought their legitimacy in a *quasi* genealogical link with an established metropole, past or present. Hence, the closest possible emulation of the metropolitan political culture served as further proof of the reality of the claimed political descent. Such a pattern, obviously, insures a considerable continuity through time of cultural forms.

THE AFRICAN FRONTIER AND THE REPRODUCTION OF SOCIETIES

This analysis has used the concept of the frontier in order to explicate (rather than, more ambitiously, to explain) certain features of African political culture. Though inspired by Turner's frontier thesis for the United States, the procedures followed have been clearly different from his, not least in *what* was being explained. In a manner typical of nine-teenth-century American (frontier?) materialism, Turner sought to leap from the material conditions of the frontier directly to American national psychology. But this leap is all the more impossible because, as we have pointed out, the American frontier stands out as a glaring exception among most frontiers in world history. Our analysis has tried to take a shorter step—from the political ecology of the frontier and its constraints to the structural setting in which African political culture was perpetuated and to the shaping in this setting of certain fundamental and very often contradictory features of that political culture. The analysis emphasized pan-African cultural unity—a reality which it is high time to begin analyz-ing and which must be made a part (even if as implicitly as European cultural commonalities are in the writing of European history) of any cultural and historical analyses of Sub-Saharan Africa. Given this emphasis on pan-African culture, we have dwelt on the conservative functions of the African internal frontier. There is no doubt, however, that the frontier concept can also serve to explicate cultural divergences *within* the African cultural continuities.

In its emphasis on continuities, the analysis has some bearing outside of Africa—namely, for Afro-American populations of the New World. Afro-American societies have played a special role in anthropological the-ory. Many scholars—most notably, Herskovits (1940, 1966)—have looked to them as examples of the dynamics of cultural persistence; in the process, they have searched for those fundamental African cultural principles whose persistence they were studying. In this enterprise, a privileged place has been occupied by independent Afro-American communities set up by former slaves. These were for the most part so-called "Maroon" commu-nities—independent settlements of escaped slaves (for a survey, see Price 1979). They were established in inaccessible and easily defended regions—in effect, natural frontier areas—such as the jungles of the Amazon (Kent 1965) or the Guianas (Herskovits and Herskovits 1934, Price 1975), or the mountain fastness of Jamaica (Kopytoff 1978). A close study of these African-derived communities from a frontier perspective would yield in-teresting comparisons with frontier dynamics in Africa, including Africa's own "Maroon" communities—the scarcely studied communities of Afri-cans who had escaped slavery within African societies, of which Cassanelli (Ch. 8) provides an example.

In presenting my analysis of the internal African frontier, I have fol-lowed an order of argument suggested by a developmental scheme of a "model" African frontier community. But the scheme must not be taken as deterministic in its direction. As Feierman (1974:167) has emphasized, the historical trajectory has not been all in one direction: states have given way to "stateless" societies no less than the other way around. In this respect, of course, African history is not different from that of other continents. One might add that short back-and-forth movements had also taken place. Innumerable social formations on the African frontier that gave the appearance of being incipient societies failed to develop and disappeared: their inhabitants broke up into smaller communities, or were annexed by another polity, or returned to their metropoles, or simply disbanded. This left political room for other attempts at social construction on the frontier. From this perspective, the ethnographic map of Africa assumes a different look: instead of being a patchwork of classic tribes, it was through the centuries more like a shimmering beadwork of repetitive patterns—hamlets, little and large chieftaincies, kingdoms, and empires— each of which was in constant structural motion as it changed its shape from one pattern to another.

Among the frontier formations that survived and grew, most stabilized into small-scale polities and remained in that condition for long periods before disappearing. Only a few experienced in full the potential cycle of growth, expansion, stabilization, further expansion, and eventual decay. This full cycle is attested to by the "shrunken" remains of previously expansive polities that had survived into the colonial period and into our scholarly awareness. Nearly all the historically known grand African polities of any degree of antiquity had experienced such a shrinkage, when they did not disappear altogether. These are the well-known "empires" that appear in African history textbooks: Kongo, Oyo, Benin, Tekrur, Mali, Ghana, to make a random list. And as they shrank, other polities rose at their frontiers and a few expanded at their expense. Similar though more modest local processes affected far greater numbers of other polities of various sizes, for most of which no records exist.

Only the early stages of the full cycle are of concern to our analysis, which has focused on the genesis of small-scale frontier polities whatever their subsequent fate. But here too it must be stressed that even this early trajectory did not lie behind every African kingdom. The development of a small old polity—whose possible frontier origins had been long forgotten—into a larger one was subject to the same forces as the growth of one on the frontier (see, e.g., the study of the growth of such an old polity in recent times by Bennett 1971). But this, in turn, does not negate the participation of these polities in the general, frontier-conditioned African political culture.

The present analysis focuses above all on the genesis of small-scale polities—an issue worthy of attention in its own right and not merely as part of the wider problem of political evolution, to which small-scale polities are interesting because they represent a transition between some assumed elementary form and full-blown states. Nor am I concerned here with some primordial past in which hypothetical "bands" became "tribes" or "chiefdoms" on the way to becoming "kingdoms." If small-scale societies were only a transition, surely the inexorable march of political evolution should have swept most of them away long ago, leaving but a few of them here and there as exemplars of some inexplicable evolutionary lag.

In the harsh light of ethnography, bands do not grow into chiefdoms, nor do most chiefdoms grow out of bands. The African societies we know were all born not "in the beginning" but as part of a continuous and variegated process of interaction and social formation—a process that involved a local political ecology that included these forms as part of the conditions in which they were created and re-created. It was an ecology that made for the fact that"states and stateless societies have existed side by side for over nearly two millennia" (Curtin et al. 1978:82)—and this time estimate may be needlessly conservative. The internal frontier was an important part of that ecology and it systemically produced innumerable small-scale polities and societies—together, to be sure, with other mechanisms that produced new social formations within the structures of mature societies.

As we have seen, small polities arose not out of archaic bands rooted in pre-history but were produced out of the entrails of existing functioning societies, of which some were small polities and some were large and mature states. Nor was the culture with which these small polities began their existence something *sui generis*; rather, it was carried by them ready-made from the metropole to the frontier. While chieftaincies did arise out of small settlements, it is equally important to stress that small settlements began, ideologically, as scaled-down chieftaincies. Instead of long lines of proliferating organic growth, in which simpler forms became transmuted into more complex ones, what we see are building-blocks of different sizes, and chips off the blocks, and the moving kaleidoscope of their grouping and re-grouping. This process has been steady and constant and consequently its products—small polities and societies—ubiquitous.

The early stages of small incipient polities, however, have been seldom available to direct observation. To recapture them, we must turn to mature societies and examine them "backwards" into their early history. Most of the societies that allow us to do this are those that presented themselves as mature societies to the nineteenth-century colonial occupiers and (having often become frozen in their mature form by colonial rule) to the twentieth-century scholars. For the most part, it is such societies that are dealt with in this book—necessarily so, since almost all of those that have failed to mature are accessible neither to historians nor to anthropologists. Together with other ethnographic data, they do, nevertheless, permit us to see the working out of the frontier dynamic in the early stages of their formation. And the understanding of this dynamic should help the historical imagination in its probing of questions for which evidence may be almost entirely lacking. As with so much else in African history, with its paucity of written records, to reconstruct from the few pieces that we know we must have a structured understanding of what we do not and may never know. This examination of the frontier peculiar to Africa has sought to present such a structured understanding of both the known and the unknown.

REFERENCES

Argyle, W.J. 1966. *The Fon of Dahomey.* London: Oxford University Press.

Apter, Andrew. 1983. "In Dispraise of the King: Rituals 'Against' Rebellion in South-East Africa." *Man* (n.s.) 18: 521-534.

Arens, W. 1979. *On the Frontier of Change.* Ann Arbor: University of Michigan Press.

Austen, Ralph A. and Daniel Headrick. 1983. "The Role of Technology in the African Past." *African Studies Review* 26(3-4): 163-184.

Balandier, Georges. 1970. *Political Anthropology.* New York: Random House.

Barnes, J.A. 1951. "The Perception of History in a Plural Society: The Study of the Ngoni Group in Northern Rhodesia." *Human Relations* 15: 295-303.

———. 1954. *Politics in a Changing Society.* London: Oxford University Press.

Barnes, Sandra. 1986. *Patrons and Power: Creating a Political Community in Metropolitan Lagos.* Manchester: Manchester University Press for the International African Institute.

Beattie, J.H.M. 1971. *The Nyoro State.* Oxford: Clarendon Press.

Beidelman, T.O. 1966. "Swazi Royal Ritual." *Africa* 36:373-405.

Bennett, Norman Robert. 1971. *Mirambo of Tanzania: 1840?-1884.* New York: Oxford University Press.

Billington, Ray Allen. 1967. "The American Frontier." In *Beyond the Frontier,* edited by Paul Bohannan and Fred Plog, pp. 3-24. New York: Natural History Press.

Binsbergen, W.M.J. van. 1981. *Religious Change in Zambia.* London: Routledge and Kegan Paul.

Bloch, Marc. 1961. *Feudal Society.* Chicago: University of Chicago Press.

Bohannan, Laura. 1949. "Dahomean Marriage: A Re-evaluation." *Africa* 19: 273-287.

———. 1958. "Political Aspects of Tiv Social Organization." In *Tribes Without Rulers,* edited by John Middleton and David Tait, pp. 33-66. London: Routledge and Kegan Paul.

Bohannan, Paul. 1954. "The Migration and Expansion of the Tiv." *Africa* 24:2-16.

Bohannan, Laura and Paul Bohannan. 1953. *The Tiv of Central Nigeria.* London: International African Institute.

Bohannan, Paul and Fred Plog, eds. 1967. *Beyond the Frontier: Social Process and Cultural Change.* Garden City, N.Y.: Natural History Press.

Bradbury, R.E. 1971. "Patrimonialism and Gerontocracy in Benin Political Culture." In *Man in Africa,* edited by Mary Douglas and Phyllis M. Kaberry, pp. 17-37. New York: Anchor/Doubleday.

Chalifoux, J.-J. 1979. "Polyandrie et dialectique communautaire chez les Abisi du Nigeria." *Anthropologie et Societes,* 3(1): 75-127.

Clark, John D. 1970. *The Prehistory of Africa.* London: Thames and Hudson.

Cohen, Abner. 1969. *Custom and Politics in Urban Africa: A Study of Hausa Migrants in Yoruba Towns.* Berkeley: University of California Press.

Cohen, David. 1977. *Womunafu's Bunafu: A Study of Authority in a Nineteenth-Century African Community.* Princeton: Princeton University Press.

Cohen, Ronald and Elman R. Service, eds. 1978. *Origins of the State: The Anthropology of Political Evolution.* Philadelphia: Institute for the Study of Human Issues.

Cohen, Ronald and John Middleton. 1970. "Introduction." In *From Tribe to Nation in Africa: Studies in Incorporation Processes,* edited by Ronald Cohen and John Middleton, pp. 1-34. Scranton, Pennsylvania: Chandler.

Collard, Chantal. 1979. "Mariage 'a petits pas' et mariage 'par vol': pouvoir des hommes, des femmes et des chefs chez les Guidars." *Anthropologie et Societes,* 3(1): 41-73.

Colson, Elizabeth. 1974. *Tradition and Contract: The Problem of Order.* Chicago: Aldine.

Commager, Henry Steele. 1977. *The Empire of Reason: How Europe Imagined and America Realized the Enlightenment.* New York: Anchor/Doubleday.

Cunnison, Ian. 1951. *History on the Luapula.* London: Oxford University Press.

Curtin, Philip D. 1984. *Cross-Cultural Trade in World History.* Cambridge, England: Cambridge University Press.

Curtin, Philip, Steven Feierman, Leonard Thompson and Jan Vansina. 1978. *African History.* Boston: Little, Brown.

D'Azevedo, Warren. 1962. "Some Historical Problems in the Delineation of a Central West Atlantic Region." *Annals, New York Academy of Sciences* 96(2): 512-538.

De Kiewiet, C. W. 1957. *A History of South Africa: Social and Economic.* London: Oxford University Press.

Douglas, Mary. 1951. "A Form of Polyandry among the Lele of the Kasai." *Africa* 21:1-12.

Durkheim, Emile. 1915. *The Elementary Forms of Religious Life.* New York: Macmillan.

Eccles, W. J. 1983. *The Canadian Frontier: 1534-1760.* Albuquerque: University of New Mexico Press. Rev. Ed.

Evans-Pritchard, E.E. 1940. *The Nuer.* London: Clarendon Press.

———. 1948. *The Divine Kingship of the Shilluk.* Cambridge, England: Cambridge University Press.

———. 1965. *Kinship and Marriage among the Nuer.* Oxford: Clarendon Press.

Fagan, Brian and Roland Oliver. 1975. *Africa in the Iron Age: c. 500 B.C. to 1400 A.D.* New York: Cambridge University Press.

Feierman, Steven. 1974. *The Shambaa Kingdom: A History.* Madison: University of Wisconsin Press.

Fernandez, James W. 1967. "The Shaka Complex." *Transition* (Kampala), 6: 53-64 (March).

———. 1971. "Bantu Brotherhood: Symmetry, Socialization, and Ultimate Choice in Two Bantu Cultures." In *Kinship and Culture,* edited by Francis L. K. Hsu, pp. 339-366. Chicago: Aldine.

Forde, Daryll. 1961. "The Governmental Roles of Associations among the Yako." *Africa* 31(4).

Forde, Daryll and Phyllis M. Kaberry., eds. 1971. *West African Kingdoms in the Nineteenth Century.* London:

Fortes, Meyer. 1953. "The Structure of Unilineal Descent Groups." *American Anthropologist* 55:17-41.

Fried, Morton H. 1968. "On the Concept of 'Tribe' and 'Tribal Society'." In *Essays on the Problem of Tribe,* edited by June Helm, pp. 3-20. (Proceedings of the 1967 Annual Spring Meeting of the American Ethnological Society.) Seattle: University of Washington Press.

Geary, Christraud. 1976. *We—Die Genese Eines Hauptlingstums im Grasland von Kamerun.* Wiesbaden: Franz Steiner Verlag.

Gerhard, Dietrich. 1959. "The Frontier in Comparative View." *Comparative Studies in Society and History,* 1: 205-229.

Gluckman, Max. 1954. *Rituals of Rebellion in South-East Africa.* Manchester: Manchester University Press.

———. 1963. "The Rise of a Zulu Empire." *Scientific American,* 202:

Goody, Jack. 1971. *Technology, Tradition, and The State in Africa.* London: Oxford University Press.

Gough, Kathleen. 1971. "Nuer Kinship: A Re-examination." In *The Translation of*

Culture: Essays to E.E. Evans-Pritchard, edited by T.O. Beidelman, pp. 70-121. London: Tavistock.

Greenberg, Joseph H. 1970. *The Languages of Africa.* Bloomington: Indiana University Press. 3rd ed.

Harris, Grace. 1978. *Casting out Anger: Religion among the Taita of Kenya.* Cambridge, England: Cambridge University Press.

Helms, Mary W. and Franklin O. Loveland, eds. 1976. *Frontier Adaptations in Lower Central America.* Philadelphia: Institute for the Study of Human Issues.

Henderson, Richard. 1972. *The King in Every Man: Evolutionary Trends in Onitsha Society and Culture.* New Haven: Yale University Press.

Hennessy, Alistair. 1978. *The Frontier in Latin American History.* London: Edward Arnold.

Herskovits, Melville J. 1938. *Dahomey: An Ancient West African Kingdom.* 2 vols. New York: Augustin.

———. 1941. *The Myth of the Negro Past.*

———. 1966. *The New World Negro: Selected Papers in AfroAmerican Studies,* edited by Frances S. Herskovits. Bloomington: Indiana University Press.

Herskovits, M.J. and F.S. Herskovits. 1934. *Rebel Destiny: Among the Bush Negroes of Dutch Guiana.* New York: McGraw-Hill.

Heusch, Luc de. 1982. *The Drunken King or The Origin of the State.* Bloomington: Indiana University Press.

Hill, Christopher. 1965. *Intellectual Origins of the English Revolution.* Oxford: Clarendon Press.

Horton, Robin. 1972. "Stateless Societies in the History of West Africa." In *History of West Africa,* edited by J.F.A. Ajayi and Michael Crowder, pp. 78-119. New York: Columbia University Press.

Isaacman, Allen. 1972. "The Origin, Formation and Early History of the Chikunda of South Central Africa." *Journal of African History* 13:443-461.

Isaacman, Allen and Barbara. 1975. "The Prazeros as Transfrontiersmen: A Study in Social and Cultural Change." *The International Journal of African Historical Studies.* 8, No. 1.

Janelli, Roger L. and Dawnhee Yim Janelli. 1978. "Lineage Organisation and Social Differentiation in Korea." *Man* (n.s.) 13: 272-289.

Kent, R. K. 1965. "Palmares: An African State in Brazil." *Journal of African History* 6: 161-175.

Kopytoff, Barbara Klamon. 1978. "The Early Political Development of Jamaican Maroon Society." *William and Mary Quarterly,* 3rd ser., 35(2): 287-307.

Kopytoff, Igor. 1977. "Speculations about the Internal African Frontier." In *African Studies Association Papers,* Waltham, Mass: African Studies Association.

———. 1981. "Aghem Ethnogenesis and the Grassfields Ecumene." In *Contribution de la recherche ethnologique à l'histoire des civilisations du Cameroun,* edited by Claude Tardits, pp. 371-381. (Colloques Internationaux du C.N.R.S. No. 551.) Paris: Centre National de la Recherche Scientifique.

Kopytoff, Igor and Suzanne Miers. 1977. "African Slavery as an Institution of Marginality." In *African Slavery: Historical and Anthropological Perspectives,* edited by Suzanne Miers and Igor Kopytoff, pp. 1-81. Madison: University of Wisconsin Press.

Kuper, Adam. 1982. "Lineage Theory: A Critical Retrospect." *Annual Review of Anthropology* 11: 71-95.

Kuper, Hilda. 1947. *An African Aristocracy: Rank among the Swazi.* London: Oxford University Press.

Lamar, Howard and Leonard Thompson, eds. 1981. *The Frontier in History: North America and Southern Africa Compared.* New Haven: Yale Univesity Press.

Lancaster, C.S. 1971. "The Economics of Social Organization in an Ethnic Border Zone: The Goba (Northern Shona) of the Zambezi Valley." *Ethnology* 10: 445-465.

———. 1981. *The Goba of the Zambezi: Sex Roles, Economics, and Change.* Norman: University of Oklahoma Press.

Lattimore, Owen. 1940. *Inner Asian Frontiers of China.* New York: American Geographical Society.

Launay, Robert. 1982. *Traders Without Trade: Response to Change in Two Dyula Communities.* Cambridge, England: Cambridge University Press.

Le Roy Ladurie, Emmanuel. 1978. *Montaillou: The Promised Land of Error.* New York: G. Braziller.

Leis, Philip. 1972. *Enculturation and Socialization in an Ijaw Village.* New York: Holt, Rinehart and Winston.

Lemarchand, Rene. 1977. "Introduction: In Search of the Political Kingdom." In Rene Lemarchand, ed., *African Kingships in Perspective: Political Change and Modernization in Monarchical Settings,* pp. 1-32. London: Frank Cass.

Lloyd, Peter C. 1960. "Sacred Kingship and Government among the Yoruba." *Africa* 30:221-237.

———. 1965. "The Political Structure of African Kingdoms: An Exploratory Model." In *Political Systems and the Distribution of Power,* edited by Michael Banton (A.S.A. Monograph 2), pp. 63-112. London: Tavistock.

———. 1968. "The Political Development of West African Kingdoms." *Journal of African History* 9(2): 319-329.

LeVine, Robert A. 1976. "Patterns of Personality in Africa." In *Responses to Change: Society, Culture, and Personality,* edited by George A. DeVos, pp. 112-136. New York: D.Van Nostrand.

Lovejoy, Paul E. 1980. *Caravans of Kola:The Hausa Kola Trade, 1700-1900.* Zaria.

MacCormack, Carol P. 1977. "Wono: Institutionalized Dependency in Sherbro Descent Groups (Sierra Leone)." In *African Slavery: Historical and Anthropological Perspectives,* edited by Suzanne Miers and Igor Kopytoff, pp. 181-204. Madison: University of Wisconsin Press.

MacMillan, W.M. 1963. *Bantu, Boer and Briton: The Making of the South African Native Problem.* London.

Mair, Lucy. 1977. *African Kingdoms.* Oxford: Clarendon Press.

Mazrui, Ali. 1967. "The Monarchical Tendency in African Political Culture." *British Journal of Sociology* 18(3): 231-250.

McIntyre, D.W. *The Imperial Frontier in the Tropics: 1865-75.* New York.

Meek, C.K. 1931. *A Sudanese Kingdom: An Ethnographic Study of the Jukun-Speaking Peoples of Nigeria.* London: Kegan Paul, Trench, Trubner and Co.

Middleton, John. 1955. "Notes on the Political Organization of the Madi of Uganda." *African Studies* 14(1): 29-36.

Miller, Joseph C. 1974. *Cokwe Expansion: 1850-1900.* rev. ed. Madison: Occasional Papers of the African Studies Committee, University of Wisconsin, No.1.

———. 1976. *Kings and Kinsmen: Early Mbundu States in Angola.* Oxford: Clarendon Press.

Mitchell, Robert D. 1977. *Commercialism and Frontier: Perspectives on the Early Shenandoah Valley.* Charlottesville: University Press of Virginia.

Muller, Jean-Claude. 1976. *Parente et mariage chez les Rukuba.* Paris: Mouton.

———. 1980. *Le Roi Bouc Emissaire.* Paris: L'Harmatan.

Murdock, George P. 1959. *Africa: Its Peoples and Their Culture History.* New York: McGraw-Hill.

Neumark, S.D. 1957. *Economic Influences on the South African Frontier.* Stanford: Stanford University Press.

Newbury, Colin. 1961. *The Western Slave Coast and Its Neighbors.* London: Oxford University Press.

Nieboer, H.J. 1910. *Slavery as an Industrial System.* 2nd ed. Hague: Nijhoff.

Njaka, Mazi Elechukwu Nnadibuagha. 1974. *Igbo Political Culture.* Evanston: Northwestern University Press.

Oboler, Regina Smith. 1980. "Is the Female Husband a Man? Woman/Woman Marriage among the Nandi of Kenya." *Ethnology* 19: 69-88.

Oliver, Roland and J.D. Fage. 1962. *A Short History of Africa.* Harmondsworth: Penguin Books.

Piault, Marc-Henri. 1970. *Histoire Mawri: Introduction à l'étude des processus constitutifs d'un Etat.* Paris: Centre National de la Recherche Scientifique.

Price, Richard. 1975. *Saramaka Social Structure: Analysis of a Maroon Society in Surinam.* Rio Piedras: Institute of Caribbean Studies of the University of Puerto Rico.

——. ed. 1979. *Maroon Societies: Rebel Slave Communities in the Americas.* 2nd ed. Baltimore: The Johns Hopkins University Press.

Rattray, R.S. 1923. *The Ashanti.* London: Oxford University Press.

Reefe, Thomas Q. 1981. *The Rainbow and the King: A History of the Luba Empire to 1891.* Berkeley: University of California Press.

Roberts, Andrew. 1967. "The History of Abdullah Ibn Suliman." *African Social Research* 4: 241-270.

Sangree, Walter. 1969. "Going Home to Mother: Traditional Marriage among the Irigwe of Benue-Plateau State, Nigeria." *American Anthropologist* 71: 1046-1057.

Smith, M.G. 1952. "Secondary Marriage in Northern Nigeria." *Africa* 23:298-323.

Southall, Aiden W. 1956. *Alur Society.* Cambridge, England: Heffer.

Stein, Burton. 1980. *Peasant State and Society in Medieval South India.* Delhi: Oxford University Press.

Tardits, Claude. 1970. "Femmes a credit." In *Echanges et Communications: Mélanges offerts à Cl. Lévi-Strauss,* edited by Jean Pouillon and Pierre Maranda, pp. 382-390. Paris: Mouton.

——. 1980. *Le Royaume Bamoum.* Paris: Armand Colin.

Taylor, George R. ed. 1956. *The Turner Thesis Concerning the Role of the Frontier in American History.* Boston: D.C. Heath.

Thompson, Edward P. 1963. *The Making of the English Working Class.* New York: Pantheon Books.

Turner, Frederick Jackson. 1893. "The Significance of the Frontier in American History." In *Frontier and Section: Selected Essays,* edited by Ray Allen Billington, pp. 28-36. Englewood Cliffs, N.J.: Prentice-Hall, 1961.

——. 1922. "Sections and Nation." *The Yale Review* 12 (Oct.), pp. 1-21.

Turner, V.W. 1969. *The Ritual Process.* London: Routledge and Kegan Paul.

Uchendu, Victor. 1965. *The Igbo of Southeast Nigeria.* New York: Holt, Rinehart and Winston.

Vansina, Jan. 1962a. "A Comparison of African Kingdoms." *Africa* 32:324-335.

——. 1962b. *L'evolution du royaume rwanda des origines a 1900.* Brussels: Académie royale des sciences d'Outre-Mer.

——. 1966. *Kingdoms of the Savanna.* Madison: University of Wisconsin Press.

——. 1978. *The Children of Woot: A History of the Kuba Peoples.* Madison: University of Wisconsin Press.

Vaughan, James H. 1980. "A Reconsideration of Divine Kingship." In *Explorations in African Systems of Thought,* edited by Ivan Karp and Charles S. Bird, pp. 120-142. Bloomington: Indiana University Press.

Verbeken, Auguste. 1956. *Msiri, roi du Garaganze.* Brussels.

Verdon, Michel. 1983. *The Abutia Ewe of West Africa: A Chiefdom that Never Was.* New York: Mouton.

Wallerstein, Immanuel. 1960. "Ethnicity and National Integration in West Africa." *Cahiers d'Etudes Africaines* I: 129-139.

Warnier, Jean-Pierre. 1980. "Les precurseurs de l'Ecole Berlitz: le multilinguisme dans les Grassfields du Cameroun au 19e siecle." In *L'Expansion Bantoue,* edited by L. Bouquiaux. II: 827-844. Paris: CNRS.

Weber, Eugen. 1976. *Peasants into Frenchmen: The Modernization of Rural France, 1870-1914.* Stanford: Stanford University Press.

Whitten, Norman E. 1974. *Black Frontiersmen: A South American Case.* Cambridge, Mass.: Schenkman.

Willey, Gordon R. and Jeremy A. Sabloff. 1980. *A History of American Archaeology.* rev. ed. San Francisco: W. H. Freeman.

Williamson, Kay. 1962. "Changes in the Marriage System of the Okrika Ijo." *Africa* 31:53-60.

Wilson, Monica. 1959. *Communal Rituals of the Nyakyusa.* London: Oxford University Press.

Wyman, Walker D. and Clifton B. Kroeber, eds. 1957. *The Frontier in Perspective.* Madison: University of Wisconsin Press.

PART TWO

Case Studies

Introduction to Case Studies

Each of the nine case studies presented here touch on most of the issues raised in Part I. These societies are scattered throughout Sub-Saharan Africa. Hence, the re-appearance in each of them of the principal themes of the frontier process reinforces the validity of the assumption, made in the analysis in Part I, that there is indeed a pan-African political culture that has both shaped and been shaped by the genesis of so many African societies on a frontier. At the same time, each case study serves to give a concrete and detailed illustration of some aspect of the frontier process or some peculiar expression of it.

The first two articles are case studies "in the round." Each deals with the genesis and development of a frontier society or a group of societies as a complete process. The first, a study of the Ekie of Zaire by Nancy Fairley, may be taken as a paradigmatic case for it analyzes a complete single frontier cycle which also dovetailed with other cycles. The study also discusses nearly every issue raised in the analysis in Part I. The second study, of the Goba of Zambia by Chet Lancaster, examines the frontier process of a single society as part of a wider regional process and of a repetitive historical dynamic.

The following four studies focus more specifically on special issues. The article on the Kpelle of Liberia, by William Murphy and Caroline Bledsoe, deals intensively with the workings at the community level of a central notion in frontier-conditioned African political culture—that of the political primacy of the "firstcomer." In his turn, Randolph Packard examines how the firstcomer complex was handled in a larger setting among the BaShu of eastern Zaire, a society that encompassed several ethnic groups, each of which laid claims to firstcomer status. The study by David Newbury, of Rwanda, takes us to the other side of the frontier-metropole nexus: it examines the metropolitan stereotypes of the frontier and their impact on metropolitan political ideology. The study of the Ningi state in central Nigeria, by Adell Patton, describes the rise of a frontier state in a setting rendered more complicated by the presence of Islam.

The last three studies deal with the persistence of the frontier process in the contemporary period and under new conditions. Lee Cassanelli examines the little-known case of former Somali slaves, originally from Bantu East Africa, who had set up frontier polities in Somalia. William Arens discusses the development of a twentieth-century polyethnic frontier settlement in Tanzania. And, finally, in the article by Sandra Barnes on the growth of a suburb of the Nigerian capital of Lagos, we see the persistence of some of the principles of African frontier organization on the modern urban frontier.

A PARADIGMATIC CASE

The rise of the Ekie state in southern Zaire, presented here by Nancy Fairley, may serve as a paradigmatic instance of the frontier process. The area in question has been a frontier twice: for the settlers who founded Ekie society and for Luba intruders, one of whom founded the Ekie state.

Before the Luba came, Ekieland had a political system that had itself grown out of an older frontier process. The first Ekie immigrants found, upon their arrival, the "original" inhabitants—Pygmy Twa—who, however, disappeared and presented no ritual problem; this allowed the Ekie to assume the status of "firstcomers" in succeeding developments. The frontier society stabilized into a politically uncentralized system of small polities, tied together by a myth of common descent and the ritual primacy of one of the polities. This suggests that the latter polity, having become the "senior line" in the mythical genealogy embracing all Ekie, was the core group around which the frontier history of the society as a whole was woven. Ekieland was the kind of frontier in which, normally, new weak immigrants were absorbed by being tacked on to the genealogy and becoming yet another segment among existing segments.

This balanced structure was confronted by the expansion of the Luba-Shankadi empire, which became the recognized metropole of the region. Like many other neighboring societies, the Ekie began to assert a historical derivation from this metropole (whatever the historical truth of the matter may be). At least twice, entrepreneurs from the metropole intruded, either as recognized agents of the kingdom or on their own as traders claiming at times to be agents. The first intrusion (which may in reality represent a narrative condensation of several such attempts) resulted in a local Luba settlement which, however, failed to expand. The second intrusion followed a typical frontier pattern: with the permission (or at least tolerance) of the local polities, the Luba immigrants became a small hunting and trading enclave that developed into a small chieftaincy under the leadership of a historically somewhat shadowy founder. Its connections with the Luba-Shankadi empire were ambiguous, probably purposely so, at this point. What is clear is that its leaders asserted their independence when dynastic disorders broke out in the empire.

The small Luba frontier polity then began gradually to incorporate neighboring polities—not by simple force of conquest but by marrying judiciously, by co-opting the Ekie ritual head, and evidently by the skillful use of their prestigeful connection with the metropole (as, for example, in conferring new titles on the leaders of other Ekie segments). This expansion of the core immigrant polity was initiated by a leader who is a historically rounded personage and who, from the Ekie perspective, was the real founder and first ruler of the new Ekie state. But the new Ekie chiefs retained their Luba identity, for ritual reasons and for the prestige it afforded, thus linking their rule with the Ekie claim of having themselves originally come from Luba country.

The established frontier state finally embarked on further expansion, this time by open conquest and domination over other polities on its own frontiers. These polities, rather than being incorporated into what now existed as an integrated Ekie kingdom, were frankly treated as political tributaries. Thus, the rise of the Luba state had generated a new frontier state which in turn became a metropole for yet another set of frontiers.

—Editor

Nancy J. Fairley

2

Ideology and State Formation: The Ekie of Southern Zaire

In Sub-Saharan Africa, state-formation has often been viewed by Africanists as a consequence of conquest. The "conquest theory" explains the emergence of political centralization as the result of one conquering group imposing a new political arrangement on another. More recently, an increasing number of students of African state-formation, such as Feierman (1974), Miller (1976) and Vansina (1978), following the initial lead of Southall (1956), have ventured beyond the conquest theory in their quest to understand the process of "secondary state-formation," that is, the recurrent emergence of states after the original ("primary") development of statehood as a form of political organization had already taken place. This paper attempts to show that actual physical force, or the threat of it, was of relatively minor importance in the process of state-formation among the Ekie of Zaire in the 18th century. Organizational, ideological, and ritual innovations were of greater significance in shaping the course of Ekie political centralization, culminating in the eventual paramountcy of a single office-holder, the king.[1]

My initial analysis of Ekie tradition also suggested that control over subsistence resources was not of central importance in the rise of the Ekie state. Feierman (1974) drew a similar conclusion about the formation of the Shambaa state in Tanzania. His contention that the accumulation of loyal subjects was the primary factor in the early phase of the process applies equally well in the formative period of Ekie political centralization. However, in the case of the Ekie, this poses the next question: how did the new rulers, who were of alien origin, manage to attract and accumulate large numbers of loyal subjects?

Charismatic authority is sometimes offered as an explanation. Thus, Shorter's study of the rule of the Nyamwezi chief, Nyungu, suggests that the king's monopolization of ritual power was crucial in Nyamwezi political centralization. "Nyungu was virtually claiming to be the only one with any right to ritual power in the countries he conquered. He alone had the charisma of a chief" (Shorter 1972:144). But the monopolization of ritual power by an individual or an office derives from more than charismatic authority: it involves social and ideological innovations. Shorter, however, concentrates on the military superiority of these kings as the main support of their charisma, and, thus, ultimately, he resorts to a variety of the

conquest theory. This approach is in harmony with much of the functionalist literature which sees religion and knowledge of the supernatural as
epiphenomenal to the political structure and social order in African societies, be they state or stateless. By ignoring the importance of history to
the understanding of social and political formations, the approach necessarily relegates religion to a supportive but essentially passive role in an
already functioning polity.

However, other ethnographic studies suggest that African religion has
historically served purposes other than merely those of maintaining the
existing power structure. For example, Wilson's work on Nyakyusa society points to the active role of religion in the development of their political
system. As she states it: "In traditional Nyakyusa society ritual played an
essential part in linking scattered political units" (1959:99). But the historical relevance of this finding remains implicit and Wilson does not provide
a historical analysis of the role of ritual in the emergence of these links.
Ogot's (1972) historical study of Padhola religion is more explicit: it
shows that the spread of a particular religious cult was a key factor in the
centralization of that society's political system. Yet, Ogot also chooses to
concentrate on the role of this cult in maintaining the newly created political order rather than on its role in the creation of it.

As Winter (1969) insists, in discussing the integrating role of religion
among the separate Iraqw territorial groups, religion occupies a more
pivotal role in the social structures of some societies than of others, and
research should pay considerable attention to religious matters in such
instances. To this, I would add that, surely, the centrality of religion in
such societies must carry historical implications, in addition to the more
commonly recognized functional ones.

Recently, Vansina's (1978) analysis of Kuba history indicated that
their ideology of kingship was closely tied to their dominant religious
ideology. During the phase prior to the emergence of the state, designated as the Age of the Chiefs, the power of Kuba chiefs was attributed
to their possession of charms and to their being chosen by nature spirits.
However, the first Kuba King, Shyaam, introduced changes into Kuba
religious ideology, which also had ramifications in their ideology of
kingship. Shyaam became a medium of the nature spirit of one descent
group within the young kingdom; as the power of the succeeding kings
increased, they came to be seen as being spirits themselves (Vansina
1978:204–207).

Let me turn now to the Ekie. Religion is more than peripheral to Ekie
social structure. To fail to take into account the dynamic role of Ekie
religious beliefs and practices in their political centralization would be to
present an incomplete historical documentation of this process.

As this paper will show, ideological innovations of a religious nature
were tools of change in their own right rather than merely means of
maintaining existing political stability. I suggest that the monopoly of the

knowledge of supernatural and religious power by the king was a key factor in the process of state-formation in Ekie society.

EKIE ORIGINS

The Ekie are one of the sixteen sub-groups of the Songye-speaking people who are located in Kasai-Oriental, a province in southern Zaire. Situated in the southwestern part of Songyeland, Ekie territory lies within the savannah region, an area of tall grass punctuated by patches of moist forest.

The Ekie distinguish between the descendants of the original settlers of their present homeland and those groups, of diverse origin, who were later incorporated into the Ekie state. This study focuses on the Ekie Lukula-Ludimbi group, which represents the oldest segment of the population-descendants of the first Ekie who migrated from what is now the province of Shaba to Kasai-Oriental. In mid-twentieth century, this segment of the Ekie numbered about 20,000 (Boone 1961:241).

Ekie oral historians all agree that in the ancient past (that is, before 1600) all of the Songye-speaking groups were one people and that they became separate political entities after they had migrated from Shaba to Kasai-Oriental. Moreover, the oral traditions of all the Songye peoples, including the Ekie, designate the Lake Samba area in Shaba as their ancestral homeland and also claim that they were once part of the Luba-Shankadi empire.

Reefe (1977) points to the frequency with which the peoples of central-eastern Zaire invent fictitious kin connections between their ruling strata and those of the Luba-Shankadi. Nevertheless, several points support the Ekie and Songye claims of this connection: (a) the Luba-Shankadi recognize the Ekie and other Songye peoples as their brothers; (b) Luba oral tradition claims that their first king, Nkongolo, was a Songye; (c) oral traditions of both the Luba and Songye peoples designate Lake Samba as the home of their ancestors; (d) archaeological discoveries by Nenquin in the late 1950's at Lake Samba have led historians such as Vansina (1966) to conclude that this was probably the cradle of Luba and Songye culture; (e) finally, linguistic evidence shows the close similarities in the grammar and structure of the Luba and Songye languages (see Guthrie 1967–1970, Samain 1923).

Ekie oral tradition presents this connection as follows. In ancient times, the Songye were part of the Luba-Shankadi at Kantu na Muanza, in present-day Shaba. The Songye left Kantu na Muanza because of serious discord with the Luba people. Ekie elders claim that the conflict was over the many detestable customs then practiced by the Luba-Shankadi; among the gravest of these was incest. Finding no way to resolve their differences with the Luba-Shankadi, the Songye decided to leave and migrated to eastern Kasai, where they settled in an area called Ejadika. This influx of Songye-speaking peoples pushed the native Twa (pygmies) westward out of this region. In their new homeland, the Songye experienced internal discord and there were more schisms, resulting in the formation of the separate Songye-speaking groups.

There is little agreement about the reasons for the schisms. According to the Ekie, they split off because of their quarrel with the Ekalebue, another Songye sub-group, over rights to a water source and the stealing of Ekie women. As a result, the *primus inter pares* of the Ekie, Makulu, led his group westward into their present-day homeland. These events may be dated to about 1600.

Ekie oral tradition suggests that, between 1600 and 1775, several crucial changes occurred in their socio-political organization. One major change was their transformation from an acephalous society into one with centralized political authority—a state society. This part of Ekie history is best understood if it is divided into two periods: (1) that prior to the creation of the office of Paramount Chief, 1600–1700; and (2) that of state-formation, 1700–1775.

PERIOD PRIOR TO THE CREATION OF THE OFFICE OF PARAMOUNT CHIEF: 1600–1700

Under the leadership of their *primus inter pares,* Makulu, the Ekie settled in the part of Songye territory which lies between Mt. Mvungulu (formerly Mt. Wissman) and the present-day town of Kabinda. Ekie territory lies astride the Ludimbi River. Groups to the east of this river are referred to as the Mudilu and those to the west as Evungu.

During the period 1600–1700, the Ekie lived in village-groups called *kavumbu.* Each kuvumbu recognized one individual, *muto-mukulu* (lit. "the oldest, the biggest"), as *primus inter pares.* A *muto-mukulu* held certain ritual privileges but had no formal political authority over other members of the village-group. Within each Ekie village-group, one village was recognized as the eldest or parent village. And for the Ekie people as a whole, the village of Mulemba, in one of the western *kavumbu,* was—and still is—distinguished as the parent village of all Ekie villages because their first *muto-mukulu* lived and died there. At present, there are 10 *kavumbu* in Ekieland, each averaging 2,000 people and ranging in size from 500 to 3,500. In the early period, the numbers were undoubtedly rather smaller.

Each *kavumbu* now contains, on the average, 5 villages, and villages range in population between 200 and 1500, with an average of 600 persons. In the early period we are considering, the political authority of each village was vested in a council of elders, composed of titled notables and the resident lineage heads, who were responsible for maintaining social order. However, one kind of title holders, the *Bana-Nkana* (sing. *Mwana-Nkana*), owners of the Kibangu staff, were specifically designated as peace-officers; they also announced council decisions, enforced the laws, and arbitrated disputes between clans and villages. The *Bana-Nkana,* it is said, did not use physical force to implement the decisions; it was believed that their power resided in ownership of the Kibangu, a staff that embodied the authority of the ancestors over the living. The highest ritual authority, the priest *Tshite,* was responsible for the investiture of the *Bana-Nkana* and he gave them sanction to use the Kibangu staff.

Tshite was the most ancient of all titles. The right of incumbency of the position was vested in a particular lineage, the Bana Kavungoi. The role was essentially religious—that of being the link between the Ekie collectively and their ancestors. In Ekie religion, as in most African religions, ancestors are attributed immense power over the living. *Tshite* performed the necessary ritual offerings to the ancestors of all the groups, appealing to them for fertility and prosperity on behalf of all the Ekie. *Tshite* did not come into direct contact with the public; the *Bana-Nkana* were his representatives.

It is thus apparent that prior to about 1700, the most important factor in delineating and integrating the various autonomous Ekie communities was the common acceptance of a ritual system "centralized" around the office of *Tshite* by way of its links with each village-group's *Bana-Nkana.* Legal sanction in Ekie society at that time rested primarily on ritual sanction. In purely political terms, however, the Ekie were an uncentralized society. They were also one of the many tributaries of the Luba-Shankadi empire (Vansina 1966). According to Ekie oral tradition, some time after they settled in Kasai-Oriental, a Luba king sent a group of his people under the leadership of *Mpibue* (hunter) Builu to establish themselves in Ekie territory. These Luba settled in the heart of Ekieland, but in a separate village-group, with their own *muto-mukulu,* independent of the Ekie *primus inter pares.*

According to Luba-Shankadi oral tradition, as recorded by Verhulpen (1936:100–103), the Ekie were forced to pay tribute to the seventh Luba king, *Mulopwe* Kadilo. Vansina (1966:156) estimates that Kadilo ruled around 1700 A.D. In all probability, the Luba-Shankadi who installed themselves in Ekieland were representatives of Kadilo's government. Kadilo fought the Ekie and other Songye groups and defeated all of them with the exception of the Kalebue, but he never directly incorporated any of these groups into his kingdom. Thus, these Songye-speaking people retained cultural identities separate from those of the Luba and simply paid tribute to the Luba kingdom.

The Luba agent Builu died and the king of the Luba sent another group, led by *Mpibue* Lubamba, to investigate the nature of Builu's demise. They did not find Builu's death to have been of a suspicious nature.

As with most other Central African traditions of genesis, Ekie tradition includes a lengthy and detailed description of how Lubamba and other members of this second group of Luba envoys came to settle permanently in Ekieland. In brief, Lubamba, who was a mighty hunter, at first traded meat with the Ekie for foodstuffs. Later, when the people of Mulemba, the Ekie head-village, were harassed by a leopard, Lubamba killed it for them. He was thereupon invited to live at Mulemba and given a wife. Eventually, when the Ekie became convinced of his good intentions, Lubamba was given a separate village for himself and his followers. Since, as a foreigner, Lubamba could not hold the title of *Mwana-Nkana,* which was hereditary, the title of *Mfuabana* was created and given to him. In the oral tradition, he is recognized as the first formally political chief among the Ekie. The Ekie also achieved thereby what they had till then unsuccessfully striven for—freedom from the domination of the Luba-Shankadi.

The presentation of these events by the Ekie must be interpreted in the light of the broader history of the region. The fact that Lubamba, supposedly a member of the Luba nobility, had been encouraged to stay in Ekieland suggests at least two possibilities: (1) that Lubamba took advantage of Luba dynastic succession problems to establish his own independence of Luba authority; and (2) that the Ekie found, in this and in their "cooptation" of the Luba warrior, the means to sever their own tributary relation to the Luba empire. We do know that Luba domination over the various Songye peoples ended after Kadilo's death, when conflict over succession to the kingship prevented Kadilo's successor, Kekenya, from retaining control over them. Kekenya's successor, Kumwimba Kaumbo, did renew attacks on the Songye, but was defeated by the Bena Milembue and this ended forever Luba-Shankadi attempts at dominating these Songye groups (Vansina, 1966:156).

THE FORMATION OF THE EKIE STATE: 1700–1775

The title created for Lubamba, *Mfuabana,* has since become the only title in Ekie society which can be acquired by any individual who is financially able to pay for it. Lubamba's title did not require investiture by the religious priest *Tshite.* Instead, Lubamba was invested by the elders at Mulemba, the Ekie head-village. And just as *Tshite* was responsible for the investiture of the *Bana-Nkana,* Lubamba became responsible for the investiture of all holders of the title *Mfuabana.* Thus, a new "secular" structure of titles arose—at first to parallel and eventually to subordinate the older structure of ritual titles.

Regardless of the various and often conflicting accounts of Lubamba's role as "chief" or *Mfuabana,* it is possible to contend that this Luba hunter was indeed first chief among the Ekie whose role was defined in political and not ritual terms. His direct jurisdiction, however, seems to have been restricted to the village-group which he had been given and not to all the Ekie. But it is possible that he had greater primacy in external affairs, especially as a buffer against Luba domination.[2]

At Lubamba's death, his son, Nkole a Lubamba, succeeded him as chief and inherited the title of *Mfuabana.* According to tradition, Nkole a

Lubamba was conceived partly through the intervention of a sorcerer, and he was considered to have special powers. It was Nkole who was the first chief, or king, of all the Ekie, in that he was the first person to unify and actively rule the entire Ekie population.

Under Nkole a Lubamba's rule, three important innovations in organization were introduced. The first was the appointment of *Tshite* as the king's principal advisor, forcing *Tshite* out of his paramountcy in the religious sphere and into subordination in the political sphere. All of *Tshite*'s ritual duties were redefined into supporting Nkole's office. The Bena Kavungoi, the lineage that corporately owned this title, resented the cooptation and left Mulemba to found their own separate village-group. Yet, because of their exclusive rights to the *Tshite* title, only the Bena Kavungoi could—and did—provide Nkole with a principal advisor of uncontestable ritual legitimacy. With this reorganization, Nkole established his control over the ritual mediation between the Ekie past and present. In his new role, *Tshite* was made responsible for the king's investiture, ritual purity and burial, and he continued to be responsible for the investiture of the *Bana-Nkana*. But these peace officers could no longer provide on their own initiative the crucial ritual services necessary for the maintenance of the social order; they could now act only at the request of the king. It was Nkole a Lubamba who took charge of all rituals for the general welfare of the entire people. The fusion of the political and religious spheres of authority around the kingship is described in Ekie as a time in history when *Tshite* became the "wife to Nkole," that is, Nkole's indispensable yet clearly subordinate partner.

The second change brought about by Nkole also crucially affected his role. He went to the sacred Lake Mbebe (the burial site of the first Luba agent, Builu) to have his new position as king approved by his own Luba ancestors. Thus, he sought ritual approval in the village-group whose origins lay in the defunct Luba-Shankadi overlordship. He offered several kinds of food to the Luba spirits in Lake Mbebe; the food did not sink and thus it was taken to be a good sign from the ancestors. Nkole a Lubamba then made another sacrifice of eight male and eight female slaves. Their drowning was taken as another sign of approval from the Luba ancestors.

The third major innovation, once Ekie unification had been achieved, was Nkole's expansionist policy at the borders. He insisted that members of the royal village-cluster create new villages and he was the first of the Ekie kings to subjugate neighboring peoples, both Songye and Luba-Kasai. While Nkole himself was satisfied merely to collect tribute from these groups, his successors sent members of the royal clan to rule over them and they became part of the Ekie state.

Under Nkole's rule, the Ekie were organized into seven village-clusters. Each of these *kavumbu* had a chief who held the title of *Mfuabana*. These *kavumbu* chiefs were hereditary and were not appointed by Nkole.

However, they could not hold the title without Nkole's approval—for Nkole, just like his father Lubamba, was responsible for the initiation of all individuals who wished to own the title of *Mfuabana*.

After Nkole a Lubamba's death, his son and successor took the name of Nkole as his title. Thus, the term Nkole acquired the meaning of King or Chief of all the Ekie, the highest ranked title in the society.

THE PATTERN OF THE FORMATION OF THE EKIE STATE

Superior military strength in the hands of one group of individuals has often been seen as a sufficient explanation for the rise of the majority of "secondary states" in Sub-Saharan Africa. But such a single-factor focus leaves other pertinent elements unexplained and unexplored.

Superior military strength is not depicted in Ekie oral tradition as having been a factor in the formation of the state. There is not, to be sure, sufficient evidence to claim that superior military force was never used by the royal lineage, and force does begin to figure in the later expansion of the Ekie state. But the central problem we are addressing is that of the initial unification of the state being successful enough to allow Nkole to begin to turn to the subjugation of neighboring peoples. The importance of superior military strength in the eventual expansion of the Ekie state does not make force a sufficient explanation of the crucial early stages of the process of state-formation. Here, in fact, ideological innovations, the manipulation of symbols, and the control of ritual loom large.

The Ekie kings maintained the state in two "circles": a core and a periphery, each requiring different mechanisms of maintenance. At the core, they attracted Ekie subjects who willingly paid them tribute but whose main value lay in their loyalty, given in exchange for protection from external threats of greater exactions. At the periphery, the Ekie kings subjugated neighboring peoples for the express purpose of collecting tribute. The collection of tribute from subjugated peoples remained a principal source of wealth for the Ekie kings until the establishment of Belgian colonial control in the latter part of the nineteenth century. No significant wealth was ever acquired by the kings through trade, which they never monopolized or even regulated. Indeed, the Ekie were only marginally connected to any major trade routes until the latter part of the nineteenth century. Power over the subject peoples required retainers at the core who were willing to participate in the attacks on their neighbors under the leadership of the royal lineage. It was in the maintenance of the core that the ritual innovations were significant. The royal lineage's monopoly of the key public rituals provided the means for keeping loyal subjects and legitimizing the power of the Ekie king. Without these means of attracting and keeping loyal subjects at the core, Ekie kings could not have maintained their state.

How did these ideological innovations reshape Ekie society? The alien Luba Nkole, the effective founder of the Ekie state, managed to monopolize the key public rituals by establishing the office of the king as intermediary between the Ekie and their ancestors—the ultimate source of the society's welfare. He did this by simultaneously linking with and subordinating to himself the office of *Tshite,* the ritual head who had an undisputable and legitimate relation to the Ekie ancestors. In a society where the living see themselves as directly dependent on their ancestors, power over the living alone cannot suffice. The dead, too, must somehow be tamed—and in this, ritual rather than military means must of necessity be used.

But Nkole had other ancestors to reckon with as well, namely, his own, and these were not Ekie but Luba. From the vantage point of his own ritual existence (as opposed to that of the Ekie), his legitimacy and success had to derive from the Luba dead. The significance of the Luba sanction was not, however, entirely limited to Nkole and his successors. The connection to Luba power also impinged on the Ekie. Even though they had rejected the overlordship of the Luba-Shankadi empire, a ritual connection to it gave prestige to the new state which was, in this context, an off-shoot of the most powerful polity in the region. Furthermore, in the internal dynamics of the Ekie state, the foreign connection also strengthened the king's position against potential subversion by subordinate Ekie chiefs.

It is clear that ideological innovations were a crucial element in the evolution of the Ekie state. This may very well also apply to other instances of state-formation in Africa, where direct evidence of it may be less apparent. While anthropologists have long recognized the relationship between ritual and political power in African societies, the explanation for the existence of this relationship has generally been offered in synchronic-functional rather than historical-processual terms. This study, we hope, has moved one step beyond the notion that the monopolization of ritual is merely a means of maintaining or reinforcing an established political structure. The Ekie case reminds us once again that in societies where military superiority tends to be problematic much of the time, ritual manipulation becomes an integral part of the process of centralization.

NOTES

1. Data were obtained during fourteen months of fieldwork conducted in Ben'Ekie territory, from January 1976 through April 1977, under the auspices of the State University of New York at Stony Brook.
2. Testimonies of Mukonkole, December 1976 and April 1977, and Majama, March 1977.

REFERENCES

Boone, Olga
　　1961　Carte Ethnique du Congo: Quart Sud-Est. Tervuren: Musée Royal de l'Afrique Centrale (Annales, Series in 8, Sciences Humaines).
Feierman, Steven
　　1974　The Shambaa Kingdom. Madison: University of Wisconsin Press.
Guthrie, Malcolm
　　1967–1970　Comparative Bantu. 4 vols. Farnborough.
Miller, Joseph C.
　　1976　Kings and Kinsmen, Early Mbundu States in Angola. London: Oxford University Press.
Nenquin, J.
　　1963　Excavations at Songo 1957. Tervuren: Music Royal de l'Afrique Centrale. No. 45.
Ogot, Bethwell A.
　　1972　"On the Making of a Sanctuary: Being Some Thoughts on the History of Religion in Padhola." The Historical Study of African Religion. T.O. Ranger and I.N. Kimambo, eds. Berkeley: University of California Press.
Reefe, Thomas Q.
　　1977　"Traditions of Genesis and the Luba Diaspora." History in Africa, 4:183–205.
Samain, A.
　　1923　La Langue Kisonge: Grammaire-Vocabulaire-Proverbes. Bruxelles: Goemaere, Bibliotheque-Congo XIV.
Shorter, Aylward
　　1968　"Nyungu-ya-Mawe and the Empire of the Ruga-Rugas." Journal of African History, 9:235–259.
　　1972　"Symbolism, Ritual, and History: An Examination of the Work of Victor Turner." The Historical Study of African Religion. T.O. Ranger and I.N. Kimambo, eds. Berkeley: University of California Press.
Southall, Aidan
　　1956　Alur Society. Cambridge: Cambridge University Press.
Vansina, Jan
　　1966　Kingdoms of the Savanna. Madison: University of Wisconsin Press.
　　1978　Children of Woot. Madison: University of Wisconsin Press.
Verhulpen, E.
　　1936　Baluba et Balubaïsés du Katanga. Antwerp: L'Avenir Belge.
Winter, E.H.
　　1966　"Territorial Groupings and Religion among Iraqw." Anthropological Approaches to the Study of Religion. Michael Banton, ed. London: Tavistock Publications.
Wilson, M.
　　1959　Communal Rituals of the Nyakyusa. London: Oxford University Press.

THE FRONTIER AS REGIONAL SYSTEM

In our analysis in Part I we saw the frontier process to be regional, involving several societies whose frontier cycles could intermesh (as they did between the Luba and the Ekie). This frontier process was more continuous and more widespread in some regions in Africa than in others. In the following study of the Goba, Chet Lancaster shows that the construction of numerous, often ephemeral, polities was a continuous process in the Middle Zambezi region, encompassing an entire group of peoples whose common ethnic identity was forged precisely by their involvement in that process within an area peripheral to the metropolitan empires of Mwenemutapa and Korekore and, later, to the Portuguese-controlled territory of Mozambique. The Goba area was thus a kind of perpetual frontier area, attracting refugees, slaves, and adventurers from both inside and outside itself. In one sense, the essay is a case study of the instabilities that are inherent in the frontier and that always threaten frontier polities.

The forces that kept the Goba area in constant flux included all those social "mechanisms of ejection" of people toward frontiers that we have discussed in Part I. Foremost among these was a particularly indeterminate system of political succession. The result was political flux, dynastic pretensions and conflicts, movements of people, usurpations of power, and the erection of new polities. All this gave a particularly strong frontier flavor to the foundation legends and charters of the various Goba polities. Rulers were defined by their subjects as immigrants, strangers, warriors, and (because they were rootless) "slaves"; this image was ritually embedded in the *basangu* complex which made them into quintessential African aliens.

Lancaster examines these processes both in their regional context and in their local expression in the Goba kingdom of NaMainga. The patterns in NaMainga are similar to those we have seen in Ekieland. But the ruler-ruled relationship was more complex here, involving more immigrant layers. The Tonga, the "oldest" existing layer, were the owners of the land and its spirits and the subjects of the rulers. The ruling layer was comprised of two sub-layers: the earlier Kasamba rulers and the later Ntombo rulers, between whom the competition for the rulership remained unresolved. NaMainga, like many other Goba statelets, never quite solidified into a mature, integrated polity (this is clearly marked in the royal installation ritual with its expressions of frank antagonism between rulers and subjects). However, the model of organization that these statelets tried to follow—with indifferent results—was clear and widely shared, and it was continuously perpetuated as an ideal by being reproduced by each new rising polity.

—Editor

Chet S. Lancaster

—————— 3 ——————

Political Structure and Ethnicity in an
Immigrant Society:
The Goba of the Zambezi

Most students of the rise of political systems have focused on the emergence of large-scale kingdoms and states, as if—as Kopytoff (1977) notes—these were the goals of an evolution in which the other political forms were only way-stations.[1] Small-scale political systems have been the object of comparative analysis (Fortes and Evans-Pritchard 1940, Lewis 1959, Vansina 1962) and, most notably, functional analysis (Middleton and Tait 1958). But the problem of the genesis and persistence of small-scale systems has received little attention.

My goal, in this paper, is to analyze the rise and persistence of the political system of the Zambezi Goba in precolonial times. The analysis is relevant to some problems raised by Middleton and Tait in their typology of "tribes without rulers" and to the general question of ethnic groups and their boundaries, as discussed in Helm (1968), Barth (1969), and Cohen and Middleton (1970). The analysis will also throw some light on the political organization of the proto-historic and historic Zimbabwe culture cluster of southeastern Africa, of which the Goba have been a part. I shall begin with a brief review of Goba political history. I shall then flesh out the bare bones of this rather abstract picture by examining the organization of a single district—the kingdom of NaMainga—which I studied intensively for two years in the field.[2]

THE GOBA: AN OVERVIEW

The term Goba designates a congerie of Central Bantu cultivators spread along three hundred miles of the Middle Zambezi Valley, in the area where the borders of Zambia, Zimbabwe, and Mozambique meet. Precolonial Goba polities in the valley existed within a wider political universe which encompassed the neighboring northern and southern plateaux and included stateless societies, chiefdoms, confederacies of more or less centralized kingdoms, and states. The Goba area presented an ever-changing mosaic of politically separate but culturally related kingdoms and statelets whose size, power, and alliances varied over time.

In numbers, the Goba probably surpass a hundred thousand. Their overall density has been relatively low—14.6 persons per square mile in

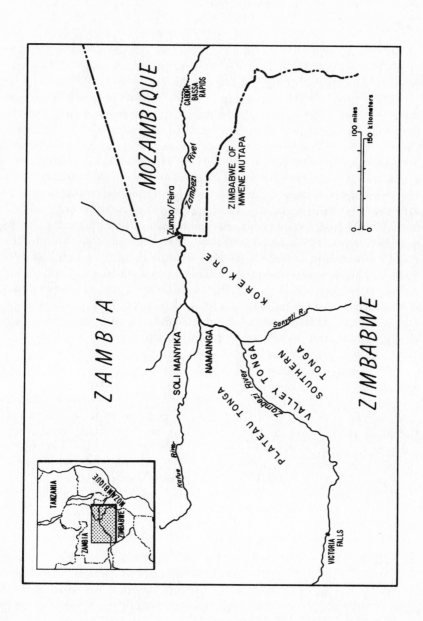

the area I studied. However, the population was (and is) distributed in rather compact clusters. The reasons are both ecological and political.

Villages were placed within daily walking distance of a year-round source of water. The shifting, slash-and-burn agriculture of the Goba typically exploited fertile alluvial soils to produce sorghum, the staple grain grown during the summer rains. Smaller dry-season gardens for greens and tobacco were made along rivers and streams. And because the plentiful game could destroy crops, these various fields and gardens had to be concentrated in fairly tight defensive clusters.

The clustering also served as protection from raids. The sparseness of the population precluded armed competition over farming land (and the tse-tse fly precluded competition over cattle and grazing land). The roots of conflict lay elsewhere. The ivory trade fostered forays by groups of armed elephant hunters, who commonly clashed with the local population. Frequent droughts and famines led to raids on granaries. The demands of the slave trade and the wish to increase one's own following created a need for captives. And finally, the rugged Zambezi Valley escarpments made the area a favored refuge for groups fleeing at various times from the disruptions by Arab and African traders, Portuguese merchants and adventurers, and Boer and British settlers. All this resulted in large nucleated villages fortified against animals and men. These in turn joined into compact and rather densely populated small polities, each with a large uninhabited hinterland that served for hunting and the gathering of foods, medicines, and raw materials. This funneling of the population into a few ecologically choice and politically important locations resulted, locally, in assimilating disparate immigrants and blurring cultural differences.

The petty kingdom of NaMainga illustrates the pattern. Its area of 535 square miles contains at present a population of about 7,800. In the 1960's, somewhat less than a quarter of the territory (22%) was arable, so that the overall population density of 14.6 per square mile rose to 66.1 on the regularly cultivated land. Yet, even then, this choice land could potentially accommodate 260 persons per square mile—over four times the present population (see Lancaster 1981). Oral traditions suggest that this limit was indeed approached from time to time in the nineteenth century, when the valley was a popular refuge area (Lancaster 1974:712-13).

THE STRUCTURE OF GOBA POLITICS

The Goba nucleated settlement clusters continuously brought together mobile groups of shifting cultivators, refugees, ivory hunters, and traders. The Goba system of kin groups helped amalgamate these varied interests and identities into small polities that gave a politically useful impression of ethnic homogeneity.

Goba society is remarkable in that its important component groups, based on common descent, emerge from conflicting principles (see Lancaster 1974a, 1981). Residential units are focused on matrilineal lines.

Counting infants, one may find as many as five generations of mothers and daughters under one roof. Men, when they marry, move in with their wives, live with their matrilocal extended families, and must engage in continuous bride-service in order to enjoy domestic life. All this gives Goba society a strong matrilineal bias, with older women having considerable authority in village councils.

But the matrilineal bias, historically, existed side by side with a strong patrilineal ideology. Goba males have tried to emulate the patterns prevalent in the prestigious Zimbabwe culture cluster south of the Zambezi, where men obtain wives not by bride-service but by paying bridewealth in cattle and where wives join their husbands who live with their fathers and brothers in extended patrilocal families. Goba men believe that a patrilineal group of senior men should be prominent in the affairs of the extended family and the descent group and balance the influence of the matrilineal group of senior women and their co-resident daughters. But while they hold these beliefs, Goba men lack the cattle for the marriage transactions appropriate to them.

As a solution, the Goba have developed a system of dual descent lines by giving preference to "brother-sister" marriages—actually, marriages between cousins and the half-siblings from the often polygynous marriages of elders. The result is a kind of "cognatic," bilateral descent grouping where ties through both mother and father are used to establish sociopolitical positions and to claim group memberships. Married women, with their children, live with their mothers and other members of their mothers' descent group. At the same time, large numbers of married sons (many married to classificatory "sisters") manage to live nearby, making it possible to organize village life in terms of both matrilines and patrilines. Such localized descent groups enjoy a large measure of economic self-sufficiency. But factional and personal rivalries scatter some of their members among a number of villages. Moreover, patrilineal and matrilineal linkages mean that a localized descent group is part of a yet larger group based on similar bilateral relations. A descent group is named after a prominent male or female member or ancestor or after the village that it dominates.

Thus, kin group membership, traced through either sex, is fluid and situational, and descent groups overlap. Gatherings of major descent groups attract 200 to 300 adults or more, including in-laws and unrelated allies. Villages also contain unrelated allies and range in size from a small family to 250 people; the prestigeful royal and chiefly villages may attract twice that number, and in precolonial times they were also swollen by slaves acquired in raids and by trade. New slaves (mostly nubile women and young children) were incorporated domestically as "children" of the descent group and eventually absorbed through marriage. Immigrants were also easily assimilated, the process aided by regional cultural similarities and the loose descent system that accommodated newcomers equally from the matrilineal north and the patrilineal south.

Local traditions and documentary evidence (Lancaster and Pohorilenko 1977) indicate that nineteenth-century kingdoms associated with trade depots (*aringa*) attracted many foreign travelers. There were three such Portuguese trading stations in NaMainga. People came to the valley seeking trade goods, medicines, and protection from the turbulent conditions on the plateaux. Others came as captives or raiders, and many stayed on. The variety in immigrant origins is impressive. From the north, there were Yao, Maravi, Bisa, Mambari, Chokwe, Luvale, Lozi and Makololo, Mbunda, Kaonde, Lamba, Lenje, Sala, Soli, Mashikolumbwe, and Plateau Tonga. From the Shona-speaking south, there were Ndebele, Shangwe, Korekore, Zezuru, Manyika, and Mbire.

Internally, Goba polities were ordered by a pattern in which various descent groupings were attached genealogically to a royal line, the latter acting as the organizational spinal cord for the kingdom as a whole. As elsewhere in Africa (cf. Middleton and Tait 1958), this allowed many unrelated immigrant groups to become part of a kin-like territorial organization. There was, here, no single, deep, all-inclusive lineage genealogy. Rather, the royal genealogy provided the spine, while peripheral groups radiated from various points in it in irregular fashion (a pattern Fox 1967 called a "merging segmentary series"). The central "royal" group (no matter how petty the scale) held the rights to the royal and chiefly offices. It also managed the state cults—communal earth-shrine cults merged with royal ancestor cults (the royal ancestors became the communal earth spirits for the kingdom as a whole). Armed warriors residing at the king's settlement provided the military and hunting-*cum*-trading cadres. Other descent groups legitimized their presence in the territory by claiming real or fictive links to the royal line. An important or ambitious descent group would claim that its links to the royal line were genealogically anterior to those of a rival group.

The royal line, however, was a concept and a valuable political fiction rather than a fact. Most political successions were ultimately based on force and usurpation by groups of warriors and traders. Local history was one of secession, dissidence, shifts in territory, conflicts over control of earth-shrines, and the arrival of new groups forging or claiming new links to the royal line.[3] The claims were embellished with free-form oral traditions in which current leaders were presented as legitimate successors of a fairly long line of rulers; the right to rule was claimed by reference to earlier heroic migrations, legitimate conquest, or primal occupation from some unchallengeable zero-point in time.

Each of the various descent groups that had successively taken power within a territory grafted onto a single genealogical construct their various ancestors and heroes. As power shifted in time among the armed groups, and new alliances, cleavages, and boundaries emerged, the royal genealogy underwent new attachments, detachments, and segmentations. Founding leading ancestors of separate groups were strung and restrung like beads on the common string of the royal line. The more powerful groups upgraded their genealogical seniority and different factions kept updating their relationship to the group in office while omitting the names of those kings that validated the claims of rival groups. Earlier kings were selectively forgotten or merged into single personages. Further genealogical complications arose because these rival descent groups intermarried. This process has continued into the twentieth century. One need hardly stress, then, the impossibility of using Goba king lists for dating—absolutely or relatively—rulers, the segmentation or replacement of royal lines, and the arrival of new groups.

This competition, fierce though it was, was nevertheless also integrative. The military technology of muzzle-loaders and spears was not massively destructive and much of the competition among groups was expressed in arguments over relative position on the royal line. This endowed the line with legitimizing powers and asserted their common relationship to it.

The integration took place within a population that was largely homogeneous in behavior, culture, and belief—a population living in a uniform, sub-arid, wooded savanna that gave self-sufficiency in subsistence but little ecological basis for group differentiation. Also, the integration took place within relatively small polities. At the Zambezi-Kafue confluence, they ranged in area from 500 to 1,300 square miles, including the large uninhabited escarpment zones. The largest kingdom probably contained at most 30,000 inhabitants. An immigrant group had no difficulty in accepting the ethnic labels, attitudes, and allegiances of its hosts. But with this ease of assimilation went the relative instability in the authority of the current ruling group. Accepting strangers added to one's power but it also created competitors who might some day dominate. Thus, alienness, clientship, and "slavery" (a metaphor for rootlessness), and the uncertainty of claims to authority were all part of the single conceptual package of rulership.

ETHNIC ZONES AND ETHNIC IDENTITIES

Each Goba polity, with its shifting boundaries and dynamic historical charters, provided its members with a complex structure of "sub-ethnic" socio-political identities. For example, in the NaMainga kingdom, the term BanaMainga, "people of Mainga," stood for its early founders from the south, as well as for their descendants, as well as for those descended from later unrelated followers, as well as for all inhabitants of the territory. At the same time, in the wider regional context, the people called themselves "Goba," and by becoming absorbed into NaMainga one also became Goba.

The term Goba itself has been used for centuries for lowland Shona-speakers and was probably first adopted as a result of an early migration from that area. But it was also applied for centuries to the populations spread along three hundred miles of the Middle Zambezi. This extensive area—that we propose to call the Goba "ethnic zone"—was broken up into many small-scale polities of different sizes, some of which would occasion-

ally be allied with or dependent on larger polities, notably the famous
Mwene Mutapa and Changamira confederacies of Shona- speakers. Culturally akin to one another, these chiefdoms and kingdoms derived their ritual
legitimacy from earth-spirit shrines and their rulers shared their authority
with councils representing local descent groups.[4]

Though many of these polities were quite small, they were structured
on the model of the larger kingdoms. Thus, even petty Goba kings had
appointees serving as palace guards, warriors, officials, and henchmen who
bolstered the power at the center. They also had territorial sub-chiefs similar to those in the East African interlacustrine kingdoms that Richards
(1960) and Fallers (1964) have called "king's men." These sub-chiefs exercised, at their more local levels, essentially the same kinds of power that the
king formally exercised over the entire territory and each maintained a more
modest version of the king's staff.[5] But the model was above all ideological.
The kingdoms' sovereignty was relative, attenuating through a series of
zones of declining central power. There was so little control over the peripheries that some of them, in practice, joined other power chains that
linked them to one and sometimes several neighboring kingdoms.

What is crucial here from a historical perspective is that the Goba
ethnic zone contained a range of structures varying in scale over time,
from petty independent kingdoms to wide alliances incorporating many
kingdoms and chiefdoms. And the ethnic terminologies reflected this.
Thus, in the late fifteenth century, at the height of the Mwene Mutapa
confederacy, the Goba around the Zambezi-Kafue confluence were probably members of the confederacy that was involved in long-distance trade
and was allied with local African and Swahili traders operating throughout
the Zimbabwe culture cluster (Lancaster 1974, Lancaster and Pohorilenko
1977). In this instance, they would have been known as Vanayi (followers,
vassals) or Korekore (followers of Mwene Mutapa), rather than as undif-
ferentiated "Goba." Others, who had rebelled and broken away from the
confederacy and taken refuge north of the Zambezi, would have been
known as Tonga ("rebels" or "independents"). By the late seventeenth
century, with the decline of Mwene Mutapa's influence, all the population
of the area seems to have been known as Tonga. In the early eighteenth
century, with the Changamira confederacy replacing Mwene Mutapa in
this region, people living south of the Zambezi became Vanayi again. But
once the Changamira confederacy was destroyed, in the early nineteenth
century, by groups uprooted by the Zulu wars, the people once again
became independent Tonga, and that is how many of them preferred to
present themselves to the British colonial officials. This gave them a
northern identity and put them closer to Northern Rhodesia, where there
were far fewer White settlers claiming land than in Southern Rhodesia.

More recently, during the independence struggle in Rhodesia (now
Zimbabwe), there was rising interest in the symbolism of association with
the long-defunct historical Zimbabwe (see Mutswairo 1974, Fry 1976).

But the attraction of the Tonga identity continues north of the Zambezi, where the Tonga are politically important (Colson 1968, 1970). Thus, "ethnic" designations continue to be as contextual and responsive to political conditions as they had been in the past. The term Vanayi conveyed an association with Shona-speaking kingdoms and "empires" to the south, and Tonga conveyed independence from them, while Goba indicated cultural affinities with other similar peoples occupying similar lowland areas along the middle Zambezi.

THE NAMAINGA KINGDOM

I shall now examine the issues I have discussed above by looking more closely at one Goba kingdom, NaMainga. Typically for Goba polities, the core inhabitants of the kingdom see themselves as immigrants. By examining the traditions that deal with the prior inhabitants of the area, the establishment of an earth shrine, the kingdom's early organization and its problems, its relations with neighboring polities, and its kingship complex, we can piece together a fairly coherent picture of an emerging Goba polity.

PREVIOUS INHABITANTS, EARLY MIGRATIONS, AND CULTURAL BACKGROUND
The BanaMainga say that the first inhabitants of the area were a few hunters-gatherers who roamed widely and had no fields or villages. Skilled, even magical, woodsmen, they could make themselves invisible and would get angry if seen at close range. They are now referred to as *bakamfwimfwi*, "short ones"; in some older accounts, they are called *vanyachisandura* or *madoma* (Lancaster and Pohorilenko 1977). Tales about such dwarf-like creatures are common throughout the region (Clark 1950, Tamayi 1959, Colson 1964). Most traditions state that they withdrew on their own, some that they were killed off or chased away. On the other hand, genetic studies (Hiernaux 1974:108-9) suggest a substantial assimilation of an old local population. Local traditions give no political significance to such a population nor any role to it in the emergence of the NaMainga polity.

The first significant populations with a tie to the land are said to have been shifting cultivators known as Tonga, who "came long ago from wars and troubles with the *Mambo* [king]" in the westerly Zimbabwe highlands. Thus, the earliest remembered "original" BanaMainga were "Tonga," Shona-speakers from the south. From time to time, other groups of Tonga—rebels against Shona kings—would move north over a wide front extending from Victoria Falls to Zumbo-Feira (Lancaster 1971, 1974). A yet later immigrant Tonga wave came from the troubled eastern lands dominated by the Korekore, bringing trade with them. And most recently, Shona-speakers are known to have fled from the south to escape European settlers and colonial taxation.

Such movements from the south no doubt took place at least as early as the fifteenth century when, after the fall of the old center at Great Zimbabwe, Mwene Mutapa established the Korekore confederacy 300 miles to the north. Further movements were triggered by subsequent upheavals—civil wars in the sixteenth and seventeenth centuries, Portuguese intrusion into the eastern valley and the Zimbabwe goldfields, Ngoni and Ndebele invasions in the nineteenth century, the closing stages of the Portuguese-British scramble for colonial territory, the Ndebele War and the Shona Uprising of 1896, the imposition of the head tax in Southern Rhodesia in 1898, and the 1917 revolt in Portuguese East Africa. Some of these migrants found permanent refuge in the strongholds of local trade leaders; others moved on. With the start of effective colonial control and peace, the trading strongholds vanished and most of the population drained away quickly, leaving behind the present low population densities.

The ethnology of the entire region suggests that all the immigrants would have practiced roughly similar methods of shifting cultivation, flood farming, small animal husbandry, hunting, gathering, and fishing. The tse-tse fly precluded serious cattle keeping and most immigrants adjusted to this by abandoning bridewealth in cattle and taking up some form of brideservice. The result was an increase in the incidence of matrilocal extended families and in the strength of matrilateral kin ties. Also, all the immigrants would also have come from areas with systems of merging segmentary descent groups that culminated, at higher levels, in local kingdoms superimposed upon a territorial organization of earth-shrine cults.

NAMAINGA FOUNDING TRADITIONS

The BanaMainga claim to have been the first of the early "Tonga" from the south to have crossed the Zambezi at its confluence with the Kafue (and some claim that BanaMainga means "those who crossed the river/ boundary"). As rebels, they came without a king (*mambo*) but with many descent group heads, warrior leaders, and magicians, who established small followings and earth-shrine realms, first on the south bank and "much later" on the northern bank. As immigration continued, some Tonga pushed into the northern highlands toward the present lands of the Soli Manyika and Plateau Tonga. The crowded valley floor near the fording places, meanwhile, became the stage for warring and competition among local and immigrant strong men "trying to build ladders to the sky" (i.e., to become famous). At this point, as legend has it, Kasamba, a powerful woman priest and medium, was called back from the land of Soli Manyika to unite the BanaMainga. Remembered history begins with her; what earlier leaders there may have been have been forgotten.

Kasamba established peace and became the first leader of all the Bana-Mainga (that is, in fact, out of her activities a new people, the Bana-

Mainga, began to take form). She installed herself as the earth-shrine priestess at Njami Hill, the oldest shrine in the country, and she selected subordinate territorial leaders. The Njami people under her were a mixture of original "BanaMainga," some BaLumbila (an early name for the people from Plateau Tonga country), and some Soli who came back with her from the north (see Chaplin 1960). It is impossible to date these events (see Lancaster and Pohorilenko 1977:15). At her death, Kasamba's powerful spirit became the main earth spirit at Njami Hill. All subsequent leaders have had to obtain the approval of her *basangu* spirit; failing this, it is said, they died.

EARLY ORGANIZATION AND POWER STRUGGLES

As new refugees continued to intrude by force, NaMainga lost some territory and finally the BanaMainga took up arms to bar the way to further immigration (and, as some say, that is the origin of their name: "those who bar the way"). The needs of defense led, it is said, to a dual leadership: Kasamba's ritual successors continued to tend the shrine at Njami Hill while a male was chosen to enforce the law and conduct military skirmishes.

Among the war leaders, the only one remembered is Ntambo. He took power at a time when some sub-chiefs had seceded and the country was torn by conflicts, pressures from new immigrants, and the intrusion of alien traders. Jealous of his Queen "Sister," he killed her "with medicines" and tried to add her ritual leadership to his military one. He moved the capital and his warriors to Chitondo, some five miles from Njami and nearer the Zambezi. Oral traditions suggest that the usurpation shows the increasing influence of the Korekore and eastern trading groups.

Ntambo's warriors turned increasingly to elephant hunting and to the ivory trade with African agents sent by the Portuguese of the lower Zambezi. The Portuguese called these agents *mussambazes*; the BanaMainga call them *vazambi* (sing. *muzambi*). Ntambo's BanaMainga around Chitondo also had access to fairly large-scale flood farming to supplement their regular cultivation of sorghum. They had large fixed villages whose population was further swollen with captives and visiting traders. But some time after the split from Njami, Ntambo's followers suffered from drought; realizing their error, many of them returned to the Njami shrine. Thus, the ancestral BanaMainga Tonga at Njami remained the recognized and respected owners of the spirits and of the land. Meanwhile, the Korekore-influenced warriors, traders, and foreigners a few miles away at Chitondo, with their Portuguese connections, trade goods, and military power, were feared and respected as "owners of the people."

Eventually, the *vazambi* traders took control at Chitondo and of NaMainga as a whole. Some became territorial chiefs, and some claimed the *mambo* title, but they are still known as *vazambi*. At Chitondo, with its floodland supporting a large population, the strongest *muzambi* Munenga secured Portuguese military support and became head of a rather powerful central kingdom surrounded by tributary chiefdoms of allied hunters, traders, and raiders.

The BanaMainga often begin their king list by reciting the names of Kasamba, Ntambo, and Munenga as if they represented a straight line of descent. But Munenga was a stranger, active in Plateau Tonga country (among the BaLumbila) before taking over NaMainga. As with Kasamba and Ntambo, he is remembered, one assumes, because he represents a significant historical turning-point and an era. Here is a typical statement about him:

> "When Munenga was king, the land was covered by fallen animals and there was much wealth. He was a strong man and gave us the law that the ivory belonged to the king. The Portuguese wanted the ivory and so he made our kingdom strong."

Munenga made the BanaMainga powerful through trade, but his enemies also remember him as a castrate and a Mwana Mambo—another name for "slave" or agent of the Portuguese. Succeeding where Ntambo had failed, he established what is still the main earth-shrine of the kingdom at Chitondo, and he appointed a male follower as its custodian, thereby demoting the Kasamba group at Njami into functionaries of a mere local shrine. But the Njami faction continued to claim to be the true owners of the land, dismissing Munenga and his successors as usurpers and mere trading go-betweens with the Portuguese. Yet, they became in time absorbed into Munenga's organization and the names of their own early leaders have been lost.

Systematic Organizational Problems

A basic organization problem, reflected in local traditions from the earliest times, has been the indeterminacy of succession to the central kingship. Since Goba descent groups were based on both matrilineal and patrilineal ties, large numbers of people could come to claim membership in them, especially in successful ones. The royal descent group of "original" Bana-Mainga, if such ever existed, became in time very large and unwieldy, and it became impossible to reckon relationships between segments within it that would be consistent and politically orderly. The genealogical disorder was compounded by many factors: irregular rates of natural increase of different segments, high rates of polygyny and reproduction among the male holders of important descent-group positions, marriages within the descent group, and sporadic assimilation of large numbers of slaves, refugees, and clients by groups in power. Formally, the kingship was supposed to pass successively to the sons of all the preceding kings' "sisters" (real and classificatory), so that all segments of the royal house shared in the power. But with numerous, unclearly defined, and unequally strong segments, most successions were in fact conditioned by strife, coalitions, intrigues, intimidation, force, and outside intervention. The picture was further confused by lingering ethnic differences and rivalries.

In the 1960's, the population of NaMainga appeared thoroughly homogenized culturally and ethnically. Yet, there was still a clear tendency to discriminate between those of Tonga and Korekore ancestry. The issue was phrased in terms of the difference between early "crossers" (descended from "true" BanaMainga from the south) and later assimilants from the east, whose claim to the kingship was weaker. There was also the Portuguese factor—the influence of those whose ancestry could be linked in any way with the Portuguese or their agents the Korekore and Chikunda. These elements acquired increasing political importance from Ntambo's and Munenga's times and held it until the late nineteenth century, when Portuguese interests began to be represented directly by a military command at the Zambezi-Kafue confluence and a trading station at Chitondo (Lancaster 1979). And later, the British Northern Rhodesian colonial administration played a political role. The colonial factor ended with Zambian independence in 1964, but its effects were a partisan issue in 1969.

Whether Korekore, Chikunda, and Portuguese links were an advantage or a taint varied with the times and situations. They were certainly an indication of late arrival in the valley, of possible slave ancestry, and of an outward orientation toward the river with its trade. They were also connected with the Ntambo-Munenga tradition of rulership. By contrast, the Kasamba-Njami tradition was embodied in "Tonga" independence and rootedness in the valley uplands. Although generations of co-residence and inter-marriage have given the BanaMainga a strong sense of unity, yet the symbolism of old Tonga, Korekore, and Portuguese associations persists in the local politics of royal succession, providing a ready-made rallying points for factionalism even though the actual descent of the rivals cannot be traced in any way. Thus, in the 1960's, each of the two factions within the royal clan claimed either the Kasamba or the Ntambo-Munenga traditions.[6] Yet, in reality, the Pax Britannica had by then drained much of the population away toward the developing White-settler dominated areas to the north and south, leaving behind a conservative and inbred population within which the old distinctions were extremely blurred. The very strength of the present symbolism of these distinctions suggests that they rest, historically, on what were politically charged distinctions.

RELATIONS WITH NEIGHBORING POLITIES

At present, only informal traditions reflect NaMainga's precolonial relations with its neighbors. They indicate that the BanaMainga, like the Goba in general, were continuously involved in a common field of political interaction that had straddled the Zambezi for a very long time.

Most BanaMainga claim that they always had close kinship links with the Korekore kingdoms to the south and with neighbors to the north. Family genealogies bear this out. It is common to find families of Shona origin, with large numbers of known relatives who remained in the south as well as those who also migrated to the northbank. Also, common exposure to the recurrent Ndebele raids from ca. 1840 to 1893 brought NaMainga into close political relations (both of alliance and enmity) with many neighbors. Finally, in times of severe drought, it was the Bana-Mainga practice to turn to the rainmaking shrines in Sikoswe, Ila, Nyamhunga, and Nyamakonde areas. Intermittent cooperation and competition marked NaMainga's relations with neighbors. NaMainga cooperated with the people of Simamba and Sampakaruma in closing to further immigration a fording place near the Sanyati-Zambezi confluence. At other times, however, they clashed.

In Ntambo's time, a magical stone, called *gabwe a chitondo*, was originally possessed by Nyamhunga, a senior king in the region. The stone was later fought over by the local kings who each wanted it for their seat (hence the local term Chitondo for royal sites). NaMainga is said to have entered a new political era when Ntambo and his warriors succeeded in wresting the stone from the people of Sampakaruma and established a new capital near the Zambezi. Thereafter, it is said, Nyamhunga and his successors installed NaMainga kings. The story suggests some kind of political or at least ritual dependence on Nyamhunga, ambiguously presented in the guise of a military victory. Nyamhunga is the only king in the region consistently referred to as *mambo*, the Shona term for paramount chief or king. He controlled a shrine to Nyanehwe Matope, the spirit of the son of Mutota, the Mwene Mutapa ("master conqueror") who established the Korekore confederacy in the fifteen century. In this way, Ntambo's NaMainga claimed to derive some of its legitimacy from outside, from the Korekore empire, even while the claim to legitimacy by Kasamba's NaMainga was local, based on its early occupation of the land. This definition of the polity and its rulership as being simultaneously a local and a foreign phenomenon found its reflection in the royal ritual.

THE SPIRITS OF THE KINGS
The Goba believe that normally, at the time of death, a *mudzimu* spirit issues from an individual who has lived an acceptable life as a free person and died in a decent manner in his own homeland among family and friends. Such a spirit may cause harm if it is neglected, and usually it is taken care of in the ancestral cult by a relative or descendant who formally assumes its name (see Lancaster 1977 for a brief introduction to the Goba spirit world).

But the outcome of death is more problematic in the case of those who have led an abnormal life, or died an abnormal death, or engaged in a dangerous calling, as in the case of mediums. This also applies to dead immigrants, adventurers, soldiers, captives, and travelers who die in foreign lands. Such persons die as rootless aliens and, therefore, "slaves." Their spirits are homeless, with no one to recognize them or befriend them, and they wander restlessly in search of a host that they might possess in order to enjoy the satisfactions of contented spirits. Such spirits are dangerous and they easily become spirit familiars to witches and sorcerers. They are known as *basangu* (sing. *musangu*) and they stand at the center of Goba conceptions of royal political power.

The *basangu* are thought to haunt the places where they lived and were buried. Hence, many *basangu* are believed to reside at former royal village sites and at the sacred royal burial grove and earth shrine at Chitondo. These numerous former alien clients, dependents, henchmen, and slaves of kings can cause trouble in death as they did in life; it is feared that the incumbent king communicates with them and it is hoped that he keeps them under control. Hence, the king is necessarily a major ritual figure in his descent group and is also feared as the country's leading witch and magician. Moreover, since the early rulers, including Kasamba herself, and many subsequent ones were immigrants, their spirits are also *basangu*, and the royal descent group as a whole, including its living members, is also referred to as *basangu*.

Every immigrant group, including Kasamba's, brought with it a new contingent of spirits and these in time became the spirits of the land. As such, they have legitimized and continue to legitimize the kings. As communal earth spirits, they are responsible for public welfare and their help is invoked when the king is under attack, and in times of epidemics, droughts, and famines. But as with living alien dependents, the relationship with them is difficult. They easily resort to force, are often cruel, and may destroy an unacceptable aspirant to the kingship. This ambivalent relationship is reflected in the rituals surrounding the selection of a new king.

ROYAL SUCCESSION

Since many precolonial kings were aliens who had come to power by force rather than by normal rules of succession, the ritual of royal succession realistically stresses the difficulty of identifying an acceptable candidate. It also stresses the reality of outside intervention and even bloodshed when a choice is being made among dangerous "strangers." Succession is seen as determined by forces beyond the control of the ordinary and "true" BanaMainga; these alien forces come from the outside world of trade, travel, and warfare—and of *basangu*. It is the *basangu* (also called "lions") at Chitondo—itself situated in a wilderness with wild game—that are said to select the king in the course of what is regarded as an ordeal. At the same time, however, the ordeal is interpreted, almost cynically, by the "true" BanaMainga as serving the needs of the people, with the king assuming the position of a sacrificial victim. Here is how the ordeal of royal selection is presented:

> Those at Chitondo eventually became slaves of the Portuguese and worked for them. We would let strong slaves be our kings and do the fighting. The strong slaves would be the ones to go, one by one, into the wilderness to brave the lions of Chitondo. If they died it was all right and we chose again. If the lions did not kill him, the slave became our king. After burying the former king we would build a small hut nearby. And the candidate must sleep in it, alone in the forest. . . . All [the installation hut] is of four poles, one on each corner, with a make-shift thatch roof, where the King-elect is placed to spend the night in the forest of wild animals. . . . In the morning after the night in the wilderness you can clearly see the footprints of the lions of the land. A big lion's footprint can be seen where it came in the night and stood over the candidate and again at each side of the open hut are to be seen the prints of the lesser lions of the land and all stood over him in the wilderness in the night. If in the early morning those returning see that the king has not been eaten it means the lions of the land have accepted him as one of them and he is now the real and true king. If they have eaten him the land is found covered with meat there at Chitondo, game that has fallen magically by the lions, and the people come and feast, for the king is dead and the spirits have spoken. We can just eat plenty and there is no king. . . .

The description is more expressive of the ideology of NaMainga kingship than of the actual process of royal selection. The ritual trial in the Chitondo wilderness has not, to my knowledge, been carried out in the twentieth century in which there have been three successions, but it is talked about as having shaped those successions.

The allegory of the "lions" is realistic. Various kinds of "lions" at different periods have been intervening in the selection and survival of the king: the Korekore paramount, the resident alien warrior-traders, the foreign slaves, the Portuguese agents, and, later, local Portuguese commanders and British colonial officers. By confronting them, even submitting to them, the kings served the people by shielding the people from them. Whether actually taking place or not, the ordeal at Chitondo sums up the process by which the king is selected and maintained in power; it is in that sense "real" and it serves to remind all concerned about the nature of NaMainga kingship. The installation of the king is completed by a ritual in which an ancient "spear of the country," made of local ore, is placed on the new king. This reasserts the important fiction of his direct descent in the royal line, a fact asserted by his having been spared by the "lions" at Chitondo.

The royal installation ceremony conveyed symbolically the complex and contradictory institution that was NaMainga kingship. The ceremony stressed both the continuity of the ancient royal line and the ever-present possibility of usurpation, both the rootedness of kingship in the local earth and its foreignness, both its local legitimacy and its legitimation by outside forces, both its awesome power and its dependence on the approval of alien and slave *basangu*, both its dominion over the people and its role as an instrument of the people's welfare.

CONCLUSION

In the precolonial Middle Zambezi Valley, the legitimacy of rulership was embodied in a line of royal succession, and ethnically disparate immigrant groups were attached to the royal line as accessory lines. This allowed assimilated groups to proclaim their legitimate pretensions to the kingship whenever they captured actual power by force and intrigue. The pattern created a dynamic regional political system in which various immigrant groups and local factions founded or appropriated chiefdoms, petty kingdoms, kingdoms, and segmentary states. Externally, these polities continuously combined, recombined, broke up, expanded, contracted, shifted their boundaries, and were absorbed by others. Internally, various factions within them succeeded one another in holding at various times the chiefly and royal positions. The larger kingdoms were confederacies of such adjacent kingdoms that were tributary to a central kingdom and they too were shaped by the same dynamic.

In this kaleidoscope, the political units at each level tended to replicate, structurally and ideologically, the units at the levels above and below them. To be sure, the central kingdoms had longer king lists and more evolved political charters, but they followed the same structural model as the smaller and more recently formed units.[7] Many kings were themselves subordinate "king's men" in a yet larger chain of authority whose links at times extended eastward toward Mwene Mutapa's home kingdom and southward toward the realms on the Zimbabwe goldfields.

Given the turbulence of precolonial times, these structures were far from stable. The political links were most brittle at the higher levels of organization—the statelet, the segmentary state, and especially the large confederacy. At the lower local levels, integration and stability were achieved by ethnic homogeneity or ethnic assimilation through the adoption of strangers and immigrants into local descent groups. Moreover, lower level units were more or less solidly "anchored," to use Colson's (1962) metaphor, by earth-spirit shrines. The fluidity of boundaries between the shifting political units made the pursuit of ethnic homogeneity a useful policy. It was also a relatively easy one to implement given the ecological uniformity of the region and the overall cultural uniformity of the population, particularly in the sphere of political values and in the flexibility of ethnic labelling.

The result was a very complicated ethnic picture. In addition to local ethnicities attached to local polities (such as, for example, the BanaMainga), certain widespread terms denoting ethnicities were also used to indicate a people's relationship to a political order or a region. Thus, Tonga also stood for rebels, dissidents, and "outsiders," Vanayi for loyal adherents and "insiders," Goba for Shona-speaking lowlanders living along the Zambezi, and Vazambi, originally applied to Portuguese agents, acquired a quasi-ethnic meaning in denoting their descendants. Because these ethnic labels varied and shifted in meaning does not mean they were unimportant; on the contrary, they did indicate important identity distinctions in various appropriate contexts.[8] Over the centuries, this resulted in fairly frequent changes in self-ascribed ethnic identities in response to the shifting alignments that took place periodically at all levels of the political structure, from chiefdoms to large segmentary states and confederacies. The formation of new polities and societies, accompanied by a variety of ethnic reclassifications, was thus a constant process in the history of the Lower Zambezi area.

NOTES

1. Service (1979) provides a good discussion of the state bias in political anthropology.

2. I conducted fieldwork among the Goba of Zambia for two years (1967-1969) in two northbank kingdoms, NaMainga and Chiava, at the Zambezi-Kafue confluence, and I focus here on this western end of the Goba area. My field research was made possible through affiliation with the Institute for Social Research, University of Zambia, and was supported by an N.I.M.H. pre-doctoral fellowship. I wish to thank Brian Fagan, David Phillipson, Harry Langworthy, Joseph Whitecotton, Tim Matthews, Aidan Southall, and Igor Kopytoff, among others, for valued help at various times in working through the Goba material. A short early version of this paper was presented at a panel organized by William Arens at the 1978 meetings of the American Anthropological Association.

3. Notable examples of armed trading groups that vied for local power at various times were the vazambi from Mozambique. Locally, they are also remembered as Barungu, KotaKota, Makua, Basungu, and Chikunda. It seems likely that each of these terms originally applied to a specific wave of traders connected at different periods with Swahili and Portuguese activities in the east (see Lancaster and Pohorilenko 1977).

4. In an age when "tribe" was a current term for ethnicity, Richards (1960) called such situations a "multiple kingdom tribe," and Middleton and Tait (1958) classified them in their analysis under their "Group III" societies.

5. Such "segmentary" states, as Southall (1956) has called them, are widespread in Africa, well-known examples being the Ashanti, Yoruba, Zande, Kongo, Kuba, Luba, and Lunda (Vansina 1962). Their structures stand in formal contrast with "unitary" states, characterized, according to Kaberry (1957), by territorial sovereignty, centralized government, specialized staff, and a monopoly by the center of the legitimate use of force.

6. In August 1974, a historian from London University (Matthews 1976:541-47) interviewed the new NaMainga king Makiyi. It is clear that Makiyi had manipulated these traditions for his own purposes. His predecessor in office, Sikaongo Chali, who reigned during most of my fieldwork (he died in January 1969), had presented himself as the leader of the Kasamba faction, while Makiyi and his supporters styled themselves as leaders of the Ntambo-Munenga faction. In his 1974 interview, Makiyi suppressed the Kasamba founding tradition, relegated Portuguese-tainted Munenga to the Kasamba tradition, and depicted himself as the heir of a glorified Ntambo. His account contains quite novel material and omits any mention of his predecessor Chali and other heroes of the Kasamba faction. Such creativity, reshuffling, and omission, typical of segmentary societies, precludes the development of a coherent historical tradition—not because of the absence of a ruling line but because each faction of that line tears down the accounts of their opponents without, however, succeeding in exclusively imposing their own.

7. In an earlier paper (Lancaster 1974:708), using a different terminology and dealing with different problems, it was suggested that present-day Goba are amorphously organized and had never been involved in a "state" system (meaning a unitary state). The present paper amplifies this view with a more precise terminology.

8. Fried (1968) points out, in passing, that politically significant functions may indeed exist for a myth of ethnic or tribal purity. But for the most part, he and other contributors to the symposium (Helm 1968) seem to be playing to an overseas audience in maintaining that ethnic labels, so often regarded by this audience as embarrassing, have little significance. But the inconsistencies and difficulties discussed by Fried *et al.* can be overcome when sufficient information exists to understand ethnicities situationally, as shown by the contributors to Barth (1969) and Cohen and Middleton (1970).

REFERENCES

Barth, F. ed. 1969 *Ethnic Groups and Boundaries*. Boston: Little Brown.

Chaplin, J.H. 1960. "A Preliminary Account of Iron Age Burials with Gold in the Gwembe Valley, Northern Rhodesia." *Proceedings of the First Federal Science Congress*. pp. 397-406.

Clark, J.D. 1950. "A Note on the Pre-Bantu Inhabitants of Northern Rhodesia and Nyasaland." *Northern Rhodesia Journal* 2:45-52.

Cohen, R. and J. Middleton, eds. 1970. *From Tribe to Nation in Africa*. San Francisco: Chandler.

Colson, E. 1962. *The Plateau Tonga of Northern Rhodesia*. Manchester: Manchester University Press.

———. 1964. "The Little People of Rhodesia." *Northern Rhodesia Journal* 5:567-287.

———. 1968. "Contemporary Tribes and the Development of Nationalism." In *Essays on the Problem of Tribe*, edited by J. Helm, pp. 201-206. Seattle: University of Washington Press.

———. 1970. "The Assimilation of Aliens among the Zambian Tonga." In *From Tribe to Nation in Africa*, edited by R. Cohen and J. Middleton, pp. 35-54. San Francisco: Chandler.

Fallers, L.A. 1964. *The King's Men*. London: Oxford University Press.

Fortes, M. and E.E. Evans-Pritchard, eds. 1940. *African Political Systems*. London: Oxford University Press.

Fox, R. 1967. *Kinship and Marriage*. Baltimore: Penguin.

Fried, M.H. 1968. "On the Concept of 'Tribe' and 'Tribal Society.' " In *Essays on the Problem of Tribe*, edited by June Helm, pp. 3-20. Seattle: University of Washington Press.

Fry, P. 1976. *Spirits of Protest*. London: Cambridge University Press.

Helm, J., ed. 1968. *Essays on the Problem of Tribe*. (Proc., 1967 Meeting, American Ethnological Soc.). Seattle: University of Washington Press.

Hiernaux, J. 1974. *The People of Africa*. New York: Scribner's.

Kaberry, P.M. 1957. "Primitive States." *British Journal of Sociology* 8:224-234.

Kopytoff, I. 1977. "Speculations about the Internal African Frontier." *African Studies Association Papers 1977*. 8 pp.

Lancaster, C.S. 1971. "The Economics of Social Organization in an Ethnic Border Zone: The Goba (Northern Shona) of the Zambezi Valley." *Ethnology* 10:445-465.

————. 1974. "Ethnic Identity, History, and 'tribe' in the Middle Zambezi Valley." *American Ethnologist* 1:707-730.

————. 1977. "The Zambezi Goba Ancestral Cult." *Africa* 47:229-241.

————. 1979. "The Portuguese Frontier in Western Mozambique, 1890." *Papers in Anthropology* 20:63-91.

————. 1981. *The Goba of the Zambezi: Sex Roles, Economics, and Change*. Norman: University of Oklahoma Press.

Lancaster, C.S. and A. Pohorilenko 1977. "Ingombe Ilede and the Zimbabwe Culture." *International Journal of African Historical Studies* 10:1-30.

Lewis, I.M. 1959. "The Classification of African Political Systems." *Rhodes-Livingstone Journal* 25:59-69.

Matthews, T.I. 1976. *The Historical Traditions of the Peoples of the Gwembe Valley, Middle Zambezi*. Unpublished Ph.D. thesis, School of Oriental and African Studies, London University.

Middleton, J. and D. Tait, eds. 1958. *Tribes Without Rulers*. London: Routledge.

Mutswairo, S.M. 1974. *Zimbabwe*. Washington, D.C.: Three Continent Press.

Richards, A.I. 1960. "Social Mechanisms for the Transfer of Political Rights in Some African Tribes." *Journal of the Royal Anthropological Institute* 90:135-150.

Service, E.R. 1975. *Origins of the State and Civilization*. New York: Norton.

Southall, A.W. 1956. *Alur Society*. Cambridge: Heffer.

Tamayi 1959. "A Visit to the Vadoma Massif." *Southern Rhodesia Native Affairs Department* 36:52-57.

Vansina, J. 1962. "A Comparison of African Kingdoms." *Africa* 32:324-335.

THE IMPORTANCE OF BEING FIRST

In the following study of a Kpelle chiefdom, by William Murphy and Caroline Bledsoe, we see the same processes, directed by the same cultural logic, as those we have seen among the Ekie and the Goba, but with a focus on the manipulation of that crucial legitimizing principle of ruler-ship—the principle of the "firstcomer."

The Kpelle frontier grew out of a larger "tidal" frontier. The region had been a backwaters area to the Sudanic belt which had, till then, been the principal stage on which the crucial events of pre-colonial West African history were played out. But the appearance of European traders on the Atlantic coast in the late 15th century began to disrupt the geopolitical configuration of West Africa, by offering new trading opportunities on the coast, reshuffling the established networks of trade, and undermining the monopolistic position of the Sudanic belt as the middleman between the Sub-Saharan areas and the Mediterranean and European markets. One consequence was a gradual movement of savanna Mande-speaking peoples toward the coast and into the Liberian-Sierra Leonean forest zone, result-ing in the rise of a series of competitive polities in constant flux. The cultural dimensions of these events have been described and analyzed by Warren d'Azevedo (1962a) in a pioneering study of an African cultural area from a frontier perspective.

We see in the following article a microcosm of the African frontier process. The area had stabilized into a "perpetual frontier"—an area of small-scale polities of more or less equal strength, separated by a network of minor frontier bands in which occasionally new polities arise, expand at the expense of existing ones, and sometimes replace them. Local power struggles led periodically to the breakdown of social order in the Kpelle and neighboring chiefdoms. The troubles both opened new areas to intru-sion and produced people willing to plunge into frontier areas in order to found new polities there. These polities would in turn succumb to neigh-bors or be broken up by their own succession troubles. The article illus-trates, again in microcosm, the cultural continuity provided by the frontier process through the back-and-forth linkage between local metropoles and frontiers.

Among the Kpelle described here, the original inhabitants of the area have been long gone. The winners in the local political struggle seek to establish their legitimacy by achieving the status of firstcomers. In this, they resort to several techniques widespread in Africa. By redefining the borders of the polity, they can claim to be first in the newly erected polity. By claiming that the land was wild, uncivilized, and disorderly, they can present themselves as the firstcomers that have brought order to it. Finally—and this is the central theme of the analysis—they affirm the political fact of their primacy by engaging in the rhetorical manipulation of the semantics of kinship and by defining some events rather than others as crucial—what the authors call "pivotal"—to the local political history. Kpelle political discourse thus becomes a series of exercises in folk historiography, analogous to the successive waves of "revisionist" history one finds in professional historiography, where facts previously ignored are stressed and those previously treated as crucial are de-emphasized.

The study makes other points that deserve special attention. It illustrates the degree to which the idiom of kinship relations provides a metaphor for political relations in Africa. It also shows that the firstcomer status is relative to a context: one can have or claim to have precedence in a hamlet, or a village, or a district, or a chieftaincy, or a region. The firstcomer at, say, the village level, after having wrested power at the chieftaincy level, can claim firstcomer status by defining the chieftaincy as an expansion of his village. The obverse of this is that the weak and the humble, seeking protection but unable to link themselves to the political hierarchy except at the lower levels, are forever in the position of newcomers at the village level, no matter how ancient may be their residence in the region as a whole. Thus, the history of a chieftaincy in terms of the politics of precedence becomes independent of the local histories of precedence. Finally, the article shows how the frontier-conditioned dynamic of the importance of firstcomer status continues to operate in the local politics of modern Africa.

—Editor

William P. Murphy and Caroline H. Bledsoe

—————— 4 ——————

Kinship and Territory in the History of a Kpelle Chiefdom (Liberia)

A widespread notion in Sub-Saharan African societies is that first occupation of a territory legitimizes the firstcomers and their descendants as "landowners" who allocate land to later arrivals and have special claims to their allegiance. At the same time, marriage and kinship ties between firstcomer and latecomer groups also structure their relations. Among the Kpelle of Liberia, territory and kinship provide the basic historical reference points in their political life. However, in accounts of the past and in political discussions of the present in Tiapa, a Kpelle chiefdom, we were struck by the fact that kinship and territory had many overlapping meanings and could be used interchangeably.[1] We shall argue here that this fusion is possible because the apparently straightforward history of settlement on the one hand and the seemingly clearcut jural system of kin relations on the other are, in fact, the outcome of strategically managed definitions of ambiguous past events. Both kinship and territorial relations constitute semantic resources which are put to rhetorical use in the political process.

The underlying premise of this paper is semiotic: that kinship and territory are cultural constructs expressed in a code of categories, beliefs, values, and symbols. Neglect of this fact accounts for some of the shortcomings of many models of the evolution of kinship and territory in society, models that treat as mutually exclusive and contrasting cultural realities that are semantically complex and potentially negotiable. After an overview of Kpelle society, we shall closely examine the Kpelle semantics of kinship and territory and then turn to cases illustrating how these meanings are politically managed.

ETHNOGRAPHIC AND HISTORICAL BACKGROUND

The Kpelle—the largest of some sixteen ethnic groups in Liberia—are slash-and-burn rice farmers in an equatorial forest.[2] In recent decades, many of them have become engaged in cash-cropping and in wage labor, especially at rubber plantations and in mining. The Kpelle are organized into a dozen "paramount" chiefdoms which, traditionally, were more fluid in composition and size than they have been since the national administration drew their boundaries in the early twentieth century. Although the language spoken in Tiapa chiefdom is predominantly Kpelle, the population is in fact quite heterogeneous in its ethnic origins.[3]

Authority in a Kpelle chiefdom has generally been divided between the secular offices—mainly those of "land chiefs" and administrative chiefs—and the ritual offices of the secret societies, both kinds being controlled by a ruling "landowning" lineage that traces its ancestry to the founding settlers of the area. The two most important secret associations are the male Poro (pɔ́lɔŋ) and the female Sande (sàneŋ),[4] into which all youth are expected to be initiated.

Patrilineal descent, polygyny, patrilocal residence of sons, and virilocal residence at marriage are cultural ideals, but the variations from these norms are considerable. Moreover, relations within a patrilineage (kala) are not necessarily solidary. Lineage solidarity is strained by various tensions, particularly in high-status lineages where political and economic stakes are high. And while political succession is ideally by a man's oldest son, it is actually frequently contested. Hence, a chiefdom's history is usually one of constant rivalry among political leaders and their patrilineal relatives competing for alliances, followers, territory, and trade. In this rivalry, a key strategy is to secure followers and patrons beyond the patrilineal network.

The concern with supporters, allies, and patrons is deeply rooted historically in external and internal threats. Before the 15th century, the equatorial forest along the Upper Guinea Coast had a very sparse, primarily hunting and fishing population.[5] The disruption of the great trading kingdoms of the Upper Niger basin during the 15th and 16th centuries and the appearance of European trade on the coast led to a major sociopolitical restructuring in the rainforest. Slaves, ivory, and food were the African products exchanged for manufactured metals, weapons, and utensils. Local groups competed to control this commerce and the trade routes, and massive migrations occurred as people moved in search of allies or patrons and of refuge in more peaceful and empty lands. This political flux produced local confederacies consisting of fragmented groups, often of different ethnic origins, that united to control and protect their territories. Since military and political factors were more important than linguistic or even kinship affinities, the groups that emerged were ethnically diverse and politically unstable. Indeed, competition among kinsmen was a common cause for group fission. It is against such a background that the rise of Tiapa chiefdom must be considered.[6]

THE SEMANTICS OF PIVOTAL HISTORICAL EVENTS

History in Tiapa is culturally partitioned into separate sets of narratives, each relevant to a particular territorial level. At the highest level are narratives about the chiefdom as a whole and its early settlers. At each succeeding lower level, history deals with a district, a village, or a quarter, each settled by later arrivals who—though latecomers to the territory as a whole—are seen as firstcomers in their respective sections. These demarcations are expressed in Kpelle by modifying the general term for "history"—*mɛni-pɔ̂lɔ* ('old matters').[7] History at the chiefdom and district levels is *lɔi mɛni-pɔ̂lɔ* ('land old matters'), the context indicating which unit is referred to. *Taa mɛni-pɔ̂lɔ* ('village old matters') refers to the settlement of the village and the interaction of the founding settlers with previous inhabitants and later arrivals. *Koli mɛni-pɔ̂lɔ* recounts the development of a village quarter. History at each of these levels is "owned" by the elders of the group that owns the relevant area and it legitimizes their dominance by highlighting the role of their ancestors in the events leading to its foundation.

Evans-Pritchard's (1940:105ff) concept of "structural time" may help to understand the sociopolitical structuring of Tiapa history. Evans-Pritchard argues that Nuer time-reckoning derives not from an abstract scale of measurement but from a cultural ordering of ongoing sociopolitical relationships. Time is measured by the "structural distance" between social units, such as lineage segments, age sets, and tribal sections. Similarly, in Tiapa, if political position is seen as concomitant with length of residence in the area, then one's present position in the hierarchy (whatever the manner in which it came about) will tend to be seen as a marker of the time-depth of one's political presence. In effect, time markers and social-structural markers become fused, so that one defines the other.

A related notion, developed by Cunnison (1951), is also relevant here. "Perpetual kinship" refers to the permanent labelling of the relationship between immigrant groups and their descendants by an event pivotal to the emergence of the relationship. Cunnison describes it for the Luapula area of Central Africa: "By this [event], people who have been in a certain relationship at some crucial point in history pass the relationship on to the next holders of their names, no matter what the actual relationships may have by this time become. . . . If a brother of the first X forms [another] village, he and his successors are all brothers of X and of his successors . . ." (Cunnison 1951:33).

As in Nuerland and Luapula, historical narratives in Tiapa are concerned with establishing pivotal points in time and space around which subsequent relationships among immigrant groups can be framed. But there are in any history many important events, so that some events must be strategically selected over others out of the flux of events and *made* pivotal. But by the same token, these events are subject to subsequent redefinitions. In a society like the Nuer, with its equal lineages, pivotal events may define only a "structural distance" among equals. Among the Kpelle, they define a hierarchical distance expressing political dominance and subordination. In the three sections that follow, we shall first outline the Kpelle cultural semantics of pivotal territorial and kinship events and then examine how these semantics are used as resources by political actors.

THE SEMANTICS OF TERRITORY

The Kpelle see carving a new territory out on the frontier as an escape from troubles in the old territory and as a promise of safety and opportunity to homestead, farm, fish, and hunt. But the frontier is also a place of uncertainty and danger. A space, defined as wild, unsettled, and unordered, must be made politically secure, while its unfamiliar spirits must be ritually confronted and brought under control or driven out. In this process, several initial events can be seized upon in historical accounts and made into pivotal points for defining subsequent political relationships.

A new territory is 'born' (nɔ̀ii ŋɔkáa-pèrei ɓe ŋí, lit. 'this is the land's manner of birth') by the forceful action of a strong leader who is variously said to 'open' or 'clear' or 'name' the land. As the founder of the new territory, he is its 'landowner' (lɔi-nâmu). He allocates its farmland, accepts or rejects new immigrants, banishes wrongdoers and rivals, and generally oversees its secular and ritual administration. This ownership and authority is theoretically shared by all his patrilineal kin and inherited by his patrilineage. But formally, the term 'landowner' is applied to the lineage head and it is supposed to be inherited patrilineally and through primogeniture.

Later arrivals in a territory are classified by their political importance to the founding group. The most important are those who bring with them some prestige and power, especially military power in the form of followers and warriors. Such latecomers become close though subordinate allies of the landowners. In contrast, a latecomer able to offer only labor and a few followers becomes a 'client' (íyéeì ŋá-nùu, 'in-your-hand person') or even, in former times, a 'slave' (luɛ) entirely dependent on the protection and patronage of the landowner.[8]

Powerful latecomers help landowners secure the territory by building settlements within it. The opening of these districts is conceptualized in the same idiom as the founding of the whole territory: they are also 'born,' 'opened,' 'cleared,' and 'named' by the firstcomers to them; and they, in turn, grant residence and farming rights to their own dependent latecomers. Areas at the periphery of a territory are particularly seen as frontiers needing political consolidation and settlement, and the internal frontiers between districts are similarly regarded at their level. Each territorial level, then, has it own historical pivotal events for defining relationships among its own settlers. What emerges from this is a hierarchical polity in which subsidiary hierarchies arise within hierarchies. The result has usually been called a "nested" structure, in which a unit at any level "nests" within a similarly-structured unit at the next higher level.[9] The hierarchy is reflected in the unidimensional terminology of territorial "ownership" by the different levels of leadership. At the chiefdom and district levels, the landowner is lɔi-nâmu. Next is the 'village-owner,' taa-nâmu. Then the 'quarter-owner,' koli-nâmu. And finally the 'household-owner,' pére-nâmu.

The incumbents of the positions of 'owner' and administrative 'chief' are often the same person. But the positions *qua* offices are separate. Very frequently, the landowner, especially as he gets older, appoints a younger middle-aged man—often his sister's son, real or classificatory—to act as the chief of the territory, thus relieving himself of the day-to-day administrative chores.[10] Again, the traditional terminology reflects the levels involved. The paramount or district chief is *lɔi-kâloŋ*, 'land-chief' (also, *kâloŋ kétɛ*, 'big chief,' or *kâloŋ maa-ŋuŋ*, 'first chief'). Below are the *taa-kâloŋ*, 'village chief,' and the *koli-kâloŋ*, 'quarter chief.'[11]

The territorial units in themselves are also hierarchically ranked. The headquarters-village (of the chiefdom or district) is called *taa kétɛ*, 'big village.' Within a district, villages are regarded as satellite developments of the headquarters-village. Within every substantial village, the main quarter is historically antecedent to its satellite quarters. And finally, each quarter has its own founding household. (And within each household, among its sub-units of wives-with-children, the senior wife's is the "founding" one.)

Ritual control of a territory operates in the same way. As a household is protected by sacrifices to the family's ancestors and by special "medicines," so at the quarter and village levels sacrifices are made at their respective shrines or founders' graves. At the district or chiefdom levels, the ritual protection of the land is achieved through the Poro and Sande societies, which jointly control the powerful 'land medicine' (*lɔi-sâle*) of the chiefdom or district. The mystical equilibrium of a territory can be easily upset by individual acts, such as the shedding of blood, suicide, incest, or warfare (it is said of a victorious war leader that he 'broke up' or 'beat/destroyed the land').[12]

In Tiapa, every district has its own Poro and Sande chapters, each with a head *zóo* ('ritual specialist') and chiefdom-wide Poro or Sande activities are each governed by its respective supreme *zóo*. But these offices are not usually occupied by chiefdom or district landowners. Rather, as with secular authority, the landowner uses an agent—for Poro leadership, usually a "sister's son"—to look after the ritual affairs of his territory.

THE SEMANTICS OF MATRILATERAL KINSHIP

Besides the order of arrivals, the other set of pivotal events in the history of a territory lies in the marriage transactions used to incorporate important latecomers. When an important leader migrates into an area, he is allowed to set up a separate quarter in the landowner's village or to build a new village in a section that lies in the direction of his homeland. He is given the right to allocate farmland in this area to his own followers and to newcomers seeking his patronage. He becomes the leader of his section and is consulted by the chiefdom landowner on important matters affecting the whole territory. In return, he pays tribute in goods and services and displays loyalty to the landowner. Most important, the landowner gives him a wife—usually a sister, a brother's daughter, or some other close relative. The newcomer, his kin group, and their patrilineal descendants are thereby transformed into an 'in-law' (ɓɔlɔ) group. And through the offspring of the marriage, the two kin groups become one bilateral group (káyɔ).

The landowner's "sister" becomes the mother of the newcomer's children and, by extension, the "mother" of the newcomer's growing descent group as a whole. The landowner's kin group is now in the position of kêra, 'mother's brother' (hereafter designated as MoBro) to the newcomer's kin group, which is its mâleŋ, 'sister's son' (hereafter SiSo). Everyone in the host lineage is in the category of MoBro to everyone in the newcomer's lineage. The initial marriage is thus considered a pivotal event in determining the (theoretically) perpetual hierarchical relationship between the two groups.

The result is a small two-tiered pyramid, with the landowners at the top linked to several newcomer groups under them. But this pyramid is part of a still larger nested structure of similar pyramids. For the newcomers, in their turn, receive and incorporate, also through wife-giving, latecomers in their own areas; and these become SiSos to the chiefdom landowners. The nested structure of hierarchical MoBro-SiSo ties ramifies throughout Tiapa Chiefdom, which is sometimes called by Tiapa people in English "the land of uncles and nephews." The saliency of these matrilateral ties even misled one of the first ethnographers of the Kpelle, Westermann, to identify them as matrilineal (see Sibley and Westermann 1929).

The essential political quality of these matrilateral relations lies in the combination of hierarchy and support, in contrast to the competition and rivalry that often permeate relations within the patrilineages. Ideally, SiSos defer completely to their MoBros. In oral tradition, a MoBro landowner could ritually sacrifice his SiSo to obtain success in war. If a chief had to surrender in a battle, his SiSo was typically assigned the dangerous and humiliating task of carrying the plea of surrender to the enemy (Swingle 1965-68). In ritual matters, a male SiSo is considered the most appropriate person to dig a MoBro's grave, a task fraught with mystical danger, and he makes the important sacrifice of a chicken on the last day of the wake.

The MoBro's is his SiSo's nuu-namu, 'person owner.' As such, he is the patron who provides political and economic help and can demand labor and support in return. He is the crucial intercessor for his SiSo when the latter gets in trouble or is involved in important matters, such as marriage negotiations or disputes. And the MoBro is his SiSo's broker in dealings with those at higher political levels.

Matrilateral kinship provides the unifying metaphor that binds the entire political structure. The founder of the whole chiefdom or his successor is MoBro to all the latecomer groups at all levels, from district to village quarters. And even in relations between autonomous contemporary paramount chiefdoms such as Tiapa, a *MoBro-SiSo* relationship sometimes marks historical antecedence and implicit political subordination in the past. The matrilateral idiom also structures the relations between the landowner and the administrative chief, whom he appoints and refers to as his *SiSo* (which, in fact, he often is).[13] And the relations among these administrative chiefs at different territorial levels are also often expressed in the matrilateral idiom; for example, the administrative chief of Tiapa is often *MoBro* to the district administrative chief, who is in turn *MoBro* to the village chief, and so on. Finally, the areas within the chiefdom are similarly designated. This serves to mark which area was established first and, hence, where the politically dominant group resides.

Matrilaterality similarly structures ritual authority. At the founding of a new territory, a *SiSo* acts as the main ritual consecrator (often in conjunction with a Muslim ritual specialist), and thereafter the ritual guardianship and administration of the land is given to those from *SiSo* descent groups. The particular man chosen is called the 'nephew of the land.' These general ritual obligations of the *SiSos* are institutionalized in the Poro society, whose leadership is largely in their hands.[14] Within the ritual hierarchy, matrilaterality is again employed as a metaphor for rank. Westermann (1921:343) notes that the head *zóo* of Poro is referred to as "uncle" (that is, *MoBro*) by the "speaker," who is his deputy and spokesman.[15]

Burial patterns also intertwine with the hierarchy of matrilateral relations. Most people are buried in a graveyard outside the village. But the founder of a territory, his important patrilineal descendants, and the leading figures of important *SiSo* patrilineages are usually buried inside villages within their respective quarters. Burial arrangements are thus a political activity because the location of a grave may later be pointed to as proof of the legitimacy of one's claims to higher status and it may even be appealed to later in challenging the landowners' status.

THE CODE OF ARRIVALS

The foregoing may be schematized into an ideology of what we shall call the Kpelle "code of arrivals." At its core is the matrilateral idiom, which integrates into a single hierarchical code the other idioms—territory, history, marriage, and ritual and secular leadership. The code may be outlined as follows:

1. *Insignificant previous inhabitants.* They are vaguely dealt with in history and are seen as having established no important cultural or political order in the area and no significant kin ties with any powerful later immigrants. Some may be incorporated marginally as 'slaves' or clients.

2. *Important previous inhabitants who have become SiSos.* These are larger, more established groups who superseded former inhabitants but, in turn, became incorporated by powerful newcomers whose "new" territory encompassed their settlements. They become subordinate *SiSos* by

receiving a woman from the new landowners and serve as secular and ritual administrators of their area for them.

3. *MoBro "firstcomer" founders.* They established the currently recognized territory, consolidated pre-existing settlements, drove out or incorporated previous inhabitants, and imposed themselves as landowners.

4. *Important SiSo latecomers.* They are powerful later arrivals who allied themselves with landowners through marriage as subordinate groups. They serve as secular and ritual administrators for their *MoBros.*

5. *Insignificant latecomers.* They are powerless later arrivals, clients greatly dependent on the landowners. They may receive low-status women from the landowners, who are unwilling to admit them as close *SiSo* relatives. They would eventually reciprocate by giving a woman to the landowner or his successor, but the latter's use of her (e.g., as a concubine to attract other clients) symbolizes the low political regard in which these unimportant latecomers are held.[16]

The "code of arrivals" conflates several institutional domains. The term *MoBro*, for example, connotes at once that status of firstcomer, founder, landowner, and wife-giver; that of *SiSo*, of supportive but dependent later arrival, wife-receiver, and assistant to the *MoBro*. Being a non-*SiSo* client indicates very low status. Residence in a particular village or quarter also conveys a set of kinship and political identities.

THE MANAGEMENT OF DEFINITIONS OF PIVOTAL HISTORICAL EVENTS

Invoking the past necessarily involves selecting particular events in it as significant, for the past is seldom unambiguous and the present seldom unproblematic. We shall examine here several cases to show how historical accounts of pivotal events are strategically selected and altered in order to restructure current sociopolitical relations.[17] The cases concern four generations of leadership in Tiapa Chiefdom, beginning with Lete, its founder, followed by his son Kana and grandson Pokpa, and Pokpa's *SiSo* Selen, and ending, finally, with the ouster of Lete's descendants from local political offices by the new Liberian regime. The events range from the second half of the 19th century to after the military coup of April 1980.

CASE 1: THE FOUNDING OF TIAPA CHIEFDOM

Oral history defines Lete as the first Tiapa leader of political significance. But Case 1 shows that this historical "fact" was produced by redefining past pivotal. The redefinition focused on Lete's role in establishing and consolidating the territory and on his marriage and kinship relations with previous inhabitants and later arrivals.

Warfare was a constant threat in Tiapa's early history. Lete, a Gola warrior, migrated into the area that was to become Tiapa with a band of warriors and relatives to escape wars in his own homeland. On the way, the band met other small, recently settled Gola groups. Continuing northeastward, it came to a large Kpelle village headed by a man named Kpolo. Kpolo allowed Lete's group to settle in the village, hoping that Lete, a powerful warrior, would give the village additional protection. To cement this tie, Kpolo gave his sister to Lete as wife. After establishing his followers in the area, Lete brought in more people from his homeland. Soon disputes arose between the Gola immigrants and the Kpelle village leaders. Lete then built a new village Letetaa ('Lete's village') on top of a hill about four miles from the Kpelle village and he also formally named the new wider territory that he claimed for his own: Tiapa lɔi ('Tiapa land').

Another reason given for the move was that the new village was in an area of higher forest that is better for rice farming. During a hungry season, many people from the Kpelle village came for rice to Lete's village and stayed, hoping for a better life, ties with a successful patron, and a better protection, for Letetaa, already enjoying its hilltop position, was also fortified with several palisade walls. With these advantages and strong leadership, Letetaa grew and prospered.

Eventually, Lete assumed undisputed leadership over a wide area which included the major Kpelle village where he first settled. Kpolo, his erstwhile host, finally accepted Lete's dominance—a dominance largely based on the implicit threat of attack by his growing band of warriors. Also, a Gola landowner to the southwest had accepted Lete's authority and, at his death, bequeathed his territory to him. Lete was now the ruler over an amalgamated territory of Kpelle on the northeast and Gola on the southwest.

Another important group of immigrants then entered the chiefdom, led by the Loma warrior Topu. Kpolo, the original Kpelle chief, gave his granddaughter to Topu as wife, and Lete gave him a sister's daughter. Topu soon became an important local leader and even served as the administrative chief of Letetaa.

Sometime after Lete died, his oldest son Kana became Tiapa's chief. Kana married Nakpa, the daughter of the Loma warrior Topu. Nakpa's 'mother' (real or classificatory) was the woman that Kpolo had given to Topu when he first arrived. One of Kana's sons from this marriage was Pokpa, who later succeeded to his father's chiefship.

So much for the main actors and their relationship to one another (see Figure 1). As this case shows, the territorial founder or landowner need not be the earliest to have physically arrived in an area. The status depends on a political redefinition of the area, its boundaries, and previous inhabitants. In his claims to landowner status, Lete used the idiom of a frontier territory. He defined himself as the consolidator and protector of a new territory and as the first with any real political legitimacy in it. Lete's group's initial residence in Kpolo's village signfied that they were strangers, politically subordinate to Kpolo. By establishing and naming his

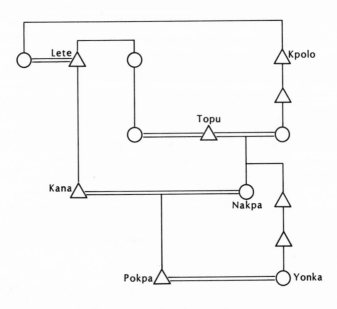

Figure 1

own village, Lete took the first step toward independence. The move was a pivotal event in the political inception of a new territory.

Marriage and the new kin ties it generated signified the inception of perpetual kinship relationships. Again, however, the process is not mechanical. Strategic choices can be made about which of these ties are to be defined as pivotal. Kpolo's giving a woman to Lete should signify Lete's and his descendants' political subordination, as latecoming *SiSos*, to Kpolo and his patrilineage. But this marriage now receives little attention in the oral histories we have collected. In fact, one elderly woman insisted that Kpolo had not given Lete a wife at all. The marriage now being given pivotal significance is that of Lete's 'sister's daughter' to Topu, the powerful Loma warrior who arrived after Lete. Here, Lete appears as the *MoBro* landowner, and the marriage led to a matrilateral tie that united Lete's and Topu's patrilineages into a perpetual political relationship. Regardless of several subsequent reverse intermarriages, Lete's lineage continued to be the *MoBro* group.

The continuation of this "perpetual" tie appears in the definition of the relationships of Lete's son and grandson to Topu's descendants (see Figure 1). By genealogical reckoning, Kana's son Pokpa is to Topu's descendants both a *MoBro* (since Pokpa's grandfather gave Topu a wife) and a *SiSo* (since his father married Topu's daughter). Conversely, Topu's descendants are both *MoBros* and *SiSos* to Pokpa. In practice, however,

Pokpa refers to Topu's lineage as *SiSos* and they to him as *MoBro*, thus perpetuating the hierarchical relationship established by the initial marriage transaction between Lete and Topu. Furthermore, Pokpa later married Yonka, Topu's granddaughter, who was both his classificatory *MoBro*'s daughter and 'father's sister's' daughter; predictably, however, Yonka was now defined as the latter, thereby affirming the perpetual *SiSo* status of her kin group to Pokpa's group.

The successive intermarriages among the three patrilineages—Lete's, Kpolo's, and Topu's—represent a series of politically conditioned decisions. But they have also created a multistranded network of kin ties amenable to further political management. Thus, the assignment of genealogical and marital labels to the relationships is not a matter of merely fulfilling normative or semantic prescriptions. A good illustration of this is the marriage history of Nakpa, the wife of Lete's son Kana and the daughter of Topu. Normatively, Kpolo's gift of Nakpa's mother to Topu established the *MoBro* status of Kpolo's lineage. However, Nakpa's relationship to Kpolo is now minimized in the history. What is emphasized is her status as Topu's daughter; and her marriage to Kana is defined as mere reciprocity for Kana's earlier gift of a woman to Topu. Thus, an earlier affinal relationship is ignored while the affinal relationship between Topu and Lete is cast as the pivotal event that was reaffirmed in the subsequent marriage of Nakpa to Kana.

Several Tiapa residents pointed out that no one nowadays in Tiapa traces his ancestry back to Kpolo. The political waning of Kpolo's group and the ascendancy of Lete's and Topu's groups are now embedded in contemporary genealogical constructions. From this and other cases (see Bledsoe and Murphy 1980), it is clear that genealogical amnesia is less a matter of faulty memory and more one of strategic reconstruction that defines and redefines as pivotal those events that best legitimize the new political arrangements.

CASE 2: RITUAL INCORPORATION OF A NEW TERRITORY

This case shows how matrilateral ties can be expressed in a ritual relationship in order to expand the territory and incorporate newcomers.

During Kana's rule, the boundaries of Tiapa chiefdom expanded further by incorporation of a section of an adjacent chiefdom. The people of this section had been complaining that their leaders demanded too much labor from them. They came to Kana and told him: "We want you take care of us." When Kana agreed, they gave him a woman and a ritually powerful cane to show his responsibility to "hold and protect them." Kana sent one of his *SiSos* to their main village to act as its ritual leader. The village then became identified as the *SiSo* village to the headquarters of Tiapa, Letetaa, the latter becoming its *MoBro* village.

Here, both a marriage transaction and a ritual exchange define the pivotal events in the incorporation of a new territory. Both events signify the dominance of the landowner and the subordination of the "newcomers" (that is, political newcomers to Tiapa). But the matrilateral link here is not created through a marriage but rather by a *SiSo* becoming the ritual leader of the new territory, thereby conferring the *SiSo* identity on it.

Meanwhile, the new subjects' gift of a woman to Kana did not make—as genealogical norms alone would—Kana's descendants through her into their *SiSos*. It is the political setting that defines the meaning and implications of the marriage. A marriage may be noted or ignored, or even, when circumstances change, invested with a political significance opposite of the one it had when it took place.

CASE 3: PATRILINEAL RIVALRY AND MATRILATERALITY

The frequent competition and hostility between lineage mates (particularly between male siblings) may provoke one of them into setting off with his family and followers to try and establish a new section within the old territory or an entirely new territory and polity. The distinction between the two is not clearcut and the status of such a settlement is ambiguous. This case illustrates the political jockeying within the patrilineage that follows such a split and the solidarity of the matrilateral tie.

To minimize threats to his dominance, Kana tried to keep his brothers from gaining independence. However, one younger brother, Sia, was particularly envious of Kana. Sia took his followers, moved to a more distant location in Tiapa, built a new village there, and established control over the area. When Sia later became sick, however, Kana had him brought back to Kana's headquarters-village, where he died and was buried. To succeed Sia, Kana installed one of his (Kana's) *SiSos* as the administrative chief of the territory that Sia had established within Tiapa.

Sia's migration was a show of independence that compromised Kana's authority in the territory. The installation, after Sia's death, of a *SiSo* as administrative chief unambiguously defined the new section of Tiapa as a *SiSo* territory. Moroever, by making sure that Sia was buried at the headquarters-village of the lineage, Kana recreated the outward signs of political solidarity in the lineage. Had Sia's followers managed instead to bury him in the new territory, they would have created a potential ritual argument for independence. Their offerings at Sia's grave could later be interpreted as confirming that Sia's establishment of the village was the pivotal event in the founding of a new territory.

Sia's territory was the only large section of Tiapa to be headed by a rival from within the ruling patrilineage rather than by a *SiSo*. Significantly, Kana's actions changed that. From then on, the entire structure of the chiefdom rested on a pyramid of *MoBro-SiSo* relationships. As this and other cases indicate, however, such an apparently normative matrilateral structure was in fact the outcome of incessant strategic actions about the past and preventive measures for the future.

CASE 4: CONSOLIDATING TERRITORY IN THE NATIONAL CONTEXT

This case and the following one bring the history of Tiapa into the modern context, when its relations—as of the Liberian interior in general—with the national government in Monrovia became more intense. The cases reveal the continuity and transformation in the national context of the traditional process of a leader consolidating a territory and legitimizing his control over it. They also show the continuing role of the matrilateral idiom in patron-client ties between leaders at different territorial levels. Finally, the cases show the transfer of this kinship idiom to relations with the national leadership.

In the early 19th century, black settlers from North America landed on the coast of West Africa and, in 1847, founded the nation of Liberia with its capital Monrovia. Like the European colonizers of Africa, Americo-Liberians (as they came to be called) saw themselves as bringing Christianity and civilization to the dark continent (for a recent study, see Schick 1980). They regarded the Liberian interior as populated by "uncivilized" and "primitive" pagans, as a frontier to be tamed, colonized, and "civilized." Land, labor, and, later, tax collection were some of the attractions of this frontier. The military instrument of these ambitions was the appropriately named Liberian Frontier Force.

For the Americo-Liberians, the history of the territory began when they arrived. They viewed themselves as founders and landowners of a new territory, not because they were the first to settle there but because they were the first to consolidate it politically and bring to it a new cultural order. Such claims required new legitimizing definitions of pivotal historical events, which national symbols and rhetoric served to enshrine. Thus, the Liberian national motto—"The Love of Liberty Brought Us Here"—celebrated the arrival of the American black settlers as such a pivotal event.

The modern phase of Tiapa history begins in the first two decades of the 20th century when the national government, notably during the administration of President Arthur Barclay (1902-12), began an active campaign to organize administratively and incorporate politically the indigenous populations. Tiapa Chiefdom provides a vivid example of the process that this initiated, not least because its proximity to Monrovia made for earlier and more intense contacts with Americo-Liberians—the national government saw Tiapa as a "gateway" to the interior. The history of Tiapa's relations with the Americo-Liberians prefigured what subsequently occurred throughout Liberia.

Indigenous leaders had to adjust to the newcomers whom they saw as they did any powerful outside stranger group: as potential competitors who might rob them of trade and laborers or as potential allies and patrons who might provide military and economic assistance in their conflicts with rival local groups. The most successful response was cooperation: it brought in new political resources that could be used in securing more followers and increasing their dependence, and in threatening dissidents and competitors for local offices and territory with economic and military sanctions (see Murphy 1981). Thus, a new tier of national patronage was added to the top of the traditional pyramid of patron-client ties.

In 1906, Kana, the son of Lete, brought his son Pokpa to Monrovia to be raised as a ward in President Barclay's household; this was in appreciation for the President's assistance in a dispute with a neighboring chief. Kana also wanted his son to learn the language and customs of the coastal settlers and to secure useful ties to them and the government.

Kana died in 1908 and one of his younger brothers became the head of the chiefdom. Pokpa returned in 1920. He had received a good education in Monrovia and his father's brother drew upon his skills to read government documents and answer government letters at a time when the government was rapidly extending its administration over the tribal areas.

Pokpa himself became chief in 1930. A few years later, he decided to have the chiefdom surveyed. This, he claimed, was to prevent Tiapa land from being privately sold the way it was being sold by chiefs nearer Monrovia to America-Liberians for cash cropping and speculation. The President at the time was Edwin Barclay, with whom Pokpa had become acquainted during his wardship in Monrovia, and the President gave Pokpa permission to carry out the survey.

A surveyor was brought in and in due time Pokpa received a survey map and deed for the chiefdom. But several neighboring chiefs were not satisfied with the results, claiming that the boundary lines of Tiapa were encroaching on their territories. Some years later, they filed a complaint with the new President, William Tubman. Tubman set up a fact-finding commission. The investigation took several years and finally President Tubman ruled that since Pokpa had a survey map and deed for the chiefdom, he had proven his claims.

In traditional logic, a leader might become the founder of a new territory by redefining its boundaries in successful negotiations with adjoining communities. Pokpa was the founder of the modern chiefdom in the new national context—by using the new idioms of surveys and deeds as well as the old idioms of politically charged kin ties in order to define the legitimacy of his territorial claims. From the local point of view, a skillful leader had secured the sovereignty of his territory through the patronage of more powerful landowners—in this case, the government—whose wider territory encapsulated his.

However, the traditional matrilateral idiom—involving the exchange of women—was less easily invoked in relations with Americo-Liberians, who professed Christianity and monogamy. A functional substitute was necessary to symbolize the alliance. It was found in wardship (foster-age)—an institution which indigenous leaders and Americo-Liberians had been using to forge ties and which had indigenous precedents. In wardship, the fostered child expands his social ties, learns new skills, and can later be a broker between the two families. Wardship was a functional equivalent of hypergamy, with children replacing women: indigenous child-givers were clearly marked as of lower status than the Americo-Liberian child-receivers.[18]

For the Americo-Liberians, wards provided labor for the house and farm and an opportunity to "civilize" indigenous children. More importantly, wardship gave the Americo-Liberians an opportunity to incorporate indigenous peoples politically in a peaceful and effective manner analogous to indirect rule. Special efforts were made to foster the sons of chiefs who, it was hoped, would later assume leadership in the traditional communities and become loyal brokers for the national government.

For the ward, his Americo-Liberian "relatives" were his "civilized" kin, to whom he could look for political and economic support when he returned to his own community. The case of Pokpa is therefore an archetypical one. It shows how the Americo-Liberians used the tie with Pokpa to extend control over Tiapa. And it also shows how an indigenous landowner lineage used the same tie to secure government support of its still shaky claim over territory that its forebears had rather recently 'named' and 'opened.'

CASE 5: PIVOTAL EVENTS AND POLITICAL SUCCESSION IN THE NATIONAL CONTEXT

In recent years, the invocation of pivotal events in Tiapa's history has marked the rivalry among several of Pokpa's *SiSos*. Two of these were especially prominent as competitors for succeeding Pokpa as the most influential patron in Tiapa. The political strategies of both exploited new forms of patronage as well as the redefinition of the territory by reference to new pivotal events. In modern Liberia, this involves resources available through government-sanctioned public offices.

Although retired from a national public office since the early 1970's, Pokpa maintained his authority as head landowner of the chiefdom. As he aged, however, two main contenders for his local power emerged: Selen and Sumo, both his *SiSos*. Selen lived in the town adjacent to the chiefdom's headquarters-village where Pokpa lived. He had been the principal of the local school and Pokpa's right-hand man. For many years, when Pokpa was busy or away, he monopolized the important role of dealing with local issues involving relations with the government. This brokering between local and national levels gave him prestige and some power, although he did not occupy the formal political office of Paramount Chief. This was held by another *SiSo* of Pokpa, a more traditional man of little education.

Eventually, Sumo, another of Pokpa's *SiSos* with a modern education, was elected Paramount Chief, and a bitter rivalry grew up between him and Selen. Sumo used his new position to punish enemies (for example, by imposing heavy fines in court cases) and to reward followers with favors, hoping to establish himself as the most powerful patron in Tiapa. One of his key strategic moves was to shift the chiefdom's official headquarters southward, nearer to Monrovia, where he performed his official duties and heard court cases, away from Pokpa's village. He presented himself in the new setting as the modern representative of Tiapa, superseding the traditional authority associated with Pokpa and the old village.

Meanwhile, his rival Selen managed to get himself appointed District Commissioner when the chiefdom was reorganized into a district—the first official administrative level above the highest traditional level of Paramount chieftaincy. Selen also succeeded in establishing the headquarters of the new district in the town where he lived. He had an impressive district headquarters built there, as well as a District Commissioner's house and a guest house. But Selen's political success was shortlived. When the military coup of April 1980 swept the Americo-Liberian government from power, Selen and Sumo were removed from their positions, and Pokpa, like others who had built up their power through the patronage of the former government, fell into government disgrace.

Despite the new idioms of power, Sumo's efforts to succeed Pokpa as Tiapa's dominant patron were very much in line with traditional notions of territorial founding and consolidation. Particularly notable was his effort to establish a new pivotal event by moving Tiapa's headquarters to a new town, where it could be directly associated with his paramount chieftaincy. But these efforts were undercut by his competitor Selen who became District Commissioner, a position formally superior to that of paramount chief.

Like Sumo, Selen also took a territorial action—the establishment of the new District's headquarters in his own town. The new location, near yet not at Pokpa's village, would both associate him with Pokpa and symbolize his supplanting of Pokpa—by then a very old man. It also redefined Sumo's moves as belonging to a lower political level. In the traditional logic of territoriality, Selen had "refounded" the territory by consolidating it in the new context of a district. It remains to be seen how the political logic we have described will operate now as a new local elite emerges as "founders" of the territory in a new administrative framework and as brokers with the new national patrons.

DISCUSSION

There are three striking features in the Kpelle idioms of matrilateral kin-ship and territory when used in defining pivotal events: (1) their use in a "nested" political hierarchy, (2) their overlapping meanings, and (3) their negotiated use in social action. We shall consider these themes in the context of a broad theoretical tradition of seeing kinship and territory as dichotomous principles of political organization.

Since the Enlightenment, Western political thought has searched for the conditions that gave rise to different forms of political order. By the mid-19th century, the answer—crystallized in the works of Maine (1861) and Morgan (1877)—was to distinguish between two bases of political order: kinship and territorial affiliation, kinship being seen as giving way to territorial affiliation as societies grew in complexity. This distinction has continued to inform recent discussions of the evolution of political systems (e.g., Fortes and Evans-Pritchard 1940, Fried 1967, Krader 1968, Sahlins 1968, Service 1975, Cohen and Service 1978).[19] In his important analysis of "stateless" societies in West Africa, Horton (1972) retains the distinction but departs in an imaginative way from the standard associa-tion of kinship with stateless societies and of territory with the state. Pointing out that most West African stateless societies are not organized on the classic segmentary-lineage model, he argues that a territorial princi-ple of affiliation, based on an ideology of historical precedence, underlies the organization of the more complex stateless societies. Thus, Horton's paper provides a sophisticated point of departure for our argument against the kinship-territory dichotomy.[20]

Horton sees kinship and territory as mutually exclusive principles that give shape to three types of stateless societies: (Type 1) a "segmentary lineage system," where solidarity is based on kinship bonds; (Type 2) a "dispersed, territorially defined community," where disparate immigrant groups define their solidarity "not in terms of a further genealogical link, but in terms of co-residence on a more or less clearly defined tract of land" (1972:94); and (Type 3) a "large compact village," where territorial affilia-tion is even more pronounced as the political role of kin ties is severely weakened by cross-cutting institutions (such as age-grade associations and secret societies) that actively combat the usurpation of power by kin groups. In this latter type, immigration engenders a political system that uses the idiom of first arrivals ("landowners") in contrast to "latecomers." The difference entails different political roles but not political inequality: the landowners allocate land to the latecomers, who reciprocate with military and political support.

Where do the Kpelle fit in this scheme? With their strong territorial-ity, secret societies, and fortified compact villages, Kpelle chiefdoms fall into Type 3—to which Horton (1972:100) indeed assigns the tribes of the

Liberian hinterland. Yet, Tiapa's political cohesion is shaped by both the territorial principle and the kinship principle of matrilateral links. Horton's model for Type 3 assumes that territorially-based societies must necessarily lack an overarching kinship principle for uniting disparate groups. But the model overlooks the possibility of using kinship ties other than those of unilineal (usually patrilineal) descent which organize Type 1 societies. In Tiapa, matrilateral ties provide an integrating hierarchical framework within which the disparate patrilineages become allied, while symbolically transforming the hierarchy into a kin-based system of support.[21]

Horton's model assumes a lack or at least a muteness of political stratification in stateless societies. But Tiapa shows that descent groups in Type 3 societies can be quite unequal and competitive, with secret societies strenghtening rather than weakening the power of the leading descent groups by providing them with the tools of ritual control.[22]

Descent groups in Tiapa are far from being politically moribund. Indeed, matrilaterality is so strongly emphasized precisely because it can provide supportive yet hierarchical links among strong patrilineages. This is in keeping with two other analyses that deal explicitly with incorporation and matrilateral kinship: Gough's (1971) and Leach's (1954, 1961).

In her reanalysis of Evans-Pritchard's data on the Nuer of the Sudan, with its emphasis on the egalitarian order among Nuer patrilineal segments, Gough focuses on the historical process of Nuer conquests, expansion, and incorporation of outsiders. Evans-Pritchard (1940:226-227) reported that strangers and captives were attached to dominant clans through women, as sisters' or daughters' sons (analogous to the Kpelle *SiSos*). Hence Gough argues that while patrilineal principles underlay the relations among "aristocratic" (locally dominant) lineages, matrilateral ties marked the very unequal relations between such a lineage and subordinate captured, conquered, poor, or immigrant people (Gough 1971:103).[23] Thus, while in Horton's categories, the Nuer are a Type 1 (segmentary) society, the processes by which people are politically incorporated are very similar to those among the Kpelle. Matrilateral links as a vehicle for hierarchical relations have also been examined by Leach (1954, 1961) in his analyses of the Kachin of Burma. Here, an initial marriage between patrilineages ranks the wife-giver over the wife-receiver, and such marriages become the idiom for structuring the political relations among chiefs, headmen, and commoners.

These views of matrilaterality as a structural principle of political hierarchy contrasts with another view of it—most notably expressed by Fortes (1949:281-332) in his analysis of the Tallensi—as largely a personal bond of amity outside the jural-political order. In the same vein, Turner (1969:114) sees matrilaterality as a form of "communitas," an unstructured mode of interaction that contrasts with the jurally constrained order of patrilineality. These views are no doubt related to Radcliffe-Brown's (1950) view of the *MoBro-SiSo* relationship as an extension of the mutual sentiments of personal concern and amity that exists in the mother-child relationship. There is, to be sure, an aura of this in the idiom in which matrilateral relations are presented among the Kpelle, but the relationship is also potentially competitive, with the more powerful *SiSos* waiting for their chance to supplant the dominant *MoBro* group as the landowning group of the area.

The common jural view of kinship and territory as mutually exclusive principles of organization neglects their possible semiotic functions. Typologically, Tiapa Chiefdom can be classified either as a territorially based polity (Horton's Type 3) or as a kin-based one, with emergent territoriality (in Service's evolutionary scheme, 1971:163, a "chiefdom-level" society, intermediary between segmentary lineage systems and states). But, as we have seen, the semiotics of kinship and those of territory need not constitute distinct systems of meanings; they can overlap, blend, and even represent a single set of meanings for marking political rights to land, people, and authority. In Tiapa, to invoke territory is necessarily to say something about kinship, and vice versa.

The jural model, in which the cultural code of categories, rules, and beliefs directly reflect social action (e.g., Fortes 1969) or directly determine it, has recently been challenged (see, notably, Comaroff 1978, Cohen and Comaroff 1976, Comaroff and Comaroff 1981, Comaroff and Roberts 1981). Our argument shares with this challenge concern with a dimension which the jural model neglects: the achievement of sociopolitical outcomes through the strategic management of cultural meanings. For example, in their study of the politics of rule manipulation among the Tshidi (a section of the Tswana), Comaroff and Comaroff (1981) show that the extensive intermarriage among aristocratic lineages creates a situation in which a particular marriage can be construed in several ways—e.g., as marriage with a "mother's brother's daughter," or a "father's brother's daughter" (in the classificatory sense). Men advance their political careers by labelling a marriage as being of one or another type or even by reclassifying it with changing circumstances. Similar kinds of ambiguities in Kpelle marriage norms have been discussed by Gibbs (1963:568).

In Tiapa, political ends are achieved by the strategic selection of one marriage rather than another as the pivotal event defining a supposedly perpetual hierarchical relationship.[24] As with the Tshidi, a network of multiple kin ties among the patrilineages allows one to construe the same relationship over time as patrilineal, or matrilateral, or even as a non-kin patron-client relationship. People seeking close but non-competitive subordinate roles can stress their *SiSo* ties to the landowning lineage, while the ambitious descendants of a latecomer will seek to put him into a *MoBro* position to others.

The incompleteness of Horton's (1972) analysis of firstcomers and latecomers in West African stateless societies stems from not allowing that these cultural notions are politically managed. The functionalist logic of the jural model, in which firstcomers dispense land and latecomers help maintain territorial integrity (Horton 1972:96, 99), wishes to see balanced functioning rather than inequality and conflict. But the firstcomer and latecomer roles are not unambiguous, semantically or socially. In Tiapa, while the vast majority of immigrants have remained dependent *SiSos* or even low-status clients, the "nested" arrangement of territorial levels means that some latecomers to Tiapa may be firstcomers in their respective sections. And firstcomer status itself is not an outcome of actual first arrival, as jural rules would have it. Rather, being a first arrival is an outcome of various political transactions and semantic manipulations accomplished in the face of others trying to construe the same events to their own advantage.[25]

All this does not mean that the Kpelle are singularly manipulative in comparison with other people. While the politics of meaning management undoubtedly varies in different societies, it would probably be misleading to create a dichotomy or continuum between "manipulative" and "non-manipulative" societies, or between societies with ambiguous and clearcut social rules. The idea that categories, rules, and beliefs could ever function in a straightforward manner in *any* society distorts the role of meaning in social life. Cognitive selection is inherent in the process of imposing meaning on any social behavior.[26]

Finally, by emphasizing meaning and its political management, we are not dismissing the importance of jurality in favor of the rule-less model of unfettered "manipulative man." Rather, we see cultural prescriptions and proscriptions themselves as critical resources in the strategic construals of social reality. This helps explain why people in Tiapa try to avoid the obligations and burdens of jural rules imposed by others while at the same time trying to make others accept the supremacy of these rules. Members of a powerful newcomer group try to claim they were the first to bring cultural and political order to an area, invoking thereby the notion of founder with its jural implications. But at the same time, they try to avoid submitting to the jural rules that would subordinate them to previous inhabitants by claiming that the land was a dangerous, unordered frontier before they arrived. Like categories of kinship and territory, therefore, jurality itself is also a cultural construction used in the rhetoric of sociopolitical discourse.

NOTES

1. Tiapa is a pseudonym. This essay is based on fieldwork among the Kpelle of Liberia in 1973-74. We gratefully acknowledge the support of the Foreign Area Fellowship Program, the National Institute of Mental Health, and the

National Science Foundation. We also wish to thank Harry Basehart, Ronald Cohen, Jane Collier, John Comaroff, and Louise Lamphere for their helpful comments, and Igor Kopytoff for his thoughtful editing. The responsibility for the present article, however, is ours alone.

2. For an ethnographic synopsis, see Gibbs (1965).

3. While the founder of Tiapa was Gola and most place-names are Gola, a large later Kpelle immigration has made the chiefdom Kpelle-speaking and today Gola is rarely heard.

4. The Kpelle transcriptions are based on the standard Kpelle orthography developed by William Welmers (1948, 1962). Tone and nasalization are phonemic in the Kpelle language. /´/ indicates high tone, /ˋ/ low tone, and /ˆ/ rising-falling tone. No mark indicates mid-tone.

5. This synoptic history of the region is taken from d'Azevedo (1959, 1962). See also Rodney (1970).

6. Tiapa's ethnic heterogeneity—e.g., several of its early leaders were Gola and Loma—and that of many other "Kpelle" chiefdoms underscores the fact that the patterns described here as Kpelle also apply to other ethnic groups of the Central West Atlantic cultural region delineated by d'Azevedo (1962a). The widespread political use of matrilateral ties, real and symbolic, can be seen by examining works on the region, such as Fulton (1968), Bellman (1975:59-61, 187-188) and Teitelbaum (1980:41) on other Kpelle chiefdoms, Finnegan (1965:29-30) on the Limba, Little (1967:196-197) and Abraham (1978) on the Mende, Holsoe (1967:85) on the Vai, and Massing (1970-71:184, 194-195) on the Belle.

7. We put single quotation marks around translation glosses of Kpelle terms and double quotation marks around informants' statements in Liberian English, scholarly quotations, and words used in a special sense.

8. For an analysis of similar processes elsewhere in Africa, see Colson (1970:41ff) on the Tonga of Zambia.

9. The processes are reminiscent of Bohannan's (1954) distinction between what he calls disjunctive migration and local lineage expansion among the Tiv. In the first, a group detaches itself from its area, migrates, and settles in a new area. In the second, the settled group expands locally over its area. Among the Tiv, the result was a "nested" structure without hierarchy. In Kpelleland, the structure is hierarchical.

10. The Kpelle describe the relationship with spatial metaphors: the one delegated with authority is the 'next-to person,' and the person with the true authority is in the background as a 'person behind a person.'

11. The terminological merger of the two upper levels—what we refer to as "chiefdom" and "district"—reflects the fluidity of authority in traditional times at these levels. A chief who had imposed (often temporarily) his authority over other chiefs of the area was not traditionally distinguished from them by a special title. We refer to him here as a "paramount" chief heading the chiefdom. The other chiefs thereby become "district" chiefs. This distinction became firmly established under President Arthur Barclay (1902-1912), when the Liberian government formally introduced the terms "paramount chiefdom" and "clan" (for district)—where the Kpelle used the single term *lɔi*, 'land'—with their respective chiefs. Of course, the extension of the government's authority also reduced the political flux and the ambiguity of the relations among the various chiefs.

12. The history of the encroachment of the national government on village life is also said to "break the land down," particularly through taxation.

13. With its increasing control, the national government introduced elections to these administrative chieftaincies. However, behind-the-scenes maneuvers by the traditional landowner is very influential in the outcome.

14. By the same token, the general process by which *SiSos* try to supplant the *MoBro* landowners results in the Poro society being a potential resource in these challenges. In the Tiapa area, the authority in the Sande society is typically held by *zóos* who are female members of the landowner patrilineage. Unlike male members of the patrilineage (and unlike some *SiSos*, female members usually provide political support to the male head of the landowning kin group (see Bledsoe 1980b, 1984).

15. Given Kpelle kin terminology and Liberian English usage, Westermann's German gloss "uncle" most likely refers to a *MoBro*. We thank Jutta Dale for her valuable assistance with translations of Westermann's text.

16. The commonly drawn opposition between kinship and clientship (e.g., Mair 1962) is thus overcome here by the complexity of matrilaterality (see, on this point, Bledsoe and Murphy 1980).

17. Each synoptic text, describing a part of Tiapa history, is a composite drawn from a total corpus of oral history collected in 1973-74 from about ten middle-aged and elderly men and women from different parts of the chiefdom. We would like to thank Cynthia Schmidt for doing follow-up interviews after we left the field. In addition, Warren d'Azevedo provided us with his 1956 field notes on the history of the area. Because this oral history is being presented here in the more permanent form of print does not mean that this is unambiguous and undisputed historical truth. A pragmatic, rhetorical use of history is central to Kpelle thought. In these accounts, except for presidents of Liberia, all personal names are pseudonyms.

18. A form of hypergamy did exist in the institution of "country wives"— essentially, mistresses of Americo-Liberians. Such a wife was visited in her remote rural village, away from the public scrutiny of the coastal communities where the appearance of monogamy was upheld. Although such ties through women did provide a mechanism for patron-client relations, our concern here is with the publicly legitimate ties through children.

19. These writers do not, of course, naively suppose that territoriality does not play some role in the organization of all societies; but Sahlins conveys the prevailing view when he says that only with state formations do we find "the establishment of society *as* a territory" (Sahlins 1968:6, his emphasis).

20. An early critic of the kinship-territory dichotomy was Lowie who argued that kinship and territory should be seen as co-existing mechanisms of organization in all societies, with "local contiguity" determining social solidarity "even in very humble cultural levels" (1920:380). A recent study by Thornton (1980), of the Iraqw of Tanzania, posits space and territory—and not kinship—as the forces shaping Iraqw sociopolitical structure. The ethnographic case is important in that it puts to question the exclusion of territory as an important structuring principle in stateless societies, but it may be taken to maintain implicitly the idea that kinship and territory are still mutually exclusive principles of organization.

21. Matrilaterality among the Kpelle allows varying degrees of political dependency. When political or economic conditions encourage political egalitarianism, equality among patrilineal segments can be emphasized with little cost. On the other hand, with stratification and centralization of authority, when individuals seek the protection of patrons or the support of followers, the matrilateral idiom may also be exploited for those ends.

22. The argument that ritual power counterbalances secular power is common. It has often been applied to the political role of the Poro societies (e.g., Fulton 1972, Little 1965, 1966), by taking at face value the rhetoric of leaders and followers and overlooking the political and economic inequality supported by this "religious" institution. The argument is also related to the perception of a complementary balance between ritual and secular authority in chiefdoms (e.g., Sahlins

1968). We argue, however, that the functionalist interpretations of a number of established analytical dichotomies (such as male/female, old/young, lineage/association, kinship/territory, and so on) obscure their use for political and economic domination in chiefdom polities (see, e.g., Murphy 1980, Bledsoe 1980a).

23. A Nuer *MoBro* sought to incorporate *SiSos* into his local community to build a political following (Gough 1971:103). *SiSos*, however, often tried to dissolve this dependence by founding new settlements of their own. Although Gough does not elaborate the point, it is clear that the hierarchical structure would then be replicated in the same idiom, the *SiSios* now becoming the *MoBros* to their own subordinate *SiSos*, much as in Tiapa. Similar processes appear among the LoDagaa (Goody 1959:68), who fall into Horton's Type 2.

24. The idea that meanings and rules are subject to management is accepted by the Kpelle. This is well illustrated by a story entitled "How an unpopular son of the king is removed," told to Westermann by a Kpelle man:

> If the townspeople do not like the first son (the heir apparent) of their chief and do not want him to succeed to the chiefship, they may go to the chief and tell him that there is some mystical danger threatening the community which requires the services of a diviner. The chief then calls the diviner who investigates the threat and determines that the only salvation for the community is to offer a human sacrifice. The diviner also claims that the only efficacious sacrificial victim is the first son of the chief. Reluctantly, the chief agrees and the sacrifice is performed (Westermann 1921:316, our translation).

25. For a broad discussion of indigene-stranger relations in Africa, pre- and post-colonial, see Shack and Skinner 1979.) Cohen and Middleton (1970:12, 13) note that while African societies perceive "indigenousness" as a political marker, it seems to have "little systematic effect upon the outcome of group relations." We interpret this fact to mean that while the empirical fact of sequence of arrival may not be significant, the cultural semantics of indigenousness and their rhetorical management importantly shapes the political process. D'Azevedo (1962b) similarly emphasizes the cultural context and political uses of historical retrospect in his article on Gola history.

26. We share many of the "ethnomethodological" assumptions about the normative order as a cognitive system for persuasively construing conduct. The moral code is used not so much to describe behavior as to create a way to view the behavior (see Wieder 1974).

REFERENCES

Abraham, Arthur 1978. *Mende Government and Politics under Colonial Rule: A Historical Study of Political Change in Sierra Leone, 1890-1937.* Freetown: Sierra Leone University Press.

Bellman, Beryl L. 1975. *Village of Curers and Assassins: On the Production of Fala Kpelle Cosmological Categories.* The Hague: Mouton.

Bledsoe, Caroline H. 1980a. *Women and Marriage in Kpelle Society.* Stanford: Stanford University Press.

———. 1980b. "Stratification and Sande Politics." *Ethnologische Zeitschrift* 1:143-149.

———. 1984. "The Political Uses of Sande Ideology and Symbolism." *American Ethnologist* 11:455-472.

——— and William P. Murphy 1980. "The Kpelle Negotiation of Marriage and

Matrilineal Ties." In *The Versatility of Kinship*, edited by Linda S. Cordell and Stephen Beckerman, pp. 145-163. New York: Academic Press.

Bohannan, Paul 1954. "The Migration and Expansion of the Tiv." *Africa* 24:2-16.

Cohen, Anthony P. and John L. Comaroff 1976. "The Management of Meaning: On the Phenomenology of Political Transactions." In *Transactions and Meaning*, edited by Bruce Kapferer, pp. 87-107. Philadelphia: Institute for the Study of Human Issues.

Cohen, Ronald and John Middleton 1970. "Introduction." In *From Tribe to Nation in Africa: Studies in Incorporation Processes*, edited by Ronald Cohen and John Middleton, pp. 1-34. Scranton, Pa.: Chandler.

Cohen, Ronald and Elman Service, eds. 1978. *Origins of the State: The Anthropology of Political Evolution*. Philadelphia: Institute for the Study of Human Issues.

Colson, Elizabeth 1970. "The Assimilation of Aliens among Zambian Tonga." In *From Tribe to Nation in Africa: Studies in Incorporation Processes*, edited by Ronald Cohen and John Middleton, pp. 35-54. Scranton, Pa.: Chandler.

Comaroff, John L. 1978. "Rules and Rulers: Political Processes in a Tswana Chiefdom." *Man* 13:1-20.

—— and Jean Comaroff 1981. "The Management of Marriage in a Tswana Chiefdom." In *Essays on African Marriage in Southern Africa*, edited by E.J. Krige and J.L. Comaroff. Cape Town: Juta.

—— and Simon Roberts 1981. *Rules and Processes: The Cultural Logic of Dispute in an African Context*. Chicago: University of Chicago Press.

Cunnison, Ian 1951. *History on the Luapula*. London: Oxford University Press (Rhodes-Livingstone Papers, No.21).

d'Azevedo, Warren L. 1959. "The Setting of Gola Society and Culture: Some Theoretical Implications of Variations in Time and Space." *Kroeber Anthropological Society Papers* 21:43-125.

——. 1962a. "Some Historical Problems in the Delineation of a Central West Atlantic Region." *Annals of the New York Academy of Sciences* 96:512-538.

——. 1962b. "Uses of the Past in Gola Discourse." *Journal of African History* 3:11-34.

Evans-Pritchard, E.E. 1940. *The Nuer*. Oxford: Oxford University Press.

Finnegan, Ruth 1965. *Survey of the Limba People of Northern Sierra Leone*. London: Her Majesty's Stationery Office.

Fortes, Meyer 1949. *The Web of Kinship among the Tallensi*. London: Oxford University Press.

——. 1969. *Kinship and the Social Order: The Legacy of Lewis Henry Morgan*. Chicago: Aldine.

—— and E.E. Evans-Pritchard, eds. 1940. *African Political Systems*. London: Oxford University Press.

Fried, Morton 1967. *The Evolution of Political Society: An Essay in Political Anthropology*. New York: Random House.

Fulton, R.M. 1972. "The Political Structures and Functions of Poro in Kpelle Society." *American Anthropologist* 74:1218-1233.

Gibbs, James L., Jr. 1963. "Marital Instability among the Kpelle: Towards a Theory of Epainogamy." *American Anthropologist* 65:552-573.

——. 1965. "The Kpelle of Liberia." In *Peoples of Africa*, edited by James L. Gibbs, pp. 199-240. New York: Holt, Rinehart and Winston.

Goody, Jack 1959. "The Mother's Brothers and the Sister's Son in West Africa." *Journal of the Royal Anthropological Institute* 89:61-88.

Gough, Kathleen 1971. "Nuer Kinship: A Re-Examination." In *The Translation of Culture: Essays to E.E. Evans-Pritchard*, edited by T.O. Beidelman, pp. 70-121. London: Tavistock.

Holsoe, Svend 1967. *The Cassava-Leaf People: An Ethnohistorical Study of the Vai with a Particular Emphasis on the Tewo Chiefdom.* (Ph.D. Dissertation in Anthropology, Boston University).

Horton, Robin 1972. "Stateless Societies in the History of West Africa." In *History of West Africa,* edited by J.F.A. Ajayi and M. Crowder, vol. 1, pp. 78-119. London: Longman's.

Krader, Lawrence 1968. *Formation of the State.* Englewood Cliffs, N.J.: Prentice-Hall.

Leach, Edmund R. 1954. *The Political Systems of Highland Burma.* (1965 edition, Boston: Beacon Press).

———. 1961. "The Structural Implications of Matrilateral Cross-Cousin Marriage." In *Rethinking Anthropology,* by E.R. Leach, pp. 54-104. London: Athlone Press.

Little, Kenneth 1965. "The Political Function of the Poro (Part I)." *Africa* 35:349-365.

———. 1966. "The Political Function of the Poro (Part II)." *Africa* 36:62-71.

———. 1967. *The Mende of Sierra Leone.* London: Routledge and Kegan Paul.

Lowie, Robert H. 1920. *Primitive Society.* New York: Boni and Liverwright.

Maine, Henry Sumner 1861. *Ancient Law.* London: J. Murray.

Mair, Lucy 1962. "Clientship in East Africa." *Cahiers d'Etudes Africaines* 2:315-325.

Morgan, Lewis Henry 1877. *Ancient Society.* New York: H. Holt.

Massing, Andreas 1970-71. "Materials for a History of Western Liberia: The Belle." *Liberian Studies Journal* 3:173-205.

Murphy, William P. 1980. "Secret Knowledge as Property and Power in Kpelle Society: Elders Versus Youth." *Africa* 50:193-207.

———. 1981. "The Rhetorical Management of Dangerous Knowledge in Kpelle Brokerage." *American Ethnologist* 8:667-85.

Radcliffe-Brown, A.R. 1950. "Introduction." In *African Systems of Kinship and Marriage,* edited by A.R. Radcliffe-Brown and Daryll Forde, pp. 1-85. London: Oxford University Press.

Rodney, Walter 1970. *A History of the Upper Guinea Coast, 1545-1800.* Oxford: Clarendon Press.

Sahlins, Marshall 1968. *Tribesmen.* Englewood Cliffs, N.J.: Prentice-Hall.

Service, Elman R. 1971. *Primitive Social Organization.* New York: Random House.

———. 1975. *Origins of the State and Civilization: The Process of Cultural Evolution.* New York: Norton.

Shack, William A. and Elliott Skinner, eds. 1979. *Strangers in African Societies.* Berkeley: University of California Press.

Shick, Tom W. 1980. *Behold the Promised Land: A History of Afro-American Society in 19th Century Liberia.* Baltimore: Johns Hopkins University Press.

Sibley, J.L. and D.H. Westermann 1929. *Liberia: Old and New.* Garden City, N.Y.: Doubleday and Doran.

Swingle, Albert E. 1965-68. Unpublished Fieldnotes, collected in Liberia.

Teitelbaum, Michele 1980. "Designation of Preferential Affinity in the Jokwele Kpelle Omaha-type Relationship Terminology." *Journal of Anthropological Research* 36:31-48.

Thornton, Robert J. 1980. *Space, Time, and Culture among the Iraqw of Tanzania.* New York: Academic Press.

Turner, Victor 1969. *The Ritual Process.* Chicago: Aldine.

Welmers, William E. 1948. *Spoken Kpelle.* Liberia: Lutheran Church of Liberia.

———. 1962. "The Phonology of Kpelle." *Journal of African Languages* 1:69-93.

Westermann, Diedrich 1921. *Die Kpelle.* Gottingen: Vandenhoeck and Ruprecht.

Wieder, D.L. 1974. *Language and Social Reality.* The Hague: Mouton.

THE MANY WAYS OF BEING FIRST

Among the Kpelle, the principle of firstcomer authority structured relations between chiefs and subjects. In the following article by Randall Packard on the BaShu of Zaire, some 2,500 miles away, the same principle governs relations among different ethnic groups—a striking illustration of the pan-African distribution of this feature of political culture.

The BaShu exemplify with particular clarity the characteristic multiplicity of origins that underlie most African societies. In their case, the clarity is related to the fact that their mountainous area harbors several ecological zones, each of which came to be exploited by the different groups that now constitute BaShu society: forest hunter-gatherers, forest root-crop cultivators, forest-clearing seed-agriculturalists from the grasslands, and herdsmen, also from the grasslands. Though the present society is culturally quite homogeneous, each of the constituent ethnic strands continues to recognize its different origin and sees its political status vis-à-vis the others in terms of it.

The political constitutions of African societies were usually cast in the idiom of historical accounts of their genesis. We have seen how the different strata of a society—such as the rulers and the subjects—brought their own perspectives to this constitution, particularly to the thorny question of who was the "firstcomer" and who the "latecomer." The BaShu illustrate very well the point that the question is not simply chronological, for the sequence of the arrival into the area of the different ethnic strands is not in dispute. What is at stake, ideologically, is the relation of this sequence to firstcomer status. A Kpelle chief may claim firstcomer status by insisting that it was his kin group that brought civic order to an area. This cultural logic is shared by all the BaShu ethnic groups. Each of them confers on itself the status of firstcomer by claiming that its particular characteristics are the ones most directly relevant to civilization.

While each of the ethnic groups holds to its own version of history, a political *modus vivendi* is insured by each one publicly agreeing on the main events of the past while retaining a different interpretation of the meaning of these events. The *modus vivendi* is further insured by the existence of a number of complicated and varying versions of events, by a pragmatic disinterest in reconciling whatever inconsistencies these different versions may contain, and by the fact that each locality's specific history is different enough to make a single overall history impossible in any case. As the author points out, these complexities and the various possibilities of interpretation are such that "everyone can claim in some respect superiority over others."

—Editor

Randall M. Packard

5

Debating in a Common Idiom: Variant Traditions of Genesis among the BaShu of Eastern Zaire

The study of social interaction in multi-ethnic or immigrant communities in Africa has received considerable attention in recent years. Most of this attention, however, has focused on contemporary social relations in urban areas (Epstein 1967, Cohen 1969, Parkin 1969, Mitchell 1969). Yet the interaction of culturally diverse groups in a geographically limited environment is not restricted to the urban world. To the contrary, historical research has shown that many, if not most pre-colonial states in Africa were a product of the migration and settlement of socially and culturally diverse groups into a single region. This can be seen in the histories of the Nyoro, Ganda, Alur, Tallensi, Zande, Bemba and Kuba. Nonetheless, little attention has been given to the mechanisms by which social integration was achieved and maintained within these immigrant states. The present study will examine one such mechanism: traditions of genesis or foundation myths.[1]

Historians and anthropologists have long recognized that traditions describing the origins of states represent mythical charters which serve to define and legitimize political relationships within the state and give expression to the political and cultural values upon which these relationships rest. As such, foundations myths serve as instruments of social integration and political legitimation within the state or polity (Malinowski 1955, Beattie 1972, Feierman 1974). On the other hand, it is also recognized that foundation myths can take a variety of forms within a single society and that the details and narrative arrangement of the myth may differ markedly from region to region or from sub-group to sub-group. While some of these variants reflect the tastes of individual tellers of the myth, others clearly represent the teller's attempt to express the interests and status of the group from which he comes. In telling these variants, therefore, each narrator expresses his group's separate identity as well as the groups membership in the state.

Given these variant traditions expressing local interests, how can foundation myths also serve to reaffirm the overriding identity and unity of the state? The present study attempts to answer this question by employing Max Gluckman's notion of "debating in a common idiom" in

order to examine variant traditions of genesis which describe the establishment of the BaShu chiefdoms of eastern Zaire.

In his analysis of Swazi royal rituals, Gluckman (1954) argues that the
major public rituals associated with Swazi kingship provide a vehicle by
which diverse social groups within the Swazi state express their rights and
identity vis-à-vis the king and the state. He concludes, however, that
because these expressions of hostility and division occur within the context
of a set of commonly accepted cultural and political values, i.e. within a
common idiom manifested in the rites themselves, the rituals reinforce
these values and thus the unity of the state.[2]

I suggest that variant traditions of genesis among the BaShu operate
in a similar fashion. While each variant is designed to present the foundation myth in such a way that it serves to assert each group's claim to status
within the state, and give expression to its separate identity, each claim is
presented in terms of a commonly accepted set of cultural and political
values. In asserting their separate identities, therefore, each group reaf-
firms these values and thus their common identity as members of a single
moral community. In this way, the BaShu foundation myth helps to
resolve the problem faced by members of all immigrant communities of
being one and yet more than one at the same time, of having common and
yet diverse interests, and thus serves to integrate the diverse membership
of the community into a single cohesive unit.

The BaShu occupy an area of some 800 sq. km. in the Mitumba
Mountains to the northwest of Lake Edward in what is now the Kivu
region of Eastern Zaire. They are a section of a larger linguistic and
cultural group known as the BaNande in Zaire and as the BaKonjo in
neighboring Uganda. Like their Nande and Konjo relations, the BaShu are
primarily mountain cultivators, growing crops of elusine, plantain bananas, beans, and cassava along the slopes of the Mitumbas. Coffee cultivation accounts for their main source of cash income, though in the higher
altitudes wheat is also grown commercially.

Politically, the BaShu are divided into several closely related chiefdoms, each of which is ruled by a family of chiefs who claim to be
descended from a common ancestor, said to have emigrated from BuSongora in Uganda at the beginning of the 19th century and to be descended
from the BaBito rulers of BuSongora, Toro, and BuNyoro. Today, the
BaShu chiefdoms form an administrative district, or 'collectivity', under
the authority of a *grand chef,* a position created by the Belgians during the
colonial era and incorporated into the present administrative system of
Zaire.

While the BaShu formerly lived in dispersed homesteads, the members of a single agnatic lineage (*nda*) occupying all or part of a ridge
(together with a few non-agnatic neighbors, often related through marriage), they have lived in multi-lineage consolidated villages since the
1930's.

The present BaShu population is descended from three distinct cultural groups, each of which settled in the Mitumba Mountains sometime prior to 1850. The first group to occupy the Mitumbas were the Ba-'Sumba, a forest Bantu people who combined root crop cultivation and the growing of plantain bananas with hunting and are said to be related to the BaPakombe and BaPere of the Ituri forest. Today the forest begins to the west of the BaShu region. However, formerly, it covered all of the Mitumbas. It is impossible to date the arrival of the BaSumba since they have no traditions of having lived elsewhere.

The second group of migrants to arrive in the Mitumbas were Ba-Nande seed-agriculturalists from the Western Rift Valley, which runs along the foot of the Mitumba Mountains to the east of the BaShu region. The majority of this group were also Bantu speakers, though there is some evidence, in the form of rainmaking practices and linguistic data, that at least a portion of these later arrivals were Sudanic speakers related to the Lendu and Lugbara of northern Zaire and Uganda. The Nande began settling in the Mitumbas in small groups, clearing the forest, around the middle of the 17th century, or perhaps earlier.

The third group of migrants were BaHima pastoralists who came to dominate the Western Rift Valley during the eighteenth century.[3] These herdsmen extended their grazing activities on to the lower slopes of the Mitumbas during the early years of the 19th century in order to gain access to important dry season pastures located there. This extension brought them in contact with the BaNande and BaSumba who had preceded them into the mountains and led to their involvement in mountain affairs. As a result, some of their descendants became incorporated into BaShu society.

Intermarriage and social interaction among these three cultural groups has produced a population that exhibits a high degree of linguistic, physical, and cultural homogeneity. Nonetheless, the members of each of these groups maintain their separate traditions and claim certain rights and privileges vis-à-vis the members of the other groups. For example, while many, and perhaps most, of the former forest Bantu population of the Mitumbas retreated to the west in response to the forest clearing activities of the BaNande, those BaSumba families who were assimilated into the society created by the later migrants claim and are accorded certain rights and prerogatives in recognition of their status as the autochthonous population of the region. Thus, only a MuSumba may relight the royal fire following the death of a chief (*mwami*) and preceding the investiture of his successor. Moreover, because of their former association with the forest and 'bush', the BaSumba are thought to have special powers over this world, which the BaShu in general view with some trepidation and fear. It is for this reason that a MuSumba is chosen to kill the flying squirrel, a ritually dangerous animal, used in the construction of the mwami's crown (*mbita*).

While recognizing the pre-eminent position of the BaSumba in certain ritual contexts, the BaNande stress in other contexts their own status as *avakonde*, descendants of those who first cleared the forest. This status gives a person special ritual influence over the productivity of the land and thus rights to social and economic privileges *vis-à-vis* later settlers.

Finally, while the descendants of some of the BaHima pastoralists who settled on the lower slopes of the Mitumbas became completely assimilated into the dominant agricultural propulation, others of the Ba-Bito clan succeeded in establishing their political dominance over the prior occupants and became the present BaShu chiefs. They thus claim and are accorded political rights over the previous inhabitants of the region.

Within each of these major groups there are further social distinctions and associated claims to status based on kinship, ritual skills, and relative length of residence in an area. It is, in fact, safe to say that nearly every localized lineage among the BaShu can and does claim in some respect a certain degree of social superiority over other lineages. These claims are voiced in each group's traditions describing their migration and settlement in the Mitumbas. More importantly, however, some of these claims find expression in the central myth of Muhiyi which describes the establishment of the present ruling family as chiefs among the BaShu.

Many BaShu elders present one of the official versions of this myth, that is, a version recognized by the chiefs themselves. However, certain lineages, residing in the area in which these chiefs first established their control and who participated in this development, advance disparate variants of the myth—variants that are designed to stress their role in the founding of the present political system and their consequent privileges within the system. These variants conflict with one another and with versions related by the chiefs and their supporters.

The myth of Muhiyi, therefore, provides numerous groups within BaShu society with a vehicle for asserting their separate rights and statuses through the presentation of differently structured versions of the myth. At the same time, however, the myth reinforces the society's values and essential unity, for each group's claim to rights and status depends on a set of commonly accepted values concerning social status in BaShu society. Thus, in presenting their conflicting claims, these groups are "debating within a common idiom." In the remainder of this essay, I shall describe four major variants of the Muhiyi myth and show how the tellers of each variant alter the narrative structure of the myth to serve their own purposes and how, despite these alterations, the myth serves to unify BaShu society.[4]

Before examining the major variants of the myth, it is useful to review briefly the actual sequence of historical events which each variant claims to describe. The area of BuNyuka, in which these central events took place, is located in the Isale region of the Mitumbas. In contrast to the surrounding areas, it rises gradually from the plains, providing relatively easy access to the mountains, and was, therefore, the scene of successive local migrations. BuNyuka was first occupied by members of the Bito clan (not to be confused with the present ruling BaBito clan) who were Nande agriculturalists. The Bito may have been preceded into the region by BaSumba, but I was unable to locate any descendants of the BaSumba in this region. In any case, the Bito were the first group here to clear the forest. This is attested to by the traditions of other clans, which refer to the Bito as *avakonde,* as well as by their pre-eminent ritual position in any activity involving the land. For example, when the present chiefs of BuNyuka bury a member of their lineage, it is the Bito who must choose the burial plot. If the chiefs wish to build a hut, the Bito must place the center pole. And in the performance of planting rituals, the Bito must make the first sacrifice.

The Bito were apparently followed into BuNyuka by several other groups, including the followers of a man named Mutsawerya, who is generally identified with the hunter Muhiyi, the central figure of the founding myth. It is unclear whether Mutsawerya's people were agriculturalists or pastoralists. For despite the references to pastoralism in their variant of the myth, there are no collaborative traditions among the pastoral groups who formerly occupied the Rift Valley to support this claim, while supportive traditions do exist for other BaShu groups who claim to have formerly been pastoralists.[5] What is clear is that Mutsawerya and his people succeeded in establishing their political authority over the Bito and other groups in BuNyuka, and Mutsawerya's descendants are still subchiefs in this region. It is also clear that this development occurred before the arrival of the family of the pastoral chief Kavango, the ancestor of the present BaShu ruling line. The primacy of Mutsawerya's family is indicated by a number of independent traditions that acknowledge Mutsawerya's prior occupancy and by the presence of the following verse in a number of BaShu narrative songs: "The day the chiefs left Kitara they came one by one, Muhiyi was the first to leave." The priority is also supported by the social relationship which exists between the descendants of Mutsawerya and Kavango. For example, Kavango's descendants pay token tribute (*muhako*) to Mutsawerya's descendants, thereby acknowledging their having received land from Mutsawerya.

Kavango's group established settlements on the lower slopes of the Mitumbas near BuNyuka at the beginning of the nineteenth century. Kavango initially acknowledge Mutsawerya's authority over BuNyuka in order to gain his support against a rival chief, Mukirivuli, who claimed authority over the land on which Kavango settled. With Mutsawerya's support, Kavango's family established themselves in Isale and eventually succeeded in becoming the dominant chiefly family among the BaShu.

This then is the sequence of events around which the myth of Muhiyi was constructed. We can now look at how these events are presented in four separate variants of the myth.[6]

The first two variants are from descendants of Kavango, the ancestor of the present ruling family. These variants support the political position of the present chiefs and have the widest distribution.[7]

Variant 1:

> Muhiyi lived with his father Kavango in the village of Kavarola in Uganda. Kavango had many cattle which Muhiyi herded. One day, Kavango noticed that the milk which had been placed in a special hut for him was missing. This continued to happen for several days. Finally, Kavango accused Muhiyi of having stolen the milk. Muhiyi, although innocent, was afraid of his father's anger. He therefore took his spear and hunting dogs and set out across the plains. Muhiyi followed the tracks of a buffalo (in some traditions it is an *embara,* which is a type of antelope) and when he reached the Kalemba (Semliki), he crossed by means of a fallen tree (in other versions he crossed at a ford). Muhiyi continued his journey until he reached the foot of the Mitumba Mountains at a place called Kaviro. There, he succeeded in killing the animal he had been tracking. Muhiyi butchered the animal and dried its meat. He left some of the meat on a rock and the rest he carried home to his father. On arriving home, he presented the meat to his father, who welcomed him, for Kavango had discovered that a serpent had drunk his milk. Muhiyi then told his father about the new land he had discovered on the other side of the Kalemba. His father said that he wished to accompany Muhiyi to this new land for there was no more room in their present land. Together they set off across the plains. When they reached the foot of the mountains, they settled at Kaviro. Kavango then gave Muhiyi the land of BuNyuka in the mountains as a reward for having discovered the new land and for having given him the meat from his kill. Kavango himself settled at Kivika. Together, Kavango and Muhiyi chased away the BaSumba who lived in the mountains and cleared the mountains of forest.

Variant 2:

> Kyavambe lived in Kitara. He liked meat very much, but there were no animals left in Kitara. So he sent his servant Muhiyi to search for game. Muhiyi took his dogs and spear and crossed the Kalemba. On the other side of the Kalemba he found a beautiful country with many animals to hunt. He did not wish to return to Kitara and so took the route to Vutungwe (BuNyuka). Later, Kyavambe took all of his family, along with his cattle, sheep and goats, and crossed the Kalemba. He eventually arrived at Musagya Muguru, a hill in the plains. It was there that Kyavamabe's wife gave birth to Kavango. Meanwhile, Muhiyi thought of his master and set out to return to Kitara. When he reached Musagya Muguru, he met Kyavambe, who asked him why he had not returned. Muhiyi begged his pardon and said that he had found many animals. Muhiyi then killed two *embara* for Kyavambe. After this, Muhiyi returned to BuNyuka, which Kyavambe gave him in return for the *em-*

bara. Kyavambe died at Musagya Muguru and Kavango took the route to Kaviro and then Kivika, where he was invested *mwami w'embita* after his father's death.

The third variant comes from the descendants of Mutsawerya. The distribution of this variant is limited to the chiefdom of BuNyuka.

Variant 3:

> Muhiyi lived in Kitara with his father Kyavambe. Kyavambe owned many cattle and Muhiyi was in charge of herding them. One day, the milk which was placed in a special hut for Kyavambe began to disappear. Muhiyi's elder brother Kavango accused Muhiyi of stealing the milk. Muhiyi, in his anger, took his dogs and spear and left his father's home. After he had left, it was discovered that the milk continued to disappear and that it was being drunk by a serpent. Kyavambe ordered a herding boy to destroy the hut and the serpent. After this, the milk no longer disappeared. Meanwhile, Muhiyi had crossed the Semliki, tracking a buffalo. When he reached the hill named Kaviro, he succeeded in killing the animal. Muhiyi saw that the land in the mountains was good and he decided to settle there. At that time, there were BaSumba living in the mountains, which were covered with forest. Muhiyi chased away the BaSumba and began to clear the forest for planting. Muhiyi was later joined by Kavango and other groups of BaShu. Muhiyi gave them land and they gave him goats as tribute (*muhako*) in return. Muhiyi took a Mwito as his first wife and she bore him Kisoro who succeeded Muhiyi.

The fourth major variant comes from the Bito (sing. Mwito) clan of BuNyuka, who claim to have welcomed Muhiyi when he arrived in Isale. The distribution of this variant is limited to the Bito of BuNyuka and to members of this clan living outside BuNyuka.

Variant 4:

> (This variant follows the basic plot line of Variant 3 up to the point where Muhiyi arrives at the foot of the Mitumba Mountains. It then continues:) Muhiyi killed the animal he was tracking. He then built a fire and began roasting the meat from his kill. At this time, there was a man named Sine, a Mwito, living in the mountains above where Muhiyi had camped. Sine saw the smoke rising from the plains below and took some of his men to go and see who was there. He found Muhiyi eating meat. Since he and his men were hungry, Sine asked Muhiyi for some meat. Muhiyi distributed the meat from his kill and they all ate together. After they had eaten, Sine noticed that Muhiyi was living in the open without a hut. He therefore invited Muhiyi to come and stay in his village in the mountains. Muhiyi agreed and accompanied Sine to Vungwe. Muhiyi stayed with Sine a long time and Sine gave him some

land on which to grow crops. He also gave him one of his daughters as a wife. This wife bore a son named Kisoro who was invested *Mwami w'embita* of BuNyuka.

The differences among the variants of the myth are summarized in Chart 1.

CHART 1: *DIFFERENCES IN THE MAJOR VARIANTS OF THE MUHIYI MYTH*

	Relationship of Muhiyi to Kavango	Cause for Muhiyi's departure	Route followed by Muhiyi	Prior occupants of the Isale
VARIANT 1	son	stolen milk	crosses plains & returns	Basumba
VARIANT 2	servant of Kavango's family	sent to search for meat	"	"
VARIANT 3	younger brother	stolen milk	crosses plains & settles	"
VARIANT 4	none or son[8]	"	"	Bito clan

A comparison of the myth's major variants reveals that each group arranges the narrative elements of the myth to support a claim to first occupancy while undercutting similar claims made by other groups. Since the status of first occupant confers on its holder considerable influence over the well-being of the land and thus political authority over subsequent occupants (primarily in the right to tribute, *muhako,* which first occupants may demand of later settlers), the establishment of this claim is important. Accordingly, the Bito emphasize the role they played in welcoming Muhiyi and thus establish their prior occupancy vis-à-vis Muhiyi. Muhiyi's descendants, for their part, counter this Bito claim by populating Isale with BaSumba, whose claim to first occupancy is limited because they did not clear the land. They also assert their claim to prior occupancy vis-à-vis Kavango's descendants by stating that Kavango followed Muhiyi and received land from him. Finally, Kavango's descendants attempt to establish their own claim to first occupancy by: (1) populating Isale with BaSumba; (2) having Muhiyi return to Kavango before actually "settling" in Isale, so that Kavango and Muhiyi settle in Isale at the same time; and (3) having Kavango give land to Muhiyi. In the second Kavango variant, the process of undercutting the claim that Muhiyi preceded Kavango to Isale is more complete. Here Muhiyi is a servant of Kavango's family who is sent to find a land with more animals. This denies the independence of Muhiyi's actions and implies that if he discovered Isale, he did so on the orders of Kavango's family. This may be a later variant reflecting an increase in the authority of Kavango's descendants over those of Muhiyi.

To the extent that each group alters the myth to assert its historical claim to special political status, the myth gives expression to social divisions within BaShu society. On the other hand, the fact that each group's claim to status is based on their common acceptance of the principle of the ritual and political importance of prior occupancy, acts to reinforce this principle. This in turn strengthens the society as a whole, for universal acceptance of the principle of prior occupancy plays a central role in ordering political relations in BaShu society and in integrating the BaShu chiefdoms.

The important role played by the principle of prior occupancy in the integration of BaShu chiefdoms is reflected in the history of BaBito political expansion over the BaShu region under the leadership of Kavango and his descendants during the nineteenth century. BaBito domination of the BaShu region was accomplished primarily through the use of wealth in livestock, and particularly goats, which were the basis of BaShu bride-wealth, to create alliances with existing local ritual specialists—rainmakers, healers of the land, and clearers of the forest—who possessed ritual authority over the land and whose cooperation was viewed by the BaShu as critical for the continued productivity of the land and society. These alliances undermined the authority of existing chiefs while strengthening that of the BaBito, and ultimately led to the overthrow of the former chiefs during periods of famine in which the loss of local ritual support destroyed their credibility and caused their followers to turn to the BaBito for salvation from the famine.

The BaBito chiefs subsequently incorporated not only their ritually influential allies but also the chiefly families they had replaced into the political and ritual hierarchies of their chiefdoms in recognition of the critical role these prior chiefs played in insuring the well-being of the land. Thus, while the BaBito performed certain important ritual functions and were politically dominant, they recognized earlier sources of authority. Recognition of the ritual authority of prior occupants gave these prior occupants a vested interest in Babito chiefship and helped to integrate their chiefdoms. This process of integration can be seen in the history of BaBito expansion into the Vusekuli area of Isale during the middle years of the 19th century.

When Mutsora, a great-grandson of Kavango, settled in the Vusekuli region of Isale, he initially recognized the ritual and political authority of an existing chief named Ghotya. However, using his wealth in livestock and his reputation as a descendant of Kavango, Mutsora slowly expanded his influence in the region by making alliances with important lineage and ritual leaders. He eventually succeeded in appropriating Ghotya's position during a major famine in which the people of the region turned to him for help. Mutsora, however, did not eliminate Ghotya, or even relegate him to obscurity. Instead, he acknowledged Ghotya's prior ritual authority over the region and incorporated him into his own ritual and political system. Today, Ghotya's descendants must be present at rituals performed by Mutsora's descendants for the productivity of the land and perform their own sacrifice before Mutsora's descendants perform theirs.[9]

The process of incorporating earlier sources of ritual authority was evidently followed by yet earlier migrants who, like Mutsora, recognized the ritual authority of their predecessors, while establishing their own claims to authority. Thus, Ghotya himself had evidently usurped the position of an earlier family of chiefs headed, during Mutsora's time, by a man named Kahindolya. Like Mutsora, Ghotya had acknowledged the ritual authority of Kahindolya's family and incorporated them into his chiefdom.

As a result of this successive incorporation of pre-existing leaders, dictated by common acceptance of the importance of prior occupancy, one finds at present, a hierarchical chain of social relationships linking together earlier and later arrivals into a unified system of ritual interdependence. This hierarchy of ritual relationships is reflected at the investiture of Ba-Bito chiefs among the BaShu. Before a chief can be invested, the family of chiefs which his ancestor had replaced must invest their own chief. This ceremony must in turn be preceded by the investiture of still earlier families of chiefs. This sequence of investitures was described by a Belgian colonial official who witnessed the investiture of a chief named Mahashu, a descendant of Kavango.

> In 1941 . . . the region of Muhashu was disturbed by a series of small festivities and parties. These were the ceremonies preceding the customary investiture of Buanga [according to the official, the people had assumed that Buanga would be invested and were surprised to learn that it was his brother Muhashu who was actually invested]. These ceremonies begin in each clan with the smallest notable. The latter has his forehead tied with a piece of barkcloth which is the symbol of his *mbita* (crown). After this he carries to the notable immediately above him the same symbol of authority only a bit larger. And so it goes up to the investiture of the chief of the clan. All of the clan heads and notables thus invested, the ceremony for the *grand chef* can begin.[10]

The hierarchy of ritual relationships was further illustrated, in 1975, by the performance of a major sacrifice intended to deter a plague of locust which was said to be moving south from the region of Lake Mobutu (ex-Albert). This sacrifice, directed by Kavango's descendants, was preceded by a series of smaller sacrifices performed by various lineage heads and ritual leaders whose families had preceded Kavango into Isale. Each of these leaders performed his sacrifices in the order of his family's arrival and settlement.

The disparity between the order of primacy reflected in the performance of public ritual and that reflected in each group's claim to prior occupancy, so apparent to the outside observer, is less apparent to the BaShu themselves. There are two reasons for this. First, with the exception of those officiating the performance of public rituals, none of the participants are aware of their position within the entire sequence of investitures or sacrifices which make up these rituals. Secondly, each group, while tacitly recognizing the prior occupancy of other groups through their actions—the giving of tribute (*muhako*), receiving emblems of authority—reduce the discrepancy created by these indicators of primacy by giving them different meanings. Thus, for example, the group receiving an emblem of authority during the accession process from a group who had preceded them into a region may interpret this action as indicating that the emblem givers, who were previously invested, are socially inferior: "Does not a chief require a servant to go before him and cleanse his intended path?" Alternatively, the receiving group may simply reduce the disparity by putting it into a neutral idiom. Thus, several informants explained the prior investiture of another group through the use of a Christian idiom, i.e., "Can one be baptized by one who has not already been baptized?" This question does not eliminate the primacy of the emblem-giving group, but simply clouds the issue. Finally, the giving of tribute (*muhako*) may also be reinterpreted in this way. Thus, Kavango's descendants claim that the tribute of goats they give annually to Mutsawerya's descendants is simply a gift, and does not represent tribute though they can give no explanation why the gift is given. In these ways, the indicators of actual prior occupancy do not conflict too sharply with each group's own claim to this status.

The myth of Muhiyi, by reinforcing the principle of prior occupancy, can thus be seen to support the ritual structure that ties BaShu society together even while it provides a vehicle for individual groups to express their separate identities. The myth thus helps solve a problem faced by the BaShu and many other immigrant societies—that of being one and yet more than one at the same time.

Finally, it should be noted that the myth of Muhiyi, is a variant of the Hunter-King tradition that has a wide distribution in eastern Africa, similar myths being found in BuNyoro, BuGanda, Kimbu, Nyamwezi, Sukumu, Shambaa and Lunda. Locally, the culturally-related BaKonjo people of the Ruwenzori Mountains tell an almost identical genesis myth. I suggest that widespread familiarity with this particular genre in regions surrounding the BaShu chiefdoms may have facilitated the adoption of the myth of Muhiyi by sucessive immigrant groups, which travelled to the BaShu region from areas which had similar traditions, and that this ease of adoption made the myth a particularly useful instrument for integrating immigrant groups into BaShu society. To the extent that Hunter-King myths served similar functions elsewhere, their wide distribution may have facilitated the integration of migrants in other societies. Certainly, the existence of highly similar traditions of genesis eased the movement of

BaNande-BaKonjo peoples back and forth across the Semliki Valley at various times over the last two centuries.

NOTES

1. An earlier draft of this chapter was originally presented at the Annual Meeting of the African Studies Association in Houston in 1977. The chapter is based on research carried out in Belgium and Zaire under a grant from the Fulbright-Hays Dissertation Year Abroad program and the University of Wisconsin. I wish to thank Ivan Karp, James Vaughan, and Igor Kopytoff for their comments on this earlier draft.

2. To be sure, Beidelman (1966) has suggested that Gluckman's analysis suffers from a superficial understanding of Swazi symbolic thought and behavior and that the tensions described by Gluckman have other meanings for the participants. Nevertheless, he does not rule out the possibility that symbolic behavior can have a variety of parallel meanings and, thus, that Gluckman's analysis, while incomplete, may highlight an important aspect of Swazi royal ritual.

3. I use the term 'BaHima' here in the sense in which it is used by the BaShu to designate people who live primarily by cattle-keeping as opposed to cultivation. It does not necessarily imply the existence of any particular physical or cultural characteristics, though many of the BaHima in the Semliki Valley appear to be related to the BaHima of Western Uganda.

4. This is not the only purpose which the myth of Muhiyi serves. Like all genesis traditions, the myth of Muhiyi operates at a number of levels. Thus, as I have shown elsewhere (Packard 1980), the myth, from a structural viewpoint, reflects certain important cultural values. At the same time, the myth's central structural theme—the social death and rebirth of the hero and his transformation from a herdsman into a cultivator—represents a distillation of the long-term political process which led to the establishment of the present BaShu chiefdoms.

5. These traditions were collected by Belgian colonial agents prior to the evacuation of the Semliki Valley on account of sleeping sickness in 1932. Cf. Renseignements-Politiques Kasindi 1908–1913, Archives Zone de Beni, Kivu-Nord.

6. I collected eighteen variants of the Muhiyi myth. This does not include numerous versions which were highly abbreviated. Of these eighteen, there were seven versions of variant 1, three versions of variant 2, four versions of variant 3, and four versions of variant 4.

7. Variant 1 is also told by some non-chiefly groups in Isale and neighboring areas. All three versions of variant 2, on the other hand, came from Kavango's descendants.

8. While most variants of the myth indicate that Kavango and Muhiyi were kinsmen, this is not supported by genealogical evidence collected independently of the myth. Moreover, the history of Mutsawerya and Kavango's subsequent interaction in Isale indicates that they were at best distantly related. The claim to kinship may reflect the important role which Muhiyi's (Mutsawerya's) family played in the initial establishment of Kavango's family in Bunyuko.

9. For a detailed discussion of these events see Packard (1981).

10. F. van Rompaey "Les Règles coûtumières regissent la succession des chefs Bashu," Correspondence, Archives de Zone de Beni, Kivu-Nord.

BIBLIOGRAPHY

Beattie, John. 1972. *The Nyoro State*. Oxford.

Beidelman, T.O. 1966. "Swazi Royal Ritual." *Africa* 31:373–405.

Cohen, Abner. 1969. *Custom and Politics in Urban Africa*. Berkeley.

Epstein, A.L. 1967. "Urbanization and Social Change in Africa." *Current Anthropology*, 8, 4:275–296.

Feierman, Steven. 1974. *The Shambaa Kingdom*. Madison.

Gluckman, Max. 1954. *"Rituals of Rebellion in Southeast Africa."* Manchester.

Malinowski, B. 1955. "Myth in Primitive Psychology." In *Magic, Science, and Religion*. New York.

Mitchell, J.C. 1969. *"Social Networks in Urban Situations,"* Manchester.

Packard, R.M. 1980. The Study of Historical Process in African Traditions of Genesis: The Bashu Myth of Muhiyi." In *The African Past Speaks,* ed. J.C. Miller. London.

———. 1981. *Chiefship and Cosmology: An Historical Study of Political Competition*. Bloomington.

Parkin, David. 1969. *Neighbors and Nationals in an African City Ward*. London.

THE VIEW FROM THE METROPOLE

The preceding studies have dealt with the metropole-frontier relationship from the perspective of the frontiersmen. The following study by David Newbury takes the opposite perspective—that of the metropole. It shows that, whatever the objective conditions that make an area into a potential frontier (such as a moderate population density or a lack of political central-ization), an actual frontier is a metropolitan creation. To its own inhabitants, an area is always a homeland. It becomes a frontier when it comes to be so defined from outside and by outsiders. The author focuses on the ideological effects on a metropole—the Central African kingdom of Rwanda—of having chosen to treat the lands beyond its borders as frontier areas.

The dynamics at the edges of the Rwandan frontier are familiar. Political refugees and adventurers from Rwanda itself, or from areas in-vaded by it, established themselves among the indigenous populations, bringing with them the pastoral culture and political values of the metro-pole. As in other such cases, they also tried to exploit their ties to the metropole they had left. What is different from the cases we have seen is that the immigrants did not become founders of lasting new polities be-cause immediately behind them came the expanding Rwandan state. The ties between immigrants and metropole worked out to the metropole's advantage: the immigrants became its advance agents and eventually ad-ministrators. This intrusion of state power into the frontier process trans-formed the Rwandan frontier into the moving edge of conquest, making it structurally similar to the tidal frontiers of expanding states, as in the case of the American or the Russian frontiers.

When the metropole is so intimately and continuously involved in the frontier, one may expect the development of a frontier ideology by the metropolitan culture. This is the central theme of Newbury's study. Previ-ously, we have seen the culture brought from the metropole by frontiers-men shape the rising frontier society that later became a metropole in its own right. Newbury's study examines the reverse flow of influence across the frontier—the reflexive impact on a metropole of its own frontier.

For all the differences in process and scale, the perspective of the Rwan-dan state was analogous to that of immigrant settlers bent on establishing an expansionist frontier polity. Like them, the Rwandan state needed to incor-porate new subjects yet distance itself from them, and it had to justify in culturally acceptable ways its domination over the subjects. The solution was one we have already seen: the rulers saw themselves as the carriers of civilization, as the cultured "firstcomers" to an area dominated by chaos and savagery. As we have also seen elsewhere, on the frontier itself where the intruder had to deal face to face with his potential subjects, such claims had to be made carefully and diplomatically. In the case of Rwanda, the claim of cultural superiority was made most eloquently at the Court, far from the actual frontier and its constraints. The claim was moreover made by a stratum of society that had developed an arrogant aristocratic military ethos and an artistically elaborate oral tradition—hence the elegance of style and the harshness of content in the contemptuous stereotyping of the "savages" at the frontier. This stereotyping of the outsider, Newbury stresses, served to define its reciprocal—the self-stereotyping of Rwanda culture as the civilization that the "savages" tried so awkwardly to emulate. But emulate it they did, with the result that these values of the metropolitan culture spread in turn to the frontier, enhancing the cultural continuity between metropole and frontier.

Newbury's study emphasizes the relativity of the frontier concept—a relativity that is both geographical and socio-political. Like the American, the Rwandan frontier moved like a tide across the land, leaving behind it areas being assimilated to the metropolitan culture even while it moved on farther out to new areas. There was thus a sequence of zones, each of which saw itself as part of the Rwandan homeland and in contrast to the uncouth frontier that it perceived as beginning at the next zone beyond it. This zonal organization is reminiscent of the structure of the American frontier as Turner saw it. But as with the latter, the geographical structure was confounded by the socio-political structure. In America, the metropole assimilated the frontier by bringing to it metropolitan features in a layered manner as the trappers were joined (rather than displaced outright) by the following waves of cultivators and cattlemen, prospectors, tradesmen, bankers, teachers, and so on; frontier elements thus co-existed in the same place with metropolitan elements. Similarly, in Rwanda, elements of the "Central Court" culture were brought to the frontier by Rwandans and co-existed there with elements of local culture. Moreover, some of this layering occurred in the Rwandan core area as well. In this hierarchical society, the "true" stereotypic Rwanda culture was created and existed above all at the Court; the other, more "uncouth" social strata in the core area exhibited elements that Court stereotyping attributed to the far frontier zones. Again, the structure is not dissimilar to the distribution of cultural refinements between the East and the frontier areas in nineteenth-century America.

But these similarities in structure go hand in hand with dissimilarities in content and process. In America, the frontier enhanced and elaborated existing egalitarian principles for the metropole and the society as a whole, even if withholding equality from the culturally and physically different indigenous population of the frontier area. In Rwanda, what was enhanced and elaborated was a hierarchical tradition, which reinforced an aristocratic culture at the center and set it in contrast to both the Rwandan lower strata and the culturally kindred frontier populations.

—Editor

David Newbury

———— 6 ————

"Bunyabungo": The Western Rwandan Frontier, c. 1750–1850

The concept of the frontier is paradoxical. Although distinct from the metropolitan society, a frontier society can only be defined and perceived in relation to the cultural heartland of which it is an extension. This relationship between frontier and metropole is critical, differentiating the frontier from other types of "peripheral" areas, such as the "Bush" or "Outback." From the perspective of the metropole, Bush or Outback are seen negatively, as truly peripheral areas; the frontier, on the other hand, is usually seen positively, as only geographically peripheral but not unimportant. Bush and Outback are not seen as areas of external expansion for the metropole, while the frontier often is; nor are they seen as crucial to the cultural identity of the heartland, while the frontier often is.

But while identified by the metropole, the frontier is a zone where the cultural values of the metropole are very much at issue. By providing alternatives to metropolitan culture—in the form of different cultural values or even a perceived lack of culture—the presence of the frontier may well threaten the harmony and hegemony of metropolitan values. Consequently the frontier zone is a region on which the essential values of the metropolitan society are projected with great intensity, creating an identity for the frontier in relation to the metropole that reinforces or justifies the metropole's claims to the frontier. Yet these projected values need only focus on the core area's ties to the frontier, but not replicate those of the core area itself. The values used to shape this identity are therefore selective values, determined by conditions within the metropole and not by the realities of the frontier. They are therefore often idealized values that may be declining or even absent in the cultural heartland. By thus reinforcing the ideological underpinnings seen as constant and enduring within the heartland, the created identity link between frontier and metropole may obscure the tensions of a society in rapid change.

The idealization of the American frontier, for example, became important approximately with the "closing" of the frontier and the late nineteenth-century transformation of the eastern cities. In the "land of the free" on the western frontier, it was argued, individual initiative was rewarded with wealth and status, even while in fact the lives of those on the frontier were often marked by physical hardship and violence. But the myth of the West grew in the east, and the characterization of the "freedom" on the western frontier came to be reflected back onto the metropolitan areas, and eventually applied to the polity as a whole. In this case, therefore, the metropolitan areas adopted the perceived values of the frontier zone as their own, even though these may in fact have been as far removed from the reality of life in the metropole as they were from that of the frontier.

The above deals with the images of the frontiersmen, who are seen as an extension of the metropole into the frontier zone. But there is also another aspect of the frontier—represented most directly by its indigenous population. For societies expanding through conquest, the concept of the frontier also lends itself to ideologies which justify the expansion and rationalize the incorporation of new groups. The most common form of this ideological construction is found in the opposition between the metropolitan values and the cultural stereotypes of those to whom the frontier zone is their homeland. By juxtaposing two cultural ideals in a polarized form, the humanity of the metropolitan culture is invariably stressed in opposition to the inhumanity of the "barbarians." As illustrated below, the choice may be posed in stark terms: culture or chaos. Consequently, such an attitude often justifies the inhumane treatment of the "barbarians" by the representatives of "civilized" society. The conceptual paradigm of the frontier, then, is as much a product of the perceptions of other cultures generated by political conditions within the metropole, as it is a product of the ethnographic realities on the ground.

The history of the central African kingdom of Rwanda provides an example of the association between the growth of the frontier concept and the westward expansion of Rwandan social and political structures. It illustrates how values, initially strongly anchored in the military expeditions to the west, came to be incorporated as essential elements of the political ideology of the Rwandan Central Court, and applied even within (perhaps most strongly within) the central regions. Historical traditions provide abundant evidence of the strength of the oppositions between Rwandan culture and non-Rwandan culture: regardless of their origins, emigrants to the west from the Rwandan culture area were seen by both the original inhabitants of the region and by the Central Court of Rwanda as "Rwandan" relative to those who lived in the western highlands. Similarly, the culture of the inhabitants of these regions is portrayed in the Rwandan literature in monolithic terms, as a single culture, invariably associated with the cultural stereotypes applied today to peoples living farther west still, west of Lake Kivu.

The inhabitants of these areas were collectively known as "Banyabungo" (or "Bashi") to the Rwandans, though in fact several distinct ethnic groups were represented in the region. Therefore, although today applied to areas west of Lake Kivu, the term "Bunyabungo" (the locative form of the personal plural nominal "Banyabungo") can be taken as historically representative of non-Rwandan societies of the western areas in general, including the regions west of the Nile-Zaire Divide, now part of western Rwanda. Indeed the people of central Rwanda often refer to the inhabitants of western Rwanda, even today, as "Banyabungo." Rather than referring to a precise cultural entity, then, the term is used exclusively in the classificatory sense of a relative category, in opposition to the concept of "Rwandan-ness." And it is almost invariably used in a derogatory manner, to mean "non-cultured" as well as "non-Rwandan." The term "Bunyabungo" therefore encodes the basic opposition inherent in the Rwandan conception of the western frontier.

But the significance of these concepts was not limited to the frontier zone. Most analyses of the Rwandan state emphasize the expansion of state institutions, stressing the impact of Rwandan structures on conquered areas. Less attention has been given to the transformations which occurred within the Rwandan heartland; it is assumed that, except for changes in scale, central Rwandan institutions remained largely unaltered as a result of the western frontier experience. In fact, the expansion of the western frontier had significant repercussions on the internal development of Rwandan society. The hierarchical administrative forms and the cultural distancing so apparent on the western frontier appear to have developed roughly at the same time in central Rwanda, as the values associated with the Rwandan expansion became more deeply embedded within Rwandan Central Court institutions in metropolitan areas. In this way the western frontier in Rwanda had a profound impact on the internal development of Rwanda, not only through expansion itself but in terms of wider political and cultural changes, as the inclusion of large numbers of culturally distinct populations provided a model for social interaction throughout the areas where Rwandan state structures were found. These changes therefore were a product not of unidirectional cause–effect relationship, but of mutual reinforcement between center and periphery.

In pursuing these themes, the discussion will first focus on the westward expansion of the Rwandan state, using published historical traditions. This will provide the political context within which to examine the development of Rwandan cultural stereotypes applied to the west. The second section illustrates the nature of these cultural stereotypes by drawing on examples of Rwandan Court literature. I will argue that defining non-Rwandan cultural traits in ways that portray non-Rwandans as "a-cultural" beings reinforces the concept of Rwandan-ness. Thus the frontier becomes not simply a geographical place, but also a conceptual field for a set of attitudes towards identity and culture, attitudes generated in a particular political context. The third section examines the types of interaction that occurred across the "Cultural Divide" delineated in the literary productions of the court. The same people who (in some social contexts) stress the barbarous nature of their western neighbors also trade with them, marry with them, and move to settle among them. These forms of interaction bring into question the set of conceptual oppositions portrayed in the Court literature and emphasize the contingent nature of such characterizations. The significance of the context in generating these stereotypes reinforces the conclusion that such portrayals speak more to the nature and conditions of the central areas that generate them than they do to the nature of the people they purportedly describe.

I

The state of Rwanda emerged in its earliest forms near Lake Mohazi, on the open savannah areas between Lake Victoria and Lake Kivu. This was pastoral country *par excellence,* and the various states which gradually took shape there were originally built on the alliance of pastoralist groups. Rwanda was, in the beginning, one state among many in this region, and through several centuries of turbulent political history, the nucleus of this state was gradually displaced westward until it was located in the area near the Nile-Zaire Divide—a forested highland area, geographically quite different from its original homeland in the east. Although there had been some contact between the Rwandan Central Court and the areas farther west (even as far as Lake Kivu) in earlier periods, it was not until the reign of Cyilima Rujugira in the mid-eighteenth century that there appears to have been a permanent Rwandan presence in the area between the Divide and Lake Kivu.[1]

As the Rwandan state grew and as its center of power gradually shifted westward, its state structures also came to encompass a greater variety of ethnic groups, distinguished as much by their relative social positions and access to power in the Rwandan state as by cultural or geographical factors. In later years, as the state structures took stronger form, these ethnicities were categorized essentially in bipolar terms, as "Tuutsi" and "Hutu" (though there were important differences within each group, and individuals could move, gradually, from one category to another). The Tuutsi shared essentially pastoralist cultural values, and virtually all positions of political authority within the Rwandan state were held by Tuutsi. The Hutu were, in general, associated with agriculturalist values (though many Hutu owned cattle as well); as the state structures expanded and rigidified, "Hutu" were increasingly excluded from positions of effective power.[2]

During the reign of Rujugira, Rwanda faced the combined military threat of three of its most powerful competitors in the region, Burundi to the south, Gisaka to the east, and Ndorwa to the northeast.[3] Eventually, Rwanda was able to prevail over its rivals—although, in various forms, the struggle with Ndorwa and Gisaka was to extend over several reigns and even into the period of colonial rule. But the history of these wars is not in itself important to this discussion. What is important is the internal administrative reorganization, the new conception of the state, and the inclusion of different cultures within the state which resulted, for the changes brought about by these wars had significant repercussions on Rwanda's later expansion to the west.[4]

Two of these alterations proved particularly important: the military reorganization and the internal administrative restructuring. More armies were formed under the reign of Rujugira than under all the kings before or (with one exception) since: together, armies formed by Rujugira represent

about one-third of all the armies for which historical records remain today (Kagame 1963:72–125 and *passim;* Kagame 1972:135–53; *Historique et Chronologie* 114–115, 159–161).[5] Associated with this growth in army formations was a new policy of posting armies permanently to certain areas, thus making these units suitable for occupying a conquered area as well as for raiding. At the same time, this policy provided a more enduring continuity to the *umuheto* group, the corporate groups performing military/administrative functions within the Rwandan state structures (Kagame 1963:10 and *passim*). Although drawn from geographically diverse areas— another policy which became increasingly prevalent under Rujugira— army members (assigned by the Court) joined together for several years of common service in areas outside their home regions; the lack of geographical concentration to recruitment enhanced the armies' common focus on the Court [*Historique et Chronologie* 159–161]. In addition, the very expansion of the army organizations provided positions of leadership and recognition for the Court to distribute among its favorites. Control over the distribution of prestige in this manner was one of the most valuable resources in the hands of the Court.

Originally, this change in policy towards permanent army postings was dictated by military necessity, but over time other functions served by the new policy became more important. Chief among these was socialization to the Rwandan state norms and the development of embryo administrative structures channeling family prestations to the Court—and thus also providing a means of accumulating material goods in the hands of the Court elite. As the educational and administrative functions of these hereditary "social armies" became increasingly important from the time of Rujugira, the armies themselves became the principal mechanism for incorporating new populations into the administrative structure of the state. Formerly, booty seized during raids was sent to the Court while individual families were required to send provisions to their members in the army; but over time these differences between booty seized from raids and resources accumulated from individual army members blurred. Increasingly (and especially from the mid-nineteenth century) the armies included some lineage groups which supplied prestations on a regular basis, regardless of the state of military mobilization, and thus these transfers gradually took on more of the characteristics of tribute. In addition to provisions for warriors, these included prestige goods—bracelets, mats, artifacts—which were sent to the Court; over time, the army leader (appointed by the Court) became increasingly an administrative official responsible for prestations rather than a military leader renowned by the spoils of war delivered to the Court. Administrative prestations from within the *umuheto* group therefore came to replace the earlier spoils of military raiding outside the territorial domain of Rwanda, and the administrative functions of these *umuheto* groups came to predominate over the military functions.

At the same time, army organization itself became more hierarchical as army membership came to include virtually all social groups. It is from the time of Rujugira, for example, that the first "Hutu" sections of armies are noted (Kagame, 1963:77, 79, 102, 103; *Historique et Chronologie*, 114–115, 121–125, 149–152, 161–162). Not all were warriors, however; many (and this applied especially to "Hutu" groups) were simply associated with army administrative structures and thus required to provide prestations. Thus, the army played a paradoxical role—it served as a means of assimilation to Rwandan forms for some, but it also served to keep others from full assimilation (by the hierarchical structures of its internal organization) and these groups continued to provide prestations on a permanent basis. This form of army organization created and reinforced social distance with inhabitants of new areas even while spreading Rwandan norms to these areas. In this way, the army came to serve as an ideal administrative structure for the expansion of the Rwandan state, combining military, administrative, and educative functions, while being closely controlled, politically and ideologically, by the royal Court.

With this consolidation of power, the state was no longer dependent on alliances with various groups, each of which drew their political strength from resources essentially outside the control of the Central Court. Instead, the Court became the dominant political actor with a preponderant role in the distribution of political resources among the various factions in the country. This concentration of power meant that the Court was increasingly able to demand services and goods from the various social groups of the country, and to punish those that did not comply with these demands. Equally important, it was able to withhold rewards from those (often "Hutu") whom it defined as outside the immediate political system and whose former autonomy had previously made it possible for them to accumulate goods independently of their status at the Central Court. What was important in this process was the relationship of interdependence which emerged between military expansion and administrative consolidation. This augmentation of power at the center through internal reorganization resulted from, as well as facilitated, Rwandan expansion to the west.

Growing Rwandan military capacity and the increasingly exclusive character of the central political arena also had important repercussions in the frontier areas that are today western Rwanda. In the wake of expanding Rwandan hegemony in the east, those who fled Ndorwa and Gisaka to search for refuge from Rwandan state power often moved west, into the highland areas of the Nile-Zaire Divide. Despite occasional military forays, these areas had, for the most part, remained until then outside of Rwandan control. The arrival of refugees with cultural characteristics similar to those of the Rwandan Central Court changed this relationship. Since most refugees were apparently from the military war zones of Ndorwa and Gisaka, they were not, strictly speaking, "Rwandans." But they nonetheless shared attributes which made them appear Rwandan to the peoples of the highland areas. Their very presence may have attracted more direct Rwandan military thrusts into the area; often, indeed, they did develop later ties to the Central Court of Rwanda, serving as the vanguard in establishing Rwandan administrative structures in the area. Consequently, in retrospect, they were often seen as "Rwandan" from the beginning, politically as well as culturally. In addition, within the context of Rwandan westward expansion, these refugees from Central Court power were also claimed as Rwandan colonizers by the Central Court, especially where they later came to serve as the nucleus for the growth of new army organizations. (M. C. Newbury 1974, 1975:*passim;* Pagès 1933:634–700).

The expansion of this western frontier is difficult to trace with precision because the Tuutsi "colonists" (originally "refugees") did not move into the area in any regular pattern. Instead, their slow penetration over several generations created a loose series of intersecting ties that eventually became incorporated within the political network of the Central Court. But these ties did not form a continuous web; many areas remained independent of this network, and in some cases "Tuutsi" refugees continued to move farther west still, to Itombwe and Gishari in the mountainous highlands west of Lake Kivu (Spitaels 1953, Maquet 1955, Kajiga 1956). In other cases, small polities along the Nile-Zaire Divide remained autonomous of the Central Court until well into the period of colonial rule (Pauwels 1962, de Lacger 1939:82–89, Nahimana 1979, Pagès 1933:328–345, *Historique et Chronologie*:94–169).

The general pattern of this penetration of Central Court norms into the western areas can be followed through the Court traditions relating to army expeditions (sometimes only raids) and through the settlement patterns of Tuutsi families. Tuutsi movements were first directed west from Nyantango, near the bend in the Nyabarongo River and near the ritual centers of the kingdom at Rukoma and Bumbogo. From Nyantango, the armies pushed westward through the lower areas across the Divide towards Lake Kivu, reaching the lake in the area of Bwishaza and Rusenyi, in present Kibuye Prefecture (Vansina 1962:88–89; *Historique et Chronologie*:96–97). Initial Rwandan presence in these areas may date to long before Rujugira's reign,[6] but it seems clear that the patterns of continuous settlement and continuous claims of the court in these areas date only from the reign of Rujugira. Traditions from the areas themselves (which differ from Central Court claims) and army locations also indicate the recent nature of this expansion of Central Court power.[7] Subsequent military expeditions were made south to Kinyaga (the provinces of Impara and Biiru) and north to Bugoyi (Vansina 1962:79–80, 86–90; M. C. Newbury 1975: Chapters II and III).

The history of the Abagwabiro lineage illustrates the gradual nature of Tuutsi penetration into the western areas. Originally from Ndorwa, this family moved first to the area of Bunyambiriri along the Nile-Zaire Divide, just west and southwest of the Rwandan heartland in Nduga, probably during the reign of Rujugira. From there, they moved north into what is today Gisenyi Prefecture (the area of Bugoyi) in northwestern Rwanda (Pagès 1933:141–3, 598–652; Reisdorff 1952:Enquête No. 31; Vansina 1962:88; de Lacger 1939: 111; *Historique et Chronologie* 121–3). This pattern of movement suggests that here was a family seeking autonomy from the Rwandan Central Court, rather than serving as its agent (as the Court sources imply). Furthermore, in most sources, Macumu, the lineage head, is described as "Hutu" (i.e., not a direct participant in Central Court politics) while Central Court traditions describe him as "Tuutsi" (i.e., one of their own). But whatever their early status, in later generations the Abagwabiro were to forge ties to the Central Court. Perhaps their tenuous position as eastern refugees without a foothold in local political networks, in an area of strong interaction with areas further west, made them willing as well as likely candidates for this role. Their orientation towards Rwandan cultural values provided a basis for later claims by the Rwandan court that they had always been "official representatives" in the area.

Similar patterns of incorporation are found in Kinyaga, in the extreme southwest of the country, where a significant proportion of the present population claims to have arrived from farther east, especially from Ndorwa and Gisaka, during the reign of Rujugira or his successor Ndabarasa.[8] Although the precise war leading to their exodus is not cited in these traditions, the process conforms to that described above, and the timing of these wars would confirm the general agreement noted in the sources that many of these groups arrived during, or just after, Rujugira's reign. Subsequently, many of these immigrants were instrumental in forging ties between this remote region (Kinyaga) and the Central Court political arena.

The very intensity of the military struggles to the east, with Gisaka and Ndorwa, has obscured the historical record of Rwanda's military ties with the west. But even the murkiness of this record has its lesson to convey: military records, army postings, the nature of later Central Court alliances with "Tuutsi" refugees (from the defeated states),[9] and even the nature of the terrain and the structure of earlier political groups—all these lead to a common conclusion that this area was not one where a clear military front was in evidence, as had occurred in wars to the east. This area became part of Rwanda not by a once-for-all campaign and the subsequent redrawing of political boundaries. Conquest in the west occurred piecemeal, gradually. Rwandan penetration here was discontinuous—both geographically and temporally. This was an area of the slow absorption of varying degrees of Rwandan (i.e., Central Court) penetration, often an area of refuge for those seeking autonomy from Central Court power but carrying with them Rwandan norms of language, dress, and consumption. Most of all, this Rwandan character was conveyed in a quality of social behavior: in the turn of a phrase, in the type of poetry recited over the evening fire, in the nature and mechanism of social alliance (cattle contracts often, rather than blood pacts or marriage ties), perhaps also in religious concepts. The spread of Central Court power was especially evident in the aloof social bearing of the elite, a bearing bred in court etiquette, nurtured in army training, and matured in contacts with the west.

Thus, while we lack the military details, the cultural implications of this move west are clear—and they were as important to the Central Court arena as to the incorporated western areas themselves. For complementing the growth of administrative structures was the growth of increasingly rigid categories of social classification; in fact, the concepts of social distancing appear to have intensified with the expansion of the Rwandan state into areas which did not share its basic cultural norms. It was a period in which Rwandan society was becoming strongly hierarchical. And just as the material spoils from western raiding strengthened the court, it seems very likely that the norms and classifications developed in the western conquest areas—where cultural differences were more marked, political structures more rigid, and social differences hence more accentuated—were carried back into the central areas to serve as a model for the general structural development occurring throughout the Rwandan kingdom.

II

The literature of the Rwandan Court articulates these concepts of social distancing and demonstrates the norms inculcated by Rwandan army training—the glorification of military prowess, of personal heroism, and of the invincibility of the state. These values appear vividly in the individual praise poems by which a warrior celebrated his own virtues before his army colleagues or before the Court. Such *ibyivugo* (sing., *icyivugo*) are recited rapidly and at full voice, with great formality, often with the speaker brandishing a spear. The artistry is evidenced by the number of syllables pronounced in a single breath, the complexity of the poetic allusions, and the audacity of the deeds claimed, as well as by the presence and bearing of the speaker (Kagame 1969:15–55; Coupez and Kamanzi 1970:96–112).[10] Two examples, illustrating some of these aspects of Rwandan praise poems, follow. (The French version below, coming from Kagame, a Rwandan, conveys the flavor of the original best. An English version by me is given in the Appendix).

> I. *Poem about Rushenyi, son of Ntoranyi—reign of Gahindiro, early nineteenth century. (Kagame 1969:16–17)*
>
> Le Perforateur des peltes,
> (race) de Piqueur-des-boucliers
> Je suis un virtuose de l'arc
> Un Muhunde vint se balançant avec un bouclier:
> Je lui décochai une flèche et il tomba de tout son long,
> Sans qu'il fut possible de le ranimer,
> tel celui qu'aurait touché la foudre
> Il y eut de remous parmi les porte-bouclier (ennemis)
> et je me plantai seul au milieu du sentier,
> tandis que les ennemis étaient en train de trier les craintifs.

> II. *Poem about Gahunde, son of Nyakaja—reign of Rwabugiri (Kagame 1969:18–19)*
>
> Le Frappeur-de-coups-à-même-le-corps
> (race) du Viseur-aux-endroits-mortels.

> La javeline à la lame blanche
> je l'ai projetée contre un Muhima, à Gakirage
> tandis qu'il en admirait la beauté parfaite,
> moi je le livrai à sa merci et elle le dévora,
> tel un male de lion en pleine force
> voyant qu'elle le dépeçait je me moquai de lui,
> en disant: "Eh bien! ce n'est pas toi seul!
> celui aussi du Bunyabungo
> je l'ai traité de la même façon!"

The features so apparent in these poems—the militaristic ethic, the training in Court etiquette, the glorification of the power of the state, and the stress on individual achievement in the conception of heroism so characteristic of Court culture—are even more apparent in the "dynastic poetry" (*ibisigo;* sing., *igisigo*) glorifying the kings and especially their military deeds, and in so doing denigrating the conquered peoples (Kagame 1954:*passim;* Kagame 1969:151–245; Coupez et Kamanzi 1970:159–197). These poems, too long to include here, detail the reigns of each of the last sixteen kings to figure in the royal genealogy. They form an important body of warrior literature, asserting Rwandan values at the official level of the Court in the same way that the individual praise poems do for the armies and their members.[11]

In other types of literature, such as the *ibiteekerezo* historical narratives, the contrast in Rwandan perceptions between their own cultural values and those of the western peoples is similarly marked. This opposition is apparent both in the political distinctions made between western kings and those of Rwanda (as they are portrayed in the Rwandan narratives) and in the cultural features which the traditions commonly attribute to the western peoples. Among such traditions, the best known relate to Ruganzu Ndoori, a Rwandan king who appears as the quintessential epic hero of Rwanda (Pagès 1933: 128–9, 228–345; Vansina 1962:86–87; Kagame 1972:93–109; de Lacger 1939:107–8; Coupez and Kamanzi 1962:texts 12–14, 16). One of the most widespread traditions dealing with his reign concerns his rivalry with a courtier named Muvunyi, son of Karema. It is an exciting tale of intense competition between friends, a story filled with espionage, temptations, and daring. It is told through a text replete with hyperbole, cultural allusions, references to magical power, and humor. Of particular interest here is the way in which these stylistic elements relate to Rwandan perceptions of the western cultural frontier. Before discussing these textual elements, however, it will be necessary first to sketch out the main lines of the story.[12]

> (1) The story tells of a western king, Gatabirora, son of Kabibi, son of Kabirogosa, "the Mushi" with his teeth filed to a point . . . Gatabirora, son of Kabibi, son of Kabirogosa who was tied by a string to a chicken, and thence to his mother so that she might know when her son had died.

(2) One day Gatabirora sent a message to Ruganzu, the Rwandan king, summoning him to build for him an enclosure of the same dimensions as his own, and requiring him to send enough butter to make a drinking trough for his cows, as they were tired of always drinking from a trough made of sand. All this because, according to Gatabirora, Ruganzu lives in the country of his father, Kabibi.

(3) On their arrival at Ruganzu's court the messengers are stupefied with awe at the size and fine construction of the enclosure, and at the numbers and bearing of the courtiers. Realizing the danger they would be in were they to relate the message as given, they simply say they have come to pay their respects on behalf of Gatabirora. Ruganzu thanks them initially, but by a clever ruse—aided by generous quantities of the honey beer of the court—he tricks them into conveying the message in its entirety.

(4) Ruganzu responds to their true message with a long praise poem (*icyivugo*). He then mutilates the messengers and sends them back to Gatabirora.

(5) Ruganzu then publicly offers his wager—a challenge to anyone at the court to kill Gatabirora before he does. Muvunyi accepts the challenge by placing his spear next to that of Ruganzu and drinking from the same urn as Ruganzu—drinking it dry, in fact. [These are actions which in most contexts would be considered acts of lèse-majesté; indeed, they can be considered as such here.] Muvunyi then leaves the court and his father sets him obstacles to overcome to prepare him for his coming ordeal.

(6) On Muvunyi's departure from the court, Ruganzu makes plans to distract Muvunyi by providing him with beer, dancing, and women. Ruganzu then leaves immediately for his confrontation with Gatabirora, though the agreement was that they would set out on the eighth day.

(7) Ruganzu meets Gatabirora, and they begin by sparring. Finally, Gatabirora hurls his spear. It misses Ruganzu, but the force from it as it flies by knocks Ruganzu unconscious and sets the forest ablaze.

(8) Muvunyi learns of Ruganzu's departure, and sets out in all haste towards Gatabirora's. After many adventures en route, he arrives just as Ruganzu falls unconscious. After reciting his own *icyivugo*, Muvunyi kills Gatabirora and leaves, having cut off the head and testicles of the western king.

(9) On awakening, Ruganzu finds that Muvunyi has killed Gatabirora. He is at first angered at having lost the wager. But in the end Ruganzu is placated by Muvunyi's father, and the two warriors are reconciled, the one achieving status and fortune, the other retaining his kingdom against the insolence of "Gatabirora, son of Kabibi, son of Kabirogosa, the Mushi with the filed teeth."

The story is of interest not only because it is one of the best-known of Rwandan stories of this kind,[13] but also because it deals with the problem of the conceptual differences by which Rwandans set themselves apart from western cultures. (It also includes certain thematic and stylistic elements which reappear in other traditions, as will be discussed below.) The story as a whole is interesting because it talks of a western king seeking to alter—even to invert—the structure of relationships between himself and Ruganzu by demanding prestations from the Rwandan king. Significantly, this is expressed through a contest in a domain in which the Rwandan court prides itself as clearly superior to its western neighbors, that of material culture. The western king seeks to build a thatched house and cattle troughs equal to those of the Rwandans.

(1) But the tenor of the narrative is set even before the story begins to unfold, with the announcement of the names "Gatabirora, son of Kabibi, son of Kabirogosa." "Gatabirora" and "Kabibi" are representative of common names found in the west.[14] "Kabirogosa," however, is even more explicitly tied to the west, as a Rwandan deformation of the (more recent) Havu dynastic name, Kamerogosa. He is identified as "a MuShi," one of the names applied to mean "those of the west" and carrying very strong perjorative connotations in Rwandan usage. He is characterized as having filed and pointed teeth, a custom disdained by Rwandans whose cultural norms do not allow for any form of bodily mutilation for ornamentation or for ritual purposes. In fact, filed teeth are not common among the Havu or Shi; they are most closely associated with the forest cultures west of the Mitumba Mountains, west of Lake Kivu. Thus, this protrayal combines elements from many cultural groups—some even beyond the immediate frontier—to create a single outgroup category in opposition to Rwandan norms.

Finally, Gatabirora's own masculinity and independence are questioned by the use of a metaphor common in this type of story: his genitals are tied by a string leading to a chicken who would inform his mother of his death.[15] (Other versions of this tale note that the string was held directly by Gatabirora's mother without any intermediary.) Aside from the obvious suggestion of dependence on the mother (an allusion, perhaps, to the tendency to matrilateral succession in royal practices in the west[16]), the metaphor also carries the implication that Gatabirora will die alone in the forest, with no one to bring news of his death but a chicken. There is also an allusion here (which is in fact the basis of the metaphor in question) to the form of dress of the "uncouth" forest peoples of the west, who formerly used a loin-cloth tied between the legs and around the waist.

Nor does Gatabirora's mother escape the caustic tone of the Rwandan narrative: she is portrayed as hiding monkeys and cockroaches between her legs. The characterization ends with a phrase of gibberish KiHavu, a language used in areas west of Lake Kivu, repeated at intervals throughout the narrative. In many respects, then, the initial portions of this tale establish the tone by which the western cultures will be characterized throughout.

(2) The parody of western character continues as Gatabirora assembles his messengers. There are seven of them, as we find out later. This is a deformation of the conventional numerical scheme applying to royalty, which is associated with multiples of four (most frequently eight). Seven, then, represents non-royalty, or perhaps pretentious and gauche attempts to claim royal status on the part of the hopelessly inept Gatabirora.[17] This image is reinforced by the nature of the meal offered them on their arrival at Gatabirora's home. The meal consists of taro, a root plant closely associated with forest cultures but disdained as food by the Rwandans. To serve this food to others, especially as part of a formal presentation to his own men, would be, in the eyes of most Rwandans, either a bad joke or a most pointed insult.

Following the meal, Gatabirora informs the messengers of their mission: to demand of Ruganzu a new house and a new drinking trough for cattle. All this is phrased in mock KinyaRwanda (the language of Rwanda), filled with mispronunciations: "Ruganzu, king of Rwanda," for example, becomes "Rugamvu ga Gwanda."[18] Gatabirora offers a long recitation of his own self-characterization, similar in form to the praise poetry of Rwanda, but including elements that would be anything but heroic to Rwandan audiences and with a hilarious transformation of the conventional *icyivugo* form: "Go and tell Rugamvu ga Gwanda that it is Katabirora [who speaks], Katabirora son of Kabibi son of Kabirogosa, the MuShi with the pointed teeth, who comes drawing with him the string [tied to his genitals], who brings with him the chickens cackling in the forest . . . [then there is more gibberish KiHavu]. It is he, Katabirora, who sends you these messengers. You will say to him 'Leta seke, leta seke' (a deformation of the KiHavu imperative "leta soko," bring tribute or offer prestations). . . ." The command is explicit, as is the threat of punishment for disobedience: for failing to pay court in this manner, Rugamvu ga Gwanda will be chewed up and spit out like so much tobacco (a northern commodity, but also associated in Rwanda with western trade networks). All this is based on the assertion that "Rugamvu ga Gwanda" lives on the land of Gatabirora's father, Kabibi.

(3) The next episode describes the reaction of the messengers from the forest to the court of Ruganzu. It illustrates the simple naiveté of these men, overawed by the splendor of the Rwandan courts. They are stupefied and see that the simple home of Gatabirora could not begin to compare with the grandeur of the court of Ruganzu. And so they decide to change their message; in fact they invert it, by saying that they bring the greetings of Gatabirora, that Gatabirora seeks to come to Ruganzu bearing prestations of the forest (mats, *ubutega* fiber bracelets, hoes), and that the land that Gatabirora inhabits is not the land of his father Kabibi, but of Ruganzu's father Ndahiro. Such an inversion illustrates the lack of char-

acter of these forest bumpkins; but Ruganzu's reaction to it and his careful distrust of such flattery also shows the cunning intelligence of the court milieu.

In other versions of the story, this theme is drawn out at greater length (Vansina, n.d.[b]). The messengers arrive and no one understands them when they speak their own language; they are portrayed as walking up to various courtiers and addressing them as Ruganzu, mistaking the noble bearing of person after person at the Court (never having seen such before) for that of the king.[19] These forward, uncultured visitors, lacking all finesse and social grace, then eat rotten food offered them and drink the dregs of others—food and drink no one at Court would deign to touch. Having filled themselves like gluttons, they fall asleep and in their sleep break wind in such volume that Ruganzu himself is awakened by the noise. Flatulence is, in fact, a common perjorative theme applied to westerners within the Rwandan court context—the epitome of the uncultured barbarian (it thus serves as another core-cliché, as discussed in note 15). The Vansina version of the narrative continues with the men awakening and speaking, again, in gibberish or pidgin KinyaRwanda. In both versions discussed here, there is reference to Gatabirora, the son of Kabibi of Kaberogosa, the MuShi who lived in the forest of "Nzira," a reference to yet another narrative tale dealing with westerners.[20] Once again, as with the theme of flatulence, the manner in which this theme is intertwined with the main story forms an important element in the meaning conveyed. By thus relating this narrative to other traditions dealing with westerners (or, in the case of Nzira, to unsuccessful Hutu opposition to Tuutsi expansion), the superiority of the Tuutsi Court culture is further stressed by allusion to the larger corpus of traditions on the common theme.

Ruganzu then shows his pleasure (and his sarcastic turn of mind) by summoning each of his warrior courtiers separately and reciting in turn their praise poems, recounting their military exploits and heroic deeds. He ends each recitation with "Have you heard how this MuShi has sent me a good message!" Finally, after Ruganzu has finished showing his gratitude to the messengers and extended a formal invitation to Gatabirora to visit his Court, one of the messengers breaks down and reveals the true message. He begins with gibberish KiHavu, and continues by noting that since Gatabirora had provided them with such a sumptuous feast of delicious taro before sending them off, the messengers cannot betray him by hiding the truth. He then tells Ruganzu what Gatabirora had asked for: "Leta seke [give tribute]!" In the second version considered here, the messengers add that if Ruganzu does not obey, Gatabirora will take off the clothes of his mother, the one who chases monkeys and hides cockroaches between her legs. Such a statement of course is an unimaginable, unthinkable blasphemy in the form of a barbaric oath, and emphasizes once again the disgusting, crude nature of these western "Banyabungo."

(4) Ruganzu then responds with a long praise poem of his own, by

implication contrasting the glories of the Rwandan regime and the refinement of the Rwandan language with the blunt straightforwardness of the uncultured "BaShi." Included in this response are many references to the western areas and themes shared with other *ibiteekerezo*. One such fragment, drawn from a story well known to Rwandan audiences, tells of the formation of Lake Kivu from an indiscretion on the part of Nyiransibula, a western woman serving at the Rwandan court. One day, while sweeping the courtyard, she creates a scandal by breaking wind—loud and clear—before the assembled courtiers pondering the affairs of state. (As in the story of Gatabirora's messengers, there is ample latitude here for a graphic performance in the telling of this tale.) Exiled from the court, she throws out her chamberpot; where it breaks, there issues forth a gigantic flow of water, flooding the entire surrounding area and eventually creating Lake Kivu. By magical means, Ruganzu is able to halt the rising waters and thus save Rwanda (Pagès, 1933:238–243, 251–253; Vansina, n.d. (a,b); Bigirumwani, 1971:100ff.; Smith, 1975:313–319). Finally, to return to the story of Gatabirora, Ruganzu terminates his response to the western messengers—but in reality addressing his own warriors—with: "Have you heard the dog of a MuShi come to insult us here!" (In KinyaRwanda, there is a play on words between this phrase and the phrase he repeated earlier: "Have you heard the good news," thus dramatizing the contrast between the two responses all the more.)

In the account given here, Ruganzu then kills all but one messenger (again a common theme in these stories) whom he mutilates and sends home to Gatabirora. After limping home—falling, crying out, and lamenting on the long road back to his king—the messenger finally enters his compound, where he begins once again with his gibberish KiHavu and goes on to tell Gatabirora how Ruganzu responded. "He is here, he is here, and you will burn, you will die, you will die." He faints, and to revive him, the courtiers bring bells to ring in his ears. Although bells are used in some Court ceremonies in Rwanda, they are most frequently associated with the anti-Court Ryangombe rituals; they are also, of course, used on hunting dogs, perhaps the strongest connotation (associated with western cultures) drawn to mind in this context.

After hearing his laconic story, Gatabirora looks up in fright and asks "Where are they coming from? Where will they pass amongst my nettles, amongst my seeds, amongst my taro plants?" This final reference, of course, serves as yet another reminder of the forest milieu and the staple food attributed to these simple and hopelessly uncultured BaShi of Gatabirora. In another version, Ruganzu mutilates each messenger in a different way, cutting off a leg of one, an arm of another, an ear of a third. He then hands each the severed part, saying: "Here, these are your provisions for the return trip. Go and tell Gatabirora I shall be there."

The remainder of the narrative (sections 6 to 9 in the synopsis above) deals with the competition between Muvunyi and Ruganzu—the drama of

the wager, the cunning of Ruganzu's tactics, the excitement of the race to
Gatabirora's, and the heroics of Muvunyi in assuring Gatabirora's death. It
is entertainment at its most intense. But these later sections concern us less
here, for they do not directly offer a parody of western cultures, so effectively portrayed in the earlier sections.

The important point of such comparisons between western cultures and
Rwanda is not just that these stories portray western peoples as uncouth, but
that they relate to elements deemed central to Rwandan culture. The references to such uncultured behavior, such unrefined language, such unthinkable foods, are all framed as deformations of accepted Rwandan etiquette
rather than valid characterizations of western peoples. In reality, then, the
parody also serves as a commentary on Rwandan norms, reinforcing Rwandan identity by stressing the non–Rwandan quality of the western cultures.
To be sure, there are allusions to western traits in the names, the literary
themes, the foods; but these are taken out of context and thus can only be
judged in the context of the Rwandan cultural norms of the listener. It is this
perspective which makes them seem so ridiculous, not the inherent quality of
the traits alone (though allusions such as those to the cockroaches or the
flatulence are clearly derogatory on their own account). The portrayal of
western cultures in the narratives therefore need not be valid in itself to have
its maximum effect; it need only provide oppositions to Rwandan culture.
The major role of the allusions to the west is to make the story plausible (and
entertaining), to provide some kind of narrative line to hold together the
images offered. Although ostensibly a cultural commentary on western
peoples, the terms employed are not always terms of ethnographic ascription; instead, they are terms generated by a particular context of oppositions
and used to enhance those oppositions. It is thus the nature of the relationships which defined the "frontier," not the presence of some "objective"
frontier which defined the relationships among groups.[21]

III

The literary sources, however, reflect only one aspect of the frontier concept: they speak for the ideology of the Rwandan Central Court alone.
The influence of these norms was of course very strong; even the local
non-royal traditions tend to pick up the stereotypes of social categories as
defined by these Court perceptions. But such a view of the frontier—
stressing idealized norms and polarized oppositions—tends to overlook, or
even to contradict, the day-to-day behavior of westerners, which reflected
the strong linkages at work both within the area (which today forms part
of western Rwanda) and with areas farther west still. Looked at from the
point of view of interaction networks, there was no clear hiatus dividing
Rwandan and western norms; in fact, the evidence at hand suggests that
until quite recently non-Court Rwandan people had closer ties with the
west than with the east, the area of most intensive Court culture. The

most significant forms of social distancing were those that separated the Court milieu from non-Court milieu within Rwanda itself. To illustrate this important difference in Court perceptions and local perceptions, three forms of linkages between western Rwanda and areas further west will be discussed briefly here—commerce, marriage ties, and mobility.

Recent research has altered our understanding of the intensive commercial networks which existed in this region, at least in the late nineteenth century and probably from well before (Lugan, 1977a, 1977b; D. Newbury, 1980b). What is particularly pertinent to the present discussion—and the feature that apparently hid this commercial activity from earlier researchers—is that it was conducted outside the Court milieu. But even before these studies were undertaken, there were suggestions of significant levels of commercial contacts which included a wide network of ties throughout the western region of Rwanda. Though markets were present (indicating the intensity of the trade in some areas), commercial interaction mainly occurred through many individual traders, dealing with trade partners linked to them by kin ties, blood-pact ties, or other more informal social ties. Typical of the testimony from the western areas are these descriptions from Ijwi Island (in Lake Kivu, just west of Rwanda), by participants in the trade from more recent periods.[22]

> [The people of Ijwi] took beans and sorghum to Rwanda for goats and bulls. They then [the Rwandans] took them to Nduga to buy livestock, Nduga and Nyanza. [Nduga is the general area of central Rwanda; Nyanza was the location of the royal capital during colonial rule but is often used in a metonymical sense to refer to the royal Court.] The food we grew here—in great quantities. . . . The beads we bought in Karhana, Kabare, Ngweshe, Kaziba [all to the west and southwest of Lake Kivu]. The *burhega* [fiber bracelets] we made ourselves, here on Ijwi. We made them from vines in the forest called *ndambagizi* and *ntunda*. After cutting them and drying them we wove them, wove them, wove them . . . like this . . . in a special pattern so they look nice—so! Then we took goats to Butembo, to the land of Ndalemwa [Mubuu, west of the Mitumba Mountains in Zaire] to look for *burhega*. We took goats and bought *burhega*; we took sorghum and bought *burhega*. . . .

> The Batembo bring *burhega* made of vines (*ishuli*) and we carry them to Rwanda. That was before the *amafranga* [European money] arrived; there were no *amafranga* then. They brought *burhega* and we took them to Rwanda to buy goats. On returning from Rwanda we took the goats to Irhambi [on the western shore] to sell them there. But this was done with friends. In those days whosoever did not have a friend was not able to buy anything.

> There were no markets but one could go [to Rwanda] to look for a friend. Then you could ask for a cow or a goat. One had to have a friend to trade.

[Summary:] Migamba, a man of the Ishaza clan came from Rwanda [to Ijwi] to buy things here. Rubenga [the interviewee] was looking for goats and goatskins for his wife [or for "his marriage"]. So Migamba told Rubenga to come to Rwanda to look for skins there. When he [Rubenga] went there, they made a blood pact in Rwanda. He took beer and beans and went to look for goats in Rwanda. There in Rwanda he traded cultivated crops and food and "harvests" and hoes for goats. When he made friendship he did not actually make a blood pact but only exchanged things like beans [except for the bloodpact with Migamba].

Thus the trade passed through many hands, and included many families in an informal network. These testimonies, to be sure, refer to the early years of the colonial period, that is, to the early years of the twentieth century. But because there were no barriers to earlier involvement in this type of network, it seems reasonable to see in these descriptions a model of commercial ties in the area for as long as the demand conditions held. Given the mobility found in this sub-region (a matter discussed below), local trade was undoubtedly a part of this regional interaction, even though trade directly with the Court milieu may have developed only more recently.[23]

The most important items mentioned in the sources (both oral and written) are the ornamental *ubutega* anklet/bracelet which Rwandan women wore by the hundreds on their legs.[24] Traded in the thousands in Rwanda, these delicate items of raffia or other fiber woven into a distinctive design were fabricated in the areas west of Lake Kivu. Because the trade in *ubutega* was strongly influenced by Central Court demand, trade patterns for these commodities are not representative of the overall network of local trade patterns within the region. Nevertheless, because they are so distinctive and hence are so often mentioned in both oral and written sources, *ubutega* trade patterns are useful in tracing the extent of this broader commercial network; included were regions stretching from far to the west of Lake Kivu to the area of the Rwandan Court east of the Nile-Zaire Divide (Biebuyck and Kahombo 1971:13, 47, 51, 55, 109, 127; Barnes 1923:115, 116; Pagès 1933:22–23, 636–637, Plates Ib, XXIa). People in most areas in between were also included as producers, consumers, or intermediaries. Although *ubutega* are the most frequently cited commodity in this commercial network, many other products were traded as well. Important among these were tobacco, salt, hoes, and foodstuffs from the north and northwest, and mats, hoes, and foodstuffs from the southwest. Livestock—goats and, more rarely, cattle—were the most frequent Rwandan return item traded for *ubutega* and other goods from the west.

Essentially similar commercial mechanisms prevailed for all such items. Although hoes (and sometimes *ubutega*) travelled with specialized traders—and travelled greater distances—most of this localized trade appears to have involved short distances between each transaction, moving from hand to hand within the commercial web. Mutual dependence, even trust, was essential in such a commercial network, one that included many participants and into which entry was easy. Commercial relations in this area, therefore, convey no sense of the clear-cut oppositions (posed in terms of culture/barbarism) so prevalent in the Court traditions applying to this region. In fact, they underscore the importance of linkages, not oppositions; these linkages are demonstrated both by the fact of widespread commercial interaction and by the nature of such interaction, characterized by face-to-face transactions where friendship networks were important in facilitating material transfer.

Marriage ties also seem to cut across the cultural barrier posited by Rwandan literary sources. Precise data on this are scanty, but the message is clear. While marriage ties on a hierarchial axis—between Court families and local residents—appear to have become more and more rare,[25] marriage ties both between different regions of present-day western Rwanda and between those regions and areas further west still, around and beyond Lake Kivu, were neither difficult to arrange nor infrequent.

One social sector for which data on such ties are preserved (although incompletely preserved) is that of the local ruling families among the many small autonomous polities which existed in the area before Rwandan penetration and incorporation. These political units, numbering well over a score, expressed their autonomy through the ritual authority of their rulers or *abami* (sing., *umwami*).[26] Though the data on marriage ties are very incomplete, it is clear that these *abami* sometimes married among themselves. Rugaba, the *umwami* of Mpembe, for example, is said to have married women from Bugoyi in northwestern Rwanda and Bukunzi in southwestern Rwanda.[27] Other sources mention the marriages between people from Bukunzi and Bumbogo (Pagès 1933:296–298, 465), and between Mashira, the *umwami* of Nduga in central Rwanda, and a woman from an unnamed polity on Buzi, a peninsula in the northwest of Lake Kivu (de Lacger 1939:103). Bukunzi data add that the kings there maintained marriage ties with the Shi kingdoms to the west. Mobility patterns would also indicate that there were few barriers to marrying within the region, as new immigrants to an area apparently had little difficulty in establishing themselves.

If there were few obstacles to marriage among the different regions of what is now western Rwanda, the same is true for marriages between people in this area and regions farther west. This was especially true for women marrying out, from areas of western Rwanda towards western areas. It was a general characteristic of this network of exchange that women moved west. It is not uncommon to find Rwandan-born women married on Ijwi, but rare to find Ijwi-born women married in Rwanda. The same general trend is found west of Ijwi, where Ijwi women are married on the Zairean mainland, but few women from the west marry on Ijwi.

Without data on the massive scale required to establish this point, such an observation can only be suggestive. Nonetheless, these observed tendencies mesh with both marriage institutions and ideological explanations. Bridewealth is greater in the west, and hence it is financially beneficial to the family, generally speaking, to marry women west; conversely, it is disadvantageous to marry women east. Ijwi ideology explains this tendency to marry women west in another way: there is not enough food in Rwanda; Ijwi women who marry in Rwanda will starve, say the Bany'Iju, and eventually they will return home (interviews with Migayo Shamahanga, 12/2/73; Kakomera, 21/6/74). Such an explanation obviously agrees with the Ijwi practice of constantly sending food to family members in Rwanda. At the same time, it serves as an Ijwi commentary on how stingy Rwandans are in terms of food exchange.[28]

The general movement of women towards the west is a phenomenon that blends with the third element considered here, the mobility of people within the region. Both trade and marriage presuppose some forms of mobility, but these were probably less indicative of the linkages within the region than were movements which led to permanent settlement in new areas. Indeed, trade and marriage ties were in part a result of the movement of people, both eastward and westward. There is a great deal of evidence suggesting movements into northwestern Rwanda (Bugoyi) and southwestern Rwanda (Kinyaga) from regions farther west. For Bugoyi, Pagès notes that "les Bagoyi . . . sont presque tous originaires du nord-ouest du Lac Kivu. . ." (Pagès 1933:636).[29] In the list he gives of "clans et sous-clans" of Bugoyi, almost one-half (27 of 57) claim a western origin (Pagès 1933:644–645); and he provides numerous examples of this immigration to Bugoyi from the west (Pagès 1933: 653–659, 666, 668, 671, 676, 682).

In more recent periods, however, the overall trend of this movement seems to have been reversed, and it is now generally towards the west. It is possible that this shift was associated with the political pressures connected with the expansion of the royal Court structures into this area. Many people moved from present-day western Rwanda onto highland areas known as Gishari, northwest of Lake Kivu, from at least the nineteenth century (and probably considerably earlier), and this movement continued well into this century, both as part of colonial policy and for less formal reasons (Kajiga 1956; Spitaels 1953). Similarly, the immigration of families from western Rwanda onto Ijwi Island is noticeable from about the middle or late eighteenth century, and intense communication between Ijwi and areas east of Lake Kivu through family ties, blood-pact ties, and commercial channels has continued in some instances into the present (D. Newbury 1979: Ch. V, VI). Such an enduring historical pattern apparently met with few obstacles—a testimony to the strength of cultural continuities in the region. Even during the wars directed against Ijwi in the late nineteenth century by the Rwandan king Rwabugiri, these local-level contacts across the lake continued virtually uninter-rupted—indeed, they flourished. They were to play a part in the war itself and in the subsequent administration, as recent immigrants who could claim ties to Rwanda were often favored as appointed administra-tive authorities during the Rwandan occupation (D. Newbury 1975).

The reality of such linkages east and west therefore challenges the categorical polarization and regional differentiation portrayed in the tradi-tions of the Rwandan Court. This again illustrates the relativity of the concept of the frontier. It is a relative concept in terms of geographical distance (held mostly in the central Court milieu, well removed from con-tact with the west) and, perhaps more significantly, in terms of the social class in which such perceptions originated. It was predominantly those tied to the Court milieu (as soldiers, narrators, or even servants) who articulated this set of frontier perceptions. But the frontier concepts were important not only as they were applied to the "frontier zones" themselves; they had internal applications as well. The categories applied to the frontier were also applied within Rwandan society, a society marked by a high degree of social stratification. Indeed, the concept of the frontier, drawn in such stark terms, could be used to reinforce and perpetuate the internal structures of Rwandan social hierarchy, as noted earlier.

The dual implication of these perceptions went farther still. As the populations of the west gradually adopted Rwandan cultural norms, they adopted also the form of expression and hence the mode of characteriza-tion implicit within Court perceptions (D. Newbury 1980a). Thus, the literary genres of the court—which included such core-images as we have noted above in the Gatabirora tale—were adopted, recounted and enjoyed by the people of these regions even while the people continued with the activities which belied such a stereotypical characterization. The literary models provided a good tale, whose hilarity to the westerners may have partly resided in the frivolity of such a portrayal. In these areas, in fact, such stereotypes may have acted to discredit or to parody the Rwandan heroes themselves, serving as Rwandan versions of *Don Quixote*. As Rwandan Court perceptions gradually penetrated the area, however, these people west of the Nile-Zaire Divide—who were themselves included among the original referents of the tale—increasingly accepted such por-trayals as "true," but applied the stereotypes to others farther west still. In so doing, of course, they reinforced their own identity as Rwandans, in this polarized context opposing "us" to "them." For each people, there-fore, the "barbarians" always lived farther west.[30]

The relativity of such a frontier concept, then, lies not only in geo-graphical or social parameters, but in situational parameters as well. The frontier is not defined by objective intrinsic elements of a situation alone, but in a concept generated by political perceptions of the day and phrased in terms of clear cultural oppositions, even polarization. The arbitrary aspect of the frontier concept applies even where the frontier zone is located in an area perceived as "empty" (though often such a categorization simply neglects the presence of other inhabitants, as illustrated in the western frontier of the United States or the Canadian Far North), for just as there is always continuity between cultures, so there is always continuity between culture and nature, and to oppose empty areas to inhabited areas is to deny this continuity. The oppositions implied in the frontier discourse, then, are a product of perceptions generated outside the frontier area itself, not emerging from it. The "frontier" metaphor speaks more to the metropolitan area than to the apparent locus of reference, the frontier zone itself. This may in part explain the problems involved in "defining" the American frontier, and the long debate which has followed from such definitional problems.

Literary genres such as those discussed above have an important place in the shaping of the frontier image. Often, the action in such tales takes place on the boundaries of the real and the fictive, on the frontiers of culture (Propp 1968). By continuously exploring the cultural boundaries which define the social group and the limits of acceptable cultural features and behavior, such stories are constantly redefining "us" by defining "them." The frontier concept itself differed little by social and geographical context—after all, the people in the west had stereotypes of other people farther west still. But the political significance which these images and these clichés acquired did vary, for these images were embedded in political activity and the clichés justified political action. And they did more than that. The power that made such clichés effective came in part from the metropolitan elite's sense of cohesion and cultural arrogance, themselves a product of the contrasting cultural universes portrayed by the images of the frontier. In Rwanda, as elsewhere, the concept of the frontier was thus both cause and effect of specific kinds of political interaction.

APPENDIX

AUTHOR'S TRANSLATIONS OF TWO IBYIVUGO (PRAISE POEMS)
(Kagame 1969:16–17 and 18–19)

I. The hunter who pierces animal skins,
   I am of those who pierce shields,
   I am a virtuoso with the bow:
   A Muhunde approached warily with a shield:
   I shot an arrow at him and he fell full length
   And could not be revived,
   As one struck by lightning.
   Consternation reigned amongst the enemy shield-bearers,

and I stood alone in the middle of the path
while the enemies were withdrawing their cowards.

II. One who strikes blows at the body,
I am of those who aims for fatal places.
The javelin of the white blade
I hurled it at a Muhima, at Gakirage,
while he was admiring its perfect beauty,
I put him at its mercy and it devoured him
As if he were a lion at the height of his power.
Seeing that it eviscerated him, I mocked him,
Saying, "Do not fret! You are not the only one!
The one from Bunyabungo,
I also dealt with him in the same manner!"

NOTES

*I am grateful to Elizabeth Traube of Wesleyan University
for her comments on an earlier draft of this paper.*

1. There is disagreement on the precise chronology of Rwandan kings. The two major chronological schema are A. Kagame 1959, *passim* and J. Vansina 1962:42–57. I have followed the general analysis proposed in the latter, although absolute dating is not essential to the argument advanced here. The basic social institutions of Rwanda are described in M. d'Hertefelt 1962. For reviews of recent research and how this has altered earlier portrayals of Rwandan social structures and history, see Bishikwabo and Newbury 1980 and D. Newbury 1980a.

2. Of course, a "Hutu" who held such a position of power for any length of time (especially if he also adopted Tuutsi social norms) would most likely gradually come to be seen as sharing "Tuutsi" status. The literature on ethnicity in Rwanda is as diverse as it is vast. Most analyses, however, neglect the dynamics of the Rwandan system and fail to account for changes in the conceptual patterns associated with the terms "Hutu" and "Tuutsi." For a recent consideration of this question for western Rwanda, see M. C. Newbury 1978.

3. The period of time involved may in fact have been longer than that implied by reference to a single king. Rujugira himself may have usurped the throne from his predecessor and brother Rwaaka (Vansina 1962:51–52). Kagame reverses this relationship, stating that Rwaaka pre-empted the rightful heir, Rujugira, and was therefore the usurper, though Rujugira later attained the throne (Kagame 1972:129–131). All sources, however, agree that they were brothers, that Rujugira removed Rwaaka from power and that subsequently Rujugira has been recognized as the only legitimate king of this generation (corresponding to the ideal of one-king-per-generation). Consequently, these two kings are considered as part of a single reign in the dynastic chronicles, and are so considered here; the "reign" of Rujugira refers in fact to the rule of two persons.

4. Raiding outside the core areas and especially into the agricultural areas of high population densities clearly had an important role to play in the internal transformations summarized below; it provided resources (in the form of booty),

prestige in raids, important new political functions for the Central Court (spoils to distribute and positions to dispense), and a new purpose to the state (expansion). Therefore, the alterations discussed here were not simply internal transformations in response to an external threat; they were a product of the changing relations with Rwanda's neighbors, especially those to the west. Such raids made the internal changes possible as well as desirable. To neglect the external interactions—so important in understanding the accumulation of political resources (material and prestigious)—is to seriously distort the nature of historical processes of change within Rwanda.

5. Although it is not used as a nominal in KinyaRwanda for these "social armies" the term *umuheto* (pl. *imiheto;* literal translation: "bow" or "arc") is constantly associated with army functions. Thus an army chief is *umutwaare w'umuheto* (sometimes *umutwaare w'ingabo*) and army prestations are *amakoro y'umuheto*. I have therefore adopted this nominal from time to time to refer to the corporate army group.

6. Kagame 1972:118–119, for example, notes Rwandan presence in the Bwishaza-Nyantango-Budaha area (the central corridor from the Rwandan heartland west to Lake Kivu) from the reign of Yuhi II (eight named kings before Rujugira) and even earlier for raids. But such references are to be treated with caution.

7. *Historique et Chronologie;* Kagame 1961; Kagame 1963; army placement during the reigns of Mmazimpaka, Rujugira, and Ndabarasa are considered in greater detail in my "Kings and Clans," Chapter III.

8. This is clear in many of the interviews conducted in Kinyaga by M. C. Newbury. Among others, see Bakomeza 27/7/70; Bagaruka 11/2/71; Gihura 10/7/70; Nyiramandwa 11/7/70; Rwaambikwa 18/2/71.

9. Here I use the term Tuutsi to refer to those who shared Rwandan state norms, though perhaps not originally tied to the Rwandan Central Court.

10. The standard orthography of Kinyarwanda has been retained here; *icy-ivugo* is pronounced *ichyivugo* in English phonetics. These poems are not usually passed down from generation to generation. Therefore, it is impossible to assign specific *ibyivugo* to specific time periods, or to trace the evolution of the genre. They are included here as representative of the ethic of military service, however, and by their close association to a set of cultural perceptions which I trace, by other data, to the period under discussion. The two poems reproduced here were selected because they include specific references to western peoples: "*Muhunde*" in the first (BuHunde is the area just northwest of Lake Kivu), "Bunyabungo" in the second (Bunyabungo is a general term referring to all the western areas, but most specifically to the area of BuShi, southwest of the lake). Because of the complexity of the language I have reproduced them in French as they appear in the published works cited; the original KinyaRwanda can be found in the same sources.

11. While it is not surprising that more poems are retained from more recent reigns, the pattern of these retentions, even if only suggestive, is still significant in terms of the timing of the processes proposed here, with a marked concentration around the reign of Rujugira. The figures are: Ruganzu, 2; Semugeshi, O; Nyamuheshera, 3; Gisanura, 6; Mazimpaka, 11; Rujugira, 30; Ndabarasa, 4; Seentabyo, 21; Gahindiro, 12; Rwogera, 30; Rwabugiri, 41. (Kagame 1954:*passim;* Kagame 1969:16 also mentions the importance of Runugira's reign in the emergence of this type of poetry.) The pattern of these poems indicates that changes in the ideology were associated with the political changes.

12. The fullest version available to me, and the one followed here, is that which appears in Bigirimwami 1971, No.23, V:68–75. Other versions are found in Vansina n.d. (a,b), Johanssen 1912:141–145, Pagès 1933:298–311, and my inter-

view in Kinyaga of Bagaruko 11/2/71. Rutungwa and Rubanza interviews, 17/2/71, apply this tale to nineteenth-century Rwandan campaigns to the west. Bogaruba notes that Gatabirora was a "Shi" from "Buhunde"; and in his *ecyivugo*, Ruganzu notes "I am Ruganzu, he who constantly seeks to attack the Bahunde."

13. Pagès 1933:298 notes that it is "Un de ceux [des récits] qui sont les plus goutés des Banyarwanda." Partial confirmation is given by the number of times it reappears in the published collections.

14. "Kabibi" may be a reference to "Mbeba"—"Ka" being the diminutive (or generic) prefix. "Mbeba" is the name of a legendary culture hero commonly associated with the Havu areas, but more directly associated with the forest-culture Tembo peoples who preceded the Havu in these areas west of the lake.

15. This theme also reflects a common image found among the western forest cultures which form the object of the parody here. See, for example, D. Biebuyck and M. Kahombo 1971, where Mwindo, the epic hero of the Nyanga, communicates with his aunt by means of a rope: pp. 27, 28, 99–100, 102, 106, 110, 114. See also p. 94, where Mwindo sets out on one of his adventures; he carries with him a rope, but leaves one end with his aunt, telling her: "You, my aunt, you stay here in the village of your birth . . . here is the rope. Remain with one end, holding it in your hand . . . if one day you feel that this rope has become still, if it does not move any more, then pay no more attention to where I have gone. Lo! The fire has dwindled—I am dead then." The repetition of this theme, a literary technique well illustrated in the various versions of this text, both relates the narrative to a larger corpus of Rwandan oral literature and demonstrates the way in which these stories are constructed, by reformulating certain "core images" to fit different narrative contexts. This literary device is considered in detail in Scheub 1971:*passim*. He summarizes the use of these core-images on page 3:

> The core cliché is the remembered element of the *ntsomi* tradition, the stable element; it is recalled during the production by means of a complex process of cuing and scanning whereby an artist dips into her rich repertory of *ntsomi* images and brings into performance appropriate images and image-segments which combine to create the finished work.

In their literary style, the *ibiteekerezo* also constantly remind the reader of the central role of the dramatic performance in their creation and retelling, another element stressed by Scheub in his analysis of the *ntsomi* form.

16. D. Biebuyck 1955, 1956–57.

17. Seven is also the perfect number in the cosmology of the western cultures, as indicated in both the content and stylistic features of their oral literature (Biebuyck and Mateene 1971:42n.4 and *passim*, Biebuyck 1979). This reference in the Rwandan text is therefore an accurate reflection of western cosmological patterns.

18. In fact the "Rw-" of the term "Rwanda" is pronounced so that it sounds somewhat like "Gw-", but the "Rw-" of Kinyarwanda is regarded as much more refined than the simple "Gw-". To pronounce the word in this way would be the equivalent of speaking "pidgin" in this language.

19. This tradition therefore reflects the widespread perception that the "cultural order" (in this case represented by the Court milieu) is signified by a proliferation of distinctions. The "chaos" of the forest, on the other hand, is shown in the abolition or ignorance of such distinctions, the essence of culture. The same discrepancy is shown in the culinary code noted below, where the forest peoples are associated with rotten food and its decay.

20. Published versions of the Nzira tale are found in Bigirimwami 1971, No.14, No.14:35, No.21:49; Pagès 1933:178–181; Coupez and Kamanzi 1972:222–254; see also Vansina n.d.(a).

21. The relativity of ethnic terms has been argued in many other contexts. For one noteworthy example, see James 1977.

22. The quotations, in order, are from my interviews with the following informants and on the following dates: Ntamati 6/2/73; Gahangamira 17/2/73; Rubanganjura 28/4/72; and a summary of Rubenga 4/5/72. For additional Ijwi accounts similar to those cited below, see Shabalikwa 3/3/72; Kasi 27/4/72; Kayirara 24/5/72; Gahangamire 17/2/73; Musemikweri 19/2/73; Rwanga 20/2/73; Gashoku 29/4/74; Gashina 6/5/74; Binombe 13/5/74; Kanyeju Kahise 18/5/74; Ntamusige 25/5/75. European observation concurs: "Kwidjwi est pour ainsi dire le grenier du lac. D'énormes quantités de produits agricoles sont exportées chaque année." R. Kandt 1904:578 (cited in Lugan 1977b:185).

23. I have argued elsewhere that one determinant of demand for ornamental commodities such as *ubutega* (discussed below) was the nature of the social hierarchy and social stratification associated with the internal evolution of royal court structures in Rwanda (D. Newbury 1980b). But while the demand for prestations for the royal court appears to have been effectively enforced in northwestern and southwestern Rwanda (Bugoyi and Kinyaga) only during the nineteenth century, local patterns of trade east and west across Lake Kivu (particularly at the northern end of the lake) are clearly much older, especially local trade in foodstuffs. The Court traditions sometimes distort these trade patterns in two ways. One is to portray all trade in goods ultimately destined for the royal Court as "prestations" whereas in fact they were traded through many hands; not all links in this chain of transfer were prestation-payers to the Rwandan Court. The other distortion in the Rwandan presentations is the common assumption that Court influence existed in the region for as long as the trade in such items existed—as proved (in the eyes of Court officials) by the fact that these items were "prestations." Data from recent research in the west and in Kinyaga demonstrate that such blanket claims are extravagant.

24. For illustrations of these see Pagès 1933, Plates Ib, XXIa; for references in the written sources see Pagès 1933:22–23 and 636–637. Other references to *ubutega* and their trade are found in D. Newbury, 1980b.

25. Early Tuutsi immigrants from the east appear to have married into local families, often those of higher social standing in the area. For examples of this in Kinyaga see M. C. Newbury, 1975.

26. These rulers are invariably referred to in the Rwandan Court literature as "abahinza," a term apparently retroactively bestowed (after conquest). The "abahinza" of at least two of these conquered "principalities," Busoozo and Bukunzi (both in southwestern Rwanda in its present boundaries) were always referred to locally as "bami." F. Nahimana argues similarly for the northern pre-Tuutsi kingdoms (Nahimana 1979:8–11). For other sources on these polities see Pagès 1933:335–345 (including genealogies of the ruling families of 16 of these Hutu "toparchies"), de Lacger 1939:82–89, Rennie 1972:15–25; and especially Pauwels 1962:*passim*.

27. My interviews on Ijwi with Nkrursiiza Kabulibuli 26/5/72; Gasarahinga 30/3/72; Ndengeyi 2/6/72. "Rugaba" was the last of the Mpembe *abami;* the use of the term here may well be anachronistic, since Rugaba is often used to refer to all such *abami.* Marriage ties between Mpembe and Bukunzi are also mentioned in Kinyaga interviews conducted by M. C. Newbury.

28. Rwandans also "explain" the westward movement of women in terms of their own ideology: only unmarried women who become pregnant are sent west, they say, onto the islands in Lake Kivu (Pagès 1933:52, Bourgeois 1954:424, Lestrade 1972:3–4). Sometimes this is said to be Ijwi itself, but people from Ijwi indicated yet another small island, Cihaya, south of Nkombo. When Rwandans

placed their pregnant unmarried women on the islands in this fashion, the Bany'Iju explain, they would go and save these women and marry them into their own families. Despite the disparaging tone in such Rwandan traditions—a reflection of literary themes—associated with sending women west, it is notable that the phenomenon apparently occurred frequently enough to require an explanation.

29. Further references to the close cultural ties binding the populations of Bugoyi with those west of Lake Kivu are found in Pagès 1933:661–662, 667, 676, 682. For Kinyaga see M. C. Newbury 1975:74–76.

30. In regions west of Rwanda, the polarizations between metropole and frontier were nowhere as strong as they were on the Rwandan frontier, as Central Court institutions penetrated the western areas. The people on Ijwi, for example, refer to those who live in the mountains west of Lake Kivu as "Babindi," a term of opprobrium. The same term is applied to people living on remote mountainous areas of Ijwi itself. The presence of such stereotypes, however, meant that there existed the potential for constantly expanding the frontier west—not by extending the definition of barbarian to yet new peoples farther west so much as by creating a polarized context in which those on the immediate border were continually seeking to identify themselves as "Rwandan," adopting an identity opposed to those further west.

BIBLIOGRAPHY

Barnes, T. A. 1923. *Across the Great Craterland to the Congo.* London.

Biebuyck, D. 1955. "Die Mumbo Instelling bij de Bonyanga (Kivu)," *Kongo Overzee* XXI, 5, 441–448.

———. 1956–1957. "Organisation politique des Nyanga: La Chefferie Ihana," *Kongo Overzee* XXII, 45, 301–341 and *Kongo Overzee* XXIII, 1–2, 58–98.

———. 1979. "Stylistic Techniques and Formulating Devices in the Mwindo Epic from the Banyanga," *Cultures et Développement* XI, 4, pp. 551–600.

Biebuyck, D. and M. Kahombo. 1971. *The Mwindo Epic.* Berkeley: University of California Press.

Bigirimwami, A. 1971. *Ibitekerezo.* Nyundo.

Bishikwabo, C. and Newbury, D. 1980. "Recent Research in the Area of Lake Kivu: Rwanda and Zaire" *History in Africa* VII, 23–45.

Bourgeois, R. 1954. *Banyarwanda et Barundi, II.* Brussels: ARSOM.

Coupez, A. and Kamanzi, Th. 1962. *Récits Historiques Rwanda.* Tervuren: MRAC.

———. 1970. *La littérature du cour Rwanda.* London: OUP.

d'Hertefelt, M. 1962. "Le Rwanda," in M. d'Hertefelt, A. Trouwborst, J. Scherer, *Les anciens royaumes de la zone Interlacustre Méridionale* (Tervuren).

de Lacger, L. 1939. *Le Ruanda.* Kabgayi.

Historique et Chronologie du Rwanda n.d., n.p. [Kigali].

James, W. 1977. "The Funj Mystique: Approaches to a Problem of Sudan History," in *Text and Context* (R. K. Jain, ed.) Philadelphia: ISHI.

Johanssen, E. 1912. Ruanda. *Kleine Anfänge-Grosse Aufgaben der Evangelischen Mission im Zwischenseengbeit Deutsch-Ostafrika.* Bethel bei Bielefeld.

Kagame, A. 1951. *La Poésie dynastique au Rwanda.* Brussels: ARSOM.

———. 1959. *La notion de génération appliquée à la généalogie dynastique et à l'histoire du Rwanda dès Xe–XIe Siècles à nos jours.* Brussels: ARSOM.

———. 1961. *Histoire des armées bovines dans l'ancien Rwanda.* Brussels: ARSOM.

————. 1963. *Les milices du Rwanda précolonial*. Brussels: ARSOM.

————. 1969. *Introduction aux grands genres lyriques de l'ancien Rwanda*. Butare: Editions Universitaires du Rwanda.

————. 1972. *Un abrégé de l'ethnohistoire du Rwanda*. Butare: Editions Universitaires du Rwanda.

Kajiga, J. 1956. "Cette immigration séculaire des Ruandais au Congo." *Bulletin Trimestriel du Centre d'Etude des problèmes sociaux Indigènes*, XXXII (1956) 5–65.

Kandt, R. 1904. *Caput Nili*. Berlin.

Lestrode, A. 1972. *Notes d'Ethnographie du Rwanda*. Tervuren: MRAC.

Lugan, B. 1977a. "Les réseaux commerciaux au Rwanda dans le dernier quart du XIXe Siècle," *Etudes d'Histoire Africaine* IX–X, 183–212.

————. 1977b. "Les poles commerciaux du lac Kivu à la fin du XIXe Siècle," *Revue Française d'Histoire d'Outre Mer* 64, 176–202.

Maquet, J. J. 1955. "Les pasteurs de l'Itombwe," *Science et Nature* VIII, 3–12.

Nahimana, F. 1979. "Les bami ou roitelets Hutu du corridor Nyabarongo-Mukungwa avec ses régions limitrophes," *Etudes Rwandaises* 12 (numéro spéciale), 1–25.

Newbury, D. 1975. "Rwabugiri and Ijwi," *Etude d'Histoire Africaine* VII, 155–173.

————. 1979. "Kings and Clans: Ijwi Island, c. 1780–1840." Ph.D. dissertation: University of Wisconsin-Madison.

————. 1980a. "The Clans of Rwanda: An Historical Hypothesis" *Africa* L, 4, 389–403.

————. 1980b. "Lake Kivu Regional Trade in the Nineteenth Century," *Journal des Africanistes* L, 1, 6–30

Newbury, M. C. 1974. "Deux lignages au Kinyaga," *Cahiers d'Etudes Africaines* XIV, 1, 26–39.

————. 1975. "The Cohesion of Oppression: A Century of Clientship in Kinyaga, Rwanda." Ph.D. dissertation: University of Wisconsin-Madison.

————. 1978. "Ethnicity in Rwanda: The Case of Kinyaga," *Africa* XLVII.

Pagès, A. 1933. *Un royaume hamite au centre de l'Afrique*. Brussels: ARSOM.

Pauwels, M. 1962. "Le Bushiru et son Muhinza ou roitelet Hutu," *Annali Lateranensi* XXII, 19–40.

Propp, V. 1968. *Morphology of the Folktale*. Austin: University of Texas Press.

Rennie, K. 1972. "The Precolonial Kingdom of Rwanda: A Reassessment," *Transafrican Journal of History* II, 2, 11–53.

Reisdorff, I. 1952. "Enquêtes foncières au Rwanda." n.p.

Scheub, H. 1975. *The Xhosa Ntsomi*. London: OUP.

Smith, P. 1975. *Le récit populaire au Rwanda*. Paris: Armand Colin.

Spitaels, R. 1953. "Transplantation des Banyaruanda dans le Nord Kivu," *Problèmes d'Afrique Centrale* VI, 2, 110–116

Vansina, J. 1962. *L'évolution du royaume Rwanda dès origines à 1900*. Brussels: ARSOM.

————. n.d.(a) "*Ibiteekerezo:* Historical Narratives from Rwanda," Chicago: Center for Research Libraries (CAMP). Among the relevant texts see Reel 1, Rugaanzu Ndori texts 6 and 8; and Reel 4, Ndahiro Cyaamatare text 14, Rugaanzu Ndori texts 14, 29, 42, 49, 51, 53, 57, 71, 87, 92.

————. n.d.(b) "*Ibiteekerezo:* Historical Narratives of Rwanda." On file at the Musée Royal de l'Afrique Centrale, Tevuren, Belgium; these texts differ from those noted above in n.d.(a).

BUILDING A STATE ON AN ALIEN FRONTIER

In the preceding case studies, the cultural differences between the frontiers-men and the host societies had not been profound; they have ranged from insignificant (Kpelle, Goba) to marginal (Ekie), to moderate (BaShu, Rwanda). This kind of cultural affinity between frontiersmen and their hosts characterized most of the internal African frontier. There were, nevertheless, instances when the cultural distance was considerably greater. Within the historic past, deep cultural contrasts on a frontier stemmed from the impact of outside forces that brought in new cultural identities. The next three articles are concerned with that kind of frontier. Two of them deal, respectively, with communities of escaped Bantu slaves in Somaliland and with a twentieth-century polyethnic community of settlers in Tanzania. The other, which follows, is a study by Adell Patton of the building of the Muslim Ningi state in the institutional vacuum of a "pagan" frontier area in northern Nigeria.

The immigrants were Muslim divines (*mallams*) and their families. Espousing a reformist quasi-millennial ideology, they moved, in protest against what they regarded as unjust taxation, to the frontier areas of a Muslim state. Here, they planned to build a community based on their convictions—an example of frontiersmen as utopians, but one that needs to be qualified and rigorously stripped of any Western connotations of the term "utopian." For the utopianism here was well within the local Muslim metropolitan cultural mold: the ideology (a term, when one deals with Islam, preferable to "religion") included a trading-and-raiding ethos, a consciousness of belonging to the cosmopolitan world of Islam, a militant and militaristic outlook, and a political culture that did not preclude ex-pansionist state-building. This cultural configuration stood in contrast with the host societies on the frontier—non-Muslim, pagan, parochial, and politically fragmented. The cultural isolation of the immigrants was exacerbated by the fact that the mallams knew that they were unlikely to be joined by others like them. At the same time, the integration with the local population could only be minimal. The resulting society was thus necessarily different from those we have seen built on culturally less alien frontiers.

The course taken by the mallam polity (which came to be eventually known as the Ningi state) exemplifies a series of paradoxes. The mallams tried to detach themselves from what they saw as an illegitimate Muslim social order, and set out to build a pure Muslim community; but it was the only social order that furnished them with a model for social construction

and the only one with which they shared a moral universe. Yet the very
hostility of the neighboring Muslim metropoles and the immigrants'
weakness meant that they had to seek refuge among pagan populations.
They sought to reproduce on the frontier a polity that would take its place
among the great metropolitan polities in the region from which the mallams came, but the polity lacked an urban base and had to rely for its
political and military recruitment on the local parochial societies. Their
dependence on pagan subjects *cum* allies made them accept these supporters as they were and precluded an aggressive imposition of Islam on
them; instead, the mallams sought to insure their support by magic perfor-
mances. This, in turn, precluded moral ties with the pagan supporters and
their ideological integration into the fledgling state. The relationship that
was built was one of instrumental cooperation: the supporters' uncertain
loyalty had to be paid for with booty. And to obtain booty, one had to
turn to raiding neighboring Muslim states.

The historical trajectory began with dreams of a reformist frontier
community and ended with a powerful predatory state. The state was
Muslim-ruled; but resting on a pagan base, it was increasingly dependent
in its dynastic politics on pagan sub-chiefs and alien slaves even while
modelling itself on the metropoles. In this respect, the story of Ningi
illustrates very well the role of the frontier as a reproducer of political
forms: whatever new social forms the frontiersmen may originally have
had in mind for the institutional vacuum that the frontier ideally represented, the success and growth of the community necessarily involved it in
the regional system, with all the conformities that such involvement imposed. The peculiarity of Ningi lay in that it had to deal with two regional
cultural traditions and it tried to reproduce one while having to build on
the other. In the other cases we have seen, there was no such cultural
disjunction.

—Editor

Adell Patton, Jr.

—————— 7 ——————

An Islamic Frontier Polity:
The Ningi Mountains of Northern Nigeria,
1846-1902

Frontier areas often provide refuge for those in rebellion against the metropolitan society. But once on the frontier, they face certain organizational problems. If there is a local population, they may meld into it, or keep apart from it, or try to use it for their own purposes. And the immigrants are often forced, sooner or later, into some kind of relationship with the metropolitan centers. This paper examines the case of a group of Hausa mallams (learned men) who fled their own society and established a polity on the fringe of the Sokoto Empire, in the Ningi mountains of the Jos Plateau of northern Nigeria. They came to live in an area occupied from time immemorial by vigorous but small-scale "pagan" societies, with rudimentary forms of organized political authority. At the same time, the immigrant mallams had not withdrawn entirely from the reach of the organized states—emirates led by the Sokoto Caliphate. Thus, paradoxically, this Muslim reformist polity came to depend on an alliance with its new non-Muslim neighbors in order to survive pressure from the Muslim states with which it had immensely greater cultural affinities. The contradictions that this entailed are at the heart of our story.

THE MALLAM REVOLT IN KANO

Kano Emirate was perhaps the most important of all the emirates in the Fulani-dominated Sokoto Empire that emerged after the successful Fulani *jihad* of 1804-1808. By the mid-nineteenth century, Kano had become not only an outstanding metropolitan center of Islamic learning but also the financial entrepot for the Caliphate. But like many empires, Sokoto began to suffer from the costs of expansion and its citizenry responded in various ways to the increasing burdens of rents and taxes. Most, to be sure, remained loyal; others joined dissident brotherhoods; and some fled to the fringes of the empire (Last 1970:345-357).

At the end of 1846, some sixteen Hausa learned men (mallams) and their families, led by Mallam Hamza, left the Islamic center of Tsakuwa in Kano Emirate, pursued by Kano forces for their refusal to pay the land tax (*kurdin kasa*)—a tax from which they had been exempted before the Fulani

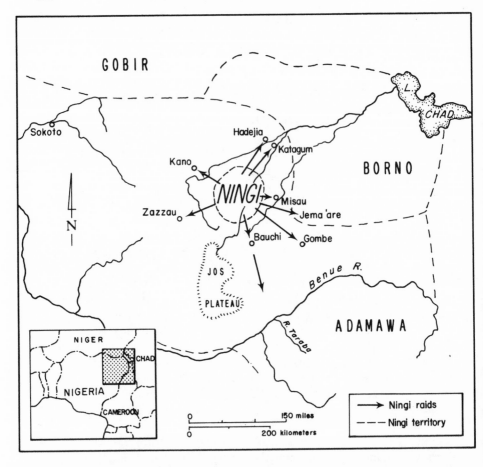

conquest (Patton 1975:125-179). The community (*jama'arsa*) established
itself in the Ningi mountains, a frontier area at the fringes of and surrounded by such Sokoto vassal states as Kano, Zazzau, Bauchi, Gombe,
Jema'are, Misau, Katagum, and Hadejia.

    The nucleus of Hamza's following came from a guild of free entrepre-
neurs. In time, this nuceleus developed into an informal Sufi religious
body. From its beginning in Iran in the eighth century, the Sufi tradition
contained elements of protest against social injustices and obsession with
material gain and worldly affairs; and it harbored ideas of salvation
through asceticism and spiritual discipline. In time, Sufism developed particular patterns of communal organization, various Sufi communities arose
over the centuries within Islamic societies, and Sufism became a subsidiary
but well established current within the broader Islamic stream (Jah
1973:93-96). Oral traditions at Tsakuwa and Ningi hold that Hamza had
prayed in seclusion for long periods of time in search of "The Way"
(Patton 1975:146). But unlike many Sufi movements, the one led by

Hamza never developed into a cohesive brotherhood (*tariq*). Instead, its retreat into a non-Muslim area on the frontier of Islam made it the founder of a predatory polity.

THE NINGI FRONTIER ZONE

The area into which Hamza's mallam community moved was peripheral to the Islamicized metropolitan centers of northern Nigeria sociologically, culturally, ethnically, politically, and geographically. In this sense, it may be regarded as a frontier zone. The Ningi area is the northernmost extention of the Jos Plateau massif. It is mountainous, incised with valleys suitable for plain and terraced agriculture. Most of it is some 2,000 feet above sea level, the central area rising to 3,000 feet and peaks reaching 6,000. The Ningi area of our story nearly coincides with present Ningi Division, which is just under 2,000 square miles. The area experiences a completely rainless season and it generally shares in the hardships of the "famine zone" of the Western Sudan (Renner 1926:583-596).

Even in the remote past, Ningi appears to have been an isolated fringe area from the perspective of the flatlands on which arose the old Hausa city-states. It shows a great deal of cultural and linguistic diversity and it had never developed, within historic times at least, important integrative networks among its communities. It is impossible to know what the population of Ningi was when the mallams arrived. The first assessment in colonial times, done in 1908 (Groom 1910), gave a total population of some 21,500, some 17,000 of these being of "original" stock. Among these, the largest groups were the Warji (ca. 7,000), the Pa'a (ca. 5,000), and the Buta (over 3,000); the other groups were each in the range of a thousand or less. These figures suggest that the non-Muslim population that the mallams found and that came to represent their "reservoir" of economic and military strength was in the range of a score of thousands.

What historical population movements we can reconstruct appear to have consisted of small groups of migrants who sought out unoccupied areas and often absorbed previous inhabitants or were absorbed by them. The result was the presence, in historic times, of several ethnic groups, the chronology of whose appearance in the area can be roughly established. The Buta (with their relatives the Ningi, who, though few in numbers, gave their name to the area) seem to represent the most ancient, non-Hausa-speaking stratum; they are the northernmost extension of the Benue-Congo language family. The Warji belong to a branch of the Afro-Asiatic languages concentrated around Lake Chad. The Siri are Chadic speakers from the Kano area, and they arrived in the Ningi area well before the 1800's. The Chama and Basa, of the Benue-Congo family, followed. The Chadic Pa'a came next, from Bauchi, sometime in the early nineteenth century. Thus, the migration of the Hausa mallams from Kano in 1846 was but the last important influx of outsiders into the Ningi frontier.

Surviving oral traditions tell us nothing of the history of these groups; they do not even yield myths of origin or commonly accepted founding heroes; and the earlier arrivals did not always allow subsequent immigrants to assimilate (Patton 1975:45). Slave raiding by the old Kano kingdom and, in the nineteenth century, by neighboring emirates served to reduce the population and probably confuse the mythical charters of the Ningi societies (Patton 1979b:18). And the establishment of the Ningi state by the immigrant mallams from Kano and the consequences of this intrusion brought further confusion into historical self-perceptions.

The political systems of the Ningi plateau peoples were highly localized (Patton 1975:56-58), though there existed a few supra-ethnic networks of social relations: some ethnic groups were connected by institutionalized "joking relationships," most of them exchanged wives, and all were connected to trade networks. Villages were autonomous and the process of fission within them often led to secondary settlements at some distance from parent villages. Each settlement was dominated by its founding patrilineage. The lineage head was usually its most senior male member, and he acted on behalf of the autonomous village community in its dealings with outsiders and as its priest of the land cult. Above several such lineage heads stood what was the highest local authority—a *tsafi*, the ritual head of the sacred shrine center linking several autonomous villages and himself usually the head of his own patrilineage.

The shrine thus provided the only formal basis for a certain degree of socio-political integration above the village level. Within the territory of a shrine, people came to consult about crop planting, famines, and judicial matters; they also mobilized for defense against external threat. The parochial nature of political relations can be seen from the fact that, for example, the Warji people (numbering perhaps 5,000 in the mid-nineteenth century) were under the jursidiction of seven tsafi (Izard 1918a,b). One of them, at Beima, was the civil and ritual senior over the others, and another, at Ranga, acted as the head in times of war. Some competition no doubt existed among the tsafi within a single language cluster. While the overall hierarchy followed the sequence of the foundation of settlements and their shrines, succession struggles among autonomous lineages did take place when a senior tsafi died.

For the surrounding emirates, the position of these plateau societies was broadly defined by Muslim law, which allowed them either to enslave populations refusing to convert to Islam or require them to pay *kharaj*, land tax (Khadduri 1955:46-47). Oral traditions in Ningi hold that the Sokoto Caliphate pursued a policy of taxation when possible, while raiding those many villages that refused to pay tribute. The Buta and Warji sometimes organized themselves, each into a temporary quasi-federation, in answer to incursions from Kano and the Caliphate, but the organization remained a purely military one. In time, the military leadership solidified among the Buta: Gwarsum began (ca. 1807) a line of nine leaders which stretched into the early twentieth century. When the Emir of Kano Ibrahim Dabo (1816–1846) invaded Buta territory, Gwarsum defeated him at Basshe. Gwarsum's victory was not decisive but it did set the stage for continuing resistance to the emirates that flared up periodically through the nineteenth century.

It should be noted that the opposition was not strictly that between the mountaineers on one side and the Muslims on the other. For example, Kano and Bauchi Emirates competed in their efforts to impose tribute on the mountaineers. The Buta around Marra and Dua villages paid tribute to Bauchi; those around Burra paid it to Kano, as did the kindred Ningi people and the Kuda. The nearby Pa'a, on the other hand, successfully resisted Bauchi while themselves imposing tribute on the Sira. Thus, the mountaineers were not strangers to relatively complex tributary relationships, nor were they entirely on the receiving end of predatory activities. Nor was the movement of the mallams into their area in 1846 without precedent. When the Sokoto Caliphate established its rule over Hausaland in 1808, some Hausa leaders fled to the fringes of Ningi with their followers, and some of these joined the Buta in their resistance to Sokoto.

THE RECEPTION OF THE MALLAMS BY THE MOUNTAINEERS

Hamza's progression into the Ningi interior was gradual. At the end of 1846, the mallams settled in the hills of eastern Burra. Burra at that time was headed by tsafi Gira and it was under Kano control. During the dry season of 1847, the mallams moved completely beyond Kano control and settled among the Buta at Dua, under Bauchi jursidiction but under the direct control of Dan Daura, the Sarki (chief) of Marra and a Fulani. Dan Daura welcomed them. In Hamza, he saw a learned man who knew many secrets and whose blessing would be beneficial; Hamza would be a good teacher for his son and would enhance Marra's prestige. Dan Daura even took Hamza to Bauchi to introduce him to Emir Ibrahim, who granted Hamza permission to stay at Dua. But the Emir warned Dan Daura: "Some day these mallams will prove too strong for you; you better leave them with me." Nevertheless, Dan Daura returned to Marra with Hamza and gave him food and lodging, and the mallams settled at Dua.

The Buta first and then the other mountaineers easily accepted the new mallam settlement in their midst. As metropolitan attempts at oppression were growing, the mountaineers became more open to the idea of larger-scale organization and more receptive to the idea of leaders knowledgeable in the affairs of the neighboring states and their modes of warfare. While their own political culture militated against a centralized organization arising from among themselves, they seemed to be open to the idea of a profitable alliance with an alien organization.

There was also, it appears, a certain messianic element in at least some local groups that made the mallams welcome. Buta traditions speak of prophecies in the past that foretold that mallamas with "little black bags"—leather satchels containing the Qur'an—would come to liberate them from tributary servitude (Sarkin Dua 1973). Some of these stories of prophecies are undoubtedly *ex post facto* elaborations; but it is also not unlikely that some echoes of utopian Islamic thought in Hausaland had reached the mountaineers through individuals acquainted with metropolitan affairs. Such prophecies should have found fertile ground in the anxieties of the mountaineers as they saw the power of the emirates closing in on them. In 1832, yet another emirate, Misau, was established by Fulani from Borno, followed two years later by Jema'are—both on Ningi's eastern flank. The inexorable course of events may well have been making the peoples of Ningi ready to accept new leadership that promised them salvation.

There were reasons, then, why the mountaineers should have welcomed Hamza and his mallam community. Hamza had come from cosmopolitan Kano, he possessed full knowledge of Caliphate affairs and its mode of warfare, and the polity he was about to found could therefore help them to resist Sokoto expansion (Vansina 1973). And there may also have been an element of sympathy: the people knew that Hamza had broken the law of the Caliphate in the same way that some of them had from time to time when they refused to pay tribute.

THE VISION OF THE NEW STATE

In 1848, the Hamza movement took on millennial overtones that echoed the millennial currents in Islam that began to gather strength in the eighteenth century. The impending appearance of the Mahdi and the end of the world were expected, and injustice, oppression, and social disorder were all signs of the Mahdi's coming. The situation in which Hamza and his community found themselves no doubt reinforced such a view of the world. They were in the midst of non-Muslim mountaineers and at the mercy of a small provincial Sarki, in stark contrast with their previous position, when they enjoyed privileges, close ties to the pre-jihad dynasty at Tsakuwa, a successfully developing Sufi community, respect in Qur'anic circles, and independence as free producers. They could observe the Buta paying tribute to the Sarki and may have seen the new setting as not very different from the one they had fled.

The strains of their new situation appear to have plunged Hamza into a psychological crisis and he entered into communion with God (for a discussion of this dynamic, see Brenner 1973). However he might at the time have perceived his mission, Hamza began preaching to the Buta, calling on them to fight for their freedom. The millennial character of Hamza's preaching is preserved in the following oral text collected at Dua, in which Hamza says to the mountaineers:

Some people, red people will be coming and they will conquer everyone
and stop you from fighting one another . . . and take power from you.
No one will have the right of enslaving anyone nor the right to fight
Kano and Bauchi. After the red people again another group will come.
They will be black, and they will fight and defeat all (Sarkin Dua 1973).

Whatever concrete actions Hamza now wished to take, it had to be in
a setting dominated by military power, and that power was overwhelmingly on the side of the neighboring emirates who saw the Ningi area as a
natural source of captives and tribute. In brief, the state power of the
enemies had to be countered by some kind of state organization.

THE CREATION OF THE NEW STATE

At the end of 1848, Hamza and his mallams began the moves by which
they would eventually transform the acephalous societies around them
into a centralized polity without resorting to conquest (which, in any case,
would probably not have succeeded). Hamza built a mosque and word of
his presence spread. He combined traditional Islamic practices with traditional Ningi ones into an appealing amalgam with magic (*Sihr*) at the
center of it. He also began to side with the Buta in their perennial disputes
with Dan Daura. The latter thereupon accused Hamza of intriguing
among his subjects and mustered his troops. In the first confrontation at
Dua, the mallams and the Buta defeated the Bauchi troops and Dan Daura
had to flee for his life.

Hamza now turned to political action on a broader scale. His messengers propagated among the mountaineers the mystical meaning of his
victory. The people of Burra, Tiffi, Ari, Guda, Badunga, Rabi, Kuluki,
and other places came to Hamza, and he shared the victory booty with
them and offered their leaders positions of responsibility. He told them:

You have now succeeded because you have found amongst you a person
like me; come to my fold and I will deliver you from the obligations to
the Fulani— the Fulani who are unjust, the Fulani who impose upon you
a lot of duties and impose upon you things which you cannot pay
(Imam Mahmud 1957-62:168).

As Hamza continued to call upon the mountaineers to rebel against
the Caliphate, he combined his preaching with his Sihr magic. Word of his
extraordinary powers spread: he could throw paper in the air which would
remain suspended; he could mount a mat floating in the air; he could
stretch his tongue around his head like a turban, or stretch his leg to the
length of two spears and bring it back to normal size, or resurrect dead
ants. Hamza would have someone kill ants, have them placed in baskets,
and resurrect them. He would then tell the people: "Even if the Fulani kill
you, that is how I will return your lives to you; nobody will ever be able
to defeat you as long as I am amongst you" (Imam Mahmud 1957-62:169).

The Emir of Bauchi sent troop reinforcements to Dan Daura for an attack on Hamza at Dua. Hamza's own troops now numbered probably well over two hundred; he also had weapons and horses captured at the first encounter and additional troops from newfound followers. Hamza set a pattern in these encounters, one that was followed by his successors. As the troops formed for battle, Hamza stayed behind, reciting prayers for victory from the Holy Book. Being his own *Sarkin Yaki* (war chief), he would, upon completing the recitation, rush out in front of the troops toward the enemy (Patton 1975:158-159). When the Bauchi forces arrived at Dua, Hamza appeared before them and showed them his magical skills. This apparently astonished them, and some of the troops retreated. The bulk of the Bauchi forces were routed and Dan Daura was killed. This victory marked the foundation of Ningi as a state. The new state incorporated with varying degrees of firmness and reliability most of the mountaineers, with the exception of the people of Sonoma valley and the Warji (Patton 1975:149).

News of Hamza's activities reached Sokoto during the Caliphate of Amir al-Muminin Ali ben Bello (1837-1859). In the educated circles of Sokoto, Hamza was acknowledged as both a learned man and a magician (Houdas 1966 [1899]:356), and his new activities were no doubt seen with great apprehension by Sokoto and the other emirates. Indeed, Hamza had already begun to raid. He burned the town of Gau, an important fief of Bauchi, forcing the inhabitants to resettle farther away from Ningi. His raiders attacked fiefs and estates that had an abundance of food, cattle, horses, and people to enslave. This established the basic raiding style which Ningi warriors were to follow throughout the 19th century.

About 1849, Emir Ibrahim of Bauchi made preparations for war against the mallams. The latter had built a number of compounds surrounded by walls of rock at Dua, which they did not want to risk being destroyed. Hence, Hamza decided to confront Ibrahim at Jengere rather than at Dua. But the Ningi forces were no match for the Bauchi and were routed. How exactly Hamza met his death remains unknown—his body was never found. Local tradition explains the failure of Hamza's magical powers in this instance. As the battle was about to unfold, it is said, the Pa'a troops rushed out to fight before Hamza could complete his prayers and incantations. As the war leader, Hamza felt compelled to lead the attack. Mounting his horse prematurely and brandishing his spear, he rode out in front of his troops toward the enemy and to his death. He was about sixty years old.

THE FOUNDING OF THE SECOND MALLAM STATE

The Hamza period of the mallam state ended in 1849, after two years at Dua. Hamza's fragile state, still tied ambiguously to millennial hopes, had collapsed and the mallams now faced a number of problems: sheer survival, the need to select a new leader, and the fear among their new non-

Muslim adherents that Kano and other emirates might join Bauchi in stamping out all signs of Ningi rebelliousness. Indeed, the tsafi leaders of the Buta, Kuda, and Pa'a quickly withdrew to their own areas, leaving the leaderless mallams virtually alone. It was clear that the mountaineers' adherence to the mallam state was opportunistic and that they were mainly interested in booty. A new and more viable state would thus require institutional intervention in mountaineer affairs in order to insure loyalty.

The mallams and their families—altogether probably a little over fifty men, women, and children—decided to move some twenty miles away from Dua into the less accessible mountain interior. They chose Tabela, a Pa'a village. Hamza's widow Atta played a decisive role in the informal process of selecting the new leader (and she continued to exert her influence in Ningi affairs for the following quarter century). Since Hamza's sons were too young to rule, leadership passed to Mallam Ahmadu, Hamza's brother. The non-Muslims of the original alliance accepted the new leader.

The reformist features of Hamza's original vision had by now almost completely receded. Rather than move in the direction of a Sufi brotherhood—as it probably would have had it remained in Kano—the community was on the way to becoming a predatory frontier polity. Ahmadu gave the fledgling state an outright military cast. He made forays into Bauchi territory and the renewed Ningi belligerency caused some concern in Kano. Barth, who visited the area in 1851, observed that the Buta of Burra continuously seized Kano couriers en route to Bauchi and confiscated the messages (Barth 1965 [1857]: 618). Bauchi finally responded with a war that lasted nearly seven years and in which it lost some 7,000 men. Bauchi received incidental help from another European traveler who visited the Emir's war camp outside of Tabela. In December 1855, Dr. Edward Vogel wrote to his father in Germany an account of his encounter with the mountaineers:

> On a scouting trip which we made to the enemy city situated on a rock, we fell into ambush and were greeted with a hail of poison arrows. My Fellata [Fulani] companions fled and left me behind to cover their retreat. I was able to do this with a gun, killing one of the attackers and causing the other to flee. The Sultan sent me a fat wether [sheep gelding] that evening for the deed. You must know that I can use guns skillfully now, and can shoot hens and ducks with a bullet if I don't have buckshot (Wagner 1860:279).

Mallam Ahmadu did not outlast the war and died about 1855. But the emir's siege of Tabela was unsuccessful, the losses were costly, and the task of suppressing the mountaineers appeared impossible. The war dragged on for nearly another two years before the Emir of Bauchi withdrew his forces. The cessation of the open hostilities gave time to both sides to attend to much neglected business.

Mallam Abubakar Dan Maje emerged as the successor of Ahmadu. Though unrelated to Hamza, he was a logical choice: the circumstances called for an able warrior, and Dan Maje had fought and had been wounded at Jengere in the battle against Bauchi. Dan Maje decided that Tabela was no longer safe as headquarters for the weakened mallam state—its non-Muslim allies were now reduced in the main to the Pa'a, the Kuda, and the Buta. Since each group had its own area of settlement, the mallams sought a similar area of their own, one that would provide added protection and would also be almost exclusively Muslim. The move may be seen as further "naturalization" of the mallams in Ningi—a step toward becoming another "ethnic" group among others and a realistic admission of the need for its own territorial base. But it also implies a retreat from the supra-ethnic stance of Hamza's early efforts. With the help of several hundred Kuda warriors, Dan Maje took over the "fortress" of Lungu, a geological cubbyhole surrounded by high mountain walls, expelling the fewer than 300 Ningi who were occupying it—an action that brought little or no outcry from the surrounding groups. The mallams then resettled in their new impregnable capital and from here Dan Maje organized his administration. His council consisted of the Hausa scholars (*ulama*) only, less than a dozen in number. The senior counselor was also the war chief, Sarkin Yaki.

In about 1860, Dan Maje conquered the Warji and established with them a tributary alliance. Once the mallam state's control over the surrounding countryside was achieved, raiding could be conducted from a secure base. The Warji were useful allies that joined him en route to raids on Katagum and other eastern emirates. The frankly military state grew remarkably in power under Dan Maje's guidance: toward the end of his rule, he had nearly 3,000 horsemen under his command.

In 1870, after losing two of his war commanders while plundering southern Bauchi, Dan Maje himself died in an engagement at Toro from an arrow wound behind his ear. His followers buried his body in a secret place to prevent it from falling into Bauchi hands and being used to immobilize his spirit. But the secret spot, in the Kwandon Nkaya vicinity, was discovered by a Bauchi official who exhumed the corpse, cut off the head, and took it to the Emir of Bauchi.

THE MALLAM STATE AT ITS ZENITH

It is a measure of the strength the Ningi state had achieved that Dan Maje's death had no effect on its stability. Indeed, the state reached its apogee in the following decade under the leadership of his successor, Haruna Karami.

There were new factors to strengthen the cohesion of the new state. A bureaucratic structure gradually developed. The office of *Mallam*—as the ruler of the state was called—had become institutionalized by the 1870's.

The Mallam now determined who would be the leader of each of the non-Muslim peoples, and he thus stood at the top of the Ningi hierarchy. And the military character of the state and of the Mallam's leadership meant that there was no hesitation to use force against any transgressor against authority, be he an ordinary mallam or a tsafi.

The scholars, ulama, served as the supreme council to the Mallam. The raids were not undertaken haphazardly but were a matter of carefully examined policy. The council planned the raids and also engaged in divination to determine whether a raid would be successful. A consensus was required on most issues, and the Mallam and the ulama also consulted the tsafi of the non-Muslim peoples. The territorial segments thus participated in the state processes and often the decisions sanctioned at the top came from the bottom (Patton 1975:93,196).

Other offices were consonant with the predatory character of the state, and Haruna himself introduced some changes in offices and created a number of new ones. The office of the war chief, Sarkin Yaki, was detached from the Mallamship, its incumbent now being one of the senior counselors to the Mallam. The military offices of *barde* initially reflected a segmented military system: every compound in the mountain fortress had its own barde, more or less equal to and autonomous of any other. Haruna put all the barde under a single head, and these accomplished warriors now formed the front ranks in battle. The barde system also became the vehicle for the distribution of booty. The booty was divided into five parts; besides the Mallam, the participants in the raids, the elder leaders in the capital, the junior ulama, and the barde themselves received, each as a group, one part. By dispensing the booty further down, into the compounds, a barde could gain followers and sometimes divert loyalties from the Mallam. Since the power of the barde decreased whenever raids were discontinued and peace prevailed, they tended to align themselves with the more warlike factions in later struggles over succession.

Slaves held certain offices. Mohammed Yayo, a slave seized in a raid at Maganni in Kano, occupied the office of *Maga Yaki*, concerned with the surveillance and scouting that preceded a raid. One important function of scouting was to spy on the movement of tribute to Sokoto in order to capture it. The scouting reports of the Maga Yaki went directly to the barde who collectively decided whether to mount a foray. Another slave held the office of *Shamaki*, in charge of all the palace slaves, who were quite numerous in Haruna's time; this office became influential in later palace politics. Ordinary slaves did maintenance work and some farming, and served in Haruna's army.

The mallam state was not without its share of internal troubles—primarily succession troubles. There were no precise rules of succession to the Mallamship. To become leader, one had to be a Hausa scholar but not necessarily the eldest scholar. In contrast to the hereditary system of the emirates, it was merit in war that primarily determined who led in Ningi.

However, there were always several mallams who were experienced warriors and who might be tempted to bid for power. And there were always the sons and relatives of the deceased ruler who were apt to feel that they had a special, even if not exclusive, claim to the Mallamship.

When the electoral council chose Haruna to be the ruler in 1870, the sons of Hamza, the founder of the state, contested the selection. When two of them realized that their pretentions had no hope, they went away to raid in Zazzau and died there. Hamza's third son, Iboro, stayed in Ningi; but failing to gain palace support, he went to Tutu, the vassal chief of the Buta at Burra, and obtained his adherence. In the fight that ensued, the retired chief Zeriya of Burra came to the aid of Haruna and Tutu was defeated and removed from his position as Sarkin of Burra. Haruna thereupon restored the chieftaincy to the Gira family, then living in exile. The new chief, Abduraman, became the first Buta chief to convert to Islam. In the meantime, Iboro prevailed upon the Pa'a to revolt against Haruna. Haruna killed a number of Pa'a in battle before the opposing forces made peace by swearing on the Qur'an, and Iboro too swore fealty to Haruna. These facts suggest the continued precariousness of the non-Muslim adherence to the Ningi state. While the state had the power to impose chiefs on these subordinate groups, dissension at the core could quickly radiate out to the vassal peoples and, in times of crisis, they could play a significant part in the outcome.

The relations between the Ningi state under Haruna and the non-Muslim mountaineers continued to be tributary. They supplied the mallams with food and, as the state's foundations were strengthened in Dan Maje and Haruna's time, the annual tribute from these people came increasingly at the end of Ramadan or of Salla. The mallams themselves did not farm in this period, and administrative offices were not based on fiefs. "Warring was their farming" according to Ningi informants (Patton 1975:235-236). The Warji, however, always posed a problem. A flat agricultural plain separated their plateau from the mallam state, and they were farther from it than from the powerful emirates. It is for this reason, it appears, that the Warji maintained a fragile balance in their relations with Ningi on the one hand and Kano on the other, while each of these engaged periodically in re-conquering the Warji to insure their loyalty.

The Ningi government levied no taxes on its citizens and vassals, preferring instead to collect gaisuwa (gifts) in the form of chickens, goats, foodstuffs, and the like. This brought it new adherents. Thus, some Fulani and others, fleeing oppressive taxation, came to Ningi from Katagum, Gombe, Zazzau, and Kano, and they were able to provide Ningi with information about places that were rich and raidable. These events indicate Ningi's increasingly more aggressive political—rather than merely military—posture in the local inter-state system.

It was Haruna's achievement to routinize the predatory functions of the Ningi state. Reacting to what promised to be Ningi's permanent presence in the area, the emirates tried to contain it physically: Bauchi and Kano built *ribats* (frontier fortresses) as a barrier to raids and appear to have resettled some of the non-Muslim populations who resided within the radius of Ningi raiding. But the emirates had also to contend with Ningi's skillful use of their common Islamic traditions as diplomatic and strategic weapons. Foremost among these was the concept of "peace," *aman* (see Khadduri 1955:163-166 and al-Mawardi 1915).

Haruna negotiated (*aman*), "the peace," first with Kano and then Bauchi in the mid-1870's. The peace legitimized Ningi as an independent state and it ushered in new peaceful relations with Sokoto as well. For in Islamic theory, the aman placed Ningi in a peaceful relationship with all the other surrounding emirates. This periodic interest in compromise involved Ningi in some long-distance diplomacy. Arabic documents show that Ningi messengers went as far as Sokoto once in the early 1870's and on several occasions to Kano with diplomatic immunity (Kanoprof Vol. 1,#17:161).

Sokoto's conditions for peace stipulated that the Kano merchants would not go to Ningi with horses for sale and that Ningi would not purchase horses in Kano. The non-Muslims in the Ningi area did not own horses before the mallams set up their state. Islamic law forbade selling horses to them and it was Caliphate policy to extend the prohibition to the ever troublesome Ningi, with its amalgam of Muslim and non-Muslim. Horses, of course, brought some parity to the parties in a war—Ningi's possession of horses explains much of its success in its forays against the emirates. Dan Maje could produce a force of 3,000 horsemen, and under Haruna the number reached 4,000. For the emirates, there was no hope of neutralizing, let alone defeating, Ningi unless the trade in this critical military resource could be stopped. However, at the time, the Caliphate area was experiencing monetary instability because of the inflation of cowries that had begun in the 1850's, and captives from raids came to constitute for Sokoto a subsidiary currency. It appears that this led some wayward Fulani princes in search of slaves to take horses to Ningi to trade them there for slaves.

In practice, the peace of aman provided Ningi with the time to heal its wounds from the losses it suffered at the hands of Caliphate forces. Ningi usually appealed to aman after military losses to its principal adversaries, Bauchi and Kano, and it returned to the attack when there was renewed promise of success. Thus, in the late 1870's, when succession problems festered in Zazzau, Kano, and Katagum, Haruna broke the peace and resumed raids against the emirates. With an army of nearly 4,000 horsemen, the Ningi state had become haughty and apparently even began to harbor hopes that the crisis prevailing in the metropole might provide it with an opportunity to seize control at the center. In effect, the frontier state was in a position to take a political offensive against the metropole and began to see itself as part of it. It may well be, of course, that the mallams had in fact seen themselves all along as being only in temporary exile.

Ningi began to form external alliances with factions within the emirates. In 1878, Ningi lent a helping hand to the *Galadima* (senior titled official) Suleimanu, a Hausa who had tried without success to become Emir of Zazzau. Rival aspirants to the thrones of both Zazzau and Bauchi had also offered Haruna substantial holdings in slaves and territory for his help (Patton 1975:236). During the Bauchi civil war of 1881, several dissident groups allied themselves with Ningi. A vassal people, the Gere, joined Ningi and threw off Bauchi domination. And some Fulani dissidents fled Bauchi City and formed an alliance with Ningi in order to maintain their independence.

About 1880, following another Ningi peace request to Amir al-Muminin Mu'adh of Sokoto, the mountaineers agreed to desist from fighting Muslims "in the East, West, South, and North" (Arewa House 1973). This suggests that at one time or another Ningi had taken on all of the neighboring emirates and, further, that in Haruna's time Ningi was apparently recognized as an autonomous power by the Amir who dealt with it directly.

Mallam Haruna is regarded as the most powerful leader in Ningi history, one who made Ningi in the 1870's into a local power to be reckoned with. Under him, Ningi had, again and again, cut off Kano from its usual source of captives for use on its plantations and as a kind of currency (Last 1970:349, Lovejoy 1978:343). And by successfully resisting and attacking Sokoto, as well as negotiating with it on terms of equality, Ningi asserted its position vis-à-vis the highest legitimizing power of the region. In the oral history of the Caliphate, "Ningi" became a common term for the place from which raiders were to be expected (Patton 1980:6).

TRADE

If Ningi's political relations with the emirates were in a constant state of flux because of the predatory nature of the mallam state, so was its trade with them. Before the mallams settled there, trade in the Ningi area was apparently relatively desultory despite the fact that Ningi was linked into the trade route network that also involved, among other centers, Kano and Bauchi (Izard 1918a:13). The commodities that the Ningi peoples could offer to the outside were few; their terraced agriculture served essentially their subsistence needs and their area was relatively deficient in natural resources. Internally, however, barter trade was ubiquitous in Ningi, with iron and medicines being of special importance (Sirawa Elders 1973:2, Butawa Elders 1973:4).

The coming of the mallams and especially Dan Maje's rule (ca. 1856-1870) introduced a new dimension to trade activity in Ningi and on the Plateau in general. Although Gerhard Rohlfs, who visited Bauchi in 1867, reported that the decade of 1856-66 was a peaceful one (Rohlfs

1874:153), peace did not mean an end to hostility between Ningi and Bauchi. The earlier freedom of travel was gone and there was insecurity and fear both within the Ningi mountains and along the trade routes. About 1868 or earlier, Dan Maje disrupted the trading activities of the Hausa tin-smelters at Ririwai-n Kano, and disrupted them twice again as they kept moving their settlement (Roberts 1918, Tambo 1979:5,12, Morrison 1974).

In spite of the military instability, neutral cosmopolitan markets nevertheless appear to have developed in the Jos area and at Sanga (Lovejoy 1979, Morrison 1976:195-197,203). Before or about 1875, cowries reached the area to become the basic currency. Sanga, according to Morrison, was also the only center in the area for trade in captives (generally, captives went north and big horses went south). Ningi increased its revenue by releasing captives, caught in raids, for ransom in cowries at these neutral markets.

UNRESOLVED INTERNAL PROBLEMS OF THE NINGI STATE

The mallam state at its zenith did not succeed in resolving a number of internal problems, the foremost being that of succession. Haruna's death about 1886 was followed once more by a succession dispute among three candidates: Gajigi, Haruna's younger brother; Inusa, son of a Ningi mallam; and Usman Dan Yaya, holder of the powerful office of Head Barde and possibly Sarkin Yaki in Haruna's time. The candidates were first-generation Ningians. In the competition, Gajigi gained the support of the powerful palace slaves, who in turn secured the support of the surrounding tsafi. The slave leaders slew Inusa, while Dan Yaya fled the capital and settled among the Pa'a.

As Mallam, Gajigi raided only once. He pursued a policy of peace and sent letters to Bauchi and Kano, requesting aman. The reasons for Gajigi's unwarlike stance remain unclear. Millennial thought continued to reach Ningi throughout its history, and Gajigi may have been influenced by the *Isawa mallamai*—believers, in the context of Islam, in the Second Coming of Jesus, *Isa*—who had been given refuge by his brother Haruna in 1870 and who were Gajigi's own devoted palace supporters. In the new relaxed climate, the mountaineers began to move freely and unmolested between Bauchi and Kano as in the old days before the Ningi state. But the movement toward economic integration with the surrounding emirates was soon cut short.

Dan Yaya, who had retained the office of Head Barde, did not want peace with Sokoto and began to intrigue against Gajigi and gained widespread support. Both Haruna and Gajigi had allowed much of the booty to remain in the Head Barde's hands, and Dan Yaya proceeded to distribute gowns, cattle, women, and slaves to the non-Muslim mountaineers, particularly to the Kuda warriors. He also got himself elected chief (sarki) over the Pa'a. Failing to gain the support of the Buta and Warji, he managed to prevent the annual gifts (gaisuwa) and various supplies from reaching Gajigi, and this caused a famine in the capital.

Dan Yaya also persuaded Gajigi's nephews to join forces with him, and to mask his own ambitions, he began to support one of them, Adamu Da, who was hoping to obtain the Mallamship for himself. He accused Gajigi of ineptness and held that if the state was to survive, Gajigi had to be deposed. In 1889, the supporters of Gajigi and Dan Yaya clashed outside the palace. The Kuda locked out Gajigi, preventing him from taking refuge inside the palace. Some of his supporters fled and the abandoned Gajigi was stabbed to death by his nephew. Thereupon, in an about face, Dan Yaya warned the ulama not to entrust the leadership to one who had killed his blood uncle; with their support, he entered the palace as the new leader of Ningi. Several of the remaining sons of Haruna fled Ningi and turned to raiding the Birnin Gwari, perhaps joining Ningi's enemies among the emirates.

Dan Yaya began to consolidate his power by killing a large number of Gajigi's supporters, including one of the Isa mallams, or chasing them from Ningi. To avenge Gajigi's selling of his mother Ramata into slavery, Dan Yaya sold Gajigi's children (Malam Yahaya 1973). Dan Yaya turned to a warlike policy. Needing a frontier lookout to guard against Kano raiders from the north, he cleared a large area of bush and made it into a slave farming estate known as Kafin Dan Yaya. He was now ready to raid.

He broke the peace by raiding in several directions—against Hadejia, Katagum, Kano, and Bauchi emirates. To end the Warji's tributary alliance with Kano, he defeated them at Chan-Chan. But the introduction of firearms into the Caliphate put the Ningi cavalry at a disadvantage, and it turned to terrorizing surrounding villages. When, in 1891, Kano administered a stinging defeat to Ningi, Dan Yaya requested aman, "peace," from Emir Muhammad Bello of Kano. The conditions for peace set by Kano required that Dan Yaya desist from raiding in Gombe, Misau, Katagum, Dilara, Shira, Hadejia, and Zazzau. Dan Yaya's reply survives in a letter in Arabic, and it shows him to be literate as well as diplomatic:

> From the Khalifa of Ningi, Usman Dan Yaya, son of Malam Haruna Baba, best greetings, good will and respect to the Sultan of Kano, Muhammad Bello, son of the late Ibrahim Dabo. Your letter has reached us and we have read it and understood what is in it completely. And as for me, I ask peace of you, peace between us and you; for peace [aman] is in the hands of God and his Prophet [i.e., you cannot avoid making peace because it is God's will]. And if there is recognition of justice between us, send to us one of your servants of whom you approve, and I will make the covenant with him for this aman, which will not be broken if God wills. This is the extent of my desire. This is all Peace (Bauprof Vol. 1, #58:65).

As before, Ningi was resorting to the strategy of peace when the balance of forces had become unfavorable. But the balance had not shifted so far as to make aman unattractive to Emir Bello as well and from 1891 to 1893, when Bello's reign ended, Kano and Ningi were once again briefly at peace.

From 1894 on, Dan Yaya's unpopularity with his own people grew. The resumption of hostilities with Kano brought no rewards. While Ningi's defenses weakened, Kano built up its own line of interlocking towns that protected successfully its own borders against raids. Finally, in 1895, Emir Aliyu of Kano invaded Ningi and followed this up with another raid in 1898. In one of these raids, he reportedly took 1,000 slaves; and he burned the granaries of the Kafin Dan Yaya estate and destroyed other crops (Robinson 1896:205-8). But in the long run, the forces remained in balance. While insecurity grew and trade came to standstill, the raiding and counter-raiding between Ningi and the surrounding emirates went on intermittently until the coming of British rule.

THE END OF INDEPENDENT NINGI

The colonial expeditionary force left Bauchi for Ningi on July 23, 1902—a seventy-five man detachment of the West African Frontier Force, equipped with one Maxim gun, led by Captain Monck-Mason, and aided by Bauchi (S.N.P. 15, 1902:1-17). When the force arrived in Ningi, Dan Yaya refused its offer of peace, declaring that they must either go away or stand and fight: "Your lies are finished (karyanku ya kare)," he said. But Dan Yaya's forces were no match for the new enemy: the colonial troops entered the town and sprayed it with bullets. Ningi suffered some fifty casualties, mostly among the palace guard. It was now clear to all the mountaineers that Dan Yaya's rule was at an end. The Buta turned against him and Dan Yaya fled his capital. He was found by the Buta of Sama on July 25. Sitting under a tree, he told the Buta to send a small boy to shoot him with a non-poisonous arrow, since special charms protected him from poisonous ones. The boy came and did as he was told. Thus, like most Ningi rulers (with the exception of Haruna, who died in the palace) Dan Yaya died a violent death. The local frontier on which Ningi's history had been made was now gone, swept up by the larger moving frontier of colonial rule.

SOURCES AND REFERENCES

Adamu, Ahmadu 1974. Personal Correspondence (Ningi Local Authority). Kano.
al-Mawardi, Ali ibn Muhammed 1915. *Les Status Gouvernementaux*. Alger.
Arewa House 1973. Arabic Manuscripts—Uncatalogued. Kaduna.

A.R.N.N. Document 1904. "Famine in Ningi." National Archives, Kaduna.

Barth, Heinrich 1965. *Travels and Discoveries in Central Africa*. Vol.1. London [orig. ed. 1857].

Bauprof Vol. 1, Outward Correspondence #58. "Letter from the Khalifa (the agent) of Ningi, Usman Dan Yaya (1890-1902), Son of Malam Haruna Baba, to the Sultan of Kano, Muhammad Bello" [in Arabic]. National Archives, Kaduna.

Brenner, Louis 1973. "Methods and Concepts in the Study of African Islam" (Unpublished Paper at a Conference at Boston University).

Butawa Elders 1973. *Butawa Oral Traditions*. Burra, Ningi.

El-Masri, Fathi Hasan 1968. *A Critical Edition of Dan Fodio's Bayan Wujub Al-Hijra 'Ala 'L-'Ibad with Introduction* (Ph.D. Dissertation, University of Ibadan). Ibadan.

Groom, A.W. 1910. Report on Ningi District June 18 to August 18, 1910. S.N.P. 7, 6137. National Archives, Kaduna.

Houdas, O. 1966. *Tedzkiret En-Nisian*. Paris [orig. ed. 1899].

Imam Mahmud b. Muhammad Bello b. Ahmad b. Idris 1957-1962. Tarikh 'Umara Bauchi. Arewa House. Kaduna.

Izard, G.W. 1918a. Burra Independent District Assessment. S.N.P. 10, 113pp. National Archives, Kaduna.

———. 1918b. Assessment Report Warji District. S.N.P. 10, 111pp. National Archives, Kaduna.

Jah, Omar 1973. *Sufism and Nineteenth Century Jihad Movements in West Africa: A Case Study of Al-Hajj 'Umar Al-Futi's Philosophy of Jihad and its Sufi Bases* (Ph.D. Dissertation, McGill University). Montreal.

Kanoprof Vol.1 Outward Correspondence #17. "Letter from Sultan of Kano, Abdullahi b. Ibrahim to amir al-masa wali al-nasa'ih, the great Wazir Ibrahim al-Khalil (1859-1874)" [in Arabic]. National Archives, Kaduna.

Kanoprof Vol.1 Outward Correspondence #58. "Letter from the Sultan of Kano Muhammed Bello b. Sultan Ibrahim to Amir al-Muminin Umar b. Ali (1881-1891)" [in Arabic]. National Archives, Kaduna.

Kanoprof Vol.1 Outward Correspondence #161. "Letter from Galadima Kano, Yusufu b. Sultan Abdullahi to amir al-masa lih Wali al-nasa'ih, the learned Waziri Ibrahim al-khalil (1859-1874)" [in Arabic]. National Archives, Kaduna.

Khadduri, Majid 1955. *War and Peace in the Law of Islam*. Baltimore.

Last, D.M. 1970. "Aspects of Administration and Dissent in Hausaland, 1800-1968." *Africa* 40:345-357.

Lovejoy, Paul E. 1978. "Plantations in the Economy of the Sokoto Caliphate." *Journal of African History* XIX:341-368.

———.1979. Personal Correspondence.

Malam Yahaya 1973. Interview at Ningi Town on July 25 (Fieldnotes).

Middleton, H. Hale 1926. Principal Famines in Hausaland. S.N.P. 17, K. 2151. National Archives, Kaduna.

Morrison, James H. 1974. Personal Correspondence.

———.1976. *Jos Plateau Societies: Internal Change and External Influence 1800-1935* (Ph.D. Dissertation, University of Ibadan). Ibadan.

Patton, Adell, Jr. 1975. *The Ningi Chiefdom and the African Frontier: Mountaineer Resistance to the Sokoto Caliphate, ca. 1800-1908* (Ph.D. Dissertation, University of Wisconsin). Madison.

———.1972-73. Fieldnotes.

———.1979a. "Ningi: The Rise and Fall of an African Frontier Chiefdom, ca. 1800-1908" (Unpublished MS.).

————. 1979b. "Oral Tradition in the Reconstruction of Ningi History, ca. 1880-1908." *Kiabara: Focus on History. Journal of the Humanities.* Vol.4, No.2:105-126 (Harmattan 1981).

————.1980. "The Name Ningi and Pre-Colonial Developing Citizenship: A 'Non-Tribal' Perspective in Nineteenth Century Hausaland." *Afrika Und Ubersee*, 6:No.4:241-252.

Renner, G.T. 1926. "A Famine Zone in Africa: The Sudan." *Geographical Review*, Vol.16, No.4:583-596.

Roberts, Trevor 1918. Report on Tin-Smelting at Lirui-N Delma. S.N.P. 7, 286B. National Archives, Kaduna.

Robinson, Rev. Charles H. 1892. "The Hausa Territories." *Geographical Review* VIII(3 September):201-221.

Rohlfs, Gerhard 1874. *Quer Durch Afrika Reise von Mittelmeer Nach dem Tschad-See und Zum Golf von Guinea.* Leipzig.

Sarkin Dua Hamidu Audu 1973. Interview at Ningi Town on September 28 (Tape #28, Fieldnotes).

Sirawa Elders 1973. *Sirawa Oral Traditions.* Ningi Town.

S.N.P. 15 1902. Ningi Expedition. National Archives, Kaduna.

Tambo, David 1979. "The Pre-Colonial Tin Industry in Northern Nigeria" (Unpublished Paper).

Vansina, Jan 1973. Personal Correspondence.

Wagner, Herman 1860. *Reisen und Entdeckungen in Central Africa: Dr. Eduard Vogel.* Leipzig.

THE DISTANT FRONTIER AS REFUGE

Like the Muslim mallams of Ningi, the frontiersmen in the following study by Lee Cassanelli were also refugees. Unlike them, they were strangers not only to the frontier but also to the metropoles around them. These frontiersmen in Somaliland were former slaves of the Somali, usually escapees, originally from Bantu East Africa. Their social construction took place in isolation, in a marginal area, empty except for a miniscule population of hunter-gatherers who quickly vanished, and without nearby models of independent polities relevant to their condition. Such an instance of African social construction is, in a sense, a "test case" of cultural persistence and cultural reproduction on the frontier. It gives us an opportunity to see the extent to which the principles of organization that we have seen operate in traditional frontier settings also operated on a less usual kind of frontier—an almost perfect institutional vacuum in which the frontiersmen were thrown entirely on their own cultural resources.

As Cassanelli points out, the configuration we see here is reminiscent of Afro-American independent "Maroon" communities, created by escaped slaves in the New World. Africa too has seen its share of settlements established afresh by Africans whose lives have been wrenched by the experience of slavery—thus, the "Creole" communities of Sierra Leone and Liberia and the various communities—still largely unstudied—of local African slaves emancipated from their African masters, mostly in the nineteenth century. These communities too were built on frontiers, geographical or sociological or both. But compared to the African frontier societies we have examined here so far, the populations of former-slave communities were likely to be less local in origin, to draw upon a larger ethnic "catchment" area, and consequently to be confronted more directly with the problem of ethnic differences both among themselves and with their hosts.

The slave origins of these communities usually stigmatized them in the eyes of the surrounding African population and this constrained their political fortunes. Paradoxically, in the present case, the sharper cultural divide between the metropolitan Somali society and its Bantu ex-slaves seemed to have given greater freedom of political initiative to the former slaves when they began to build their communities. It may be that the stigma of slavery inhibits action less when the former slave is less immersed in the wider society and less constrained by its judgments. The Maroon communities of the New World were also apt to be founded by African-born slaves who were—more than those born locally—deeply alien to their surroundings. Another reason, in this case, was ecological: the slaves sought refuge in areas that were inhospitable to their pastoral

Somali masters and their communities could consequently incubate and eventually prosper in relative safety.

The feat of social construction was, in this case, probably more original than in the other cases we have seen. There, the model that was brought to the frontier was parochial and relatively invariant—or, in the case of Ningi, a consciously devised variation on the local pattern. Here, the model was looser since the former slaves came from different parts of Bantu East Africa, had had experience as slaves in a radically different social order, and were facing entirely novel problems. What we see, as a result, is an interplay between the persistence of familiar African principles of organization and the exigencies of rather extreme conditions of an isolated frontier. One such exigency—the shortage of women—was more starkly evident on this frontier than on those we have seen before. The response to it seems to have been the typical one of erecting a complex system of rights in women—complex enough to defy the comprehension of European observers.

Among other familiar items, we see the working out of the first-comer principle: the founders of communities became their heads and allocated their lands. And since at the beginning and during much of the subsequent history of these communities, the frontier remained open, there was a great deal of mobility (enhanced by local famines and occasional Somali raids). Because the dissatisfied could easily leave, the relations between aspiring rulers and potential subjects remained flexible. Thus, in the earlier stages, the organization appeared relatively "democratic" (that is, the kinship model of organization prevailed). But as new layers of immigrants were inserted, the organization became more "oligarchic," with earlier comers frankly exercising control and common ethnicity providing political bonds. Finally, in one region, Gosha, a chieftaincy arose which acquired an increasingly patrimonial and eventually despotic cast. The further development of this chieftaincy was stopped by the intrusion of colonial powers. But it had probably reached in any case the limits of expansion that the charismatic leadership of Nassib Bunda could give it. For this was indeed a different kind of African frontier. As an agricultural Bantu enclave of former slaves in the midst of a pastoral, warlike, and culturally haughty Somali society, Nassib's polity had no chance of ever moving politically into metropolitan areas. As Cassanelli points out, these frontier communities began to approach, in the end, the centuries-old pattern in which politically semi-dependent "oasis" agriculturalists live in economic symbiosis with the pastoralists.

—Editor

Lee V. Cassanelli

—————— 8 ——————

Social Construction on the Somali Frontier: Bantu Former Slave Communities in the Nineteenth Century

During the second half of the nineteenth century, two new "frontier" societies emerged in southern Somalia, composed almost entirely of runaway or freed slaves who had come originally from the Bantu-speaking regions of East Africa.[1] One developed along the lower Juba River in the region known as Gosha (from the Somali word for "forest"). The other, Avai, grew up about one hundred miles to the east, near the point where the Shabeelle River disappears into swampy marshes not far from the Indian Ocean coast. Neither of these remarkable experiments in social reconstruction has received serious scholarly attention, although many similar communities of runaway slaves, known as "maroons," have been studied in the Americas (see Price 1973). And Cooper (1977) has recently discussed the appearance of such settlements elsewhere in nineteenth-century East Africa. As in these better-documented cases, the ex-slaves of Somaliland constructed their communities in relatively uninhabited areas, beyond the easy reach of the slave-holding population. They cleared land, organized production for subsistence, and evolved a political system that maintained internal order and a diverse set of external relations.

Here as elsewhere, such communities were a peculiar variant of "frontier societies" in that they grew in part out of the peculiar culture that characterizes plantation life. Having been already required to adapt to enslavement, the escaped slaves brought to the frontier a combination of plantation culture and their previous ethnic traditions. Reconstructing slave society and culture in Somalia is itself problematic, not least because most of our information comes from the dominant group, whose views naturally differ from that of the slaves. And since the slave population of nineteenth-century Somalia derived from at least a dozen different East African peoples, one cannot even be certain of where to look for sources of cultural survivals.

What makes the Somaliland examples particularly interesting is the wider setting in which these communities took root and to which they had to adapt. Both Gosha and Avai grew up on the fringes of a predominantly pastoral society that always looked upon cultivation with a certain disdain, preferring the "freer" and "nobler" (though no less demanding) life of transhumant pastoralism. This prevalent Somali attitude helps explain why slaves had been used as cultivators in the first place and why, even after the runaway communities were established, they and the pastoralists continued to interact in a distinctly symbiotic way. Former masters and former slaves gradually constructed a set of linkages reminiscent of those found between herdsmen and farmers in many other parts of precolonial Africa. This and the material conditions of life in a semi-arid environment had shaped these frontier societies as much as did their slave origins.

Another distinctive aspect of the Somaliland case derives from the larger historical context: the escaped slaves who built Gosha and Avai had been brought to Somalia at a time when it was being drawn into an international economy. The plantation products, harvested under the supervision of Somali and Arab masters, were destined for the expanding markets of Zanzibar, Europe, and Asia. Given the pastoral orientation of the Somali—even slaveholders continued to maintain substantial investments in livestock—the agricultural slaves provided the major productive link with the larger commercial world. When they escaped to found their own communities, the ex-slaves continued to participate in the export economy—to a greater extent, I believe, than did the New World "maroon" communities. This contributed to the internal consolidation and the external recognition of these frontier societies on the eve of the colonial occupation and division of Somalia by Britain and Italy.

For a coherent picture of the development of these communities, it has been necessary to piece together data from a wide range of sources. Most of the information comes from the observations of European travelers, administrators, and ethnographers, made from the late nineteenth to the mid-twentieth century, well after the major formative processes had been completed. The earlier travelers' accounts are extremely fragmentary and sometimes contradictory, while subsequent fuller descriptions of the frontier societies—made after the establishment of colonial rule—clearly reflect changes brought about by colonial consolidation itself. Fortunately, a number of oral traditions transmitted by members of the ex-slave communities were recorded by these European observers, and they provide an internal interpretation of the early frontier experience. These published traditions are supplemented by a few oral fragments which I came across in the course of my own fieldwork among the neighboring Somali. Perhaps, systematic oral research could add to the picture drawn below. However, recent reports (Prins 1960, Andrzejewski 1969) indicate that the former Bantu-speaking populations of Somalia are rapidly becoming assimilated linguistically and culturally to the numerically dominant Somalis.

Following a brief section on the geographical and historical background, the essay summarizes the available evidence on the origins and development of the Goshaland settlements from about 1840 to 1900. This is followed by a discussion of Nassib Bunda, the legendary ex-slave of Yao origin who was, for two decades, the leader of the entire confederation of Gosha freed-slave villages along the Juba. Then comes a section on Avai, founded in the 1870's, with its many similarities as well as some revealing differences with Gosha. The essay concludes with a review of some recurrent themes of community building as they are distilled in the oral traditions of Gosha and Avai.

GEOGRAPHICAL AND HISTORICAL BACKGROUND

Somalia is predominantly a land of nomadic and semi-nomadic pastoralists. About two-thirds of the country's four million inhabitants are engaged exclusively in rearing camels, cattle, sheep, and goats—a proportion that has changed little since the nineteenth century. The remaining third is divided between part and full-time cultivators. Most of the part-time cultivators belong to livestock-owning Somali lineages; they practice farming during the spring rainy season in the plains between the Juba and Shabeelle Rivers while their kinsmen move about the rangelands with their animals. Such dryland farming helped supplement the normal pastoral diet of meat and milk but it rarely produced an exportable surplus.

Most of southern Somalia's full-time farmers lived along the Shabeelle River, whose low-lying banks permitted year-round irrigation agriculture. Here were clusters of permanent villages and cleared fields extending a few kilometers from the river's edge, their outer boundaries shading off into the vast grazing lands beyond. From the lower Shabeelle, which runs parallel to the Indian Ocean coast for more than a hundred miles, came harvests of grain and beans that for centuries helped supply the populations of the old trading towns of Muqdisho, Marka, and Baraawe. Between 1600 and 1900, parts of the Shabeelle plain were occasionally incorporated into loosely structured sultanates and the cultivators were forced to pay tribute; but for most of that period, relations between nomads and farmers, nomads and townsmen, and townsmen and farmers were conducted through dyadic ties of alliance, patron-clientship, or commercial exchange.[2]

Most scholars agree that the earliest riverine cultivators were ethnically distinct from the Cushitic-speaking Somali. They appear to represent the remnants of the northernmost extension of Bantu-speakers who migrated into the adjacent regions of East and Central Africa during the first millennium A.D. (Cerulli 1957:54-57, 1959:115-121; Grottanelli 1975:61-68). Their physical features do distinguish them even today from most of the pastoral Somali, although centuries of intermarriage have blurred these distinctions in most of southern Somalia. Culturally, most of the farmers have been "Somali-ized"—they speak Somali, they are Muslims, and they maintain genealogies usually linking them to Somali ancestors. Nonetheless, until recently, they were considered inferior by the "pure" (bilis) Somali, both because of their agricultural pursuits and their presumed racial origins. With respect to the new ex-slave communities, these traditional farmers, then, provided both a model for a corporate identity as socially inferior cultivators vis-à-vis the pastoral Somali and a precedent for the assimilation of many aspects of Somali culture.

Toward the middle of the nineteenth century, Somalia was drawn into the growing East African slave trade, whose center was the cosmopolitan island port of Zanzibar, off the Tanganyika coast. Somalia's role was less that of a supplier of slaves than, at first, that of a transshipment center and, later, of a buyer of slaves. Arab dhows, filled with slaves captured on the East African mainland and destined for markets in Arabia and the Persian Gulf, often landed along the Somali coast for provisioning. A few slaves then were generally purchased by wealthy Somali or Arab townsmen. For example, Guillain (1856, II:537) noted that 600 were sold in Muqdisho in 1846.

When, in the 1860's, the British navy patrols off East Africa began to enforce the prohibition on slave trading, increasing numbers of slaves were sent overland from Lamu to the Somali ports, from where they could more easily be reexported to the Middle East. In 1866, the German explorer Brenner counted six slave caravans in four days passing through Baraawe (Kersten 1871:349). By the 1870's, the British consul in Zanzibar estimated that 10,000 slaves were taken across the Juba annually into Somalia.[3]

It is clear that not all of these slaves continued north. Many were absorbed into the agricultural economy of the lower Shabeelle, where new land was being cleared for the cultivation of durra, sesame, orchella (a lichen used to make a crimson textile dye), and cotton—products in demand at the coast and in Zanzibar. The new ready supply of labor meant that the Somali clans along the river could participate in the commercial boom. Elsewhere, I have documented in greater detail the emergence and brief flourishing of this southern Somali plantation economy (Cassanelli 1982:166-178). While one cannot know the exact number of slaves imported into Somalia during the second half of the nineteenth century, the remarkable growth of Goshaland suggests that they numbered in the tens of thousands.

THE GOSHA COMMUNITIES

While it is possible that small groups of cultivators were living along the lower Juba River before 1800, there is no direct evidence that runaway slaves began to settle there before the middle third of the nineteenth century. The various oral traditions available to us suggest that the earliest refugees arrived in the 1830's and 1840's, and that the only inhabitants they encountered were scattered bands of hunters and gatherers known as Waboni (Zoli 1927:149, Grottanelli 1953:254). Somali herdsmen did not approach the river in this area because it was a breeding ground for the tse-tse fly, fatal to livestock.

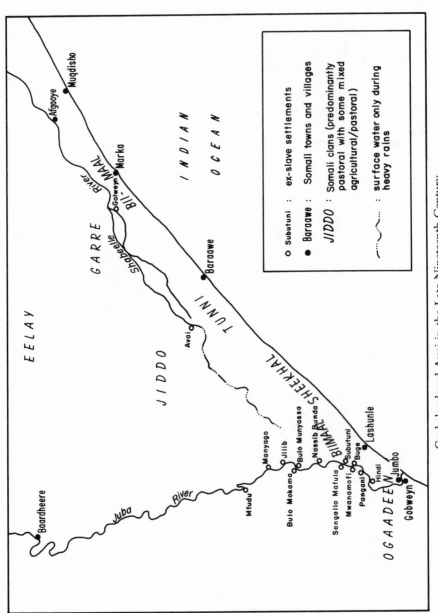

Goshaland and Avai in the Late Nineteenth Century

The first runaway slaves to reach Goshaland represented a number of ethnic groups from the coastal hinterland of East Africa: Ngindo, Nyassa, Yao, and Zigua. The Zigua seem to have predominated in the early years of the settlement: they are the only ethnic group mentioned explicitly by Guillain (1856, III:179-180), and the von der Decken expedition of 1865 encountered at least six Zigua villages along the Juba, with an estimated population of 4,000 (Kersten 1871, II:303-304, 306). Since the Zigua represent one of the earliest constituent populations of Goshaland, traditions of Zigua settlement can reveal much about the initial conditions that faced the runaways. Fortunately, we have two independent oral traditional accounts of these early years which enable us to sketch out a Zigua view of their frontier experience.[4]

The group in question left their homeland in the eastern part of what is today Tanzania during a severe famine known in Zigua tradition as "Kidyakingo." Entire families "sold themselves" at the coast to traders from Baraawe in the hope of finding food and a place to live until the famine was over.[5] Only when they reached Somaliland did they learn that they were being taken into slavery. After a short period of enforced agricultural work, they conspired to escape, resolving to trek overland to their homeland. When they reached the river called Gosha (the Juba), they built villages on its bank and were soon joined by others of their countrymen who had also fled enslavement.

While exploring the surrounding bush, some of the settlers encountered a shepherd of the semi-sedentary Tunni clan, from the small Somali village of Lashunle near the coast. A few Zigua accompanied him to his village, where they made a pact promising Zigua assistance to the people of Lashunle should they need it against other Somalis. In return, the Zigua were given seeds of all kinds—maize, millet, beans, and vegetables—and a goat to seal the alliance. But they got a more hostile reception from the local Waboni hunters, who are said to have killed a Zigua leader named Majendero with a poisoned arrow near a place remembered as Mkwama. After this, the Zigua pioneers attacked the Waboni on every possible occasion. One hunter was taken captive and held for a long time. The Zigua asked him how to cross the Juba, which was always deep. The hunter asked for an axe and built a raft with it. The Zigua then crossed the river and built a large village on the right bank which they called Mwanamofi.

After Majendero's death, leadership was assumed by a woman remembered as Wanakuka, a renowned *mganga* or seer. It is said that Wanakuka saw in a dream that her people would never return to their homeland; hence, she directed them to build villages along the Juba. Under her command, the Zigua skirmished successfully with nearby Oromo (Galla) and Somali pastoralists, then made peace with both. At her death, leadership passed to Makoma Maligo, identified only as the son of one of Majendero's companions (thus presumably a descendant of one of the first settlers). Under Makoma, the Zigua defeated and beheaded a Somali shaykh in a major encounter that secured Somali recognition of Zigua autonomy.

This narrative encapsulates the main elements of Zigua traditions about their early settlement, remarkably similar in the two accounts. The traditions go on to talk of the founding of other villages and the handing down of authority to Makoma Maligo's patrilineal descendants. The position of tribal leader may have been an innovation of the early days; by the twentieth century, the Zigua chief's authority was nominal. Also, in 1950, each locale had its own *mganga* or religious specialist, usually enjoying purely local prestige (Grottanelli 1953:254-256).

By the late 1860's, former slaves began to arrive in Goshaland in increasing numbers. Some fled from plantations along the Shabeelle. Others had been emancipated by Somali shaykhs after faithful service as domestic servants or artisans in coastal towns. Still others had been liberated by British anti-slavery squadrons at sea. Thus, in late 1867, one naval commander freed 322 slaves off the coast of Baraawe, including some Nyika, Nyamwezi, Yao, Nyassa, Makua, and Ngindo (Sullivan 1873:153-172 *passim*). Finally, there were no doubt slaves that had escaped during the overland trek from Lamu, for the caravan route crossed Juba not far from the southernmost Gosha settlements.

Though we lack traditions as detailed as those for the Zigua, we can piece together something of the way these new groups organized their communities along the Juba frontier. Fragmentary traditions gathered by administrators and ethnographers in the early twentieth century suggest that many of the earliest settlements were each occupied by refugees of the same ethnic group. A settlement frequently took the name of its founder (e.g., Songollo Mafula or Nassib Bunda) or of a place or figure remembered from one's homeland (e.g., Buge or Ngambo).[6] New arrivals would seek out villages of their own ethnicity, such as the Makua village of Subutuni or the Yao village of Kolokoto (Colucci 1924:64, Zoli 1927:149, 181). This tendency was no doubt reinforced by the influx of liberated or escaped slaves fresh from their homeland.

But some settlements were ethnically heterogeneous. As early as 1865, von der Decken (1871:302) described the large village of Hindi as being made up of Zigua, Nyassa, Yao, Bisa, Makua, and natives of Zanzibar. Some villages were founded by comrades who had served as slaves in the same locale or been owned by masters from the same Somali clan. Thus, the town of Jilib is said to have been founded by escaped slaves from the Jiddo, a Somali clan which inhabited much of the territory between the lower Shabeelle and the Juba. Mokama was founded by slaves of the Tunni clan from around Baraawe, and Manyago by those of the upcountry Eelay (Colucci 1924:64-65). Somali traditions suggest that in the earliest days of frontier settlement, villages tended to be ethnically homogeneous and that only later did mixed villages begin to appear (Colucci 1924:64-65; Zoli 1926:181-182). But other facts suggest that different patterns of organization—based on origin, place of enslavement, early or later ethnic mixture, and new political ties—existed side by side by the turn of the century.[7]

In 1891, the British naval officer F.G. Dundas (1893:214), who sailed up the Juba as far as Baardheere, estimated Goshaland's population at between 30,000 and 40,000. This figure seems high when compared to the later estimates of Italian colonial officials: Perducchi in 1901 (30,000), Ferrari in 1911 (15,000 on left bank only), and Tozzi in 1932 (23,500). But it is possible that Goshaland's population decreased after 1900. Dundas's voyage occurred during the peak years of Goshaland's growth, following the official abolition of slave trading in East Africa but preceding the imposition of effective colonial administration. Once colonial authority was firmly established, ex-slaves could move more freely about the colony and found it less necessary to seek sanctuary along the Juba.

The size of individual Gosha settlements varied considerably. Von der Decken estimated the population of Hindi in 1865 at between 600 and 700. In 1891, Dundas (1893:213, 216) said that some villages reached 600 to 1,000 inhabitants, while a newly established settlement on the extreme northern frontier of Goshaland had only about 30. In fact, small settlements seem to have been the most common: of the 60 villages listed in Ferrari's census (1911:82-84), 41 had fewer than 100 inhabitants and 28 fewer than 50. Thus, the overall pattern appears to have been that of a few large settlements and several hundred mostly small dispersed hamlets, some of which were virtually contiguous and cooperated in military matters.

The ecology of the Gosha frontier—and perhaps the cultural preferences of the slaves who came from societies with dispersed settlements—tended to promote this pattern of small scattered hamlets. The protective forest and dense bush country extended no more than a few kilometers from the banks of the Juba, and the pioneers tried to leave a safe barrier of uncleared land between their settlements and the open grazing lands of the Somalis. Most of the cultivation was done in *desheks*, or depressions, adjacent to the river banks. Cleared and burned, the *desheks* were watered either by the river's overflow in the rainy season or, more commonly, by small rivulets that fed into the Juba. This required no elaborate irrigation works and it promoted the constant clearing of new *desheks*. As the population grew, therefore, new settlements sprang up in two narrow ribbons of land along both sides of the Juba.

Many of the East African societies from which the slaves had come and on which they may have modelled their frontier organization were organized into small villages whose component kin groups (particularly in matrilineal societies like the Yao) were apt to fragment periodically and give birth to new settlements. But this argument for cultural continuity is made difficult by the absence of data on the kinship systems of any of the Gosha communities, though it is apparent that in some ethnic groups, such as the Zigua, affiliation with named patrilineal groupings was independent of one's village of residence (Grottanelli 1953:256). This suggests that village fission—hinted at by Dundas (1893:216)—did contribute to the multiplication of settlements.

We have some information on the political organization of Gosha—a matter of interest both to early colonial officials, who sought to co-opt it, and to the descendants of the early settlers themselves, who saw in it the roots of political legitimacy.

The earliest colonial administrators reported that each village had a headman, typically its founder or a descendant of an original settler. The headman apportioned land to new arrivals and represented the village in its dealings with outsiders. He was assisted by a council of elders from the major subdivisions of the settlement. In ethnically homogeneous communities, these subdivisions were lineages or lineage segments. In ethnically mixed villages, the structure was often more complex. In some, we find officials known as *sagale* (a Somali title for a community leader's representative in a segment of the community). Each ethnic group or cluster of new immigrants had a *sagale* to provide liaison with the headman and his council of elders. He oversaw the internal affairs of his segment and might also make village proclamations and organize local ceremonies. Groups of *sagale* mediated in controversies within the village, regulated dikes and irrigation canals where these existed, and advised in wartime (Zoli 1926:187-188). We do not know whether specific ethnic groups tended to fill particular specialized roles. It seems probable that precedence in settling in the community, rather than ethnic affiliation as such, determined the order in which functions were allocated to particular *sagale*.

Oral traditions clearly show that before colonial rule most Gosha communities formally distinguished between their original founders (*gamas*) and later arrivals (*majoro*). Usually, only the *gamas* and their descendants could elect and become village headmen and council elders (Zoli 1927:181-182)—an understandable precaution in the face of periodic influxes of runaways of different ethnic origins. The system also had economic and political implications, for the *gamas* allocated and revoked rights to land near the settlement. This further explains the proliferation of settlements: dissatisfied *majoro* would be tempted to break off and found villages of their own.

As long as there was plenty of land available along the river banks—as there was into the twentieth century—the prerogatives of each settlement's *gamas* did not provoke conflict with later-arriving settlers. Nor did it lead to ethnic stratification within villages. Rather, the open frontier made possible the perpetuation of distinct ethnic identities as each new settlement took on the character of its own ethnic founders. Thus, in the 1920's, the Bantu of Goshaland still referred to nine original *gamas* communities as constituting the heart of their confederation (Zoli 1927:181, 187; Colucci 1924:148) and these identities were maintained at least until the mid-century (Grottanelli 1953:252). The nine original *gamas* are generally agreed to be Yao, Nyassa, Makua, Ngindo, Makale, Mushangolo, Nyika, Molema, and Nyamwezi. Interestingly, the Zigua—the very first comers—stand apart in this, as an autonomous society with a distinct political structure of its own.

According to Zoli (1927:187), representatives of the nine *gamas* traditionally chose a territorial chief from among the Yao notables. The leaders of each *gamas* gathered and the newly elected chief was made to sit on a bed of skins covered with cloth and elevated on a wooden platform. The new leader's relatives surrounded the platform while dances and songs were performed in his honor. However, it should be noted that there is no evidence of this accession ritual in the precolonial sources and it may be that the custom of selecting a Yao successor was established at the death in 1906 of the most famous Gosha leader, Nassib Bunda.

While the availability of land and the exclusion of newcomers from local authority worked to give a polyethnic cast to Gosha society, other factors promoted the emergence of a Gosha-wide culture. Demographic, economic, and political realities all contributed to this integrative process.

Although the data do not tell us about the rules of residence after marriage and their effects on population movements, what is clear is that intermarriage between the different ethnic groups was not uncommon. Since fellow tribals were not always available as mates and there was a general shortage of women among refugees, mixed marriages were virtually essential if family life were to be reconstituted. Only the Zigua— whose early settlements included, if we are to believe tradition, entire families—were able to increase steadily while marrying primarily their own and the Zaramo, a neighboring people in their Tanganyikan homeland (Grottanelli 1953:256).[8] Some groups originally prohibited the taking of wives from the Yao, Mushangolo, and Nyika because they did not practice female infibulation (Zoli 1926:204); but there is nothing to indicate that the Yao, Mushangolo, and Nyika men did not marry out (a situation that theoretically should have favored their increase). The great imbalance in the sex ratio, particularly before the official abolition of slavery in Somalia, militated against any tendency toward ethnic endogamy. Runaways, it appears, took wives where they could find them, often returning clandestinely to their old plantations to persuade former female companions to join them.

Several other factors ensured regular population movements along the Juba river corridor. Traditions clearly indicate that the early pioneers would resettle several times: in his lifetime, an individual might live in three or four localities on both sides of the Juba (Rossetti 1900:31-32). Migrations could be prompted by the threat of Somali raids, infertile or flooded farmlands, local population pressure, or political schisms within existing settlements. Such recurrent crises also produced regular interaction among the Gosha communities. Moreover, by the 1890's, the Gosha farmers were producing a small surplus of maize, durra, and bananas for export to Arab and Swahili traders on the coast. By river raft or overland caravan, the southern Gosha took their goods to Gobweyn or Jumbo, near the mouth of the Juba, where they exchanged them for cloth, hardware, and guns (Dundas 1893:214).

Since virtually all the runaways came originally from the Bantu-speaking regions of East Africa and many of the slaves captured in the coastal regions of Tanganyika probably already spoke Swahili as a second language, it is not surprising that, as Dundas (1891:214) confirms, Swahili was spoken throughout the Gosha region toward the end of the century. Also, between 1890 and 1910, many of the settlers converted to Islam, thereby furthering cultural integration along the lower Juba. While many of them had no doubt been exposed to the Faith during captivity, the effective penetration by Islam of Goshaland appears to have been the work of itinerant Somali shaykhs who were active throughout southern Somalia in the second half of the century. A certain Shaykh Osmana, for example, is remembered as having set up a small religious settlement at Jilib, in the heart of Goshaland, in the mid-1880's. He married a freed slave, converted a number of prominent Gosha leaders, and become renowned both as a man of learning and as an intermediary between the settlers and their Somali neighbors (Rossetti 1900:36, Ferrari 1911:81).

The emergence of a Gosha-wide culture did not preclude, as we have seen, the perpetuation of some ethnic distinctions among the settlers. As in much of East Africa, so here several ethnic groups, living within a rather uniform physical setting, maintained their linguistic and genealogical identities while interacting in a way that created broadly shared cultural and political values. This may be partly explained by the need to maintain social order under conditions of territorial mobility. The constant comings and goings of different groups within the single region required the rigorous maintenance of genealogical distinctions as markers of precedence, priority, and seniority, and as a way of maintaining stable sets of relations when physical boundaries were constantly changing.

But in addition to these systemic integrative factors, there was a historical one: the effort by the remarkable former slave Nassib Bunda to forge a confederation of settlements under his command. Nassib Bunda came to prominence in the last quarter of the nineteenth century, during the peak years of Goshaland's growth, and he has become one of the legendary heroes of this period. His story provides insights into many of the processes of community formation that have been discussed. The story is also one of the building and consolidation of political power in a frontier setting.

NASSIB BUNDA

The little evidence we have suggests that the future Nassib Bunda was born a Yao in northern Mozambique in the 1830's; his original name was Makanjira.[9] An old comrade recollected how he and Makanjira were captured in a raid on their village by "the warriors of Tippu Tib," carried to Somaliland by dhow, and sold to Somalis of the Ogadeen clan in the vicinity of Baraawe. This probably occurred in the late 1850's or early 1860's, when Makanjira would have been about twenty years old. After an escape attempt, Makanjira was beaten and left to die by his owners. He was rescued and restored to health by a Tunni shaykh from Baraawe who, according to some accounts, gave him freedom and, according to others, took him in as a servant. From this shaykh, who may be the same Osman who was later to found the religious settlement at Jilib, Makanjira apparently received his first lessons in the Koran and took the name Nassib, "good fortune" (the name Bunda or Bundo appears to refer to an ex-slave settlement where he lived for some time).

After his manumission—the subject of several accounts[10]—he made his way to the town of Hindi on the lower Juba, described in 1865 as a settlement of some six to seven hundred former slaves of diverse origins. There, so the story goes, Nassib charmed many of the local women and incurred the wrath of Hindi's jealous husbands (a theme that recurs in many of the accounts of his later life). Forced to leave, he and several Yao companions crossed to the other bank and founded a thriving settlement. But the influx of new runaways and the sporadic harrassment by nearby Ogadeen Somali nomads compelled Nassib to resettle once again. He founded the town named after him and soon other settlements sprang up nearby as former slaves gravitated toward this charismatic figure (Rossetti 1900, Bargoni 1931).

Nassib Bunda's emergence as a regional leader is dated by traditions to 1875. In that year, an Egyptian expedition, commanded by MacKillop Pasha, sailed into the Juba estuary with the aim of establishing a link between the Indian Ocean coast and Egyptian outposts on the Upper Nile. In seeking local authorities willing to accept Egyptian sovereignty, Mac-Killop Pasha found both Nassib Bunda and a certain Farahan Makua claiming to speak for the Gosha settlers. The details of the negotiations are unclear. But apparently with the connivance of prominent Tunni Somali notables, Farahan Makua was killed and Nassib Bunda was acknowledged as the leader of Goshaland (Zoli 1927:149-150).

Although—or perhaps because—the Egyptian forces withdrew early in 1876, Nassib Bunda continued his ascent to power. The evidence for this early period is very limited. Nassib Bunda had to compete with several rivals, notably a Ngindo leader named Songollo Mafula (who founded a village of that name) and the aforementioned Zigua chief Makoma Maligo. The rivalry probably had some ethnic significance: Yao, Ngindo, and Zigua settlers were the earliest and most numerous along the Juba. It is said that Nassib Bunda sought to put his own Yao kinsmen in charge of each settlement that pledged him loyalty. By 1885, he was recognized as the patron and protector of former slaves from Subutuni to Mfudu, though some villages and tracts of territory always refused to acknowledge his authority.

Tradition attributes to Nassib Bunda many of the institutions and customs noted by the early colonial authorities in Goshaland. It is said that he sought to reinstate the practice of organizing villages along ethnic lines. He may also be responsible for the practice of appointing *sagale* to supervise newly arrived immigrants and thereby ensuring his control of the burgeoning Gosha settlements. He established certain rules of land tenure: no free Somalis were allowed to settle in Goshaland, for example, and land abandoned for four years reverted back to the village *gamas*—its founding families. Finally, he is said to have established penalties for a number of crimes, including rape, adultery, homicide, cannibalism (witchcraft?), and injury or insult to headmen or *sagale* (Zoli 1927:149-150, 181-182, 244-245, 253-259).

From the fragmentary evidence, one can infer some of the sources of Nasib Bunda's power and the mechanisms he used to extend it over Goshaland. Some of these mechanisms clearly built upon existing beliefs of the settlers; others grew out of the peculiar circumstances of late nineteenth-century Somalia and involved alliances with elements of the surrounding Somali society.

Nassib Bunda is remembered as a courageous warrior and military leader. Many stories speak of his success in defending his followers against their former Somali masters. A string of early successes against Ogadeen and Biimaal raiding parties enhanced his reputation as both protector and magician; he was said to be able to summon the animals of the forest and river to his cause (Fieldnotes 1971, Rossetti 1900). Age-classes do not seem to have been institutionalized in Goshaland, but all able-bodied males had to give military service and each village of the confederation had a military head responsible for its contingent of militiamen. With arms acquired from Zanzibari traders in the 1880's, Nassib Bunda created a special force of musket bearers under his own command and it became the core of his fighting forces, supported by a second line of archers and spear bearers (Zoli 1927:198). Firearms enabled Goshaland to take the offensive in the last few years of the century: on one occasion, Nassib Bunda directed an attack against a Somali *zariba* (nomadic thorn enclosure) in retaliation for a Somali raid on a friendly caravan trader (Robecchi-Brichetti 1899:209).

But it was not only military success that secured Nassib Bunda's reputation. He was an acknowledged master of the mystical arts, combining Islamic and African practices in exercising his leadership. His reputed ability to command animals in defending Goshaland has already been mentioned. Rather less popular was his supposed power over the crocodiles of the Juba, which he used against Gosha rivals; and he supposedly threatened family heads with gory death if they refused to give him their daughters in marriage.[11] Given the unfamiliar surroundings with its unknown spirits, it is not surprising that the settlers should emphasize their leader's supernatural powers. Religious specialists often play an important role in frontier situations, as in the already noted instance of the Zigua *mganga*'s. What Nassib Bunda did was to combine supernatural expertise with military prowess.

His claim to Islamic mystical knowledge contributed further to his prestige among his overwhelmingly illiterate followers, for it suggested control in the world of their former masters. Islamic trappings also provided a source of political legitimacy that transcended ethnic ties. It is not surprising that after 1885 Nassib Bunda styled himself "sultan" of Goshaland and was recognized as such by Zanzibar and, later, European authorities. In the 1890's, an Italian traveler found in Nassib's employ a learned Muslim secretary who served him as adviser and correspondent with Muslim authorities in Baraawe and Zanzibar (cited in Rossetti 1900:36).

Nassib Bunda's policies were conditioned by the proximity of other political communities. A shrewd diplomat, he effectively used external alliances with neighboring Somalis and with Arab representatives of the sultans of Zanzibar. In his earlier years, it appears, Nassib Bunda was hostile to all Somali clans save the Tunni, one of whom had rescued him from slavery and whose notables helped him gain recognition from the Egyptian expedition. Peaceful relations with the Tunni involved trade and the diffusion of Islamic learning. On at least one occasion, Nassib and some followers visited Baraawe, a center of the Qadiriya Muslim brotherhood and the main trading town of the Tunni (Rossetti 1900:33).

More surprising, however, is the apparent accord that Nassib Bunda reached with segments of the Biimaal and Sheekhal Somali. These largely pastoral clans had occupied the coastal plains between Baraawe and the Juba River about the time Nassib Bunda first settled in Goshaland, and they had periodically attacked isolated hamlets and taken former slaves captive. After several indecisive skirmishes, Nassib Bunda apparently decided to neutralize them. He agreed not to admit to his settlements any runaway slaves from these clans and it is said that he even cooperated in restoring some fugitive slaves to them (Zoli 1927:199). In exchange, Biimaal and Sheekhal raids on Gosha settlers diminished; the exchange of crops for livestock products became easier; and Nassib Bunda had perhaps secured external allies in his struggle for domination of the Gosha confederation. Clearly, once Nassib had achieved internal Gosha leadership, its maintenance required other kinds of skills. Having built a reputation as an ardent foe of Somali domination, Nassib Bunda sought, after 1885, outside recognition of his territorial supremacy. To do this, he needed a *modus vivendi* with his neighbors. The task was greatly facilitated by the segmentary nature of Somali politics on the one hand and, on the other, by the desire of Zanzibar's sultans—now under increasing British influence—to promote peaceful trade in their vast East African dominions.

Among the Somali, frequent feuding among lineages and clan segments encouraged a politics of limited alliances that achieved temporary balances of power in districts where resources had to be shared. Nassib Bunda adapted this system to his own needs. By allying himself with certain Somali clans, he reduced the threat to Goshaland's security and insured a certain respect from other Somali clans who recognized the strength that such alliances could bring. Thus, while internally the Gosha polity was built on social, political, and religious principles shared by most of the settlers, its external relations had to borrow from the pragmatic Somali model. There is no evidence of any ritual sanctions or supernatural explanations of these alliances.

Nassib Bunda's accommodation with the Zanzibar regime followed upon his short-lived recognition by the Egyptian expedition which Zanzibar saw as a direct challenge to its supremacy in East Africa. Nassib's policy used Zanzibar's official efforts to end the slave trade and substitute trade in other commodities. Sultan Barghash's efforts to establish trading stations along the Somali coast had found little Somali support and frequent Somali hostility. The emergence of the Gosha enclave held out to Zanzibar the prospect of a new market and a commercial corridor to the interior. Hence, by the 1880's, Nassib Bunda was able to secure Zanzibar's recognition of his authority (together with a small supply of firearms and ammunition) in exchange for his acceptance of the Sultan's right to trade up the Juba, a trade that never amounted to much.

When, in 1890, British and Italian authorities moved to enforce their respective claims to what were to become the two Somalilands, both sought support of the "Sultan of Goshaland" by promising him a stipend. However, while the European powers were interested in creating a pacific zone from which they could move out to subdue rebellious Somali clans in the hinterland, Nassib Bunda was concerned with maintaining his control over the segments of his confederation. As old rivals like Songollo Mafula threw in their lot with the British, Nassib appears to have immersed himself even more in the anti-European politics of the surrounding Somali. His followers began covertly to supply food (and perhaps firearms) to the Ogadeen Somali, then in revolt against the British. On the Italian side of the Juba, he continued to attack Somali traders, leading the Italian resident to threaten him with imprisonment. By 1903, it was reported that a belligerent Nassib Bunda was corresponding with Mohammed Abdille Hasan, the so-called "Mad Mullah" who was waging a holy war against British and Italian infidels in northern Somalia and was looking for allies in the south (Chiesi 1909:631-634). Nassib Bunda's importance in the region may be gauged from the fact that Gosha at the time represented a force of 800 to 1,000 guns.[12]

Nassib's miscalculations about the external balance of power were now coupled with errors of internal policy. Many of his followers became disillusioned with the unpredictable behavior of his last years. Traditions—including one from a sympathetic Yao companion—record the tyrannical actions of which he was accused: hoarding Goshaland's wealth, demanding young virgins as tribute from the settlements, and practicing sorcery against his erstwhile supporters. Whatever part factionalism played in these accusations, several prominent headmen, including his own son, finally appealed to the Italian resident for relief. Nassib Bunda's days were numbered. He was arrested and died in a Muqdisho prison in 1906. His death seems to have aroused no sympathy in Goshaland, though it was recorded in a poem by a Somali of Obbya—an indication of how far his fame had spread (Cerulli 1964:202-203).

This digression into the little-known exploits of a remarkable former slave reveals, I think, the significance of individual personalities in the formative process of frontier communities. A powerful figure in his lifetime, Nassib Bunda also provided a focus of historical identity for all Goshaland after his death. Yet, his very position as a symbol of his community's emergent identity has probably led to his being attributed many institutional innovations when they were in fact part of the more impersonal processes of his society's adaptation to its setting. To say this is not to deny the many tangible benefits he brought, such as Zanzibari military assistance and European trade. Perhaps the "culture heroes" of many African traditions played precisely this role: they were visible foci of authority and cohesion at the time when the community had obtained recognition from outsiders as a distinct and viable polity.

AVAI: A DIFFERENT FORM OF ADAPTATION

At about the time that the Gosha settlements were being consolidated under Nassib Bunda, the community of Avai was being founded in the sparsely inhabited bush country along the lower Shabeelle River. Runaway slaves had apparently used the region as a refuge for some time. As early as 1843, the first European to reach the river was cautioned about the danger from "the slaves or rather self-liberated free men of the interior"; the community of Golweyn "acknowledge no authority" (Christopher 1844:84). The first person to settle in Avai, downstream from Golweyn, was one Makarane, a former slave of the Somali Garre clan, who arrived there "with his family" in the mid-1870's. According to local accounts, he was joined shortly after by Dao, also a former Garre slave, and Songollo Awiva, a former slave of the Biimaal clan. Each seems to have become the head of a distinct hamlet, and they attracted other runaways from the small plantations further up the Shabeelle. Every new arrival in Avai was expected to gather the branches and thatch for building a house; the inhabitants of the hamlet helped with the construction. The work was followed by a feast in which a goat was slaughtered (Colucci 1924:258, n.1). Clearly, the newcomer's incorporation was ritual as well as pragmatic.

These early settlers are said to have allied themselves with the nearby Somali Jiddo clan, providing them with maize and durra in exchange for "protection." The arrangement may have initiated the corporate patron-client relation between herdsmen and farmers so typical of the Horn of Africa; or it may have simply been an alliance of convenience against common enemies, the nearby Garre and Biimaal. In any case, the alliance proved successful, for it is recalled that Avai inflicted a crushing defeat on a Somali raiding party, with several hundred Somalis killed or drowned in the Shabeelle. The numbers may be exaggerated, but the event did establish Avai as a security zone for escaped slaves (Chiesi-Travelli 1904:298, Robecchi-Brichetti 1904:146).

At Makarane's death, Dao became the nominal leader of the Avai settlement cluster. But real power lay with Songollo Awiva, who is remembered as a forceful and despotic leader. He is said to have prohibited trade with neighboring Somalis and the sending of surplus crops to the coastal markets. This bred a resentment that was further increased by a great famine that forced many settlers to flee. Some went to Goshaland, while others were "recaptured" by their former Somali masters. Only after Songollo Awiva's death—in one account by assassination, in another, from smallpox—did life in Avai return to normal.

In 1903, Avai consisted of six villages, with a population of some 2500 to 3000, about two-thirds of them males. This was one-tenth the size of the Gosha polity (for one thing, Avai did not initially experience the constant influx of European-liberated slaves that Goshaland, closer to the sea, did in the early stages of growth). And Avai differed greatly from Goshaland in organization. Each of the Avai settlements was build around a core of freed or escaped slaves from a particular Somali clan: two from Garre, and one each from Mobileen, Elay, Biimaal, and Tunni. The principle of social categorizing by former masters was carried further: a knowledgeable colonial resident reported that the goods of a deceased slave commonly went to a companion who had formerly been a slave of the same Somali master or of a master from the same Somali clan (Chiesi-Travelli 1904:300, Colucci 1924:65 and map 186).

All this—coupled with the fact that Avai traditions nowhere refer to any original ethnic affiliations—suggests that Somali patterns of social organization had a stronger influence in Avai than in Goshaland. Why this should be so is not clear. Avai was founded no earlier than the 1870's; hence, it had scarcely a generation to assimilate the customs of the surrounding Somali. Nor is there any evidence that its population had a high proportion of second- and third-generation slaves who had been "Somali-ized" before escaping. On the other hand, size may be an important factor in the contrast with Goshaland. Avai may simply not have had the critical population mass to organize itself on the basis of previous ethnic identities and therefore turned to the affiliations in slavery for its organizational markers.

THE WIDER CONTEXT OF FRONTIER ADAPTATION

Another hypothesis to be considered in explaining the kind of adaptation that Avai represents looks to external factors. One can see turn-of-the-century Avai as being at the crossroads of development in two possible directions. One was toward becoming a full-fledged "maroon" (autonomous escaped slave) society, like Gosha. The other direction was toward becoming a traditional agricultural client-community, characteristic of southern Somali social organization.

As mentioned earlier, minority communities of cultivators in Somalia have for centuries interacted in various ways with the dominant pastoral population. Minimally, the interaction involved the exchange of crops for meat and dairy products. But, as Cerulli (1964:75-84) has noted, these exchanges typically developed a socio-political dimension. Nomadic groups seeking access to watering points along the river often made arrangements to cross the land of the cultivators while guaranteeing the exclusion of rival nomad clans. From there, it was a short step to providing protection and exercising a limited hegemony over the cultivators. As a sign of their overlordship, the pastoralists would take a portion of the harvest as an annual tribute. Ritual exchanges and common celebrations of Islamic festivals served to strengthen the growing symbiotic link. Thus, there developed along the Shabeelle River a series of agricultural communities, each corporately linked to a distinct Somali patron clan. Each client-community of cultivators was said to "stand with" a particular Somali clan which "protected" it from depradations by other pastoralists.[13]

The importation, in the nineteenth century, of large numbers of slaves into the riverine area stimulated the bringing of new lands under cultivation. While the new laborers were the property of individual slave-owners, it is evident that in many places in the interior slaves and traditional client-cultivators worked side by side.[14] Moreover, slaves frequently intermarried with the farmers, swelling the size of the client groups (Cucinotta 1921:493-502). As a result, there was a rapid assimilation of slaves into the traditional client-communities. This helps explain why later scholars found it so difficult to distinguish in this area between the remnants of prehistoric "Negroid" populations and the descendants of nineteenth-century captives (Cerulli 1964:87-89).

Thus, when slaves first escaped to Avai and struck up an alliance with the nearby Jiddo clan, they were following a well-established regional pattern. The early Avai leaders were substituting a less severe Jiddo patronage for the oppressive control of their former masters. Later, when the leader Songollo Awiva decided to sever all ties with the neighboring Somalis, he was moving his community toward greater autonomy on the Gosha pattern—at the expense, it turned out, of its economic well-being. With Songollo's death, the new leaders began cautiously to reestablish ties with their Somali neighbors. Within a generation, then, the ex-slaves of Avai had experimented with several social models and had, by the eve of colonial occupation, settled on one that has long existed in the area. It kept Avai from the total subjugation that slavery implied, but it also kept it from achieving the sort of autonomy enjoyed by Gosha.

It is thus possible to see the communities of former slaves in Somaliland as occupying positions on a spectrum of types, the spectrum ranging from plantation slavery to self-sufficient agricultural societies. Both Avai and Gosha grew out of rejection of plantation slavery. Yet, as they crystallized into polities, they had to come to terms with the larger society around them. Avai seemed to be moving toward replicating a traditional agricultural client-community, but the process was halted with the coming of colonial rule which made Avai a refuge for slaves liberated by colonial government decree. Gosha, with a larger population, molded by a constant influx of first-generation runaways and better situated geographically to obtain arms from Zanzibar, had to pay less heed to the larger Somali society. Even so, under Nassib Bunda, Gosha began trading and making alliances with some of its Somali neighbors, many of whom maintained slaves in client villages that lay just beyond the forest fringes of Goshaland proper (Chiesi and Travelli 1904:303, 306).

The evolution of these communities illustrates a centuries-old process of social structuring along the pastoral-agricultural frontier. In this larger perspective, both extremes on our spectrum—plantation slavery and autonomous ex-slave communities—represent responses to abnormal conditions. The first followed upon the influx of large numbers of unassimilated cultivators who had to be organized for production; the second resulted from these slaves' escape to freedom. But the conditions of life in this predominantly pastoral country insured that neither of these extreme types could be maintained for long. Somali pastoralists had neither the technology nor the inclination to keep the total control over workers characteristic of slave plantations elsewhere, while the former slaves could not attain economic and military security without accommodating in some way to the pastoral society around them. Just as the Somali-dominated plantation economy proved to be an unstable construct, so did the frontier communities of runaways. Both tended, in time, to move toward becoming client-communities in symbiosis with pastoralist patrons—a type that had sanction from the larger regional culture.

ORAL TRADITIONS AND THE AFRICAN FRONTIER

In conclusion, it is worth reviewing what these two communities can tell us about common processes of society building on the internal African frontier.

In the first place, virtually all such societies have their founding heroes. I have suggested that these may be the political leaders who were ascendant at the time when the crystallizing polity had gained recognition from the larger society as a viable corporate entity to be dealt with. Like all focal personalities or events, the lives of these founding figures are subject to embellishment. We have seen how, in Nassib Bunda's case, crucial organizational practices and customs tended to be seen as his innovations. There continues to be a consensus about his central role in organizing the Gosha federation; and his centrality in tradition as the defender of Gosha's integrity is not undermined by the acknowledgment of the excesses of his later years.

The traditions also emphasize the obstacles that faced the pioneers building their new society, such as Waboni hunters, Somali raiders, absence of tools, and famines. Military victories are an important part of frontier traditions, as inspirational and unifying in the retelling as they must have been in the actual event. Equally significant is the role of religion in the adaptation to the new environment. At a time of social and political flux, the settlers required the support (or at least benign neutrality) of the local spirit world; religious leadership secured it for them. And no less significant is the endowment with supernatural powers of the early leaders, for these powers serve to legitimize the authority of current office holders—who claim to be descendants of the original leaders.

The very critical demographic problems, among them the scarcity of women in the early frontier setting, find expression in traditions concerned with marriage. Great emphasis is placed on Nassib Bunda's hoarding of women. While he may well have been unusually concupiscent, the emphasis put on this fact indicates the importance of women in creating the new society and the difficulties of obtaining enough marriage partners. Nassib Bunda's purported control of women can also represent a subtle commentary on his political dominance, for wives represented links of alliance to their kinsmen, and the more wives a leader had, the greater number of adherents he could marshall. Colonial officials commented on the seeming obsession of Goshaland's inhabitants with women, attributing it to the lack of "a religious ethic" among them and to the "absence of any coherent set of customs governing marriage" (Chiesi 1909:636-638).[15] An obsession it truly was, but hardly for the reasons tendered.

Finally, like all African traditions, those of Gosha and Avai are very concerned with delineating the relations of the new communities with the established societies around them. Each pioneer group has its own accounts of battles, of treaties, and of the acquisition of food crops or firearms from its neighbors. These episodes, significant in themselves, are also markers of the relations with the groups concerned: relations in the making, in the strenghtening, in the breaking. No new society, especially one on an internal frontier, can afford to ignore the potential enemies or allies around it; and traditions bear vivid testimony to the events on which those relations are based.

NOTES

1. The spelling of Somali clan and place names follows the new standard orthography introduced by the Somali government in 1972. In most cases, the reader should have no difficulty in relating it to earlier spelling (e.g., Baraawe for old Brava, Baardheere for old Bardera). For the ex-slave villages, many of whose names derive from Bantu words, I have used the commonly accepted English spellings, as I have also for personal names. "Somalia" and "Somaliland" have

been used interchangeably to refer loosely to the entire area that coincides with modern Somalia.

2. Details on the social organization and history of some of these southern Somali groups can be found in Luling (1971) and Cassanelli (1973, 1982).

3. There are no detailed studies of the slave trade as it affected Somalia. Brief references to the overland route are found in Beachey (1976:153-154), Collister (1961:39-68 *passim*), and Cassanelli (1982:169).

4. Grottanelli (1953) recorded local Zigua traditions during a brief visit to the lower Juba in 1951. The other, earlier account was taken in 1934 by Bakari bin Mdoe, Native Treasury Clerk at Handeni in Tanganyika, who heard it from Abdallah bin Simba. The latter was a resident of Somalia whose grandfather had been enslaved and taken to Somaliland in the nineteenth century. Abdallah had been sent from his village in Goshaland to seek out relatives in the Zigua homeland. Upon reaching Tanganyika, he provided a detailed narrative of events still widely remembered by the Zigua of Somalia. I am grateful to Professor Thomas Spear for bringing this remarkable document (Handeni District Book, 1934) to my attention.

5. East African traditions record a prolonged famine that affected much of coastal East Africa in the mid-1830's; accounts of families selling members into slavery during this period are quite common. See, e.g., Feierman (1973:137).

6. Grottanelli 1953:254, n.28. Ngambo probably recalls the eastern Usambara fortified town of Mghambo, overlooking the Zigua lowlands. Buge may well stand for Bughe, who helped consolidate the kingdom of Shambaa on the fringes of Zigualand in northeast Tanganyika (see Feierman 1973:91-93, 191, 196-197).

7. The first interpretation finds some support in a census of Gosha villages, published by Ferrari (1911:82-84). Of some 60 tabulated villages, only 14 are identified by ethnic origins, while the rest are listed as villages of the ex-slaves of the Tunni, Eelay, Jiddo, and other Somali clans. It may be that by the beginning of the twentieth century, new forms of ethnic identity, based on association with powerful Somali clans, had begun to emerge. On the other hand, Ferrari's classifications may be misleading. We know that the village of Subutini, listed as a settlement of freed Tunni slaves, contained many people of Makua origin, and there were other villages like that.

8. However, Grottanelli (1953:256) noted that among the patrilineal clan names that he recorded in 1951 were some (Bena, Lomwe) that probably reflected the incorporation of other ethnic groups into Zigua society.

9. This account of Nassib Bunda's life is pieced together from a variety of sources, the most important being Rossetti 1900, Chiesi 1909, Robecchi-Brichetti 1904, Zoli 1927, Bargoni 1931, and information provided by Sherif Haji Mohammed Jennay (Cassanelli field notes, 1971).

10. Robecchi-Brichetti (1904) records that Nassib Bunda, during a trip to the interior on behalf of his master, found a large quantity of ivory left by hunters in the bush. When he reported the discovery to his master, the latter was so grateful that he immediately granted Nassib his freedom. According to an account obtained by Bargoni (1931) from an old companion of Nassib Bunda, a pious shaykh purchased Nassib from his former masters for a few thalers and, after helping restore the slave to health, freed him.

11. The belief that certain individuals have power over river crocodiles is widespread in rural Somalia even today. Small lineages of *bahar*-most of them working as ferrymen along the Shabeelle—are often hired to work their magic on the reptiles to prevent them from harming fishermen and riverside cultivators.

12. This is noted in a report of the Italian Commissioner for Somalia to his government in June 1904. The Commissioner also reported that the partisans of

Nassib Bunda were said to be preparing an anti-government action, which apparently never materialized. *Archivo storico dell'ex Ministero dell'Africa italiana,* position 66/4, folder 43.

13. Various examples of these corporate patron-client ties between pastoralists and agriculturalists are cited in Cerulli (1959:117-118) and Cucinotta (1921:389-390).

14. For example, an escaped slave interrogated by colonial officials recalled that he had been placed in leg irons and made to work alongside other cultivators who were not chained, since they were long-time residents with families in the area. Report of the Italian Consul General at Zanzibar to the Ministry of Foreign Affairs, 8 February 1903, no. XLV, in *Documenti Diplomatici: Somalia Italiana 1899-1905* (Rome, 1906).

15. Chiesi (1909:636) quotes from a report by the resident of Goshaland in 1901: "Unions between men and women in Gosha are free and cost nothing. . . . There are many reported cases of women who are claimed by four or five husbands in the same village. Mr. McDougall [the British resident on the opposite bank] and I have consequently refused to concern ourselves with claims of this type, since it is impossible to resolve them. One Kusangia, for example, seeks to reclaim three of his wives taken by other headmen, whose wives in turn had been taken by others; and he himself has to deal with four wives and two concubines who are with him and who are being sought by some fifteen lovers and husbands spread on both banks of the river."

REFERENCES

Andrzejewski, B.W. 1969. "The Position of Linguistic Minorities in Somalia" (Paper delivered to a seminar on Minorities and Minority Problems in Africa, School of Oriental and African Studies, London).

Bargoni, Umberto 1931. *Nella Terra di Nassib Bunda.* Leghorn: Marzocco.

Beachey, R.W. 1976. *The Slave Trade of Eastern Africa.* London: Rex Collings.

Cassanelli, Lee 1973. *The Benaadir Past: Essays in Southern Somali History* (Ph.D. Dissertation, University of Wisconsin).

————. 1982. *The Shaping of Somali Society.* Philadelphia: University of Pennsylvania Press.

Cerulli, Enrico 1957, 1959, 1964. *Somalia. Scritti vari editi ed inediti.* 3 vols. Rome: Istituto Poligrafico dello Stato.

Chiesi, Gustavo 1909. *La Colonizzazione europea nell'Est-Africa.* Turin: Unione Tipografico-Editrice Torinese.

———— and Ernesto Travelli 1904. *Le Questioni del Benadir: Atti e relazione della Commissione d'inchiesta della Societa del Benadir.* Milan: Bellini.

Christopher, William 1844. "Extract from a Journal by Lieut. W. Christopher . . . on the E. Coast of Africa. Dated 8 May 1843." *Journal of the Royal Geographical Society,* 14, pp. 76-103.

Collister, Peter 1961. *The Last Days of Slavery.* Dar Es Salaam: East African Literature Bureau.

Colucci, Massimo 1924. *Principi di Diritto Consuetudinario della Somalia italiana meridionale.* Florence: La Voce.

Cooper, Frederick 1977. *Plantation Slavery on the East Coast of Africa.* New Haven: Yale University Press.

Cucinotta, E. 1921. "La costitucione sociale somala." *Rivista Coloniale*, 6, pp.389ff, 443ff, 493ff.

Dundas, F. 1893. "Expedition up the Jub River through Somali-land, East Africa." *Geographical Journal*, I, new series, pp. 209-223, map.

Feierman, Steven 1974. *The Shambaa Kingdom: A History*. Madison: University of Wisconsin Press.

Ferrari, G. 1911. *Il Basso Giuba Italiano e le Concessioni agricole nella Goscia*. Rome: B.Lux.

Grottanelli, Vinigi 1953. "I Bantu del Giuba nelle tradizioni dei Wazegua." *Geographica Helvetica*, no.8, pp.249-260.

Guillain, M. 1856. *Documents sur l'histoire, la geographie, et le commerce de l'Afrique Orientale*. 3 vols. Paris: Arthus Bertrand.

Handeni District Book 1934. "Notes on a Wazigua Colony in Somaliland." Recorded by Bakari bin Mdoe, Native Treasury Clerk, Handeni; trans. by S.B .Jones, District Officer, Handeni; narrated by Abdallah bin Simba.

Kersten, Otto ed. 1871. *Baron Carl Claus von der Decken's Reisen in Ost Afrika in den Jahren 1862 bis 1865*. Vol. II. Leipzig and Heidelberg: C.F. Winter.

Luling, Virginia 1971. *The Social Structure of Southern Somali Tribes* (Ph.D. Dissertation, University of London).

Price, Richard 1973. "Introduction." In Richard Price, editor, *Maroon Societies*. New York: Anchor Books.

Prins, A.H.J. 1960. "The Somaliland Bantu." *Bulletin of the International Committee on Urgent Anthropological and Ethnological Research*, 3, pp.28-31.

Robecchi-Brichetti, Luigi 1899. *Somalia e Benadir*. Milan: Carlo Aliprandi.

———. 1904. *Lettere dal Benadir*. Milan: La Poligrafica.

Rossetti, Carlo 1900. "Nassib Bunda: Sultano di Goscia." *L'Italia Coloniale*, I, No.10, pp.29-37.

Sullivan, G.L. 1873. *Dhow-Chasing in Zanzibar Waters*. London: Dawson's (1967 reprint).

Tozzi, Ruggero 1941. *Cenni sull'agricoltura e l'economia degli indigeni del Basso Giuba*. Florence: Istituto Agronomico per l'Africa Italiana.

Zoli, Corrado 1927. *Oltre-Giuba*. Rome: Sindicato Italiano Arti Grafiche.

A CONTEMPORARY "ANOMALOUS" SOCIETY ON THE RURAL FRONTIER

Although free settlers rather than escaped slaves, the frontiersmen of Mto wa Mbu in twentieth-century Tanganyika, described here by William Arens, shared some features with the Bantu frontiersmen of Somaliland. Both groups were, culturally, Bantu East Africans and both were of mixed ethnic origins. Their niches on their respective frontiers were similar—both were agriculturalists exploiting lands that were marginal to the pastoralists dominating the two regions. In both cases, the settlers' lands of origin were far from the frontiers and could not play the role of metropoles in the frontier process. Nor could this role be fully played by the local dominant societies (Somali in one case and Masai in the other) with whom their cultural differences were too profound; hence, as with the Bantu former slaves, social construction in Mto wa Mbu was a strikingly self-contained process. And, finally, in both instances, we are dealing with an Africa different from the one we have been considering so far: it is an Africa in which the colonial powers and their successor national states intrude more and more into the shaping of the frontier societies. The former slaves in nineteenth-century Somaliland manipulated the presence of colonial powers—British, Italian, and Zanzibari—to promote their interests. In the case of the twentieth-century settler community in Tanganyika, British colonial power and the modern state constrained its development; what manipulation has taken place had to do with ideologies rather than power politics.

Moreover, we see the two groups at quite different points of the frontier process. The former slave communities in Somaliland had gone through the full process of becoming established polities. The people of Mto wa Mbu had gone only through the very beginnings of developing a frontier community when the larger political environment—the colonial state and then the national state of Tanganyika/Tanzania—became dominant.

In the earlier stage of Mto wa Mbu's development, the half-hearted control by the British administration was strong enough to interfere with the typical overall pattern of development of an African frontier society but weak enough nevertheless to make Mto wa Mbu not untypical in many specific details. The community itself arose where it did because the existence of the British administration was sufficient to protect it in its infancy from harassment by the Masai who dominated the region. From its inception, then, the community was freed from what traditional African frontier communities had to grapple with—the dangers of the relationship with their frontiers' hosts.

Internally, we find here, as elsewhere, the familiar "firstcomer" pattern. While the earliest settlers claimed to be the founders by virtue of actual chronological precedence, Muslim settlers claim to have really founded the Mto wa Mbu community by having brought an Islamic social order to it. But the contradiction has led neither to a confrontation nor to a subtle accommodation of the kind we saw among the BaShu, because the different claims had no political consequences in a community that was not politically sovereign; the ultimate administrative power rested, even if lightly, in British hands. For the same reason, the settlers could also ignore whatever claims to primacy might have been advanced by the Masai. And, as elsewhere and as Arens points out, the availability of land no doubt had something to do with this mutual tolerance of one another's firstcomer claims.

The lack of political autonomy also affected the process of redefinition of ethnic identities in Mto wa Mbu. The various ethnic identities of its inhabitants did not disappear but they weakened, and intermarriage among the different ethnicities was increasingly frequent. In this, Mto wa Mbu resembles all other developing frontier communities. The emergent ethnicity of Mto wa Mbu became largely based, culturally, on an Islamic model of community organization brought by the dominant section of the community. And, as in other small frontier communities, the model could be followed relatively smoothly here, for the various vested interests that plague large established polities had not yet emerged (later, the arrival of Christian Chagga did affect this smoothness).

Typically, the emergent local ethnicity of Mto wa Mbu was expressed in terms of "civilization." It defined its agricultural way of life as superior to the "primitive" pastoralism of its regional hosts, most particularly the Masai. But the typical frontier process of ethnic amalgamation has so far only run a part of its usual course. No new ethnic identity had been fully created. Thus, what we find in Mto wa Mbu is one of those "anomalous non-tribes" discussed at length at the beginning of Part I—communities whose uncertain (in reality, incomplete) ethnicity, frozen by the colonial presence, made them so annoying to administrators, so uninteresting to anthropologists, and so insignificant to historians.

The further fortunes of this "anomalous" ethnicity continued to be shaped by external forces. In colonial times, the emerging Mto wa Mbu identity—no less "ethnic" in local terms than that of the Masai—had no particular significance beyond the local setting. With the coming of independence, however, this incomplete ethnicity, characteristic of young frontier communities, happened to conform to the "anti-tribal" ideals of the national government: Mto wa Mbu became an example of ethnic coexistence and polyethnic peace. Similarly, the ethnic stereotyping by Mto wa Mbu of the Masai and other pastoralists could now be cast in the national political idiom as the contrast between "civilized" agriculturalists and "primitive" pastoralists, between "progressive" polyethnic social formations and "backward tribal" ones. Thus, like other African frontier communities seeking legitimation through affiliation with large real or imaginary metropoles, Mto wa Mbu found the legitimation of its own local incomplete ethnicity in the ideological constructs of an emergent national metropole.

—Editor

W. Arens

—————— 9 ——————

Mto wa Mbu:
A Rural Polyethnic Community in Tanzania

Taken as a whole, there is little doubt that our view of historical and social processes in Africa has been overly simplistic. Though often brilliant analytically, the classical anthropological studies of African societies have generally portrayed them in a harmonious relationship to time and space. In the search for dynamics, later studies focused on the urban environment as the arena of change, adjustment, and novelty. Behind this dichotomy lingered the implicit assumption that the "tradition-dominated" African hinterland lay dormant while the European-inspired urban centers were the catalyst for change.[1]

More recent studies by historians and historically oriented anthropologists are altering this image of the continent. Yet there remains another conceptual contrast, the rural-urban one, which, although originally cast in the form of a continuum, has most often been operationalized as a polarity. Intermediate forms of community organization scattered throughout the countryside, not quite rural nor yet urban, remained unattended to by researchers until relatively recently and hence left out of our vision of African social processes. This ethnographic gap is all the more surprising when one considers that such communities paralleled in many ways the North American frontier experience, where people of one and usually several ethnic groups moved into areas far from their traditional homeland and sought to construct a workable social and cultural environment within the bounds of an encompassing state structure. The fact that in North America the state was an independent nation, while in Africa it was a newly created colony, is in some respects inconsequential while in some others important. The following is an examination of one such polyethnic rural frontier community in twentieth-century Africa.[2]

THE ECOLOGICAL AND ECONOMIC SETTING

In 1920, meandering through what was then Northern Tanganyika Territory, a British traveler commented with surprise on a little village, describing it as "inhabited by a polyglot crowd of neighbors who had emigrated from various inhabitable and barren districts, regardless of tribal distinction to place themselves in this fertile spot . . ." (Shorthose 1923:250). Such communities of internal migrants had already begun to dot the countryside during the nascent colonial period. Although the interior of East Africa had long known similar settlements astride the major trade routes to the coast, colonial rule stimulated the appearance of minor pockets of cultivators who, in a country where agriculture was often a precarious enterprise at best, sought little more than better subsistence. Not far from Shorthose's itinerary lay Mto wa Mbu, which came into existence in 1920 for just such a reason. From modest beginnings, it had grown by 1970 into a major agricultural, trading, and administrative center of 3,500 residents. The development was a gradual one and reflected at the local level changes taking place in the colony as a whole.

The village of Mto wa Mbu lies a little over seventy miles by road west of Arusha, the headquarters of Arusha region. Its name ("River of the Mosquitoes") derives from one of the perennial streams that flow through the area, and it initially referred to the settlement only. By external administrative decision after independence, Mto wa Mbu division was formed to include both the village itself and a portion of western Masailand. The commercial core of shops, a few bars and hotels, a marketplace, and the surrounding cultivated area lie at an altitude of 3,000 feet, a short distance from the foot of the escarpment in the eastern branch of the Great Rift Valley. Three miles south of the village center is Lake Manyara, one in the chain of lakes running through the Rift Valley.

If one approaches Mto wa Mbu from the east, heading toward the escarpment, the dry plains of Masailand come to an abrupt halt with the emergence of forest and intermittent cultivation that continues westward for about three miles to the base of the escarpment. The forest, formerly the preserve of wild animals, has been gradually cleared over the years. Cultivated plots and habitation stretch northward from the lake shore for some five miles, until the plots gradually disappear into bush. The amount of cultivated and used land that forms the community of Mto wa Mbu proper is about twenty square miles, but expanding as availability of water permits.

It is this water availability for irrigation that attracts settlers to the community. According to one estimate, two-thirds of Tanzania is not suitable for cultivation because of the scarcity and unreliability of rainfall (International Bank . . . 1961:11–19). This situation would also prevail in this corner of the valley if the rainfall on the plateau, plentiful and reliable, did not feed a number of small rivers and streams that eventually flow down the escarpment and crisscross the edge of the valley floor before discharging into Lake Manyara. The residents take advantage of these rivers by making irrigation furrows for their fields that, on the average, cover two to three acres. The result is a secure harvest for household consumption and a surplus that, sold to traders in the market, provides modest but steady cash for other necessities. In sum, the residents are in a relatively advantageous economic position in comparison to many of their countrymen in other parts of Tanzania.

The main crop is the banana in its many varieties. It demands a fair amount of moisture; without irrigation, it is normally grown in highland areas that receive close to sixty inches of rainfall a year. The banana is easy to cultivate; it provides food and a base for beer throughout the year; and it is a constant source of income. Every household also cultivates a vegetable plot, primarily of tomatoes and onions; these, supplemented with occasional fresh meat or fish from the market, give an adequate and varied diet. A minority of the farmers, less enamored of a perpetual diet of banana, resort to the cultivation of corn, making cornflour their staple.

The market stalls are liberally sprinkled with other items, such as lemons, avocadoes, peppers, tobacco, and fruits from the nearby fields. Although it has not always been so, the commercial arena is now dominated by those engaged in trading as a full-time occupation. Most are young men from one ethnic group, the Chagga, who arrange to transport the banana surplus to surrounding communities for a profit. Other stalls are manned by part-time farmers and traders, who restrict their commercial ventures primarily to the community.

In light of all these ecological and economic facts, it is easy to see why the area has attracted and continues to attract new settlers who are willing to pay the price of emigration and relocation. But beyond that, the ecology and economy of Mto wa Mbu have strongly shaped the character of interpersonal relations, the form of community organization, and the local interpretation of historical events.

THE EMERGENCE OF A FRONTIER COMMUNITY

Except for parts of West Africa, the large and small towns of tropical Africa appear, on present evidence, to be the result of alien influence, Arab or European (Steel 1961). In this, Mto wa Mbu is no exception. The area on which the settlement now stands was, in the early twentieth century, an uninhabited stretch of forest. Archaeological evidence, however, does indicate the existence of settled agricultural villages throughout this portion of the Rift Valley prior to the arrival of the Masai early in the 17th century (Sassoon 1967). During the immediate pre-colonial era, the plains to the east of the wooded area, as well as the highlands just above, were controlled by the ever-expanding Masai with their herds. Both the Masai and the Iraqw of the plateau avoided the woodland stretch: its tse-tse fly posed a threat to their livestock and its mosquitoes were debilitating to people adapted to a relatively malaria-free environment. At the same time, the agricultural Mbugwe, living in the lowlands just to the south, were discouraged from expanding into the area by the concentration of wild animals and an apparent desire to maintain a buffer strip between themselves and the Masai. Consequently, the potentially fertile parcel of land remained uninhabited from the seventeenth to the early twentieth century.

Colonial control—initially German and then, after the First World

War, British under a Mandate—had an almost immediate effect on such patterns of occupation throughout Tanganyika Territory. Areas within the vast expanse of Masailand that were suitable for agriculture were quickly encroached upon by other groups, who heretofore had been forced to live on the adjacent slopes overlooking the plains. It was only a matter of time before land-hungry settlers began to move farther afield, in order to exploit pockets of suitable agricultural land in the vacant interior.

Mto wa Mbu is such a case in point, though it is not possible to ascertain the founding of the community with any precision. What is clear is that the change from uninhabited forest to a small settlement of permanent residents was gradual. Each of the various groups in Mto wa Mbu now sees the emergence of what it considers to be a true community in terms of its own arrival. Representatives of coastal groups, who had been converted to Islam centuries ago, claim that their co-religionists founded the village in the sense of implanting Islam as a community ethos, where before there were only scattered individuals living in a disorganized state. On the other hand, Nyamwezi and Sukuma residents, who come from Central Tanzania, argue that their ethnic representatives were the first to settle the area. From a historical perspective, the latter claim has a physical validity, while the Muslim claim has greater social and cultural significance. During the initial period of my fieldwork there were some residents still alive who were among the earliest arrivals, and it was possible to reconstruct with some degree of assurance the founding of the village.

In 1917, during the East African campaign of World War I, which wrested Tanganyika from the Germans, a German column, composed of European officers, African *askari* (soldiers), and retainers, camped for a short time at the edge of the forest area that was to become Mto wa Mbu, before continuing their march. According to the accounts, the area was then a wilderness, but its possibilities were readily apparent to some of the African members of the column. After the end of hostilities, a small number of these former *askari* found themselves interned in Arusha. With the encouragement of the new British administration, they decided to move to the virgin site rather than return to their homeland, which they had left some years before. Not all had remained from this first cohort, but assuming these individuals to be the first settlers, the founding of the village can be dated to somewhere between 1917 and 1920.[3]

During this early period, the population increased at a slow but steady pace. For the oldest residents, the struggle with the land assumes major importance in their historical memory of these years, and the seemingly insignificant banana takes on its local cultural prominence in this context. In addition to being a basic food, the banana facilitated immigration and the continued establishment of new separate households in the new community. In the natural process of growth of the plant, the reproduction of surplus offshoots at the base hinders the growth of the parent stalk; this means that these stems are available to others for the asking. Hence, a new arrival could start his own field at little expense to himself by requesting stalks from someone already established in Mto wa Mbu. Depending upon the location of his field, the new settler could have a food supply within three to five months of arrival. Since the typical pattern was for a man to arrive on his own and put up with an acquaintance, he could shortly thereafter call on his family to join him or, if necessary, return home to marry and bring his new wife back.

The cultivation of the banana, then, had social implications that went quite beyond mere subsistence. Among the first events related by one of the oldest living members of the village, to whom I indicated my interest in its history, was the following: in the early days, when everyone had to rely for food on fish from the lake, one of the early settlers walked thirty miles through Masailand to Engaruka, a similar village of cultivators, and returned with the first banana plants. From these original stems, the few inhabitants were able to begin cultivating their own banana groves. The passing of these plants from neighbor to neighbor was therefore a primary means of creating and cementing social ties. Each man received from someone else the basis for a reliable and highly valued food supply, and eventually he passed it on to another newcomer. In a manner deeply appreciated by the older residents, the banana, ordinary as it may seem, symbolizes the unity of the earliest settlers and the emergence of an integrated community.

Although many other events of the early days are obscure or entirely forgotten, the history of the crops remains vivid. I was told who brought the first papaya plants after a visit to the coast, and who introduced the first oranges and lemons. The banana, however, is as significant in the present as it was in the past, for it continues to allow the village to persist and expand.

In the British period, the little village is first mentioned in the administrative records in 1935, a few years after the construction of a road passing through Mto wa Mbu. The road linked the large European wheat farms in the Iraqw highlands to the Great North Road, twenty miles away, and thus to the world market. The new road also attracted more settlers to Mto wa Mbu: by 1935, the settlement had an official taxpaying population of three hundred. The records also indicate at this time that the area had been designated as an "alien" (non-Masai) agricultural settlement. Moreover, since the Masai had no interest in the agricultural potential of the land, it was decided that the number of migrants would not be restricted and permits from the District Office, allowing individuals to relocate in the community, would not be required, in contrast to the usual policy governing other alien settlements in the district (cf. Masai District Book).

As indicated, the earliest arrivals were primarily from the coastal and central regions of Tanganyika. They were typical of those who had been swept up by the early impact of the colonial era and had drifted throughout Tanganyika as soldiers, porters, laborers, and low-level administrators. For most, Mto wa Mbu was the last stage in a history of wandering. The majority of them were Muslims since birth, or had been converted to the faith during their travels or after arriving in Mto wa Mbu. Thus Islam and agriculture gave the initial cultural stamp to the community.

A second distinctive wave of immigration took place in the late nineteen forties and early fifties. This one consisted in large part of individuals from the Central and Northern Regions. Most of them came directly from their homeland to Mto wa Mbu in search of better land. While there were Muslims scattered among them, the majority held traditional African beliefs. Eventually, however, they were drawn into the Islamic community through a combined process of religious adoption and conversion (see Arens 1975a). Their primary interest in agriculture and their eventual acceptance of Islam meant that, except for a population increase, the overall character of the community remained undisturbed during these years.

In the 1960s, the village experienced a third phase of expansion—this time, one that had qualitative as well as quantitative effects. This most recent stage witnessed the arrival of a large number of Chagga and Pare from Northern Tanzania, people who are overwhelmingly Christian. Many of these new arrivals came not only to farm but to trade, to open shops, and to engage in skilled labor such as tailoring, carpentry, and shoe making. As a result, this stage saw an enlargement of the market, the initiation of trade on a larger scale, and the building of retail shops, lodgings, and bars that challenged the trading monopoly of the few resident Asian shopkeepers. This period also saw the establishment of Lutheran, Seventh Day Adventist, and Catholic missions, which competed for the unconverted with the existing mosque. Consequently, Mto wa Mbu was transformed from a small Muslim agricultural settlement into a busy and culturally heterogeneous market center taking advantage of a heavily travelled road.

In considering this flow of events and the resulting social and cultural heterogeneity of the community, one might at first glance suggest that Mto wa Mbu could be conceived of as a city in microcosm. However, crucial aspects of the community organization would belie this view. Thus, most urban communities in Africa are characterized by an emphasis on the distinctiveness of their various ethnic components. In Mto wa Mbu, by contrast, such ethnic distinctiveness had failed to emerge as a major feature of social organization. I have discussed this issue in greater detail elsewhere (Arens 1973) and suggested that what urban anthropologists often refer to as "retribalization" (cf. Cohen 1969) failed to occur in Mto wa Mbu, largely because of its uniform agricultural base and reliance on irrigation. A competitive arena involving the struggle for scarce economic rewards, so common in the African urban migrant's experience elsewhere, has failed to materialize in Mto wa Mbu with its abundance of land there for the asking. Furthermore, the community's reliance upon irrigation stimulated a need for cooperation rather than competition among the residents. In short, ethnic distinctiveness was rarely an issue that could be exploited organizationally to achieve desired goals. This argument is further substantiated by the signal exception to the pattern, the Chagga, whose primary concern as a group was not agriculture but commerce. Of all the potential ethnic groups, they alone used the advantages of ethnicity in the attempt to monopolize trading opportunities. Their particular economic niche resulted in an ethnic organizational focus, in contrast to the general pattern in which ethnicity was of little consequence.

This development of a coherent community character owes much to the ecological and economic variables I have mentioned, but it is not the entire explanation, for other historical experiences lent further support to the gradual emergence of a frontier culture that stood in stark contrast both to the conservatism of other rural areas and to the patterns of change characteristic of the urban environment. In these latter instances, a continued commitment to ethnicity remained a safeguard throughout the colonial era. At Mto wa Mbu, the opposite held true, for reasons I shall now examine.

THE FRONTIER FROM TWO PERSPECTIVES

The history of the formal political-jural organization of this frontier community is a complex affair, often involving competing organizational models at various times. From the absence of official comments in the district records, it can be assumed that during the formative stage the European administrators took little interest in community affairs. As indicated, during this period Islam was the dominant religious persuasion, and from the earliest days the community had a mosque and a resident *mwalimu* (teacher) who was responsible for providing both sacred and secular guidance. Issues involving marriage, descent, and inheritance followed the Islamic code as interpreted in East Africa. A small "bride-price" was offered, polygyny was practiced, divorce was allowed, and descent was patrilineal. Minor disputes requiring mediation, which were reported to be rare, were taken to a respected neighbor or to the *mwalimu* for resolution. As to those who did not subscribe to Islam, they either returned home to marry or sought a local spouse from their own ethnic group, and they followed traditional precepts, which usually were not greatly at variance with Islamic practices. In sum, the residents were able to manage their domestic and jural affairs with a minimum of difficulty.

However, this polyethnic village in Masailand was unsettling to the colonial sense of order. The mere existence of such a community was a source of discomfort and suspicion. Rather than conclude that the migrants were simply seeking a more secure, if not better, livelihood, the Europeans saw these particular "natives" as being difficult by the mere fact of their moving from one place in the Territory to another. According to the prevailing British view of the strength of "tribalism" and the force of custom, normal Africans would not abandon their traditional homes and culture. The suspicion, then, was that this village was inhabited by drifters, tax dodgers, and assorted other deviants.

However much they might have preferred to ignore this blight on the Masai landscape, the authorities had eventually to face the task of a half-hearted official supervision. Thus, in 1935, the British designated a local Muslim resident as *jumbe* (headman), responsible to the District head-quarters. The *jumbe* was instructed to appoint other officials in the various recognized localities, who were to report to him. Their duties included tax collection, law enforcement, and the hearing of minor civil and criminal cases under the jurisdiction of a native court, which was officially estab-lished in 1938. These individuals had little traditional legitimacy, but they were accepted by the other settlers because of their local reputation as respected residents. However, peaceful social intercourse continued to be maintained by the sharing of basic values and customs that cut across ethnic boundaries, rather than by the existence of an administrative machinery. In effect, the social and cultural differences that loomed so large in the British model of African life had no such significance here. The residents, of course, recognized that others sometimes had different *desturi* (customs), but none of these was so odd as to be incomprehensible, bothersome, or threatening. At the level of interpersonal relations, the relative unimpor-tance of differences in ethnicity may be gauged by the rates of inter-ethnic marriage, which exceeded those of urban centers. Thus, seventy percent of the marriages that were contracted after arrival and that actually took place in Mto wa Mbu, occurred between persons of different ethnic backgrounds. At the same time, religious endogamy prevailed (Arens and Arens 1978). This emergence of a community culture was facilitated by reliance on Ki-Swahili as the community language. The people of Mto wa Mbu saw themselves in contrast to their neighbors on the plains and plateau, whose customs they held in rather low regard. This conception of what constitutes civilized and uncivilized behavior was and is a significant social boundary marker. At present, as further proof of their commitment to change and modernity, the residents recall with pride that they were early supporters of the independence movement in Tanganyika, and they recount how those associated with the colonial system were swept from office during an anti-witchcraft movement (Arens 1980). They point to their active local branch of TANU, the Tanzanian single party, as continuing evidence of their political awareness, and hold this in contrast to their more conservative neighbors, whose outlook they consider to be more suitable to pre-indepen-dence times.

Having established a political structure to its satisfaction, the colonial administration, to all intents and purposes, turned its back on the village. This was not surprising. Since the overwhelming majority of the residents of the district were Masai, it was their problems that assumed paramount

importance, and the meager administrative services and projects were
geared toward meeting Masai needs. This was not merely a matter of a
practical approach to government. There was also at play, here, a basic
political and philosophical outlook on the part of the administration: despite official pronouncements, great value was placed on the continuity of
indigenous societies. This orientation was further compounded, in this
instance, by the special, often romantic, attitude of many European officials toward the Masai, whom they considered a proud, independent
people, as evidenced by their unwillingness to change their ways. Other
ethnic groups, more responsive to change and more inclined to "western-
ization," were less admired. They also presented greater administrative
problems. The government was concerned with improvements in the Territory, but its policies were aimed at producing changes without intention-
ally upsetting the mode of life of the peoples involved or affecting the
pattern of relations among various groups.

In discussing British rule in East Africa, Gulliver has stated that "the
net effect of the colonial era was a marked heightening of tribal consciousness and a deepening of tribal differences" (1969b:16). Mto wa Mbu provides a striking exception to this situation, since it was established during
the colonial era and had a population that sought to deemphasize ethnicity.
As an anomalous farming community within an immense area populated
by cattle-keeping people, it was all but ignored during the British administration of the District. Also, since it was populated by migrants from
other areas and therefore lacked a traditional political structure, it had to
be dealt with in a different manner from the other parts of the District.
Given the lack of a traditional system of authority and the mixture of
residents, no single body of customary law could be applied in the community. This further compounded the European functionaries' confusion
and gave the settlement an aura of untidiness. During the entire Trust
period, no development projects were initiated, few services were provided to the residents, and official visits by administrators were infrequent
and usually full of comments on the deplorable circumstances. Mto wa
Mbu was not alone in this—the same treatment was given to all other such
"alien" agricultural settlements in Masailand.

With the coming of independence in 1961, the situation was radically
altered. The departure of the British and the installation of an African
administration was accompanied by a discernible shift in attention by the
new regime away from the countryside and to the more densely populated
rural settlements, such as Mto wa Mbu. In the Masai District, this meant
that the many pastoralists scattered throughout the area were no longer
treated as being of greater significance than the inhabitants of these agricultural settlements.

This administrative shift in outlook and values stemmed, generally,
from policies formulated at the national level by the new regime. Foremost among these was an early policy of agricultural development that

encouraged rural residents to become small-scale cultivators. This program of rural development also tried to provide greater social services to the countryside than it had previously received under the British. This meant fostering more compact rural settlements and using those already in existence as centers for social and administrative services. Mto wa Mbu was a natural site for the implementation of this policy, since it exhibited all the characteristics necessary for the purpose. With the creation of smaller administrative units below the district level, Mto wa Mbu became the headquarters for Mto wa Mbu Division, a large area that included a portion of the outlying Masai plains. In effect, part of the traditional Masai country now fell under the jurisdiction of Mto wa Mbu, while previously the opposite had been the case.

The rising importance of communities such as Mto wa Mbu goes beyond matters of explicit policy. The replacement of British by African officials meant a change in the administrative attitudes toward the Masai. The typical African administrator does not see the Masai and other conservative groups as proud members of noble "tribes" but rather as "backward" people lacking the proper consciousness necessary for contributing to the growth of a modern progressive nation. Hence, the new administration has subjected the Masai to programs to make them wear trousers and shirts in place of their traditional cloaks, to stop piercing their ears, and to abandon other practices considered unseemly in a modern society. The new communities had been important rural outposts of the independence movement. The residents of Mto wa Mbu organized the first local branch of TANU in the District, the movement spreading from there to the smaller settlements, and they continue to give firm support to the Party. By contrast, the Masai and the other groups in the vicinity, such as the Iraqw and Wambugwe, took little interest in these matters. This fact was not forgotten by the government, which involved these centers of political strength in the machinery of rural development and administration.

For Mto wa Mbu, this policy has meant the establishment of a police post and a local court with two trained magistrates, the opening of a dispensary with a small hospital, and the building of a primary school. The increased importance of the community was further marked by an influx of government employees and the stationing of various officials concerned with local development, in addition to the school staff, medical personnel, court officials, policemen, and, finally, the employees of the nearby National Park and, intermittently, the tourists visiting it. To meet the new needs, the government built forty-five housing units and brought piped water to the village, while the local economy was stimulated by the demands of an expanded market.

Under British rule, Mto wa Mbu represented, in its way, what was new and changing in the country, even if it was administratively ignored in favor of what was traditional and stable. With independence, this growing village came to represent not only what was new, but also what was now defined as desirable, and was given government support. In the new official ideology, Mto wa Mbu is the new Tanzania, much as the surrounding countryside is the old. The implications of this contrast have not been lost on the residents of the community.

The features of Mto wa Mbu culture that are held to be superior to the cultures of the surrounding areas are few and sharply drawn. First, the people of Mto wa Mbu characterize themselves as *watu wa kijiji* (townsmen), in contrast to the Iraqw and Masai, whom they disdain as *watu wa kabila* (tribesmen). Second, despite internal divisions between Muslims and Christians, the residents take pride in the fact that they are all *watu wa dini* (religious people), as opposed to the Iraqw and Masai, whose traditional religions cast them as *wapagani* (pagans). Finally, the residents take comfort in the notion that they are *waswahili* (Swahili people), which puts them into a category that is national and even international, and not a parochial one (see Arens 1975b). In addition to a proficiency in the Swahili language, this ethnic designation implies a "modern" disposition, whose expression ranges from a style of dress to a style of political expression.

In addition to maintaining an ethnic boundary marker at the local level, this self-proclaimed modern outlook serves as a cultural bridge to other villages, towns, and cities of Tanzania. The result is that, in a profound sense, the residents of Mto wa Mbu also see themselves as *wanachi* (citizens)—a further indication of their modernity, in contrast to those *watu wa kabila* who have failed to broaden their political horizons and commitments.

ON THE FRONTIER OF CHANGE

If the residents of Mto wa Mbu see themselves as the harbingers and reflectors of social change in what was formerly a colonial Territory and is now an independent nation, to what extent, we may ask, does this collective self-perception correspond to typical external definitions of their situation? Within both folk and social-science models of change and "modernity," this self-perception would be largely valid. The drive, during the colonial period, to relocate and take advantage of new economic and social opportunities bears witness to a willingness to experiment. The form of social organization that emerged followed the ethical guidelines of a world religion and deemphasized ethnicity at both the community and interpersonal levels—a further reflection of the residents' willingness to accept what was often novel rather than traditional. Although the personal attitude of local British administrators was often unfavorable, these developments did conform to the official goals of the Trust Territory government. As the colonial period drew to a close, the residents of Mto wa Mbu continued to grasp new opportunities, rejecting the local political figures identified with alien rule and replacing them with those associated with the drive for independence.

Throughout the existence of Mto wa Mbu, its people seemed ever willing to adopt precisely those features of organization and social orientation that accord with typical definitions of "modernity." Mto wa Mbu is not unique in this, for there are other such settlements in rural areas (for another example, see Guillotte 1973). And, as Gulliver (1973) has pointed out, the residents of these communities often reflect, in some respects, the ideal contemporary image of "modernity" more closely than do urban residents, who continue to maintain a strong sense of ethnic loyalty. It is thus the rural settlements in the backwaters of the interior "frontier" that often stand at the edge of the wider national frontier of change.

NOTES

1. The contention applies most strongly to Anglophone anthropology. Within it, a notable exception to the generalization is the work of Aidan Southall, whose study of the Alur focused on the process of indigenous political expansion. His co-authored study of urbanization in Kampala was also an early study of this type by social anthropologists (Southall and Gutkind 1957).

2. The field research carried out over sixteen months in 1968–1969 was made possible by a grant from the National Institute of Public Health (Grant No. MH 114414-01). A return visit to the community during the summer of 1973 was funded by a SUNY Faculty Research Award. The community is described in Arens 1979.

3. The general outline of historical events, as related by some of the oldest residents, was subsequently verified by a European farmer who settled in the Iraqw Highlands before the emergence of Mto wa Mbu.

REFERENCES

Arens, W. 1973. "Tribalism and the Poly-Ethnic Rural Community." *Man* 8: 441–450.

———— 1975a. "Islam and Christianity in Sub-Saharan Africa: Ethnographic Reality or Ideology." *Cahiers d'etudes africaines* 15: 443–456.

———— 1975b. "The Waswahili: The Social History of an Ethnic Group." *Africa* 45: 426–438.

———— 1979. *On the Frontier of Change: Mto wa Mbu, Tanzania.* Ann Arbor: The University of Michigan Press.

———— 1980. "Taxonomy versus Dynamics Revisited: The Interpretation of Misfortune in a Poly-Ethnic Setting." In *Explorations in African Systems of Thought,* edited by Ivan Karp and Charles S. Bird, pp. 165–180. Bloomington: Indiana University Press.

Arens, W. and Arens, Diana Antos. 1978. "Kinship and Marriage in a Polyethnic Community." *Africa* 48: 149–160.

Cohen, Abner. 1969. *Customs and Politics in Urban Africa*. London: Routledge and Kegan Paul.

Guillotte, Joseph V. 1973. *Becoming One People: Social and Cultural Integration in a Multi-Ethnic Community in Rural Tanzania*. Ann Arbor: University Microfilms.

Gulliver, P.H. 1969. "Introduction." In *Tradition and Transition in East Africa*, edited by P.H. Gulliver. London: Routledge and Kegan Paul.

International Bank for Reconstruction and Development. 1961. *The Economic Development of Tanganyika*. Baltimore: The Johns Hopkins University Press.

Masai District Book, Northern Province, Tanganyika Territory. Masai-Monduli District Headquarters, Tanzania.

Sassoon, H. 1967. "New Views on Engaruka, Northern Tanzania." *Journal of African History* 8: 201–217.

Shorthose, W.T. 1923. *Sport and Adventure in East Africa*. London: Seeley, Service, and Co.

Southall, Aidan W. 1956. *Alur Society*. Cambridge: Heffer and Sons.

Southall, Aidan W. and Peter C.W. Gutkind 1957. *Townsmen in the Making*. Kampala: East African Institute of Social Research.

Steel, R.W. 1961. "The Towns in Tropical Africa." In *Essays on African Population*, edited by K.M. Barbour and R.M. Prothero. London: Routledge and Kegan Paul.

THE POLITICAL DYNAMICS OF THE
URBAN FRONTIER

In American usage, the term "frontier" slides easily into metaphor. No sooner had America accepted "the End of the Frontier" than it was told that a "New Frontier" had begun, not least by probing the "Last Frontier of Space." One may ask, then, how much reality and how much metaphor there is to the notion of an African "urban frontier." In terms of the definition we have been using, the notion is very much on this side of reality. We have considered a central characteristic of the frontier to be social construction by immigrants in an area that to them represents an institutional vacuum. As Sandra Barnes points out, in the following study of Mushin, a suburb of Lagos, Nigeria, both the Yoruba cities of the nineteenth century and many contemporary urban agglomerations like Mushin grew very quickly and their immigrant populations were (as they often are now) confronted by an institutional vacuum which they tried to fill by constructing a new social order. That is, historically, the African internal frontier was not exclusively rural. Furthermore, there is a heuristic advantage to seeing many African cities as frontiers—it reverses the long dominant view of urbanization as something "imposed" upon Africa, thereby focusing our attention on the discontinuities and disruptions in African life. By contrast, a frontier implies active construction rather than passive submission to outside forces. Instead of the urbanization of Africa, the frontier perspective makes us look at the Africanization of urbanism in Africa.

The growth of urban Mushin exhibits many familiar features. It illustrates the political mobility "by levitation," discussed in Part I, in which hamlet and village heads are, so to speak, carried upward into chieftainship by the insertion under them of successive layers of later settlers. Mushin also shows the struggles over the definitions and redefinitions of firstcomers ("sons of the soil")—struggles that involved the rhetorical manipulation, akin to the one we saw among the Kpelle, of boundaries, precedents, and events in order to render them historically pivotal. We also see in Mushin the familiar contentions over what Barnes here pithily calls "titles and followers"—the titles giving external validation to the local position one achieves by acquiring followers. There is also in Mushin the frontier dialectic between the rulers' preference for ascriptive criteria of authority and the necessity for the polity to satisfy the subjects by granting some authority to achievement. Above all, what Mushin vividly exemplifies is the flux of frontier politics: the ambiguities of "seniority" that increase the ambiguities of authority, the open-ended-ness of struggles and maneuvers, and the permanent lack of finality to solutions and accommodations.

The continuity of themes that we have until now seen in historical, traditional, and rural contexts is striking. On the one hand, Barnes's analysis of the principles of Yoruba political culture serves very well to amplify the discussion in Part I of the broad principles of traditional pan-African political culture. On the other hand, we see these same principles operating in a modern metropolis and enmeshed with modern politics. If this persistence of frontier features in political culture is somewhat more striking in Mushin than it is in rural Mto wa Mbu, it is perhaps because in a modern state a city offers a larger stage on which political culture can express itself than does a rural village. For example, colonial and national authority in Mto wa Mbu deprived the firstcomer principle of much of its political substance. In Mushin, much of this substance remained and the contenders for it were far more numerous. At the same time, the presence of the Nigerian state authority gave a measure of safety to political contests. Unlike the situation in an autonomous frontier polity, one could rarely be physically knocked out of the Mushin power game; one did not have to regard loss as permanent and one could keep returning to the political fray. Hence the enhanced nature of the political flux and the saliency of the principles underlying it.

—Editor

Sandra T. Barnes

———————— 10 ————————

The Urban Frontier in West Africa:
Mushin, Nigeria

Before the twentieth century, the societies of tropical Africa were mainly rural, and the social frontier—the uncharted terrain of human relationships—was still rural. Only one percent of the population lived in cities. When economic and political opportunities shifted to the cities in this century, so did the social frontier, and by 1980 the percentage of the tropical African population living in urban places jumped to some 28 percent. Rapid growth meant that, despite the overarching administrative institutions introduced by Europeans both in the administrative and company towns they established and in the traditional cities that predated them, the colonizers' finances, manpower, and expertise were insufficient to deal with the expansion of legal, administrative, and judicial needs of the people. As a result, Africans were forced to find their own ways of maintaining order by creating various informal political structures. In the case presented here the informal structures were not politically centralized, for, as I argue, an urban frontier presents unique structural problems when there is a rapid and large expansion of population. Put briefly, urbanization and political centralization need not go hand-in-hand.

It is part of our received wisdom that cities require centralized governments to manage and control their large and diverse populations (e.g., Fox 1977:24–5; Martindale 1962:27; Sjoberg 1960:67). Indeed, political centralization has been thought to be virtually synonymous with urbanization. Centralization, to be sure, is one of those characteristics of a political system that can range from weak to strong. It refers to the control of political functions existing at the top level of a hierarchy in a political system or a field of political relationships. The more varied and numerous the functions and roles of the controlling authority at the top—be it a person or an institution—the stronger is the degree of centralization. The less varied and fewer the functions and roles are at the top—and accordingly the greater the control vested in lower levels of the hierarchy—the weaker is the degree of centralization (cf. Hunt and Hunt 1978:76–7).

In the situation I discuss here, the mechanisms for maintaining social order did not evolve slowly from a lesser to a greater degree of complexity but, of necessity, developed swiftly. As a result, the problem of order was solved initially by a number of similar political structures that co-existed in what may be called a loose urban federation that was weakly centralized—if at all—and that, despite being encapsulated within the overarching institutions of the state, continued to resist centralization despite some significant advantages to be gained by it.

When Mushin, a suburb of metropolitan Lagos, was established officially in 1955, its population had just surpassed 32,000. In less than two decades, by 1972, it had mushroomed to some 600,000. Although contiguous with Lagos city proper, Mushin was administratively separate, and there were no formal direct political ties between the two or with any of the other three suburbs. The indigenous population of Mushin—primarily of Awori Yoruba descent—was quickly reduced to a minority once the area started to urbanize, and this prevented Awori from dominating the process of developing political institutions. The incoming population represented a broad variety of Nigeria's peoples, although at least 60 percent were Yoruba-speaking. The latter were the ones who did dominate the process of building a political community.

The term Yoruba is a colonial creation applied to some 10 million people of southwestern Nigeria (and part of the Republic of Benin), who share the same language, the same traditions of common origin, and similar symbols and customs surrounding political and mystical authority. The Yoruba-speaking peoples are divided by more than ten dialects—more or less mutually intelligible—and by pre-colonial political boundaries. Most Yoruba still identify themselves according to earlier political identities, such as Ife, Ijebu, Oyo, or Ondo, which were attached to kingdoms and city-states or to dialect groups (e.g., Awori). The governmental structure of each sub-group was different. While it might be said that similar political institutions were found in many of the pre-colonial polities, the structural arrangements, the functions, and the emphases placed on each of them varied markedly from one polity to another. The Yoruba peoples who migrated to Mushin, therefore, brought with them a variety of orientations to traditional political institutions. At the same time, they brought significant cultural commonalities. The Yoruba had been urbanized for hundreds of years before direct contact with the West and most of them were exposed, directly or indirectly, to an urban political culture. Mushin's Yoruba residents, therefore, shared underlying cultural principles that acted as ideologically integrative forces in what was, at the beginning, a potentially chaotic situation.

YORUBA PRINCIPLES OF AUTHORITY

Authority in traditional Yoruba politics was based on the principle of seniority. Most social interaction carried with it a tacit evaluation of the relative seniority of each participant with respect to every other participant.[1] In a household, the most senior person present, as determined by age, sex, or social status, allocated and supervised household tasks. In the absence of a parent, the oldest sibling would assume the senior role, and so on down the line. If a dispute arose, the senior person was expected to settle the conflict.

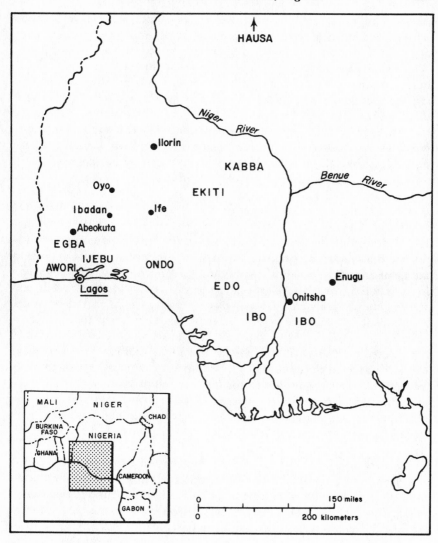

Home Areas of Major Migrant Groups in Lagos

The application of the seniority principle in community politics meant that the most senior member of a town (defined by age, sex, time of arrival, and condition by birth, say in a royal lineage) should be its highest authority figure. Whatever the context, a person knew how to rank himself or herself in relation to others on the basis of various ascribed characteristics. Seniority was not simply a matter of relative age. Returning to the household context, one's male sibling may have been the oldest person present, but the presence of one's father's brother, younger in years but senior in generation, meant that a question arose as to who was actually senior, and that priorities in seniority rules had to be established. In some cases, priorities were worked out; in most, the rules were ambiguous enough to provide some degree of flexibility to the process of evaluating and assigning senior status. The point is that when a bundle of ascriptive attributes were used to determine seniority, there were possibilities for manipulating the rules, and for arguing that certain attributes had greater weight than others. This is what made competition possible.

Authority was exercised in large measure in the adjudication of disputes, the making and enforcing of decisions, and the allocation of resources. Unlike the modern West, where judicial authorities are largely placed in a class by themselves, conflict among the Yoruba was usually resolved not by the disputing parties but by the authority vested in the most senior person present or relevant to the context where the dispute occurred.[2] The prerogatives of seniority were such that the act of acknowledging another person's seniority over oneself potentially constituted a diminution of personal sovereignty—particularly with respect to the management of conflict. As might be expected, those who competed for political power were loath to recognize the seniority of rivals and avoided contexts in which evaluations of seniority would have to be made. As we shall see, this fear became extreme on the frontier, to which individuals were often attracted precisely because of the greater opportunities it presented for competing for power. In political matters, therefore, there was reluctance to acknowledge the seniority of others if it tainted one's own claims to exercising the prerogatives of senior status.

The logical outcome of applying seniority rules was that everyone could be ranked hierarchically from lowest servant to highest chief. Theoretically, every community had one person who outranked all others and who was, therefore, the central authority figure in that place. But when political rivals refused to recognize the seniority of one person, the political pyramid was uncapped. However, this was the exception, for among most Yoruba peoples there was a central authority figure: a king, paramount chief, or headman. Beneath that person there was usually a hierarchy of titled chiefs ranked in order of importance.

Large Yoruba polities had two kinds of chieftaincy title holders: established (in a corporate group) and honorary (personal). Established titles were permanent and heritable. The incumbency of the highest established posts in a chiefly hierarchy was, in most cases, determined by ascriptive rules, the posts being "owned" by corporate descent or territorial (quarter, village) groups. But within these title-holding groups, members competed for titles by manipulating rules of seniority to their advantage. A wealthy and charismatic member of a descent group could muster greater support among kinsmen for nomination to a title than a poor and retiring one, even if the latter was—in this gerontocratically biased society—senior in age.[3] The highest titles ideally resided in the descent group of the founder, or conqueror, of a town; the lineal descendants of the founder and other people who first settled on land that came to be identified with a particular community were known as "sons of the soil." Hence, one of the most agreed-upon principles was that the highest ranking title holders of a community should be "sons of the soil."

Honorary titles were not permanent, and not group held. They were open to competition and governed by achievement-biased principles. The existence of achieved titles rested on another widely held belief, that opportunities to be a chief should be widely distributed (Biobaku 1957:88; Lloyd 1962:237; Awe 1967:19–20). Such titles were acquired by appointment (by the senior chiefs or *ǫba,* king), by election (by fellow members of organizations such as markets, age-grade associations, religious bodies, or craft guilds), or less commonly through title-taking associations. Merit could be displayed by such attributes as the size and strength of one's following, wealth, valor, wisdom, or mystical power.

The value that called for an open political field co-existed with the value that only certain members of a community were, by circumstances of birth or other status markers, eligible to hold high titles. The simultaneous application of these two principles in a polity did not pose an unresolvable contradiction. Elsewhere, in a study of politics in a Tswana chiefdom, in Southern Africa, John Comaroff found the two values of ascription and achievement to be interdependent parts of the same reality; because politics was by definition competitive, they provided a dialectic around which political culture revolved (1978:16–18). This was also the situation I found in Mushin. Assertions of seniority that rivals found untenable could be dealt with through avoidance or could be contested by an adroit re-ordering of the priorities within the larger bundle of ascriptive rules, in the case of established titles, or evaluations of merit, in the case of honorary titles. The outcome, as one might expect, was that the assignment of seniority, and especially titles, could be adjusted to reflect the realities of power.

The mere recognition that a person was the senior figure in a group was enough to confer legitimacy on that individual so that he or she could act as an authority figure. Nevertheless, holding a title in addition gave more weight to one's power. Titles were scarce and their conferral generally required a fairly broad base of assent. In a large, mobile population, where not all inhabitants were personally known to one another, a chieftaincy title gave the holder an advantage in political affairs, for it labeled him or her as an "approved" authority figure.

Legitimacy in the world of politics was thus a matter of degree. The wider the sphere of influence and the greater the number of people who assented to and were affected by one's actions, the more legitimacy the title holder enjoyed. In theory, a title holder had a greater degree of political legitimacy than a non-titled (senior) authority figure because, first, he had been singled out, in some way, by others as worthy of a named position, and, second, the status was permanent and not subject to re-evaluation in each context as it was with senior status. Some titles conferred greater prestige and more sweeping powers than others. A title holder in a traditional craft guild had a restricted sphere of operation and a narrow field of influence, despite the fact that the title was known in the community at large. A civic title holder, by contrast, had the whole community as his sphere of effective operation. Legitimacy was, after all, a matter of compliance, and the more followers who complied with, or assented to, one's use of power, the more sanctioned it was.

Legitimacy also rested on setting precedents. In Mushin, a new hierarchy of titles was created and rules governing their acquisition were established during a twenty-year period between 1955 and 1975. There were few if any precedents that could be used as a basis for establishing either the titles or the rules. Moreover, given the heterogeneous nature of the population and the diversity of succession rules the residents had experienced in their home settings, there were no pre-established bases for agreement. Political contests, as a result, involved permitting or preventing precedent-setting events; such events simultaneously validated the titles and the rules by which they were conferred, after which they were incorporated into the communal code that governed and justified, *ex post facto,* the action taken. Staging or preventing precedent-setting actions depended upon the use of power and the consent of others; and securing a title through a precedent-setting action was itself a legitimation of such power.

HISTORICAL BACKGROUND OF MUSHIN

The single most important factor in the political development of Mushin was neglect. Mushin was part of the Colony of Lagos[4] ceded to the British in 1861. The Mushin area was dotted by a few autonomous farming villages that, unlike most Yoruba settlements, were not formally drawn into a centralized state. As a result, the British administrators saw them as among the most backward in the soon-to-be Nigeria[5] and ignored them, despite the fact that all Colony residents were British subjects who were to be governed under the principles of direct rule (unlike the rest of Nigeria, which was occupied later and governed under indirect rule). Mushin, in fact, received no administrative attention until 1927 when a District Officer was posted to the area so that, for the first time, taxes could be collected from residents. The District Officer tried to make contact with the villagers and their headman and to bring them into contact with one another. But his attempts were cut short by the depression and then the Second World War, which prompted cutbacks in the colonial service and a withdrawal of personnel from all but the most critical posts.

Thus, Mushin was again left alone until 1944 when a Native Court and a Native Authority were finally established.[6] Prominent local residents were appointed to serve in each body, and two forums emerged in which ties of communication and cooperation among settlement leaders could develop. Yet, in comparison to other urbanizing places, the steps taken outside Lagos were rudimentary, and external political conditions reinforced this state of affairs. Two governmental reorganizations, in 1951 and 1954, divided the Colony of Lagos, putting the city under federal government control (in an arrangement not unlike the District of Columbia) and the remainder of the Colony under the Western Region Government. It was a move that was politically unpopular on both sides. Colony residents resented being placed under a large Regional Government with which they had no political leverage. On the other side, Western Region officials believed that the rapidly urbanizing suburbs around Lagos would inevitably be rejoined to the city, so that the metropolitan area would be governed under a single higher authority; they chose, therefore, to neglect the newly annexed territory rather than invest funds, time, and manpower into a place where no political harvest might be reaped (Sada 1968:83–4).

Thus, between 1861 and 1954, official neglect made unofficial self-help imperative. Throughout this period, order was maintained by the use of traditional authority figures. Each of the villages, and then each of the growing urban neighborhoods, recognized one person as a *Baalę*, headman. The headman was either the senior member of the dominant descent group in that settlement (if it was an older settlement), the first settler, or a senior resident. There are only a few accounts of places that did not have such a senior authority figure. The *Baalę* exercised adjudicative and decision-making powers within the settlement. Residents had the right to take disputes to the Supreme Court of the Colony, located some five to ten miles from the outlying settlements, but they appear to have preferred unofficial procedures. Distance was no doubt a deterrent, but more inhibiting was the fact that, in the Supreme Court, British legal principles often took precedence over customary principles. Hence, some matters were taken to traditional chiefs in the city (when the *Baalę* was unable to bring about a settlement) rather than to the Colony court, roughly the same distance away.

The authority structure within each of the outlying settlements was often more complex in older villages; it also became more complex in the urbanizing neighborhoods, but this took time. In the older villages, a few titles were taken by leading residents or son-of-the-soil descent-group elders, who then acted as a council of advisors to the *Baalę*. In the urbanizing areas, a council of landlords sometimes emerged to assist and advise the *Baalę*. As it was often explained to me, landlords were the logical people to form a council because they not only had a permanent vested interest in the area but also wished to maintain order in their houses, which they invariably constructed to accommodate rent-paying tenants and their families. The major duties of the neighborhood headmen and landlord councils were to settle disputes between landlords or between landlords and tenants (the individual landlords usually settled disputes between tenants in their own houses); to provide protection (to which end they often hired community night-guards); to maintain roads and paths; to insure orderly settlement; and to collect taxes. Only the latter activity was approved by the government, and even then tax collection was not statutorily mandated.

Throughout this period there were few, if any, links among the settlements, as I have indicated. After the first District Officer was assigned to the area in 1927, some settlements banded together to form Village Group Councils. Their goal was to deal with some local problems, particularly disputes, and to pressure government to solve others, especially the provision of police protection and basic urban amenities. Like the District Officer, the councils were short-lived, but they re-emerged after World War II. Representatives to the revived group councils were headmen or settlement representatives who had shown leadership qualities. The latter, generally, were migrants and relatively well educated (which, in those days, meant that they had completed primary school); they made up the pool from which Native Court and Native Authority appointments were made.

The year 1955 marked a turning point for Mushin. As Nigeria prepared for independence and an elected form of representative government, the headman-council authority structures in the various settlements were strengthened. Local sections of national political parties were formed and one of them, the Yoruba-dominated Action Group, used this pre-existing neighborhood authority system as a base on which to build grassroots party cells. Encouraged by the attention of politicians and their inclusion in party affairs, local leaders, who until then had honed their political skills in the Village Group Councils, Native Court, and Native Authority, banded together and, using party connections, petitioned government to create an official administrative authority for Mushin itself. These initiatives resulted in the establishment of the Mushin District Council, which consisted of elected representatives from the settlements, which were grouped into 30 electoral wards.

THE CREATION OF A CHIEFTAINCY SYSTEM IN MUSHIN

The first order of business for Mushin's elected councillors was to bring traditional authorities into the official bureaucratic structure of the district—a goal which, quite unexpectedly, would not be realized for ten years. Councillors proposed that chiefs have a permanent place in the Council, as they did elsewhere in Yoruba administrative districts,[7] with a view to perpetuating the ancient symbols of political authority "along modern lines."[8] To fill these roles, councillors looked to the headmen of older villages and newer urban neighborhoods, and to enhance their status their titles had to be elevated.

The names of six senior chiefs, representing six chieftaincy divisions, were accordingly sent to the Western Region Ministry of Local Government for official recognition early in 1956. Three chiefs were proposed by indigenous descent groups ("sons of the soil") that were the core kin groups of well-known villages: the Onisolo of Isolo, the Onitire of Itire, and the Olu of Ojuwoye. Two chiefs were proposed by small outlying villages whose founders were migrants from the north: the *Baalę* of Ewu and the Odofin of Ejigbo.[9] The sixth chief, the Olu of Odi Olowo, was strikingly different from the others. He was elected by the headmen of twelve urban neighborhoods, each an electoral ward in Mushin. The Olu and the eleven other headmen, who thereupon formed his advisory council, were all migrant settlers. None of the twelve attained his neighborhood headmanship position by virtue of heredity; all had achieved their positions through election. Together, they represented the most populous and urbanized area of Mushin.

The move to bring traditional authority figures into the District Council touched off a struggle that was characterized as "violent" and "vehement."[10] Up to this time, headmen had been so restricted to their separate spheres of influence that the question of whether they were indigenous "sons of the soil"—as opposed to migrant settlers—was not a matter of public concern. Once they were elevated and drawn into a higher order of community-wide political activity, the question became significant. Chiefly titles carried with them many dividends: high status, a position from which to influence local policy, access to wide-ranging networks of politically and economically influential people, and the possibility of sitting in the Western Region House of Chiefs.[11] When the Mushin District Council requested that the six senior chiefs be recognized, these positions immediately became highly prized and eligibility rules became a contentious issue, arousing the passions of those who stood to gain or lose in the recognition process. In the settler view, establishing a new chieftaincy division with a paramount chief was consistent with modern urban politics, where highly valued offices could be acquired through one's own achievements and efforts and not by virtue of ascribed status. For the sons of the soil, on the other hand, the actions of the settlers were a threat to their exclusive domination of a suddenly attractive field of political activity.

The indigenous Awori strongly protested the right of migrant settlers to hold senior chieftaincy titles. In terms of customary principles, the issue was fundamental. Both the Awori and the settlers agreed that senior titles should be limited to owners of property, that is, of land or houseplots. They disagreed, however, on the interpretation of ownership. Members of Awori descent groups argued that titles of the most senior rank should be restricted to sons of the soil, whose rights to land derived from membership in founding descent groups. In their view, it was illegal for settlers, who had merely purchased land, to establish a chieftaincy with a title equal to their own titles. The two highest titles being used for paramount figures in Mushin, *ǫǫni* and *olu,* were among the highest titles used in other traditional political systems, and according to the Awori interpretation of the principles of seniority, they should be reserved for people of the appropriate son-of-the-soil status.

Settlers countered the Awori argument on two grounds. First, they argued that by selling land outright, the Awori had forfeited the customary rights of sons of the soil to monopolize traditional offices of highest rank, since, under the new land tenure laws introduced by the British, the principle of freehold ownership conveyed legitimate and total transfer of land rights to the purchaser. Implicit in a freehold transaction, they reasoned, was a transfer of rights to full political citizenship. Second, they saw themselves as having brought into being a new social order to Mushin and therefore were entitled to full political rights in that new order. When they arrived, the settlers argued, Mushin was rural; they had transformed a backward, undeveloped area into a civilized, urban place and hence were entitled to share in its full political life. The settlers were careful not to deny the rights of Awori to hold titles of senior rank. Rather, their goal was to establish full equivalent political rights, especially the right to hold the most senior titles, for those who did not have the Awori identity. In their view, the principles determining office holding should be expanded from exclusive ascription and include the principle of achievement.

The Awori-settler dispute went to the Mushin District Council where the settler position was strongly supported by a great majority of the councillors. The power structure of the new district reflected the new demographic realities. Some three-quarters of the thirty councillors were settlers (and of these, thirteen were from electoral wards of the disputed area of Odi Olowo, including the Olu himself); they were keenly aware of the fact that a strict acceptance of the son-of-the-soil principle would render the settlers and their heirs forever ineligible to hold Mushin's senior titles. To confirm and strengthen their Council victory, the settlers held an *iwuye,* a coronation ceremony, and installed the settler Olu on March 4, 1956. Prominent citizens attended the affair and their presence signalled to the public that an important precedent had been set.

A second struggle, equally bitter, arose over attempts to unify the chieftaincies and thereby centralize the chieftaincy system. Mushin's councillors and other political leaders asked the six *ǫba* (as they had already come to be informally addressed) to select one of their number to serve as president of the Council. In effect, the selection of an *ǫba* as Council president would single out one chief as first among peers; this, it was feared, would set a precedent that could be used by the president to claim seniority over others. The strongest resistance came from the three Awori chiefs, none of whom was willing to see one gain precedence over the others. Then, one of them decided to press a claim to seniority: the Olu Ojuwoye changed his title to coincide with the district's name and called himself Olu Mushin of Ojuwoye. He argued that a century earlier the Mushin market, owned by the Ojuwoye descent group, was a central meeting place for the area, and therefore Ojuwoye rightfully deserved the most senior position in the community. Strong objections were lodged by the Isolo and Itire chiefs, who argued that their status was equal to Oju-woye's since all three descended from the same ancestor and none could rightfully claim seniority over the other. Again, the Council resolved the issue by introducing a compromise agreement suggesting that each ọba serve one year as president in a six-year rotation cycle, and it forwarded the plan to the Ministry of Local Government.

To the surprise of Mushin's leaders, the petitions for recognition of the ọba and a rotating Council presidency were rejected. Word of the Awori-set-tler conflict and the inability of chiefs "to top" their hierarchy reached the colonial government officials and prompted them to equate the lack of unity with the lack of authenticity. Furthermore, a government inspector, recalling the fact that there was no traditional central authority in the area and no long-standing cooperation among villagers and their leaders, claimed that the chiefs had not played a strong historical role in the area.

Failure to gain official recognition stimulated, rather than dampened, the activities of Mushin's *de facto* chiefs. The most important consequence was the emergence of two new settler chieftaincies: Shomolu, headed by the Jagunmolu, and now a rapidly urbanizing sector of Mushin; and Oshodi, where settlers of Lagosian (and before that, Nupe) descent, with strong ties to the city, started a settlement under the leadership of a *Baalẹ* whose title had not been elevated in the petitions for recognition. In addi-tion, another Awori chieftaincy division, Onigbongbo, claimed its rights to be recognized and its *Baalẹ* (also not elevated) was informally added to the ranks of the district's senior chiefs. Finally, a number of more junior titles began appearing in all of the chieftaincy divisions. However, for reasons unknown to me, two of the six original claimants to senior chief status, the Odofin of Ejibgo and the *Baalẹ* of Ewu, dropped out of com-munity-wide chieftaincy activities and allowed their claims to be recog-nized to lapse into dormancy.

Meantime, Mushin's chiefs joined hands as a council and met together until sometime in 1962. Meeting with them were Mushin District council-lors and party leaders who did not hold titles but who acted as the chiefs' spokesmen to government and as their supporters in an ongoing struggle to gain official recognition. Indeed, the chiefs were beholden to these leaders for their very existence and thus became their clients. By the same token, the non-titled politician leaders, in search of large blocs of clients and followers in their election struggles, were eager to serve as patrons to the chiefs in order to gain access through them to the chiefs' followers.

In a dramatic turn of events, ten years after the proposal to secure recognition was initiated, seven senior chiefs[12] were officially recognized as traditional authorities of Mushin and allocated small salaries to help them carry out their mainly ceremonial duties in the community. The govern-ment also allocated five new seats in the Western Region House of Chiefs to Ikeja Division (of which Mushin was a part) for which its chiefs could compete. The presidency of the Mushin District Council was not turned over to the chiefs, but in time the government established a Mushin Chieftaincy Committee—an advisory body to the Council—consisting of the seven ọba, and ruled that its chairman was to be elected periodically.

The successful establishment of chieftaincy divisions in Mushin had been conditioned by three kinds of political processes. First, no claim to a senior title could be made without the support of a substantial number of followers who acknowledged the legitimacy of the position and claimant's right to hold it for life. In the case of Awori claimants, support emanated from large descent groups which had, for at least a century, named a headman of the dominant kin group and of the village in which it lived. With settler claimants, support came from neighbors who had also chosen headmen—though more recently—and who united behind them in landlord associations. In this, both Awori and settlers followed the widespread Yoruba custom of acknowledging a senior authority figure in a residential group, and both supported the elevation of the headship to a senior chiefship as a logical extension of this authority.

Second, no claim to a title could be made without the consent and support of some community-wide political leaders, who operated beyond the local range of chieftaincy affairs. In essence, a chieftaincy claim by one segment (a chieftaincy division) of the community had to meet the approval of, and fit into, the community's overall power structure or it would not reach the proper forums for recognition—in this case, the Mushin District Council, the national political parties in power, and the regional (later state) government. Certainly it was possible for a claimant to have the support of local followers but not that of higher-level community leaders—which is what I suspect happened to the chiefs of Ejigbo and Ewu; in such a case, the title holder was restricted to his or her neighborhood sphere of influence and operation and prevented from operating on a full community level.

Third, no claim to the title could be upheld without community-wide affirmation of its legitimacy. The holding of a ritual coronation ceremony, an iwuye, established a significant precedent, inasmuch as, according to the customs of traditional office holding, once a title was properly conferred, it could not be taken away (except in unusual circumstances). An authentic title was conferred for life; a title holder could be promoted to a higher title, but not demoted. Without an iwuye, a title was neither legitimate nor permanent and therfore it was still open to the vicissitudes of political competition. An iwuye was a public act, performed before ordinary community members and prominent citizens who acted as witnesses and who signalled their consent by participating in the event. Ultimately, the iwuye symbolized the coming together of both kinds of support: that of followers from the separate neighborhoods or descent groups, and that of representatives of the overarching political institutions of the full community.

THE STRUGGLE TO SURVIVE

Recognition of the seven ǫba brought divisiveness to Mushin's chieftaincy system—not a united sense of victory. Recognition was achieved through party channels but, surprisingly, not through the District's councillors and those Action Group (AG) party leaders who had nurtured the chieftaincy system in its infancy or served as patrons during its years of unofficial existence. The explanation for this unexpected twist of fate lay in political events in the Western Region that were external to Mushin but which had a strong effect on its internal affairs. In 1963, a major faction split off from the AG. The AG retained its hold on Mushin, but the new rival Yoruba party, the Nigerian National Democratic Party (NNDP) took over the Western Region Government. Because it had seized power through a political maneuver, and not through elections, NNDP had no grassroots organization in places such as Mushin; to compensate for this, the NNDP government recognized a number of chiefs throughout the Region as a way of gaining support and building local power bases. In exchange for recognition, the ǫba were expected to abandon earlier AG loyalties and cross over to the NNDP. For a complex set of reasons, not the least of which was that no rewards were offered to junior title holders or other chieftaincy followers, the newly recognized ǫba were overwhelmingly scorned by their supporters and left to pursue their new allegiance alone. The Olu of Odi Olowo, for example, was ostracized by the junior chiefs and political patrons who named a regent in his place and met without him. The houses of two ǫba were burned to the ground and in one case, or so it was believed, a moneylender foreclosed a chief's mortgage so that he could not rebuild on the site. Eventually several ǫba fled Mushin and remained away until after a military coup in January 1966 put an end to partisan politics everywhere in Nigeria for the next twelve years.

However, a new threat to the existence of Mushin's chiefs came with the military regime, and, again, the challenge revitalized chieftaincy activities. Soon after taking power, the military government undertook an investigation of the authenticity of the Mushin titles. Settlers were particularly troubled. Unlike hereditary chieftaincies, where a title owned by a descent group was held by a member for the remainder of his life, title-holding rules in settler chieftaincies were not yet clearly defined. Was an elected chief a chief for life, or could he be replaced? The initial response to the defection of the Olu of Odi Olowo, after ostracizing him, was to replace him. As government investigations proceeded, however, settlers reversed their position on the advice of political leaders who believed that if investigators learned the Olu had been ousted because of an unpopular party affiliation, the recognition of the title could be labeled an instrumental partisan act rather than an attempt to perpetuate a time-honored custom. Showing that the incumbency of a chiefship was permanent was one way to demonstrate its authenticity. With this in mind, Odi Olowo leaders recalled their ọba, and in time Mushin's chiefships were validated by the authorities.

Interest in chieftaincy politics among untitled community notables intensified once the chiefly system was secure. Under the military, many avenues for political participation were closed. There were no more elected or partisan posts, and many politically oriented organizations were banned. The chieftaincy system now offered one of the few remaining outlets for exercising formal leadership and for securing prestige and status in one's community. To be sure, the government appointed civic leaders to advisory boards and committees—posts that were scarce and hence highly valued. Such appointments went primarily to people with large followings, whose leadership was clearly acknowledged in the community. Thus, when the chiefs of Odi Olowo revitalized their activities in 1966, they were joined by prominent civic leaders who during the partisan era held concillorships, court appointments, or party offices, but not titles. The new participants took an active part in chieftaincy affairs with an eye to securing what they needed in order to prove their legitimacy as community leaders: titles and followers. Until then, the principles for determining office holding in settler divisions were that chiefs were elected representatives of territorial units, while in Awori districts, they were selected from son-of-the-soil descent groups. Both the settler territorial units and Awori descent groups held rights to name established title holders. Now, in response to new pressures, most of Mushin's chieftaincy divisions began to confer honorary chieftaincy titles on prominent civic figures. As in most traditional Yoruba polities, honorary titles were bestowed for life but could not be perpetuated by succession.

The intense interest and participation of civic leaders in chieftaincy divisions brought about a struggle for power within them. It was waged over the rights to appoint and rank title holders. Again, Odi Olowo offers a case in point. In the formative years of the settler chieftaincies, chiefs looked at the former kingdom of Ibadan as a model for their division's succession rules, although none of them was himself from Ibadan. Under this system, the Olu was, of course, placed at the top of the hierarchy, and the remaining chiefs were ranked in descending order according to their seniority and were assigned titles reflecting that rank. The ranks were like rungs in a ladder. When the Olu or any other chief died, the vacant place was filled by the chief ranked immediately below, who moved up one rung of the ladder; as did each lower-ranked chief. Each of the twelve Odi Olowo titles was held by a ward, not a descent group. Hence the ward holding the vacant title elected a replacement who, then, took his position in the empty place at the bottom of the ladder.

In theory, the succession hierarchy was fixed. In practice, it was subject to manipulation (as was also true in Ibadan). Relative seniority in the hierarchy was determined by a bundle of criteria such as age, wealth, date of selection, and influence among other chiefs or politician patrons. During the first two decades of the division's existence, as the fortunes of the chiefs fluctuated, their relative placement in the chieftaincy hierarchy also fluctuated. Let me explain how this took place. The right to rank chiefs and to assign named titles to them ideally rested with the Olu. In 1962, when the Olu lost control of the Odi Olowo chieftaincy division, his functions were taken over and were retained thereafter by an executive committee of the division's most influential junior chiefs and participating civic leaders. I do not know how the Olu assigned titles or changed the assignments before this time. I do know that the committee altered the seniority rankings of chiefs on the succession ladder in order to enhance certain chiefs' statuses in the following ways:

a) In one case, a chief who was elected to replace a deceased title holder, entered the hierarchy at the same level held by his predecessor and not at the bottom of the ladder.

b) In several cases, the names of titles were changed to connote a higher status than the name previously used (which was then dropped from the division's title repertoire). In one instance, a name change enabled a chief—elected to replace a deceased title holder—to enter the hierarchy at a higher level than that of his predecessor and, again, not at the bottom of the ladder.

c) In still another case, the date of selection of a chief was changed to an earlier date, enabling the title holder to claim he has seniority over others and thus to jump to a higher rung on the ladder.

Later, the committee transferred some honorary title holders to ranked, established positions when a suitable vacancy occurred in their ward. On one occasion, a prominent leader was moved from an honorary title to the second rung in the chieftaincy ladder which meant he would succeed the Olu, should he outlive him. Another such transfer from honorary to ranked title produced dissent in the ward where the vacancy occurred, since the ward's landlord council felt that, rather than choose a candidate, it was forced to accept a *fait accompli*. While such manipulations did not occur without strong protests—as the minutes of chiefs' meetings record—the protests were ineffective.

The new honorary chiefs had, as civic leaders, established a broad base of support in the community and influence with the higher powers of the state. With titles and followers, they were in a position to obtain appointments to government bodies and thereby have access to resources and rewards that they could distribute within the community. In turn, this enabled them—with lesser leaders dependent on them—to take advantage of ambiguities in seniority and succession rules and to alter the chiefly hierarchy to reflect the changing realities of power.

The struggle among community leaders for power, followers, titles, and political appointments intensified the conflict between settler and Awori factions. This in turn intensified the activity within their respective chieftaincy divisions, and expanded their numbers and fields of action (see Barnes, in press). The most dramatic change came about when settlers successfully pressed the state to recognize Mushin's junior chiefs and thereby increase the number of legally recognized traditional authorities. Eighty-four junior chiefs, many of whom had been appointed as honorary title holders, were officially installed at a state-sponsored *iwuye* in May, 1975.[13] Once again, Awori protested the legitimacy of the chiefs from settler divisions. Previously, in 1969, they had successfully prevented Odi Olowo from holding a divisional *iwuye* for its junior chiefs; this time, they were unable to prevent the government-sponsored ceremony from taking place. During the same period, two chieftaincy divisions (one new and the other the long-dormant Ewu) emerged and applied for recognition of their ọba and chiefs. Finally in one ward, the chief conferred honorary titles on members of his landlords' council, thus giving the chieftaincy hierarchy a third tier.

Despite the expansion of the system, the chiefly divisions remained uncentralized in that they did not name a single senior chief of Mushin. They were, nevertheless, operating under a centralized administrative council and as part of the political networks of prominent civic leaders who operated at a community-wide level. Over time, the failure of the chiefs themselves to unite under a single paramount figure strengthened in some ways and weakened in others Mushin's traditional political institutions. On the one hand, decentralization allowed a greater number of people to hold the highest (ọba) titles; thus, it offered a broad field in which competition for, and the proliferation of, junior titles could take place under the auspices of each senior chief and his division. The more decentralized the system, the more the residents were able to realize the achievement-oriented traditional ideal that chiefships should be widely distributed. On the other hand, if one may be allowed some speculation, centralization would no doubt have brought official recognition to senior chiefs earlier. One of the reasons local AG politicians were unsuccessful in pressing the case for recognition was the failure of chiefs to name one senior title holder for all of Mushin.[14] Recognition would have brought an institutionalized role to the senior chief as chairman of the Mushin District Council and as member of the regional House of Chiefs; this, in turn, would have provided the entire chiefly system direct contact with high government authorities to influence them and seek their favor. Undoubtedly, such advantages would have reduced the chiefs' dependence on politicians and elected office holders, giving them more power and freedom to run their own affairs. Lack of centralization, therefore, left the title holders less powerful in the aggregate and more beholden to the power struggles around them. Yet, on the other side, lack of centralization opened the field to a large number of participants whose unofficial activities filled many gaps—dispute settlement, security, residential order—that official institutions left open.

NINETEENTH-CENTURY URBAN FRONTIERS

If the facts of the Mushin situation are seen in isolation, it can be argued that the failure of leaders to centralize the chiefly system was either an anomaly or a luxury that could only be afforded in the relatively quiescent political context in which law and order was assured by the Nigerian government. After all, colonial and post-colonial institutions did act as an umbrella over the traditional chiefly system, giving it a certain amount of freedom to indulge in segmented political competition. The need to co-alesce was not critical to survival. This argument is difficult to sustain, however, when we turn to the historical record, and to a comparison with two pre-colonial cases in the early stages of their development. The failure of Mushin's senior chief to take the principles of seniority to their logical conclusion and cap the traditional political hierarchy with a paramount authority figure appears to be consistent with conditions on *urban frontiers* and is not unique to a single time or situation.

Two Yoruba cities—Ibadan and Abeokuta—represented urban frontiers before the advent of colonial rule. Both cities were founded in the 1820s, when pervasive warfare, triggered by the slave trade and subsequent economic readjustments, brought about massive and swift relocations of population throughout the area. At least by the 1850s, when we have the first accounts, the populations of the two places had reached 60,000 to 100,000—which meant that the rapidity and the scale of the population expansion were commensurate with Mushin's. Like Mushin, they were, for their first two or three decades, urban frontiers in the sense that there were no pre-existing institutions that could govern the large, heterogeneous, and densely settled population that congregated in them in a strikingly brief period. Yet, unlike Mushin, their polities were formed in very different circumstances.

IBADAN

Ibadan[15] was founded by a heterogeneous group of people—mainly soldiers—who poured into the area in the first half of the nineteenth century. According to historian Bolanle Awe

> . . . almost every Yoruba town had a son in Ibadan. As a new town, unbound by any traditions, it offered more scope for achievement than the traditional Yoruba towns. Ambitious young men eager to achieve success, craftsmen looking for better opportunities for their trade, and rich men bored with life in their own towns came there (1967:14–15).

Theirs was a precarious existence in many ways. The political system was relatively unformed in early years, leaving the settlement in a state of near anarchy. Warfare was the principal occupation. And, as the polity took shape, there was no hereditary succession; rather, many new titles, awarded on the basis of achievement, were created by the city's budding influentials who, in creating political institutions and offices, borrowed ideas "from wherever they could be found" (Awe 1967:14–15, 18–19).

Ibadan did not begin with a strong centralized political focus. That came later. In the beginning, it was an urban federation, not of chieftaincy divisions but of large powerful descent groups. Most of the principal political functions and roles were embedded in descent groups. They dominated Ibadan's two principal resources: agricultural land and manpower. In addition to controlling slaves, "warboys," and other followers, strong descent groups acted as patrons to later-arriving kin-groups and in so doing amassed large numbers of relatively organized followers and tribute-paying clients. Individual descent groups also undertook the basic political functions of settling disputes among members and clients, allocating land, and collecting taxes. The effect on Ibadan was such that not even military endeavors encouraged centralization, for Ibadan's army was an alliance of powerful warrior chiefs each of whom recruited separate armies from among his own kinsmen, slaves owned by his descent group, or "warboys" who were his descent group's dependents. Rather than undermine descent group autonomy, warfare and the management of military units served to consolidate the powers of descent groups. Controlling hundreds of warriors as they did, descent groups were the basic war units, and Ibadan's military prowess—in fact, its very existence in this time of widespread unrest—was dependent on them.

Unifying tendencies, however, later asserted themselves as individuals strove to acquire political power in the wider community. The principles of hierarchy and seniority imposed an order on the competitive process of acquiring chiefly titles. Four hierarchical "lines" of chiefs—civil, military (2), women—were created and competition for the titles was open to all freeborn citizens. Initially, bravery as a warrior and, then, age, experience, and wealth largely determined the selection. Later, the lineal heirs of title holders claimed that once a title was gained, a precedent had been established and the holder's descent group should be recognized as a privileged group in the community. From among the heirs of these special descent groups, title holders were then selected. This system preserved to some extent the principle of achievement in title taking—the criteria for selection were varied—but it also limited choice (to an unknown extent) to an ascriptively based pool of favored citizens (Lloyd 1971:22). Moreover, once a chief became a part of the hierarchy—and at the peak of its pre-colonial strength there were, simultaneously, twenty-three chiefs in each line (Jenkins 1967:227)—rules were manipulated (just as they were in Mushin) so that competition again entered into the process of choosing which chiefs were to move up the ladder and secure higher titles as they fell vacant.

The central position of the *Baalę* was significant in the early years mainly in its weakness. Real power was diffuse. The important descent groups and, for a time, the warrior chiefs, separately controlled Ibadan's major resources and carried out many political functions within their own precincts, thus capturing many of the political roles and functions that elsewhere would reside in centralized institutions. Furthermore, Ibadan maintained a loose relationship to Oyo, the parent Yoruba kingdom from which many of its residents emigrated. It protected Oyo from being attacked by powerful Fulani war leaders and it paid tribute to the Alafin of Oyo as its titular ruler. While this relationship did not prevent Ibadan from being militarily the most powerful state in Yorubaland in the 1870s, it had an inhibiting effect on the development of a strong central internal authority.

The *Baaleship,* and indeed the entire chiefly system, became further weakened with the establishment of British rule in 1893. Searching for a strong central figure and finding only the weak *Baale,* the foreign rulers turned to the Alafin of Oyo and gave him the power to ratify Ibadan's chiefly appointments. His control expanded and he soon began to interfere in the selection process itself. In the meantime, Ibadan's own chiefs were being excluded from the community's decision-making and adjudication, despite an official policy of indirect rule. This lasted until 1934, when the Alafin's growing power, among other things, threatened to interfere with British administration. At this point, the administration separated Idadan from Oyo.

Separation from Oyo revitalized the chieftaincy system in Ibadan. The *Baale's* title was elevated to that of Olubadan in 1936, providing him with the symbols of kingship without all of the attendant rights. A City Council was re-established, but it was not until 1954 that chiefs actually began showing strong leadership in it. As in Mushin, they depended in this on the support of an elite stratum of civic leaders which came to power outside of the traditional chiefly system—largely through partisan activities. These civic leaders began to participate in the chiefly system themselves in order to strengthen it and provide themselves both with titles and with a political forum in which to nurture their local interests.

ABEOKUTA

Like Ibadan, Abeokuta[16] also came into being through warfare. The people who came together at its hill-protected site in the first half of the nineteenth century were refugees displaced by northern Yoruba peoples who had themselves been forced south into Ibadan and other former Egba Yoruba settlements. The early settlers were heterogeneous, coming from a large number of autonomous Egba towns and villages; they were soon joined by returning Yoruba former slaves (who had been caught in the Atlantic trade and freed by the British) and by migrants from many northern Yoruba towns. The newcomers congregated in at least 150 separate camps; the people did not recognize a senior authority over all of the camps because they both feared the loss of independence and believed they would soon return to their natal towns. In the meantime, each camp developed a judicial system and a way of regulating its internal affairs. It was estimated that by 1852 more than 4,000 people were involved in the process of governing the various camps (Biobaku 1957:52). Eventually, when it became clear that they were not returning home, the people amalgamated the camps into four, later five, townships.

Abeokutans failed to unite the townships under a central authority during their first seventy years. As in Ibadan, lower-level units in the political hierarchy controlled the community's valued resources. Townships and the descent groups within them controlled agricultural land, warriors, and large numbers of dependent clients, and could use the power gained from such control to exercise political functions independently. As in Ibadan, armies were the amalgamations of autonomous units of warriors, controlled by their respective descent groups. Each township regulated its own commercial endeavors. And, finally, the power to select title holders and to control internal affairs resided mainly in the separate townships, so that each of them became a competitive arena in and of itself.

The settlers of Abeokuta, too, held to the ideal that opportunities to be a chief should be widely spread and they provided for open competition in the political institutions of each township. Just as Ibadan formed four lines of chiefs, each of Abeokuta's townships had three such avenues for advancement, but they were organized as title-taking societies: one a judicial, administrative, and legislative body; the second a warrior society; the third, a marketing and trade guild. In all three bodies, promotion from one title to the next was by merit; a high title in one line helped an individual gain a higher title in another. Internal competition for titles meant a chiefly hierarchy was not fixed; adjustments in the relative seniority of title holders could take place, reflecting, as in Mushin, the realities of power in each township. Once these powerful title-granting societies were firmly entrenched in Abeokuta, each township selected a senior chief with a title connoting the status of an oba. Yet in the beginning each of these paramount chiefs functioned more as *primus inter pares* than as a strong central authority. Rights to hold an oba title were, unlike society titles, ascriptive in that only a township's descendants were eligible. Eventually these rights appeared to have devolved to specific descent groups (Ajiṣafe 1964:215).

The first successful federation of the separate townships came about with outside pressure. A treaty between Abeokuta and Britain in 1898 preserved the sovereignty of the people and created an indigenous, unified authority consisting of a coalition of traditional chiefs, educated leaders, and commercial entrepreneurs, formally embodied in a state council on which were seated the four township oba, chiefs named by the Christian and Muslim communities, and several others. When the British finally took over in 1914 they chose to rule indirectly through one of the oba—the Alake of Ake township who had long been favored by Christian missionaries—and a council of senior chiefs taken from each township, but excluding the other three oba. Because the oba of the other townships were excluded from the council—a deliberate attempt to centralize power—the action was bitterly contested and the issue has remained alive until the present time. This inter-township conflict was one of the energizing forces in chiefly politics throughout Abeokuta's history.

The Alake's success in gaining seniority rested, in large measure, on his ability to do several things: to gain support among educated elements of the community; to win favor among missionaries and other foreign representatives, who tended to reside in Ake township and who, in turn, strongly influenced the Christian leadership of the city; and, significantly, to exercise rights to confer honorary titles on influential citizens, thus bringing into being an Abeokuta-wide chiefly hierarchy, largely of his supporters.[17] Once again centralization occurred when pressure came from overarching authorities and from educated elites in whose interests it was to operate in and control a unified urban polity.

DISCUSSION

The chieftaincy systems of Ibadan, Abeokuta, and Mushin were uncentralized urban federations in the early periods of their history.[18] Control of critical resources and the exercise of political functions and roles were spread out to a large extent among similar, parallel, and largely autonomous political structures, and were not (or only weakly) concentrated in a central figure or central institution at the top of a community-wide political hierarchy. This does not mean that centralizing forces were not there, working to bring the separate nodes of power into a common system of authority. The forces of consolidation operated in constant tension with those of segmentation, to the extent that this struggle itself provided contact among the parts and thereby a certain cohesive dynamic to the whole.

When the British came onto the scene, neither Ibadan nor Abeokuta, nor Mushin, was able to demonstrate to the colonial power that it had a strong tradition of central control. The foreign rulers sought central figures and institutions, through which to govern the population indirectly. Unable to find what they desired, they imposed their own ideas of what the central authority should be. In Ibadan, the British allowed the Alafin of Oyo to exercise control over the traditional *Baale* and chiefly hierarchy, further weakening this indigenous system of authority. In Abeokuta, they put into power the senior chief of their choice; in so doing, they prevented other township chiefs of equivalent status, who were in close touch with the population, from sitting on the central council and thereby acting as spokesmen for public opinion; the resentment of these chiefs created bitter controversy and a divisiveness that never abated, but which never removed the Alake from the senior post. In Mushin, by contrast, the failure to erect a central authority resulted in delaying official recognition of chiefs and preventing them from securing direct contact with higher levels of the state. In short, the three urban communities lost the ability to control, through authorities of their own choice, certain critical aspects of their traditional political institutions that were important in fulfilling their political needs.

Nevertheless, the Colonial regime was not able to administer large urban populations without the support of indigenous political leadership. The need to carry out governmental duties that statutory institutions were unable to discharge kept traditional chiefly institutions alive, even if their ultimate powers were weak. Equally significant was the emergence of cadres of community-wide leaders who first emerged outside the chiefly systems but who served critical mediating roles between the people and the foreign rulers. In all three polities, this elite stratum was relatively well educated and used the backing of political parties and religious groups to gain high offices in their communities. Through their informal networks, these civic leaders acted as a unifying force among the separate segments of their communities and they became strong supporters and patrons of traditional authorities in the process.

Traditional chiefs now became dependent on new civic leaders who, in exchange for their support, gained some control over chiefly affairs. Once in power, elite patrons could use the traditional authority system to their own ends. Their most important strategy was to secure appointments as titled chiefs—offices that could be used to legitimate and institutionalize political roles that up to that point were exercised either informally or through relatively impermanent positions. Above all, chiefly titles gave some of the new elites permanent named positions and legitimate outlets for political participation, freeing them of the ups and downs of competitive partisan politics.

Finally, two features of the chiefly systems made them able to absorb the civic elite and thus reflect the changes in the overall structure of community power. First, each system could add new title holders through honorary appointments based on merit. Second, the rules for placing these and other title holders in a ranked hierarchy were ambiguous, as in the cases of Ibadan and Mushin, or competitive, as in Abeokuta. Relative seniority in the hierarchy was determined by an evaluation of not one but a bundle of attributes whose relative importance was not fixed but responded to flexible priorities. Depending on the context and the legalistic skills in manipulating these priorities, the statuses could be re-evaluated or rearranged, elevating or lowering the rankings of title holders.

CONCLUSIONS

I began by stating that it was a Yoruba-wide value that positions of authority be distributed as widely as possible. Indeed, it was thought that the well-being of the group depended on good government and good government rested on widespread participation in it. Yet the Yoruba believed just as strongly that titled positions of authority should be limited to those with whom one shared the moral bonds of propinquity (one's heirs, kinsmen, or neighbors) or to those who had permanent vested interests in the community ("sons of the soil" or ruling houses) as demonstrated by their control of society's valued resources, such as land, wealth, people, wisdom, supernatural sanctions, and so on.

Each value was expressed in a fundamental principle of office-holding. For nearly everyone to believe that he or she could someday be a chief, it was necessary to make achievement determine office-holding, at least in some measure. Conversely, if valued political statuses belonged more legitimately to some than to others, the determinants of authority had in some measure to be ascriptive. Each of the three polities described here used, to some degree and at some period, one or the other of these principles. Needless to say, ascriptively biased principles could be resorted to as political resources, to narrow the field of competitors, while achievement-biased principles did the opposite. Together, these principles provided a critical dynamic in the process of building and maintaining traditional authority systems.

What is striking, here, is that the determination of title-holding was largely competitive and achievement-biased during the formative years of the urban polities we have examined.

The stress on achievement and the accompanying lack of central focus is related to the special conditions associated with urban frontiers. None of the three urban places developed as a small, homogeneous core settlement that could slowly absorb newcomers by integrating them into pre-existing political institutions and processes. Instead, each burst into life out of the control of any one formative force. To avoid anarchy and chaos when vast heterogeneous populations congregate in the same place, several centers of control—often competing and overlapping—emerged. Decentralization was functional at this point, and widespread participation was necessary. The urban frontiers in this part of West Africa reinforced the ideal, more universal, frontier image of openness and opportunity. Here were places where individualistic, competitive drives for power could be given free rein, aided and abetted by the ideal that everyone should have an opportunity to be a chief. Once power had been achieved, however, it was not easily let go and the distribution of power began to narrow. Centralization in traditional political institutions of the two cities that emerged in the nineteenth century came after lengthy maturation periods and only with outside pressures. It was yet to come in the comparatively youthful, twentieth-century Mushin.

NOTES

I would like to thank Josef Gugler, Robert Hunt, Igor Kopytoff, William Murphy, and the members of the staff seminar of the Institute of African Studies, University of Ibadan, who offered valuable suggestions for improving an earlier draft of this essay. They are, of course, in no way responsible for the end product.

1. See LeVine (1976:119) for a general discussion of hierarchy in African society.

2. A council of chiefs might also be asked to settle a dispute, in which case one chief always acted as *primus inter pares* and was thus known as the senior member of the council.

3. See Lloyd (1974:54–5) on the different assessments of age and power/wealth in determining seniority.

4. The Colony was divided into Lagos Town and the Vicinity of Lagos. The territory that became Mushin lay in the latter division.

5. This reputation persisted for nearly a century (Nigeria 1952:5).

6. The Native Authority and Court were set up to serve Ikeja Division, of which Mushin was a part.

7. In most cases the ọba, king, or the most senior titled chief of a district served as president of the District Council.

8. Mushin District Council Minutes and Notes, 1955–56. Private files.

9. The ọọni or ọba is the highest authority of the traditional kingdom or city state. Olu is often the head of a town or city. The term aafin, palace, also connotes kingship. Hence the Alaafin is the title of the king of Oyo; Odofin is another variation on this theme. In Mushin the official titles of chiefs differed from informal titles. Both in addressing and referring to the senior chiefs, residents preferred to use the most widely used title, ọba. For official purposes, however, the olu, ọọni, or even Baalẹ titles were used.

10. Ibid. Private files.

11. Later local chiefs sat in the Lagos State Council of Obas and Chiefs.

12. The seven chieftaincies were Itire, Isolo, Ojuwoye, and Odi Olowo (all part of the original six) and Shomolu, Oshodi, and Onigbongbo (which asserted their rights later).

13. The eighty-four chiefs represented only five of the seven divisions. The ọba of two Awori divisions—Isolo and Ojuwoye—died before the ceremony and had not been replaced. Thus the recognition of their replacements and junior chiefs under them was delayed. Once the latter were installed the number of junior chiefs in Mushin would exceed one hundred.

14. The pressure of politicians on the chiefs to centralize their hierarchy is reflected in minutes of the Odi Olowo chieftaincy division.

15. The summary of Ibadan's political history is taken from Awe (1967), Jenkins (1967), and Lloyd (1971).

16. The summary of Abeokuta's political history is taken from Biobaku (1957), Lloyd (1962 and 1971), and Phillips (1969).

17. The Alake's success also rested on his ability to cite historical, precedent-setting events that could legitimate his claims to seniority. Before and during the colonial era, much of Abeokuta was built on Ake territory, making it possible for its early settlers to claim they were sons of the soil. Also at some time in the eighteenth century, an Alake presided over an Egba-wide court, which, like other "international" courts, could not enforce its decisions, but which was seen as having final decision-making powers (Biobaku 1952:39).

18. See Lloyd (1971:22, 30–4, and 47–53) for a more detailed discussion of the reasons for the failure of Ibadan and Abeokuta to centralize.

REFERENCES

Ajiṣafe, Ajayi Kọlawọle
  1964 History of Abeokuta, Abeokuta: M.A. Ola, Fola Bookshops, Rev. Ed.
Awe, Bolanle
  1967 "Ibadan, its Early Beginnings," in The City of Ibadan, P.C. Lloyd, A.L. Mabogunje, and B. Awe (eds.), Cambridge: Cambridge University Press and Institute of African Studies, University of Ibadan, pp. 11–25.

Barnes, Sandra T.
  1986 *Patrons and Power: Creating a Political Community in Metropolitan Lagos,* Manchester: Manchester University Press for the International African Institute.
Biobaku, Saburi
  1952 "An Historical Sketch of Egba Traditional Authorities," *Africa* XXII(1):35–49.
  1957 *The Egba and Their Neighbours, 1842–1872,* Oxford: Clarendon Press.
Comaroff, John L.
  1978 "Rules and Rulers: Political Processes in a Tswana Chiefdom," *Man* 13(1):1–20.
Fox, Richard G.
  1977 *Urban Anthropology: Cities in Their Cultural Settings,* Englewood Cliffs, NJ: Prentice-Hall.
Hunt, Eva and Robert C. Hunt
  1978 "Irrigation, Conflict, and Politics: A Mexican Case," in *Origins of the State: The Anthropology of Political Evolution,* R. Cohen and E.R. Service (eds.), Philadelphia: ISHI, pp. 69–123.
Jenkins, George
  1967 "Government and Politics in Ibadan," in *The City of Ibadan,* P.C. Lloyd *et al.* (eds.), Cambridge, pp. 213–33.
LeVine, Robert A.
  1976 "Patterns of Personality in Africa," in *Response to Change: Society, Culture, and Personality,* George A. De Vos (ed.), New York: D. Van Nostrand Co., pp. 112–136.
Lloyd, Peter C.
  1962 *Yoruba Land Law,* London: Oxford University Press for NISER, University of Ibadan.
  1971 *The Political Development of Yoruba Kingdoms in the Eighteenth and Nineteenth Centuries,* London: Royal Anthropological Institute Occasional Paper No. 31.
  1974 *Power and Independence,* London: Routledge & Kegan Paul.
Martindale, Don
  1962 "Prefatory Remarks: The Theory of the City," to Max Weber, *The City,* New York: Collier Books, pp. 9–67.
Nigeria
  1952 *Report of the Native Courts (Colony) Commission of Inquiry, 1949,* Lagos: Government Printer.
Phillips, Earl
  1969 "The Egba at Abeokuta: Acculturation and Political Change, 1830–1870," *Journal of African History* X(1):117–131.
Sada, Pius O.
  1968 *The Metropolitan Region of Lagos: A Study of the Political Factor in Urban Geography,* Bloomington: Unpublished Ph.D. thesis, Indiana University.
Sjoberg, Gideon
  1960 *The Preindustrial City,* New York: The Free Press.

CONTRIBUTORS

WILLIAM ARENS is on the anthropology faculty of the State University of New York at Stony Brook. He has done research in Tanzania and the Sudan and his articles have focused on political symbolism and ethnicity. He is the author of *On the Frontier of Change* (1979), *The Man-Eating Myth: Anthropology and Anthropophagy* (1979), and *The Original Sin* (1986), and has co-edited (with Susan Montague) *The American Dimension* (1976).

SANDRA T. BARNES is on the faculty of the anthropology department at the Univesity of Pennsylvania and has also been a visiting faculty member at Johns Hopkins University. Her publications have dealt with African urbanism, religion, politics, and history. She has been engaged in continuing research on the politics and religion, both contemporary and historical, of Lagos, Nigeria, and she is the author of *Patrons and Power: Creating a Political Community in Metropolitan Lagos* (1986).

CAROLINE H. BLEDSOE has taught at the University of New Mexico, has been a Visiting Scholar at the Population Studies Center of the University of Pennsylvania, and is now an Associate Professor of Anthropology at Northwestern University. She is the author of *Women and Marriage in Kpelle Society* (1980) and her articles have focused on politics, social stratification, secrecy, and child fosterage in Liberia and Sierra Leone, where she has done extensive research.

LEE V. CASSANELLI is a member of the Department of History at the University of Pennsylvania. He is a specialist in the history of Somalia, on which he has done research both in archival and oral sources. He has published on problems of ethnohistorical research in uncentralized and nomadic societies and is the author of *The Shaping of Somali Society* (1982).

NANCY J. FAIRLEY, an anthropologist, is on the faculty of Herbert H. Lehman College of the City University of New York. She has also taught at the University of Cincinnati and Lake Forest College. Her articles have dealt with the Ben'Ekie of Zaire, among whom she has done intensive ethnographic and historical research, with a focus on politics, economics, and religion.

IGOR KOPYTOFF is on the anthropology faculty of the University of Pennsylvania. He has also taught at Brown University and has been a visiting professor at the University of Montreal. He has done research in Zaire, the Ivory Coast, and Cameroon. His articles have dealt with African thought, social structure, and religion, and he is co-editor (with Suzanne Miers) of *Slavery in Africa: Historical and Anthropological Perspectives* (1977).

CHET S. LANCASTER has done anthropological research in Zambia and the United States and has been on the faculty of Rutgers, Tulane, and the University of Oklahoma. He is currently engaged in development work and is associated with Technoserve, Inc. In addition to his articles, focusing on ecology, social organization, sex roles, and ethnohistory, he has published *The Goba of the Zambezi: Sex Roles, Economics, and Change* (1981) and is co-author (with Jane Lancaster) of the forthcoming *Eve and Adam: The Evolution of Human Sexuality*.

WILLIAM P. MURPHY has taught at the University of New Mexico and has been a Senior Fellow in Anthropology at the University of Pennsylvania. He is now Research Scholar in the Department of Anthropology at Northwestern University. He has published extensively on his research on politics, language, and secrecy in Liberia and Sierra Leone.

DAVID NEWBURY has taught at the University of Zaire in Bukavu, the University of Wisconsin, Wesleyan University, and Bowdoin College. He is now on the history faculty of the University of North Carolina, Chapel Hill. His research has been in Rwanda and Zaire, and he has published articles on the pre-colonial history of the area around Lake Kivu. He is co-editor (with Bogumil Jewsiewicki) of *African Historiographies: What History for Which Africa?* (1985).

RANDALL M. PACKARD, a historian, is on the faculty of Tufts University. He has done research in Uganda, Zaire, Swaziland, and South Africa. His articles have focused on history and ideology, and health and society, and he is the author of *Chiefship and Cosmology: A Historical Study of Political Competition* (1981).

ADELL PATTON, JR., a historian, has taught at Benedict College and is now on the faculty of the history department at Howard University. He has done research in Nigeria, Ghana, and Sierra Leone, where he was Senior Fulbright Research Fellow. His publications and research have focused on pre-colonial and colonial African history, the African Diaspora, frontier societies, and Afro-American history.

INDEX